CONNECTICUT FAMILY LAW CITATIONS

A Reference Guide to Connecticut Family Law Decisions

Author
Monika D. Young

ISSUE 86

This issue includes family law decisions from January 1, 1979 through December 31, 2024
Discard all previous issues

2025

Filed Through:
RELEASE NO. 86 March 2025

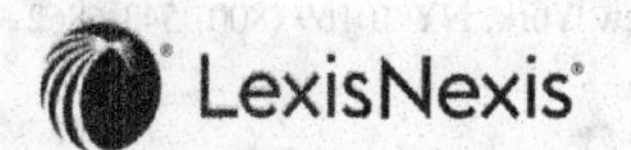

QUESTIONS ABOUT THIS PUBLICATION?

For questions about the **Editorial Content** appearing in these volumes or reprint permission, please call or email:

Cathy Seidenberg at .... (908) 673-3379
Email: .... Cathy.J.Seidenberg@lexisnexis.com

For assistance with replacement pages, shipments, billing or other customer service matters, please call:

Customer Services Department at .... (800) 833-9844
Outside the United States and Canada, please call .... (518) 487-3385
Fax Number .... (800) 828-8341
LexisNexis® Support Center ..... https://supportcenter.lexisnexis.com/app/home/

For information on other Matthew Bender publications, please call
Your account manager or .... (800) 223-1940
Outside the United States and Canada, please call .... (518) 487-3385

ISBN: 978-0-8806-3045-0 (print)

Cite this publication as:

Connecticut Family Law Citations, Sec. No. (Matthew Bender)

Example:
Connecticut Family Law Citations, § 2.02 (Matthew Bender)

Because the section you are citing may be revised in a later release, you may wish to photocopy or print out the section for convenient future reference.

Editorial Office
230 Park Ave., 7th Floor, New York, NY 10169 (800) 543-6862
www.lexisnexis.com

MATTHEW BENDER

(3/2025–Pub.80349)

CONNECTICUT FAMILY LAW CITATIONS

Summary Table of Contents

About the Author

Monika D. Young received her JD from Golden Gate University in 1997, is a member of the State Bar of California, Family Law Section, and has practiced family law in California. She is the author of VALUATION AND DISTRIBUTION OF MARITAL PROPERTY and a researcher for LINDEY AND PARLEY ON SEPARATION AGREEMENTS AND ANTENUPTIAL CONTRACTS, both LexisNexis family law publications. Ms. Young is also a former contributor to several Thomson Reuters family law publications.

Volume 1 Table of Contents

Volume 1 Table of Contents

CHAPTER 1

MARRIAGE AND CIVIL UNIONS

SYNOPSIS

§ 1.01 Marriage

[1] General Overview

1991—*Tatro v. Tatro*, 24 Conn. App. 180, 587 A.2d 154.

Changes in status such as marriage, divorce, adoption, citizenship, or religious affiliation implicate fundamental personal rights that cannot be subject to a court order.

[2] Capacity to Marry

1983—*Garrison v. Garrison*, 190 Conn. 173, 460 A.2d 945.

If neither party to a marriage intends to be married, their lack of mutual consent renders the marriage contract void.

1980—*Carabetta v. Carabetta*, 182 Conn. 344, 438 A.2d 109.

Lack of consent to a marriage is also a substantive defect derived from the common law, sufficient to avoid a marriage.

[3] Nature of Marriage

1998—*Simmons v. Simmons*, 244 Conn. 158, 708 A.2d 949.

The marriage unit is an actual economic partnership.

1990—*Cabrera v. Cabrera*, 23 Conn. App. 330, 580 A.2d 1227.

Communications made by one spouse to a marriage counselor in front of the other during joint counseling sessions are privileged and not public disclosures destroying confidentiality, however, if a spouse's mental health is in issue, the court must also find that the interests of justice require disclosure of confidential communications made to a psychiatrist.

[4] Validity

2016—*Gershuny v. Gershuny*, 322 Conn. 166, 140 A.3d 196.

Connecticut was required to recognize the marriage of two parties married in New York by an unqualified officiant which New York recognized as valid; Conn. Gen. Stat. § 46b-22 only applies to marriages performed in Connecticut.

1988—*Manndorff v. Dax*, 13 Conn. App. 282, 535 A.2d 1324.

Court had subject matter jurisdiction to invalidate a marriage through a declaratory judgment action.

1983—*Garrison v. Garrison*, 190 Conn. 173, 460 A.2d 945.

Court found marriage valid even though the license was never filed where evidence showed parties intended to be married when the marriage ceremony was performed.

1980—*Carabetta v. Carabetta*, 182 Conn. 344, 438 A.2d 109.

A marriage duly solemnized but deficient for want of a marriage license was not void for lack of a marriage license, but was voidable.

§ 1.02 Civil Unions

2014—*Mueller v. Tepler*, 312 Conn. 631, 95 A.3d 1011.

Same sex partner could assert spousal loss of consortium claim even though she was not married to her partner at the time of alleged negligent conduct, if she alleged that she would have been married or in a civil union when tort occurred if they had not been barred from doing so under state law.

2002—*Rosengarten v. Downes*, 71 Conn. App. 372, 802 A.2d 170.

Trial court lacks subject matter jurisdiction to dissolve Vermont civil union.

§ 1.03 Cohabitation

2010—*Lehan v. Lehan*, 118 Conn. App. 685, 985 A.2d 378.

Modification of alimony based on cohabitation was improper where no demonstration that living arrangements had altered defendant's financial needs and without evidence of measurable and quantifiable change.

2006—*Loughlin v. Loughlin*, 93 Conn. App. 618, 889 A.2d 902, *aff'd*, 280 Conn. 632, 910 A.2d 963.

Prior marriage between spouses and subsequent period of cohabitation are irrelevant to proper disposition of proceeding to dissolve parties' second marriage. Length of time relevant to marriage dissolution is length of marriage not length of total relationship.

The Connecticut Supreme Court held, "Based on the previously reviewed jurisprudence of this state, however, it is clear that consideration of a period of cohabitation that precedes a marriage as part of the statutory factor of 'length of the marriage' in a dissolution action is improper." 280 Conn. at 644.

2002—*Herring v. Daniels*, 70 Conn. App. 649, 805 A.2d 718.

Where parties have established an unmarried, cohabiting relationship, it is parties' conduct that determines right in property.

1999—*DeMaria v. DeMaria*, 247 Conn. 715, 724 A.2d 1088.

Court may read into separation agreement requirements of change in financial circumstances in cohabitation case even in absence of statutory reference.

1998—*Wichman v. Wichman*, 49 Conn. App. 529, 714 A.2d 1274.

Judgment providing nonmodifiable alimony until death or remarriage is not modifiable based upon cohabitation.

1996—*D'Ascanio v. D'Ascanio*, 237 Conn. 481, 678 A.2d 469.

Trial court erred in refusing to apply the terms of the modification agreement because the parties had previously agreed that once a finding of cohabitation was made, the alimony award would be reduced by one-half.

1996—*Burns v. Burns*, 41 Conn. App. 716, 677 A.2d 971.

Remarriage, cohabitation or defendant's retirement are not grounds for terminating alimony.

1990—*Miller v. Miller*, 22 Conn. App. 310, 577 A.2d 297.

Where two married individuals are living together as husband and wife and one party conveys property to the other, there is a presumption that a gift is intended.

1988—*Brochu v. Brochu*, 13 Conn. App. 681, 538 A.2d 1093.

Breach of promise to live together is actionable.

1987—*Burns v. Koellmer*, 11 Conn. App. 375, 527 A.2d 1210.

A court will not grant any relief to a plaintiff who rests his claim upon an agreement which is against public policy, for that would be to lend its aid to an illegal transaction.

1987—*Manaker v. Manaker*, 11 Conn. App. 653, 528 A.2d 1170.

The amount a housemate could contribute to former husband's common expenses was relevant in fixing alimony and support amount.

1986—*Warwick v. Warwick*, 7 Conn. App. 361, 508 A.2d 828.

Court held that there was sufficient evidence presented by former husband to indicate that his ex-wife was living with another person in a living arrangement that caused sufficient change of circumstances as to alter her financial needs thus the court modified the judgment and reduced the ex-wife's alimony payments.

1985—*Klein v. Klein*, 3 Conn. App. 421, 488 A.2d 1288.

Trial court denied former husband's motion to modify alimony payments because he had not sustained his burden of proving cohabitation for four continuous months as set forth in parties' separation agreement.

1981—*Kaplan v. Kaplan*, 185 Conn. 42, 440 A.2d 252.

The General Assembly chose the broader language of living with another person rather than cohabitation.

CHAPTER 2

LEGAL SEPARATION

SYNOPSIS

§ 2.01 Grounds

1987—*Ferrucci v. Ferrucci*, 11 Conn. App. 369, 527 A.2d 1207.

Trial court found that both parties engaged in sexual activities with others after their separation which in the context of numerous other findings led to court's conclusion that the parties were equally culpable for the breakdown.

§ 2.02 Conversion to Dissolution

2011—*Luster v. Luster*, 128 Conn. App. 259, 17 A.3d 1068.

Involuntary conservators can respond to an action for legal separation by filing a cross complaint that seeks a dissolution of marriage.

1996—*Szot v. Szot*, 41 Conn. App. 238, 674 A.2d 1384.

At time court converts a decree of legal separation into a divorce it must make a finding that the prior orders are still fair and equitable.

1991—*Mignosa v. Mignosa*, 25 Conn. App. 210, 594 A.2d 15.

When a dissolution of marriage is granted following a decree of legal separation, court must determine whether prior separation agreement is fair and equitable in light of the circumstances existing at the time of the dissolution.

1988—*Brochu v. Brochu*, 13 Conn. App. 681, 538 A.2d 1093.

Court treatment of cohabitation action as dissolution of marriage was error.

1984—*Mitchell v. Mitchell*, 194 Conn. 312, 481 A.2d 31.

Court dissolved the wife's marriage to petitioner husband by granting the husband's petition to convert an earlier legal separation into a dissolution of the marriage.

§ 2.03 Resumption of Marital Relations

1991—*Mignosa v. Mignosa*, 25 Conn. App. 210, 594 A.2d 15.

Dissolution judgment may only be obtained while a decree of legal separation is in effect thus if one party claims marital relations resumed, there must be an evidentiary hearing. If parties have resumed marital relations since a decree of legal separation, they cannot use Conn. Gen. Stat. § 46b-65(b) but must use Conn. Gen. Stat. § 46b-40 to divorce.

CHAPTER 3

ANNULMENT

SYNOPSIS

§ 3.01 Grounds

2024—*Ciarleglio v. Martin*, 228 Conn. App. 241, 325 A.3d 219, *appeal denied*, 350 Conn. 920, 325 A.3d 218.

Where the decedent had initiated an annulment action, an action by the administrator of his estate to annul the marriage following his death did not constitute an impermissible collateral attack on a legally valid marriage. By statute, an annulment shall be granted if a marriage is void or voidable. The defendant's contention that, if a party does not act to obtain an annulment from a court of competent jurisdiction prior to the death of one of the parties, the voidable defect is deemed waived, and will abate with the death of a party, was based on a false premise. The decedent did act to obtain an annulment by commencing the action in the first place.

1981—*Fattibene v. Fattibene*, 183 Conn. 433, 441 A.2d 3.

Court ruled that the husband lacked standing to collaterally attack the prior divorce decree because he had no interest therein at the time it was entered and he was not entitled to an annulment under Conn. Gen. Stat. § 46-32(b) because the alleged fraud did not relate to sexual obligations of the marriage.

§ 3.02 Void and Voidable Marriages

1998—*State v. Nosik*, 245 Conn. 196, 715 A.2d 673.

Court discusses criteria as to when marriage is void or voidable.

1988—*Durham v. Miceli*, 15 Conn. App. 96, 543 A.2d 286.

In order to be entitled to an annulment of marriage, the husband had to allege and prove that the marriage was void or voidable under the laws of the state or the state in which the marriage was performed.

CHAPTER 4

JURISDICTION AND SERVICE

SYNOPSIS

§ 4.01 Residency Requirement

2012—*Jungnelius v. Jungnelius*, 133 Conn. App. 250, 35 A.3d 359.

Court properly determined that it had jurisdiction to dissolve a marriage and plaintiff met the residency requirement where action had been withdrawn, parties moved out of CT, and action was restored to the docket on plaintiff's motion.

2010—*Schwarz v. Schwarz*, 124 Conn. App. 472, 5 A.3d 548.

Defendant failed to present facts to sustain a finding that Florida was his domicile.

1998—*Charles v. Charles*, 243 Conn. 255, 701 A.2d 650.

Native American on reservation is resident of Connecticut for jurisdiction purposes.

1988—*Cugini v. Cugini*, 13 Conn. App. 632, 538 A.2d 1060.

Jurisdiction requires domicile plus substantially continuous physical residence.

1988—*Manndorff v. Dax*, 13 Conn. App. 282, 535 A.2d 1324.

Plaintiff must be a domiciliary of Connecticut in order to bring an action to invalidate her husband's second marriage.

1985—*Sauter v. Sauter*, 4 Conn. App. 581, 495 A.2d 1116.

Decree dissolving a marriage or granting a legal separation may be entered if: (1) one of the parties to the marriage has been a resident of Connecticut for at least the 12 months next preceding the date of the filing of the complaint or next preceding the date of the decree; (2) one of the parties was domiciled in Connecticut at the time of the marriage and returned to Connecticut with the intention of permanently remaining before the filing of the complaint; or (3) the cause for the dissolution of the marriage arose after either party moved into Connecticut.

1985—*Carchrae v. Carchrae*, 10 Conn. App. 566, 524 A.2d 672.

Residency gives court subject matter jurisdiction.

§ 4.02 Personal Jurisdiction

2014—*Hornblower v. Hornblower*, 151 Conn. App. 332, 94 A.3d 1218.

The trial court retained personal jurisdiction over wife following dissolution, despite her relocation out of state.

2008—*Kenny v. Banks*, 289 Conn. 529, 958 A.2d 750.

Improper dismissal of UIFSA based on lack of personal jurisdiction: New York court entered child support judgment and parties thereafter left New York; obligee mother moved to Connecticut and the father moved to California; mother registered New York order in Connecticut for enforcement and then filed contempt motion.

1996—*Cashman v. Cashman*, 41 Conn. App. 382, 676 A.2d 427.

Once a divorce judgment is granted by a court with personal jurisdiction, neither party can escape jurisdiction in future proceedings that attempt to modify the judgment.

1996—*Pinder v. Pinder*, 42 Conn. App. 254, 679 A.2d 973.

Alimony not ordained to either party when defendant was a nonresident and court lacked personal jurisdiction.

§ 4.03 Subject Matter Jurisdiction

2024—*Ciarleglio v. Martin*, 228 Conn. App. 241, 325 A.3d 219, *appeal denied*, 350 Conn. 920, 325 A.3d 218.

Trial court did not lack subject matter jurisdiction over the annulment action commenced by the decedent. Because the administrator of the estate had a legitimate fiduciary interest in establishing the identity of the rightful heirs and a duty to carry out the wishes of the decedent, it was logical that he was permitted to continue an action to annul a marriage under the circumstances presented by this case. The purpose of the cause of action originally pursued by the decedent was not defeated or rendered useless by his death. Accordingly, the exception set out in Conn. Gen. § 52-599(c)(1) to the circumstances under which an action interrupted by the death of a litigant shall be allowed to continue by substituting the executor or administrator of the estate in place of a deceased litigant did not apply.

2024—*Hepburn v. Brill*, 348 Conn. 827, 312 A.3d 1.

The trial court improperly dismissed the plaintiff's petition for third-party visitation with her niece. The Superior Court has plenary jurisdiction over family relations matters under Conn. Gen. Stat. § 46b-1 and the 2012 amendments to the third-party visitation statute, Conn. Gen. Stat. § 46b-59(b), which provides that any person may submit a verified petition to the Superior Court for the right of visitation with any minor child. The plaintiff's amended petition alleged facts sufficient to warrant a hearing under § 46b-59.

2023—*Strauss v. Strauss*, 220 Conn. App. 193, 297 A.3d 581.

Trial court properly denied Defendant's motion filed in 2019 to vacate contempt orders made in 2014. Trial court did not have continuing authority to grant the motion because the motion represented an attempt to void, not effectuate, substantive terms of the 2014 orders. If Defendant wanted to challenge these orders, his remedy was to file a timely appeal, a timely motion to reargue, or a motion to vacate within the four months following the contempt orders (Conn. Gen. Stat. § 52-212a). In 2019, trial court did not have authority to vacate these orders on the grounds that it had improperly found Defendant in contempt five years earlier.

2022—*Hebrand v. Hebrand*, 216 Conn. App. 210, 284 A.3d 702.

Wife appealed trial court judgment denying her motion to open the 2017 postjudgment modification of the parties' 2013 settlement agreement. She claimed that in 2017 the trial court did not have subject matter jurisdiction to modify the dissolution judgment and that in 2020 the trial court improperly failed to find fraud in denying her motion to open. Appellate Court affirmed. Trial court had jurisdiction under Conn. Gen. Stat. § 46-1 to consider the parties' joint motion in 2017 to modify certain financial aspects of the 2013 agreement and to accept the stipulation they filed in 2017. Wife's arguments that Husband mislabeled his 2017 motion and did not pay the required filing fee were not jurisdictional in nature and she did not provide any authority to support her arguments. Further, Wife did not prove her allegations of fraud and her other claims had no merit. Judgment was affirmed.

2022—*Olson v. Olson*, 214 Conn. App. 4, 279 A.3d 230.

Trial court had subject matter jurisdiction to hear a motion to modify an alimony order issued in the United Kingdom. Assuming the provisions of the order were applicable, nowhere in the context of the order was it manifest that the United Kingdom retained exclusive, rather than concurrent, jurisdiction to modify the spousal support order.

2020—*Powers v. Hiranandani*, 197 Conn. App. 384, 232 A.3d 116.

In dissolution proceedings, the trial court did not lack subject matter jurisdiction over the real property defendant husband had owned with his deceased brother, which was awarded to plaintiff wife as part of the marital estate, because the court had plenary subject matter jurisdiction over legal disputes in family relations matters pursuant to Conn. Gen. Stat. § 46b-1(c) and authority to transfer property under Conn. Gen. Stat. § 46b-81. Because the trial court was required by statute to divide the marital assets of the parties at the time of dissolution, it properly ordered defendant to transfer all of his rights, title, and interest in the marital residence to plaintiff, irrespective of the status of his deceased brother's estate. Judgment as to the real property upheld; judgment reversed and remanded for further proceedings as to defendant's separate claim that the trial court failed to divide the parties' personal property.

2019—*Shear v. Shear*, 194 Conn. App. 351, 221 A.3d 450.

Plaintiff's appeal from an order of the family support magistrate was not taken from a final judgment because the magistrate did not render a decision on all of the issues. The appellate court has previously concluded that where there is a lack of final judgment the trial court fails to fully resolve the matter placed before it. The Superior Court should have dismissed the appeal for lack of subject matter jurisdiction.

2019—*Callahan v. Callahan*, 192 Conn. App. 634, 218 A.3d 655.

Trial court properly concluded that it did not have subject matter jurisdiction to require defendant to endorse insurance checks for post-dissolution property damage to the former marital home awarded to and previously distributed to plaintiff. The court could not revisit property distribution orders or make additional property orders to compensate plaintiff for the alleged reduction in the value of the home after judgment. To the extent the insurance checks are a new asset acquired pursuant to an insurance contract in effect after the parties' marriage was dissolved, the insurance proceeds are not marital property distributable under § 46b-81.

2019—*In re Adrian K.*, 191 Conn. App. 397, 215 A.3d 1271.

Trial court had ongoing subject matter jurisdiction over order of temporary custody although motion to modify dispositional order of protective supervision was filed the day after the period of protective supervision had been set to expire. An order of temporary custody necessarily modifies period of protective supervision by suspending it such that previously ordered period of protective supervision cannot expire and terminate the underlying neglect petition while the order of temporary custody is in place. Moreover, whether the timing requirement of the applicable rule of practice is mandatory or directory and whether a motion to modify protective supervision was timely filed are irrelevant to the question of subject matter jurisdiction.

2019—*Firstenberg v. Madigan*, 188 Conn. App. 724, 205 A.3d 716.

Petition for visitation by the maternal grandfather was dismissed for lack of subject matter jurisdiction because the grandfather's petition failed to include specific and good-faith allegations that parent-like relationship existed between himself and grandson and that denial of visitation would cause real and significant harm.

2018—*Reinke v. Sing*, 328 Conn. 376, 179 A.3d 769.

Trial court had the authority to entertain and determine the plaintiff's claim seeking a modification of the dissolution judgment. That authority derived not only from the court's plenary and general subject matter jurisdiction over dissolution actions (Conn.

Gen. Stat. § 46b-1); but also from its authority to assign to either spouse all or any part of the marital estate (Conn. Gen. Stat. § 46b-81(a)).

2018—*Fredo v. Fredo*, 185 Conn. App. 252, 196 A.3d 1235.

Trial court erred in granting plaintiff's motion to dismiss defendant's motion for modification of child support for lack of subject matter jurisdiction where court had subject matter jurisdiction pursuant to General Statutes §§ 46b-1 and 46b-86(a).

2017—*Fuller v. Baldino*, 176 Conn. App. 451, 168 A.3d 665.

Trial court properly dismissed the plaintiff's third-party petition for visitation for lack of subject matter jurisdiction where the plaintiff's petition failed to establish a parent-like relationship and that denial of visitation would result in real and substantial harm to the minor child.

2017—*In re Santiago G.*, 325 Conn. 221, 157 A.3d 60.

Appeal dismissed for lack of subject matter jurisdiction where intervening party did not have a colorable claim of intervention in termination of parental rights proceeding.

2017—*Richman v. Wallman*, 172 Conn. App. 616, 161 A.3d 666.

The court acted within the scope of its subject matter jurisdiction by ordering the plaintiff to agree to the terms of the two QDROs.

2016—*Weyher v. Weyher*, 164 Conn. App. 734, 138 A.3d 969.

A party may not collaterally attack an order of the court, even if said order was impermissibly made, if the order was made under proper subject matter jurisdiction and the party failed to challenge the order in a timely manner.

2014—*Devone v. Finley*, 148 Conn. App. 647, 87 A.3d 1120.

Trial court lacked jurisdiction to entertain father's application for sole legal custody of child born out of wedlock.

2014—*Perry v. Perry*, 312 Conn. 600, 95 A.3d 500.

Court had jurisdiction to hear attorney for the minor children's writ of error as an aggrieved nonparty.

2013—*Bauer v. Bauer*, 308 Conn. 124, 60 A.3d 950.

Courts may exercise continuing jurisdiction to clarify a judgment when ambiguity in language arises as a result of post-judgment events.

2005—*Fewtrell v. Fewtrell*, 87 Conn. App. 526, 865 A.2d 1240.

Trial court had jurisdiction to entertain post-judgment motion to modify where motion was to effectuate original order regarding assignment of debt.

2003—*Fusco v. Fusco*, 266 Conn. 649, 835 A.2d 6.

Trial courts always have subject matter jurisdiction over motions for modification of post-majority child support.

2002—*Crockett v. Pastore*, 259 Conn. 240, 789 A.2d 453.

Court has subject matter jurisdiction to consider maternal grandmother's petition for sole custody.

2000—*Rosenfield v. Rosenfield*, 61 Conn. App. 112, 762 A.2d 511.

Court distinguishes subject-matter jurisdiction and statutory jurisdiction.

1999—*Amodio v. Amodio*, 247 Conn. 724, 724 A.2d 1084.

Trial court always has subject matter jurisdiction over modification of child support and alimony orders; proper inquiry is whether court has power to act under decree.

1999—*W. v. W.*, 248 Conn. 487, 728 A.2d 1076.

Trial court had subject matter jurisdiction to order pendente lite child support regardless of whether child at issue was considered "child of marriage."

1998—*Miner v. Miner*, 48 Conn. App. 409, 709 A.2d 605.

Court lacks jurisdiction to modify post-majority support absent a written agreement allowing modification.

1998—*Doe v. Doe*, 244 Conn. 403, 710 A.2d 1297.

Court has jurisdiction to award custody of a child as between the biological father and his wife, who is neither biological nor adoptive parent of child born from surrogate mother.

1996—*Pinder v. Pinder*, 42 Conn. App. 254, 679 A.2d 973.

Personal and subject matter jurisdiction satisfied to grant divorce when switchboard operator signed return receipt on behalf of defendant when she had actual notice.

1996—*Muller v. Muller*, 43 Conn. App. 327, 682 A.2d 1089.

Trial court lacked subject matter jurisdiction under UCCJA; jurisdiction had become vested in California where the mother and child had lived since the child's birth more than five years earlier.

1995—*Krafick v. Krafick*, 234 Conn. 783, 663 A.2d 365.

Court can reserve jurisdiction over the disposition of property in the future.

1993—*Roberts v. Roberts*, 32 Conn. App. 465, 629 A.2d 1160.

Court had subject matter jurisdiction to enter orders post-dissolution to carry out its decision to sell marital home.

1993—*Sierra v. Lozada*, 31 Conn. App. 114, 623 A.2d 1045.

Family support magistrate does not have jurisdiction to decide contested custody claims.

1993—*Rummel v. Rummel*, 33 Conn. App. 214, 635 A.2d 295.

Failure to close the pleadings where all the parties were present and represented will not fatally affect the jurisdiction of the case.

1992—*Martone v. Martone*, 28 Conn. App. 208, 611 A.2d 896.

Court can retain jurisdiction to make alimony and property orders after it dissolves the marriage.

1989—*Albrecht v. Albrecht*, 19 Conn. App. 146, 562 A.2d 528.

Trial court does not have jurisdiction to modify post majority support provisions without written agreement of parties regarding modification.

1989—*Daly v. Daly*, 19 Conn. App. 65, 561 A.2d 951.

Litigant claimed 19 years after judgment that the court lacked subject matter jurisdiction to award wife part of a trust husband was to receive in future but court held that the need to have finality of judgment outweighed husband's claim that court lacked subject matter jurisdiction.

1989—*Mayor v. Mayor*, 17 Conn. App. 627, 554 A.2d 1109.

Court does not have jurisdiction to change a child's name in an action for dissolution of marriage.

1988—*Hurtado v. Hurtado*, 14 Conn. App. 296, 541 A.2d 873.

Court does not lose jurisdiction in custody matter because the children are removed from the country.

1987—*Carchrae v. Carchrae*, 10 Conn. App. 566, 524 A.2d 672.

Jurisdiction to grant decree cannot be determined until the date of decree. Residency gives court subject matter jurisdiction. Amendment to complaint granted to insure the pleading of facts necessary to give the court jurisdiction. Residency gives court subject matter jurisdiction.

1985—*Grynkewich v. McGinley*, 3 Conn. App. 541, 490 A.2d 534.

The court set aside the judgment that had dismissed the father's counterclaim for custody of his two minor children with the mother and remanded the case for an evidentiary hearing as to subject matter jurisdiction pursuant to the UCCJA.

1985—*Sauter v. Sauter*, 4 Conn. App. 581, 495 A.2d 1116.

Subject matter jurisdiction determined at date of decree.

1980—*Broaca v. Broaca*, 181 Conn. 463, 435 A.2d 1016.

The superior court had inherent authority to act because its judgment was void ab initio.

§ 4.04 In Rem Jurisdiction

2023—*Schoenhorn v. Moss*, 347 Conn. 501, 298 A.3d 236.

The trial court did not err in dismissing Plaintiff's action for a writ of mandamus on the ground that it was nonjusticiable as the court could not provide any practical relief. Plaintiff filed in Hartford for a writ ordering the chief court reporter in Stamford-Norwalk to produce transcripts sealed by the family court there in a separate marital dissolution action involving different parties. Because the family court had jurisdiction over the marital dissolution action, it had jurisdiction over the sealing order. Plaintiff's action constituted an impermissible collateral attack on another court's order. The Hartford court lacked subject matter jurisdiction to issue the writ.

1988—*Fernandez v. Fernandez*, 208 Conn. 329, 545 A.2d 1036.

Dissolution of marriage proceeding is an action in rem and not in personam which requires jurisdiction over defendant.

1986—*Samrov v. Samrov*, 6 Conn. App. 591, 506 A.2d 1077.

Quasi in rem jurisdiction required to make support order which can be satisfied against property in Connecticut.

1981—*Ivey v. Ivey*, 183 Conn. 490, 439 A.2d 425.

Courts of one state have no power to affect directly the title to real property located in another state because title adjudications are actions in rem.

§ 4.05 Jurisdiction Under the UCCJA/UCCJEA

2024—*Ammar I. v. Evelyn W.*, 227 Conn. App. 827, 323 A.3d 1111.

Trial court properly dismissed the plaintiff's petition for third party visitation with his biological children, with respect to whom his parental rights had been terminated. The trial court lacked subject matter jurisdiction because Connecticut was not the children's home state on the date the plaintiff commenced the child custody proceeding. It was undisputed that the children had lived in North Carolina with the defendant for more than six months prior to the commencement of this proceeding. Further, because the children had lived in North Carolina for approximately 13 months, that state possessed home state jurisdiction over visitation petitions involving them.

2021—*De Almeida-Kennedy v. Kennedy*, 207 Conn. App. 244, 262 A.3d 872.

Conn. Gen. Stat. § 46b-115l(a)(1) provides in relevant part that "a court of this state which has made a child custody determination pursuant to sections 46b-115k to 46b-115m, inclusive, has exclusive, continuing jurisdiction over the determination until . . . [a] court of this state or a court of another state determines that the child, the child's parents and any person acting as a parent do not presently reside in this state . . . ." Exclusive jurisdiction is not reestablished if, after the children, the parents, and all persons acting as parents have all left the state, the noncustodial parent subsequently returns.

The trial court properly determined that it did not have exclusive, continuing jurisdiction over the defendant's November 2018 motion for custody and his other motions related to custody and visitation with the minor children because from April 2018 to September 2018, neither the plaintiff, the defendant, nor their minor children presently resided in this state. The defendant's return to Connecticut in September 2018 did not reestablish jurisdiction. The trial court properly granted plaintiff's motion to dismiss the custody related motions. However, it improperly dismissed the defendant's other motions that were unrelated to the issue of child custody or visitation.

2021—*Swanson v. Perez-Swanson*, 206 Conn. App. 266, 259 A.3d 39.

Where the parties had entered post-dissolution agreements allowing the plaintiff to relocate to North Carolina with their children and stipulating that the court in either Connecticut or North Carolina would have jurisdiction to determine any issue relating to child custody and/or visitation, the trial court erred in dismissing the defendant's motion modify custody on the ground that it lacked jurisdiction to enter further orders regarding child custody or visitation under Conn. Gen. Stat. § 46b-115l(a)(2) because the children had resided with the plaintiff in North Carolina for at least six consecutive months. The trial court considered only one of the three statutory factors listed in § 46b-115l(a)(2). It must also consider whether the children no longer have a significant relationship with the defendant, who still lives in Connecticut, and whether substantial evidence concerning the children's care, protection, training, and personal relationships is no longer available in this state.

2020—*Parisi v. Niblett*, 199 Conn. App. 761, 238 A.3d 740.

The trial court properly applied the UCCJEA provisions to determine if it had subject matter jurisdiction to modify the Florida court's custody order. Conn. Gen. Stat. § 46b-56(a) does not automatically grant subject matter jurisdiction over a properly domesticated foreign child custody judgment; it expressly and unambiguously requires the trial court to examine the UCCJEA to determine whether it has subject matter jurisdiction to modify the foreign child custody order.

When issues of fact are necessary to the determination of a court's jurisdiction, due process requires a trial-like hearing with an opportunity to present evidence and to cross-examine adverse witnesses. The trial court improperly determined that it lacked subject matter jurisdiction because it did not afford the plaintiff an evidentiary hearing.

2020—*In re Teagan K.-O.*, 335 Conn. 745, 242 A.3d 59.

The trial court erred by denying a father's motion to dismiss a petition brought on the basis of predictive neglect because the allegations did not satisfy the jurisdictional requirements of Conn. Gen. Stat. § 46b-121(a)(1). There was no allegation from which the court could reasonably infer that the infant child born in Florida would be neglected in Connecticut. The child was present in Connecticut only because of Connecticut's action to remove her from her parents' new state of residence, Florida. Jurisdiction to make an original custody determination rested with Florida.

Because the UCCJEA does not create jurisdiction but prescribes the circumstances under which courts may exercise jurisdiction that otherwise is conferred by constitution or statute or must defer to another state's jurisdiction, it does not bar the application of § 46b-121.

1999—*State v. Vakilzaden*, 251 Conn. 656, 742 A.2d 767.

Joint custodians were held liable for abducting child.

1996—*Muller v. Muller*, 43 Conn. App. 327, 682 A.2d 1089.

Trial court lacked subject matter jurisdiction under UCCJA because jurisdiction had become vested in California where the mother and child had lived since the child's birth more than five years.

1991—*Turner v. Turner*, 219 Conn. 703, 595 A.2d 297.

UCCJA not violated where court found issues of child abuse.

1989—*Ozkan v. Ozkan*, 18 Conn. App. 73, 556 A.2d 628.

In order to achieve interstate uniformity in custody matters, the UCCJA limits custody jurisdiction to the state where the child has his home or where there are other strong contacts with the child and his family.

1989—*Perez v. Perez*, 212 Conn. 63, 561 A.2d 907.

Six month "home state" requirement under the UCCJA cannot be defeated by one parent improperly removing a child from the jurisdiction.

1985—*Benson v. Benson*, 5 Conn. App. 95, 497 A.2d 64.

The court may order either spouse to pay the reasonable attorney's fees of the other in accordance with their respective financial abilities and the criteria set forth in Conn. Gen. Stat. § 46b-82; Conn. Gen. Stat. § 46b-1 includes family matters such as custody under the Uniform Child Custody Jurisdiction Act (UCCJA).

1985—*Brown v. Brown*, 195 Conn. 98, 486 A.2d 1116.

The legislature clearly intended that the inconvenient forum issue in UCCJA cases remain discretionary.

1985—*Grynkewich v. McGinley*, 3 Conn. App. 541, 490 A.2d 534.

The court set aside the judgment that had dismissed the father's counterclaim for custody of his two minor children with the mother and remanded the case for an evidentiary hearing as to subject matter jurisdiction pursuant to the UCCJA.

1982—*Schurman v. Schurman*, 188 Conn. 268, 449 A.2d 169.

In order to implement the policy of the Uniform Child Custody Jurisdiction Act, a court may choose to overlook formal defects when the circumstances warrant such action thus the weight to be assigned to the defendant's formal noncompliance with the statute rests in the discretion of the trial court.

1981—*Agnello v. Becker*, 184 Conn. 421, 440 A.2d 172.

The Uniform Child Custody Jurisdiction Act sets forth the bases for jurisdiction of a court to make a child custody determination. In the first place, a court in the child's home state has jurisdiction, and secondly, if there is no home state or the child and his family have equal or stronger ties with another state, a court in that state has jurisdiction.

1981—*Kioukis v. Kioukis*, 185 Conn. 249, 440 A.2d 894.

The first state's exclusive jurisdiction does not continue indefinitely under the Uniform Child Custody Jurisdiction Act. At some point the child's connections with the first state become too tenuous to satisfy the demands of the statute.

§ 4.06 Continuing Jurisdiction and the Uniform Interstate Family Support Act

1983—*Morabito v. Wachsman*, 191 Conn. 92, 463 A.2d 593.

In a child support enforcement action, the issue of jurisdiction had been fully and fairly litigated when the husband specially appeared in Nevada to contest jurisdiction and was unsuccessful.

§ 4.07 Jurisdiction to Modify Support Order

2024—*L.K. v. K.K.*, 226 Conn. App. 279, 318 A.3d 243.

Trial court had subject matter jurisdiction to enter orders regarding the parties' adult child because it had jurisdiction under Conn. Gen. Stat. §§ 46b-1 and 46b-86(a) to modify the unallocated alimony and child support order. The court also had jurisdiction under Conn. Gen. Stat. § 46b-66 to enforce provisions of the parties' written dissolution agreement, incorporated into orders, for the care, maintenance, or support of a child beyond the age of 18.

2018—*Fredo v. Fredo*, 185 Conn. App. 252, 196 A.3d 1235.

Trial court erred in granting plaintiff's motion to dismiss defendant's motion for modification of child support for lack of subject matter jurisdiction where court had subject matter jurisdiction pursuant to General Statutes §§ 46b-1 and 46b-86(a).

2005—*Fewtrell v. Fewtrell*, 87 Conn. App. 526, 865 A.2d 1240.

Trial court had jurisdiction to entertain post-judgment motion to modify where motion was to effectuate original order regarding assignment of debt.

2003—*Fusco v. Fusco*, 266 Conn. 649, 835 A.2d 6.

Trial courts always have subject matter jurisdiction over motions for modification of post-majority child support.

1999—*Amodio v. Amodio*, 247 Conn. 724, 724 A.2d 1084.

Trial court always has subject matter jurisdiction over modification of child support and alimony orders; proper inquiry is whether court has power to act under decree.

1998—*Miner v. Miner*, 48 Conn. App. 409, 709 A.2d 605.

Court lacks jurisdiction to modify post-maturity support absent a written agreement allowing modification.

1996—*Cashman v. Cashman*, 41 Conn. App. 382, 676 A.2d 427.

Once a divorce judgment is granted by a court with personal jurisdiction, neither party can escape jurisdiction in future proceedings that attempt to modify the judgment.

1989—*Albrecht v. Albrecht*, 19 Conn. App. 146, 562 A.2d 528.

Trial court does not have jurisdiction to modify post majority support provisions without written agreement of parties regarding modification.

§ 4.08 Full Faith and Credit and Foreign Judgments

2024—*K.S. v. R.S.*, 350 Conn. 692, 326 A.2d 187.

Prior and during the marriage, the defendant was involved in years long litigation in

New Jersey concerning his family's business. He pledged the parties' Greenwich property and investment accounts as security for his appeal in that lawsuit and subsequently forfeited that property.

The Connecticut trial court in this dissolution action erred when it failed to afford full faith and credit to the New Jersey court orders regarding the forfeiture of the parties' Greenwich property and investment accounts. The Connecticut court was not permitted to treat that property as part of the marital estate. The defendant had submitted to the New Jersey court's personal jurisdiction over him, had voluntarily pledged that property, and was subject to the New Jersey order vesting a special fiscal agent with power of attorney over his rights to that property. There was no public policy exception permitting the Connecticut court to decline to give full faith and credit to the New Jersey orders.

2023—*Gershon v. Back*, 346 Conn. 181, 288 A.3d 602.

The appellate court held that where the plaintiff registered a New York judgment of dissolution in Connecticut and then filed a motion to open and set aside the judgment, the trial court had improperly dismissed the motion on the grounds that it lacked subject matter jurisdiction, but it had properly determined that the plaintiff was able to challenge the separation agreement only by bringing a plenary action. The New York rule requiring a party to challenge a separation agreement through a plenary action, which was explicitly incorporated into the terms of the parties' separation agreement, is substantive and not procedural. Conn. Gen. Stat. § 46b-71 and the parties' agreement required that the trial court apply this New York substantive rule to the plaintiff's motion to open. Because the trial court should have denied instead of dismissing the motion, the form of its judgment is improper. The Supreme Court affirmed, finding that the appellate court had correctly concluded the New York plenary action rule was substantive for choice of law purposes and that the trial court should have denied, rather than dismissed, the plaintiff's motion to open and set aside the divorce judgment.

2019—*St. Denis-Lima v. St. Denis*, 190 Conn. App. 296, 212 A.3d 242.

Trial court properly determined that there was a final judgment of dissolution in Brazil and did not abuse its discretion in affording comity to the judgment; the court reviewed documents submitted by both parties, including the Brazilian case overview submitted by the plaintiff, which established the existence of a final divorce decree in Brazil.

2016—*Gershuny v. Gershuny*, 322 Conn. 166, 140 A.3d 196.

Connecticut was required to recognize the marriage of two parties married in New York by an unqualified officiant which New York recognized as valid; Conn. Gen. Stat. § 46b-22 only applies to marriages performed in Connecticut.

2014—*Devone v. Finley*, 148 Conn. App. 647, 87 A.3d 1120.

Custody case discusses the full faith and credit clause.

2013—*Juma v. Aomo*, 143 Conn. App. 51, 68 A.3d 148.

Court properly rendered its own dissolution decree and did not give comity to a

Kenyan dissolution decree where the foreign action was first in time but due to the facts of the case, Connecticut had subject matter jurisdiction.

2013—*Zitkene v. Zitkus*, 140 Conn. App. 856, 60 A.3d 322.

No abuse of discretion where a court granted comity to a Lithuanian divorce decree and then dismissed a Connecticut dissolution action for lack of subject matter jurisdiction where uncontested facts stated that the parties entered into a separation agreement in Lithuania and the plaintiff already had received the benefit of that bargain.

2005—*Segal v. Segal*, 86 Conn. App. 617, 863 A.2d 221.

Uniform Enforcement of Foreign Judgments Act—modification of a previously domesticated foreign judgment in Nevada must be refiled only if change is substantial.

1998—*Lindo v. Lindo*, 48 Conn. App. 645, 710 A.2d 1387.

Connecticut court lacks jurisdiction to modify foreign matrimonial judgment entered by default.

1997—*Vitale v. Krieger*, 47 Conn. App. 146, 702 A.2d 148.

When modifying foreign matrimonial judgment, Connecticut court must apply substantive law of the foreign jurisdiction.

1994—*Colby v. Colby*, 33 Conn. App. 417, 635 A.2d 1241.

Court, in modifying judgment, must apply the substantive law of the Massachusetts jurisdiction in which the foreign matrimonial judgment was entered.

1993—*Mirabal v. Mirabal*, 30 Conn. App. 821, 622 A.2d 1037.

Entry of an appearance in the original California action by both parties is a threshold requirement for enforcement of a foreign matrimonial judgment.

1988—*Fernandez v. Fernandez*, 208 Conn. 329, 545 A.2d 1036.

The immunity of the diplomatic agent is maintained even in the matter of divorce because a divorce action under the local jurisdiction is incompatible with his dignity as a diplomat.

1986—*Rule v. Rule*, 6 Conn. App. 541, 506 A.2d 1061.

Connecticut trial court upheld the enforceability in Connecticut of the Massachusetts judgment of contempt.

1985—*Bruneau v. Bruneau*, 3 Conn. App. 453, 489 A.2d 1049.

Even if the divorce decree rendered in Mexico was jurisdictionally invalid, it was permitted practical recognition.

1985—*Lashgari v. Lashgari*, 197 Conn. 189, 496 A.2d 491.

Upon dissolution of marriage, the court awarded damages to ex-wife on her claim for breach of Iranian marriage contract.

1985—*Nielsen v. Nielsen*, 3 Conn. App. 679, 491 A.2d 1112.

Court ordered consolidation of foreign judgment enforcement action with pending Connecticut action.

1984—*Van Wagner v. Van Wagner*, 1 Conn. App. 578, 474 A.2d 110.

A foreign matrimonial judgment shall become a judgment of the court of Connecticut where it is filed and shall be enforced and otherwise treated in the same manner as a judgment of a court of Connecticut provided such foreign matrimonial judgment does not contravene the public policy of Connecticut.

1983—*Morabito v. Wachsman*, 191 Conn. 92, 463 A.2d 593.

The Full Faith and Credit Clause, U.S. Const. art. IV, § 1, requires that judgments of the courts of each state be given the same faith, credit, and effect in sister states as they have by law or custom in the courts of the state rendering them.

1983—*Burton v. Burton*, 189 Conn. 129, 454 A.2d 1282.

When modifying a foreign matrimonial judgment, Connecticut courts must apply the substantive law of the foreign jurisdiction.

1983—*Juma v. Aomo*, 143 Conn. App. 51, 68 A.3d 148.

Court properly rendered its own dissolution decree and did not give comity to a foreign dissolution decree where the foreign action was first in time but due to the facts of the case, Connecticut had subject matter jurisdiction.

1981—*Hayes v. Beresford*, 184 Conn. 558, 440 A.2d 224.

The court held that the parties could not confer jurisdiction over the separation agreement upon a court and, moreover, the jurisdictional defect was not cured by its incorporation into the Mexican divorce decree.

1980—*Krueger v. Krueger*, 179 Conn. 488, 427 A.2d 400.

The judicial proceedings of a state must be given full faith and credit in every other state.

1979—*Calig v. Schrank*, 179 Conn. 283, 426 A.2d 276.

Agreement's controlling law provision could not be relied upon to apply New Jersey law to an action for reimbursement that had no connection with New Jersey.

§ 4.09 Service

[1] Abode Service

2012—*Leftridge v. Wiggins*, 136 Conn. App. 238, 44 A.3d 217.

Trial court improperly modified child support where the obligor had not been properly served because abode service was made at a residence where he did not live.

2008—*Jeudy v. Jeudy*, 106 Conn. App. 372, 942 A.2d 476.

Motion to open a dissolution judgment denied because abode service was adequate.

1999—*Charbonneau v. Charbonneau*, 51 Conn. App. 311, 721 A.2d 565.

Although defendant was not served at his usual place of abode, court determined he had actual notice of the pending dissolution action where he admitted to having possession of the papers.

1980—*Gluck v. Gluck*, 181 Conn. 225, 435 A.2d 35.

Abode service is only a step removed from manual service and serves the same dual function of conferring jurisdiction and giving notice.

[2] In Hand Service

1993—*Cato v. Cato*, 226 Conn. 1, 626 A.2d 734.

In-hand service is sufficient to confer jurisdiction over a nonresident spouse without an order of notice under Conn. Gen. Stat. § 46b-46. An order of notice is permissive, not mandatory, and is not a condition precedent to effective, in-hand service in another state pursuant to Conn. Gen. Stat. § 52-57a.

[3] Effectuating Service of Process

2012—*Leftridge v. Wiggins*, 136 Conn. App. 238, 44 A.3d 217.

Acting on a motion that had not been properly served violated due process.

2011—*Alldred v. Alldred*, 132 Conn. App. 430, 31 A.3d 1185.

Trial court properly dismissed post-judgment motions for contempt because of insufficient service; sending copies of post-judgment motions for contempt to counsel did not constitute proper service on the plaintiff.

2008—*Finan v. Finan*, 107 Conn. App. 369, 945 A.2d 476.

A request to produce at hearing served five days in advance of a post-judgment contempt hearing was timely. Conn. Gen. Prac. Book, R. Super. Ct. § 25-56 does not require service five business days in advance of a hearing.

1993—*Cato v. Cato*, 27 Conn. App. 142, 605 A.2d 558, *aff'd*, 226 Conn. 1, 626 A.2d 734.

Order of notice is not necessary to obtain personal service under the long arm statute.

CHAPTER 5

PREMARITAL AND POSTMARITAL AGREEMENTS

SYNOPSIS

§ 5.01 Premarital or Prenuptial Agreements

[1] Validity

2015—*Chowdhury v. Masiat*, 161 Conn. App. 314, 128 A.3d 545.

Husband did not stipulate to sufficient facts for court to find enforceable contract; the stipulation did not constitute an acknowledgement by the defendant of a debt owed the plaintiff or otherwise relieve the plaintiff of her burden of proving that there was a valid, enforceable contract.

2015—*Beyor v. Beyor*, 158 Conn. App. 752, 121 A.3d 734.

Husband provided adequate financial disclosure at time premarital agreement was signed. Wife did not show premarital agreement was unconscionable.

2005—*Winchester v. McCue*, 91 Conn. App. 721, 882 A.2d 143.

Prenuptial agreement upheld where wife waived right to husband's income/alimony;

financial circumstances at dissolution were not beyond the contemplation of the parties.

1996—*Elgar v. Elgar*, 238 Conn. 839, 679 A.2d 937.

New York law applied in upholding the validity of the premarital agreement.

1980—*Crews v. Crews*, 107 Conn. App. 279, 945 A.2d 502.

Trial court improperly relied on equitable principles rather than contract law when invalidating premarital agreement.

1980—*McHugh v. McHugh*, 181 Conn. 482, 436 A.2d 8.

Antenuptial agreements relating to the property of the parties, and more specifically, to the rights of the parties to that property upon the dissolution of the marriage, are generally enforceable where three conditions are satisfied: (1) the contract was validly entered into; (2) its terms do not violate statute or public policy; and (3) the circumstances of the parties at the time the marriage is dissolved are not so beyond the contemplation of the parties at the time the contract was entered into as to cause its enforcement to work injustice. Applies to premarital agreements entered into before the enactment of Conn. Gen. Stat. § 46b-36g.

[2] Choice of Law

1996—*Elgar v. Elgar*, 238 Conn. 839, 679 A.2d 937.

New York law applied in upholding the validity of the premarital agreement.

[3] Content of Agreement

[a] Unconscionability

2021—*Grabe v. Hokin*, 341 Conn. 360, 267 A.3d 145.

It is not unconscionable to enforce a prenuptial agreement merely because there is an extraordinary disparity between the incomes or standards of living of the custodial parent and the children, on the one hand, and the noncustodial parent, on the other hand.

2020—*Bevilacqua v. Bevilacqua*, 201 Conn. App. 261, 242 A.3d 542.

The trial court properly awarded alimony to the plaintiff despite the mutual spousal support waiver in the parties' premarital agreement. The trial court properly concluded that enforcing this provision of the premarital agreement would be unconscionable because the plaintiff had been in an accident that impaired her ability to work full time, a scenario far beyond the parties' contemplation at the time they executed the agreement.

2013—*Schoenborn v. Schoenborn*, 144 Conn. App. 846, 74 A.3d 482.

Trial court properly concluded that a premarital agreement was not unconscionable.

2011—*Reizfeld v. Reizfeld*, 125 Conn. App. 782, 13 A.3d 1103.

Equitable concerns about whether the agreement was a good bargain do not enter the analysis on unconscionability.

2010—*McKenna v. Delente*, 123 Conn. App. 146, 2 A.3d 38.

Trial court did not improperly conclude that New York premarital agreement was enforceable when defendant had not asserted unconscionability as a special defense prior to the trial.

[b] Financial Disclosure

2017—*Chang v. Chang*, 170 Conn. App. 822, 155 A.3d 1272.

Defendants incorrect statement that assets were too speculative to value resulted in invalidation of prenuptial agreement.

Financial awards to the plaintiff would have been permitted even if prenuptial agreement was valid; prenuptial agreement was silent as to alimony.

2011—*Oldani v. Oldani*, 132 Conn. App. 609, 34 A.3d 407.

Premarital agreement unenforceable because plaintiff failed to disclose his income adequately, had not expressly disclosed net income anywhere on his financial disclosure attached to the premarital agreement, and did not disclose a formula for determining his income prior to execution.

1996—*Elgar v. Elgar*, 238 Conn. 839, 679 A.2d 937.

Adequate financial disclosure, waiver of a right to an attorney and no evidence of coercion were sufficient to uphold a premarital agreement.

[4] Amendment or Revocation of Premarital Agreement

2010—*McKenna v. Delente*, 123 Conn. App. 146, 2 A.3d 38.

Waiver of spousal benefits under pension plan was valid, both under premarital agreement and later modification of that contract.

[5] Enforcement of Agreement

2023—*Tilsen v. Benson*, 347 Conn. 758, 299 A.3d 1096.

Trial court properly denied Plaintiff's motion to enforce as a premarital agreement provisions of the parties' ketubah, which provided for a 50/50 division of the marital property and relieved Plaintiff from the obligation to pay alimony to Defendant, because the establishment clause of the First Amendment precluded the relief Plaintiff sought. Since the parties' ketubah was facially silent as to each spouse's support obligations in the event of dissolution of the marriage, the trial court would have had to determine those obligations from external sources concerning Jewish law and interpretations provided by the parties' respective experts regarding such law as it pertains to alimony and property division. If the trial court had given effect to the parties' ketubah, it would been required to discern and enforce what Jewish law requires with respect to property division and financial support upon dissolution.

Further, Plaintiff failed to prove that the trial court's decision not to enforce the ketubah violated his rights under the free exercise clause of the First Amendment. Considering the parties' disagreement as to what Jewish law required in their case given the breadth of the ketubah's language, making this determination as to the applicable Jewish law would have risked a violation of Defendant's free exercise rights in the name of protecting those of Plaintiff. Enforcement of the vaguely worded ketubah in the guise of protecting Plaintiff's free exercise rights would have put the trial court in an establishment clause dilemma.

2022—*Seder v. Errato*, 211 Conn. App. 167, 272 A.3d 252.

Trial court did not abuse its discretion by excluding defendant's proposed exhibit and not enforcing enforce the parties' alleged premarital agreement. Defendant did not have a copy of the alleged agreement; his proposed exhibit was an unsigned, undated, and unfinished boilerplate premarital agreement form downloaded from an online legal publisher. The court found significant portions of his trial testimony not to be credible and the credibility of both parties' testimony during the motion in limine regarding the proposed exhibit was wanting. As the fact finder, the trial court had discretion to determine the amount of weight, if any, to give to defendant's testimony. The evidence amply supported the court's finding that defendant had not established the terms of the alleged premarital agreement.

2022—*Ostapowicz v. Wisniewski*, 210 Conn. App. 401, 270 A.3d 145.

Although defendant had not specifically requested enforcement of the parties' premarital agreement as required by Conn. Practice Book § 25-2A, the trial court still subject matter jurisdiction under Conn. Gen. Stat. § 46b-1 to determine defendant's separate property and enforce the premarital agreement.

2012—*Brody v. Brody*, 136 Conn. App. 773, 51 A.3d 1121.

No abuse of discretion where trial court awarded lump sum alimony secured by title in real property where premarital agreement precluded equitable division of the property.

2011—*Oldani v. Oldani*, 132 Conn. App. 609, 34 A.3d 407.

The appellate court held the trial court improperly determined that the parties' prenuptial agreement was enforceable, the husband having failed to provide the wife with a fair and reasonable disclosure of his income before the execution of the agreement.

2011—*Reizfeld v. Reizfeld*, 125 Conn. App. 782, 13 A.3d 1103.

A premarital agreement that precluded either party from seeking "payment for liabilities from the other" in a dissolution action was unambiguous, and it precluded the court from awarding attorney's fees.

2010—*Crews v. Crews*, 295 Conn. 153, 989 A.2d 1060.

Party seeking to challenge enforceability of premarital agreement "bears a heavy burden" and appellate court properly applied plenary review in addressing enforcement of premarital agreement.

1996—*Elgar v. Elgar*, 238 Conn. 839, 679 A.2d 937.

Premarital agreement held enforceable even though it was given to wife two days before the wedding.

1993—*Ashton v. Ashton*, 31 Conn. App. 736, 627 A.2d 943.

Premarital agreement not enforced where financial circumstances of husband changed dramatically during the marriage.

§ 5.02 Postmarital or Postnuptial Agreements

2022—*O.A. v. J.A.*, 342 Conn. 45, 268 A.3d 642.

Trial court did not err in awarding plaintiff pendente lite alimony, attorney's fees, and expert fees without first determining the enforceability of the parties' postnuptial agreement. The determination of the validity of a postnuptial agreement may be made when the case is tried on the merits. The parties' postnuptial agreement addressed only alimony awarded upon the formal termination of the marriage, not pendente lite alimony, and did not address payment of the parties' attorney's fees and expert fees during a dissolution proceeding. Gen Stat. § 46b-83 authorized the trial court to award pendente lite alimony, after considering the factors in Gen. Stat. § 46b-82, to provide for plaintiff throughout the duration of the case. The court also had broad discretion to order pendente lite attorney's fees or expert fees if the circumstances require. Further, the valuation of defendant's assets is a necessary step in determining the validity of the parties' postnuptial agreement. Given the complexity of defendant's finances, valuing his assets could take a long time. If the trial court were required to determine the validity of the postnuptial agreement before awarding pendente lite alimony and fees, plaintiff would not have the means to support herself, hire an attorney, or retain an expert to analyze defendant's finances.

2020—*Yun Zhou v. Hao Zhang*, 334 Conn. 601, 223 A.3d 775.

Supreme Court held that the trial court correctly determined that the parties' postnuptial agreement was enforceable because it was fair and equitable at the time of execution and was not unconscionable at the time of dissolution. Plaintiff wife's decision to enter into the postnuptial agreement was voluntary and not the product of duress. The evidence supported the trial court's finding that she understood her rights and obligations under the postnuptial agreement notwithstanding its length and complexity, as she was highly educated, had independent counsel during the negotiation and execution of that agreement, and acknowledged in the agreement her complete understanding of the effects of the agreement. Plaintiff failed to identify a change in circumstances since the execution of the agreement that would warrant a finding that its enforceable at the time of dissolution would be unconscionable.

2016—*Antonucci v. Antonucci*, 164 Conn. App. 95, 138 A.3d 297.

An agreement between two parties and one spouse's parent, signed during the marriage, is not a post nuptial agreement. A post nuptial agreement is an agreement between two spouses. The court set out factors for the remand court to consider when determining whether the contact would be void against public policy.

2011—*Bedrick v. Bedrick*, 300 Conn. 691, 17 A.3d 17.

Postnuptial agreements are valid; however, they require stricter scrutiny than with premarital agreements.

1999—*Wilkes v. Wilkes*, 55 Conn. App. 313, 738 A.2d 758.

Midnuptial agreement upheld where court finds it to be fair and equitable.

CHAPTER 6

SEPARATION AGREEMENTS

SYNOPSIS

§ 6.01 Validity

2014—*Doyle v. Doyle*, 150 Conn. App. 312, 90 A.3d 1024.

Separation agreement and marriage dissolution decree were sufficiently clear and unambiguous to support trial court's refusal to issue a judgment of contempt.

2009—*Perricone v. Perricone*, 292 Conn. 187, 972 A.2d 666.

Separation agreement did not supersede and nullify confidentiality agreement.

1991—*Coscina v. Coscina*, 24 Conn. App. 190, 587 A.2d 159.

Action for declaratory judgment was appropriate to determine meaning of medical insurance clause in separation agreement when divorce was in Haiti.

1989—*Kronholm v. Kronholm*, 16 Conn. App. 124, 547 A.2d 61.

Where rights, duties and obligations are fully stated in a written contract between the parties, the court is obligated to determine the intention of the parties from the language used interpreted in the light of the situation of the parties and the circumstances connected with the transaction.

1989—*Albrecht v. Albrecht*, 19 Conn. App. 146, 562 A.2d 528.

Oral agreement ineffective to modify terms of separation agreement.

1988—*Nelson v. Nelson*, 13 Conn. App. 355, 536 A.2d 985.

Between two possible interpretations of contract, courts prefer the more equitable and rational interpretation.

1984—*Arseniadis v. Arseniadis*, 2 Conn. App. 239, 477 A.2d 152.

Judgment is void when one part of the stipulation is found to be unenforceable.

1982—*Baker v. Baker*, 187 Conn. 315, 445 A.2d 912.

Agreements concealed from court, such as oral agreements not presented at hearing, are void.

1981—*North v. North*, 183 Conn. 35, 438 A.2d 807.

A contract which is subject to a financing contingency may still be a valid contract.

§ 6.02 Content of Agreement; Language; Interpretation

2023—*Simpson v. Simpson*, 222 Conn. App. 466, 306 A.3d 477.

Because the Appellate Court concluded that the trial court had improperly interpreted the parties' separation agreement and reversed and remanded on that basis for a new hearing, it was unnecessary for the Appellate Court to resolve Plaintiff's claim on appeal that the trial court's articulation of its postjudgment orders had improperly changed the calculation of additional child support and alimony set out in the original judgment.

On January 23, 2024, the Connecticut Supreme Court granted an appeal on the following two questions:

"1. Did the Appellate Court err in reversing the trial court's remedial orders on the basis of its erroneous conclusion that the parties' separation agreement clearly and unambiguously relieved the defendant of the obligation to pay supplemental child support and alimony?

"2. Did the Appellate Court err in concluding that the parties' separation agreement clearly and unambiguously relieved the defendant of the obligation to pay supplemental child support and alimony when, inter alia, (a) both parties advanced reasonable and plausible interpretations of the relevant provisions, (b) the Appellate Court majority failed to give effect to the intent of the parties as expressed in the agreement, (c) the concurring and dissenting judge correctly concluded that the agreement was ambiguous and thus its meaning presented a question of fact for the trial court, and (d) both the majority and the concurring and dissenting judge noted the absence of extrinsic evidence on the issue of the parties' intent, as well as the need for such evidence in order to interpret the agreement?

Simpson v. Simpson, 348 Conn. 942, 307 A.3d 909.

2022—*Mazza v. Mazza*, 216 Conn. App. 285, 285 A.3d 90.

By transforming the funds intended for the plaintiff into nonliquid assets such as real property, the defendant forced the trial court to consider alternative remedies in order to protect the integrity and purpose of the separation agreement.

On January 17, 2024, the Connecticut Supreme Court granted an appeal on the following question:

"Did the Appellate Court incorrectly conclude that the trial court had properly determined that the parties' separation agreement, which provided that 'the plaintiff [would] receive 50 [percent] of all awards from [the] defendant's workers' compensation suit,' clearly and unambiguously included that portion of such awards representing payment for the defendant's medical expenses, notwithstanding the plaintiff's statement to the trial court when judgment was rendered indicating that she would not be entitled to a share of the workers' compensation payments intended for such medical expenses?"

Mazza v. Mazza, 346 Conn. 904, 287 A.3d 600.

2021—*L.W. v. M.W.*, 208 Conn. App. 497, 266 A.3d 189.

According to the parties' agreement, the defendant's "earned income" was to be the amount reflected on his W-2 and/or 1099 form. This definition of "earned income" contained no reference to business deductions for tax purposes. Therefore, under the terms of the agreement, any deductions made by the defendant for tax reasons was not included.

2018—*LeSueur v. LeSueur*, 186 Conn. App. 431, 199 A.3d 1082.

Trial court, in construing parties' separation agreement, properly determined that the provision governing parties' post-secondary education obligations were not limited to the cost of in state tuition at a school which is part of the Connecticut state university system.

2018—*Hirschfeld v. Machinist*, 181 Conn. App. 309, 186 A.3d 771.

Ambiguous agreement led to hearing where the prior counsel testified on the issue of intent of the parties.

2018—*Schimenti v. Schimenti*, 181 Conn. App. 385, 186 A.3d 739.

Language in a separation agreement found to be ambiguous [meaning of country club initiation fee] required a hearing to ascertain the intent of the parties "a fact bound task."

2016—*Mettler v. Mettler*, 165 Conn. App. 829, 140 A.3d 370.

The use of the phrase "agreed-upon" in relation to children's expenses was found to be ambiguous.

2016—*McTiernan v. McTiernan*, 164 Conn. App. 805, 138 A.3d 935.

The definition of gross annual earned income from employment was ambiguous.

2016—*Fazio v. Fazio*, 162 Conn. App. 236, 131 A.3d 1162.

The court erred in not finding the cohabitation language ambiguous where the agreement provided that alimony would be payable to the wife until cohabitation "pursuant to" Conn. Gen. Stat. § 46b-85(b).

2014—*Yomtov v. Yomtov*, 152 Conn. App. 355, 98 A.3d 110.

As used in parties' separation agreement, ex-husband's "gross annual income from employment" was the income actually received by ex-husband, and not the income actually received by his limited liability company.

2014—*Hirschfeld v. Machinist*, 151 Conn. App. 414, 95 A.3d 1167.

Wife was not responsible for costs related to refinancing of a line or credit or closing costs and fees in connection with the refinancing where there was no such obligation contained within the clear and unambiguous language of the relevant portions of the separation agreement.

2014—*Doyle v. Doyle*, 150 Conn. App. 312, 90 A.3d 1024.

Trial court did not abuse its discretion in applying legal principals of contract construction, rather than relying upon child support guidelines, in determining intent of parties as to payment of children's medical expenses under separation agreement.

2013—*Tow v. Tow*, 142 Conn. App. 45, 64 A.3d 128.

No abuse of discretion where the court denied a motion for contempt and where the parties lived together post judgment and the separation agreement called for direct payments of alimony and child support to the wife but the husband made deposits to a joint account to which the wife had free access.

2013—*Malpeso v. Malpeso*, 140 Conn. App. 783, 60 A.3d 380.

Trial court improperly determined that a separation agreement precluded modification of child support where agreement provided for unallocated support and precluded modification of "alimony" unless certain circumstances occurred.

2012—*Hirschfeld v. Machinist*, 137 Conn. App. 690, 50 A.3d 324.

Trial court improperly interpreted a provision in separation agreement to restrict the plaintiff's ability to obtain documents relating to the defendant's earned income where the purpose of the contract language was to require disclosure of documents to corroborate earned income, which formed the basis of a percentage-based support order.

2011—*Loso v. Loso*, 132 Conn. App. 257, 31 A.3d 830.

Educational support provision in the parties' separation agreement was clear and unambiguous.

2011—*Hirschfeld v. Machinist*, 131 Conn. App. 352, 29 A.3d 159.

Payment of "shelter expenses" under the parties' separation agreement included maintaining a swimming pool at the former marital home.

2010—*Creatura v. Creatura*, 122 Conn. App. 47, 998 A.2d 798.

Appellate Court rejected defendant's reading of a college education provision in separation agreement and found provision unambiguous.

2009—*Davis v. Davis*, 112 Conn. App. 56, 962 A.2d 140.

Trial court improperly concluded that mutual release provision in separation agreement barred a tort action for intentional infliction of emotional distress.

2009—*Isham v. Isham*, 292 Conn. 170, 972 A.2d 228.

Trial court improperly determined that an oral separation agreement was unambiguous, and it incorrectly excluded extrinsic intent evidence.

2009—*Taylor v. Taylor*, 117 Conn. App. 229, 978 A.2d 538.

Court correctly interpreted "second look" provision as permitting *de novo* post-judgment review of alimony, rather than on substantial change.

2009—*Cifaldi v. Cifaldi*, 118 Conn. App. 325, 983 A.2d 293.

Trial court should have fashioned a post-judgment order to effectuate division of pension benefits in accordance with parties' separation agreement, even though two QDROs had not been implemented.

2008—*Sutherland v. Sutherland*, 107 Conn. App. 1, 944 A.2d 395.

A clause that precluded oral modification of the separation agreement did not preclude modification of support under Conn. Gen. Stat. § 46b-86.

2008—*Dougherty v. Dougherty*, 109 Conn. App. 33, 950 A.2d 592.

Separation agreement had divided Indiana public employees' retirement fund that could not be divided by QDRO.

2007—*Monette v. Monette*, 102 Conn. App. 1, 924 A.2d 894.

Plaintiff failed to satisfy a condition precedent set forth in the separation agreement before seeking to modify child support.

1999—*DeMaria v. DeMaria*, 247 Conn. 715, 724 A.2d 1088.

Court may read into separation agreement requirements of change in financial circumstances in cohabitation case even in absence of statutory reference.

1992—*Greenburg v. Greenburg*, 26 Conn. App. 591, 602 A.2d 1056.

A term not expressly included will not be read into a contract unless it arises by necessary implication from the provisions of the instrument.

1991—*Coscina v. Coscina*, 24 Conn. App. 190, 587 A.2d 159.

Where a clause in the separation agreement is ambiguous, the court must ascertain parties' intent.

1991—*Mignosa v. Mignosa*, 25 Conn. App. 210, 594 A.2d 15.

When a dissolution of marriage is granted following a decree of legal separation, court must determine whether prior separation agreement is fair and equitable in light of the circumstances existing at the time of the dissolution.

1989—*Baldwin v. Baldwin*, 19 Conn. App. 420, 562 A.2d 581.

Intent of parties is determined by a fair and reasonable construction of the written words considering the circumstances of the execution of the writing and the object of the parties.

1989—*Albrecht v. Albrecht*, 19 Conn. App. 146, 562 A.2d 528.

Counsel fee provisions in separation agreement supersedes Conn. Gen. Stat. § 46b-62.

1988—*Nelson v. Nelson*, 13 Conn. App. 355, 536 A.2d 985.

Between two possible interpretations of contract, courts prefer the more equitable and rational interpretation.

1987—*Sweeny v. Sweeny*, 9 Conn. App. 498, 519 A.2d 1237.

Interpretation of clause in separation agreement is a search for the intent of the parties.

1986—*Masters v. Masters*, 201 Conn. 50, 513 A.2d 104.

Clause in separation agreement tainted by fraud was severable.

1985—*Klein v. Klein*, 3 Conn. App. 421, 488 A.2d 1288.

Trial court denied former husband's motion to modify alimony payments because he had not sustained his burden of proving cohabitation for four continuous months as set forth in parties' separation agreement.

§ 6.03 Incorporation of Agreement into Final Decree

2003—*Breiter v. Breiter*, 80 Conn. App. 332, 835 A.2d 111.

An agreement between divorced parties that is incorporated into a dissolution decree should be regarded as a contract. In interpreting contract items, the intent of the parties is to be ascertained by a fair and reasonable construction of the written words and that the language used must be accorded its common, natural, and ordinary meaning and usage. Where the language of the contract is clear and unambiguous, the contract is to be given effect according to its terms.

1995—*Zadravecz v. Zadravecz*, 39 Conn. App. 28, 664 A.2d 303.

Stipulated judgment is in the nature of a contract and will be interpreted as a contract.

1992—*Greenburg v. Greenburg*, 26 Conn. App. 591, 602 A.2d 1056.

Judgment incorporating a separation agreement is construed as a contract.

1986—*Pickman v. Pickman*, 6 Conn. App. 271, 505 A.2d 4.

The court held that the court properly determined that the agreement was fair and equitable and properly incorporated the agreement and that consideration was not necessary.

1985—*Guille v. Guille*, 196 Conn. 260, 492 A.2d 175.

Settlement agreements incorporated into dissolution judgments should be interpreted consistently with accepted contract principles.

1985—*Marsico v. Marsico*, 195 Conn. 491, 488 A.2d 1248.

Where the provisions of a settlement agreement have been incorporated by reference in the judgment, it is necessary to ascertain the intent of the parties as expressed in the language of the agreement rather than to construe the language of the decree itself.

1984—*Bronson v. Bronson*, 1 Conn. App. 337, 471 A.2d 977.

Where an agreement is incorporated by reference in a dissolution decree rather than its terms being included in the decree itself, the decree should be construed by ascertaining the intent expressed in the language of the agreement.

1979—*Calig v. Schrank*, 179 Conn. 283, 426 A.2d 276.

Separation agreement executed in New Jersey was incorporated into parties' divorce decree but court held stipulation that the law of New Jersey controlled its construction could not be relied upon in an action for reimbursement that had no connection with New Jersey.

§ 6.04 Modification, Alteration, Change or Amendment Generally

2024—*L.K. v. K.K.*, 226 Conn. App. 279, 318 A.3d 243.

In a post-judgment dissolution matter, the trial court did not lack subject matter jurisdiction to enter orders regarding support for the parties' adult child because the defendant's child support obligation stems from a written agreement that he voluntarily entered into with the plaintiff, which was deemed fair and equitable and was approved by the court. To the extent the parties' agreement provides for postmajority support for their children, trial courts have jurisdiction under Conn. Gen. Stat. § 46b-66 to enforce written provisions of dissolution agreements, incorporated into court orders, for the care, education, maintenance or support of a child beyond the age of eighteen.

2022—*Birkhold v. Birkhold*, 343 Conn. 786, 276 A.3d 414.

Trial court did not abuse its discretion by modifying the alimony provision of the parties' separation agreement and modifying the amount Husband was to pay Wife. Trial court based the modified award not only on Husband's past gross income but also on his long, successful career as a senior executive, broker, and consultant and on the fact that he had moved to a state with no income tax.

2022—*Dolan v. Dolan*, 213 Conn. App. 112, 277 A.3d 829.

Trial court did not abuse its discretion by modifying the definition of "pre-tax compensation from employment" set out in the parties' separation agreement because the plain language of the agreement demonstrated that the parties intended such a modification be done in accordance with the spirit of their agreement to ensure fairness, and not be done in accordance with the criteria of Conn. Gen. Stat. § 46b-82. Judgment affirmed.

2021—*Bologna v. Bologna*, 208 Conn. App. 218, 264 A.3d 598.

The trial court did not improperly modify the parties' separation agreement when it denied the plaintiff's post-dissolution motion for clarification of terms of the separation agreement regarding the marital home. The trial court's order effectuated the terms of the existing separation agreement to which the parties previously had agreed and which was incorporated into the dissolution judgment. By agreement, the parties had deviated from their separation agreement by not selling their home within the specified period of time and the plaintiff continuing to pay the mortgage. They could have but did not also agree to modify the buyout provisions, which were the subject of the plaintiff's motion.

2020—*Brown v. Brown*, 199 Conn. App. 134, 235 A.3d 555.

The trial court improperly modified the parties' separation agreement by granting the defendant's motion for reimbursement of unallocated support and ordering the plaintiff to repay the defendant a portion of the unallocated support he paid her in 2015, the year she remarried. The relevant section of the parties' separation agreement was clear and unambiguous. If they had intended to prorate the unallocated support the plaintiff received for seven months in 2015, any claimed overpayment would have been taken into account and placed on the record at the time they stipulated to defendant's child support obligation in 2016.

2016—*Malpeso v. Malpeso*, 165 Conn. App. 151, 138 A.3d 1069.

In a case where the decree precludes modification until a certain key date, the court had jurisdiction and authority to modify alimony when a motion had been filed prior to the key date, but the hearing took place after the key date.

2016—*Morera v. Thurber*, 162 Conn. App. 261, 131 A.3d 1155.

The trial court erroneously failed to hold a hearing on a request for leave on a motion for modification.

2014—*Doyle v. Doyle*, 150 Conn. App. 312, 90 A.3d 1024.

Trial court did not abuse its discretion in applying legal principals of contract construction, rather than relying upon child support guidelines, in determining intent of parties as to payment of children's medical expenses under separation agreement.

2012—*Nassra v. Nassra*, 139 Conn. App. 661, 56 A.3d 970.

Post-judgment order requiring a party to take steps to withdraw a lawsuit was an improper modification of the parties' separation agreement where the agreement only required the party to instruct his counsel to withdraw the lawsuit.

2009—*Auerbach v. Auerbach*, 113 Conn. App. 318, 966 A.2d 292.

Alleged condition precedent in separation agreement did not deprive trial court of authority to modify alimony and child support. Agreement stated payor could seek to modify if annual income fell below $475,000.

2008—*Sutherland v. Sutherland*, 107 Conn. App. 1, 944 A.2d 395.

A clause that precluded oral modification of the separation agreement did not preclude modification of support under Conn. Gen. Stat. § 46b-86.

1992—*Greenburg v. Greenburg*, 26 Conn. App. 591, 602 A.2d 1056.

Court cannot change or vary the construction and legal effect of a contract because the terms are inconvenient or even unreasonable.

1990—*DeMatteo v. DeMatteo*, 21 Conn. App. 582, 575 A.2d 243.

When agreement was silent on issue of who gets tax refunds, the court must determine the intent of the parties.

1989—*Albrecht v. Albrecht*, 19 Conn. App. 146, 562 A.2d 528.

A provision of a separation agreement precluding modification absent a writing precludes the parties, but not a court, from modifying such an agreement without a writing. Oral agreement ineffective to modify terms of separation agreement.

1988—*Nelson v. Nelson*, 13 Conn. App. 355, 536 A.2d 985.

Where the text of an agreement reasonably allows for varying interpretations, whether by the inadvertence or design of the draftsman, the need for judicial construction cannot, and may not, be avoided.

1987—*Sweeny v. Sweeny*, 9 Conn. App. 498, 519 A.2d 1237.

Clause in agreement calling for a reduction in alimony does not require court to apply statutory criteria, but to infer parties' intent.

1985—*Klein v. Klein*, 3 Conn. App. 421, 488 A.2d 1288.

Court cannot create a new agreement by disregarding the actual words.

1983—*Sands v. Sands*, 188 Conn. 98, 448 A.2d 822.

Court has the power to accept, reject, or modify.

1982—*Costello v. Costello*, 186 Conn. 773, 443 A.2d 1282.

The court has the power to change an incomplete agreement.

§ 6.05 Enforcement of Agreement

2023—*John Hancock Life Ins. Co. v. Curtin*, 219 Conn. App. 613, 295 A.3d 1055.

In an interpleader action brought by an insurance company to determine the distribution of the proceeds of a decedent's insurance policy, the trial court properly granted summary judgment in favor of the estate. The decedent's separation agreement with his ex-wife required him to maintain a $500,000 life insurance policy with his ex-wife as the primary beneficiary and his daughter as the secondary beneficiary. The separation agreement also provided that his failure to maintain such life insurance would constitute a claim and charge against his estate by his ex-wife in the face value amount of $500,000. The decedent breached the separation agreement by designating his estate as the primary beneficiary and naming no secondary beneficiary. The equitable remedy decedent's ex-wife and daughter sought in this interpleader action was contrary to and inconsistent with the remedy provided for in the separation agreement. The trial court properly concluded that, as a matter of law, the estate was entitled to summary judgment.

2022—*Scott v. Scott*, 215 Conn. App. 24, 282 A.3d 470.

Trial court did not abuse its discretion by holding that Husband was not required to reimburse Wife for her private college coach because she did not act in good faith with respect to the expense she unilaterally incurred for the coach, as required by their separation agreement. Wife's $51,500 expenditure for the coach was extravagant and unnecessary.

2014—*Watkins v. Watkins*, 152 Conn. App. 99, 96 A.3d 1264.

The mutual releases provision in a separation agreement precluded a negligence action based on behavior occurring during the marriage because the release provision was not ambiguous and therefore only susceptible to one reasonable interpretation.

2003—*Bijur v. Bijur*, 79 Conn. App. 752, 831 A.2d 824.

Party obligated to continue paying monthly periodic alimony under separation agreement even though party had retired.

1991—*Coscina v. Coscina*, 24 Conn. App. 190, 587 A.2d 159.

Action for declaratory judgment was appropriate to determine meaning of medical insurance clause in separation agreement when divorce was in Haiti.

1987—*Goold v. Goold*, 11 Conn. App. 268, 527 A.2d 696.

Clause in separation agreement awarding counsel fees if one party breached agreement requires fees to be ordered without regard to Conn. Gen. Stat. § 46b-62.

1986—*Niles v. Niles*, 9 Conn. App. 240, 518 A.2d 932.

Court can fashion an appropriate remedy to protect the integrity of the original consent judgment.

1985—*LaVigne v. LaVigne*, 3 Conn. App. 423, 488 A.2d 1290.

College education provision enforceable by civil suit in damages.

§ 6.06 Standing

2018—*Hamburg v. Hamburg*, 182 Conn. App. 332, 193 A.3d 51.

Counsel for deceased plaintiff's estate did not have standing to pursue descendant's claims against the defendant. However, the defendant's daughter had standing to pursue the descendant's financial claims that related to the daughter.

CHAPTER 7

GROUNDS FOR DISSOLUTION OF MARRIAGE

SYNOPSIS

§ 7.01 Grounds for Dissolution—No Fault

2020—*Nietupski v. Del Castillo*, 196 Conn. App. 31, 228 A.3d 1053.

The trial court did not violate the Free Exercise Clause of the First Amendment by rendering a judgment of marital dissolution pursuant to Conn. Gen. Stat. § 46b-40(c)(1). The statute does not in any manner infringe on the plaintiff husband's right to exercise his religious beliefs merely because it permitted defendant wife to obtain a divorce from him against his wishes.

1985—*Eversman v. Eversman*, 4 Conn. App. 611, 496 A.2d 210.

Conn. Gen. Stat. § 46b-40(c)(1) provides that a decree of dissolution of a marriage shall be granted upon a finding that the marriage has broken down irretrievably; the determination of whether a breakdown of a marriage is irretrievable is a question of fact to be determined by the trial court.

1983—*Sweet v. Sweet*, 190 Conn. 657, 462 A.2d 1031.

In accordance with Conn. Gen. Stat. § 46b-51(a), if the parties execute a written stipulation that their marriage has broken down irretrievably and submit an agreement concerning the custody, care, education, visitation, maintenance or support of their children and concerning alimony and disposition of property, then the court must make a finding that the marriage has irretrievably broken down.

1982—*Carpenter v. Carpenter*, 188 Conn. 736, 453 A.2d 1151.

Trial court stated that in making the awards it considered the finding that the parties were equally at fault for the irretrievable breakdown.

1980—*Posada v. Posada*, 179 Conn. 568, 427 A.2d 406.

Where the wife argued the trial court should have considered the causes for the dissolution of marriage, the court disagreed stating that no fault divorce does not mean that the causes of the marital breakup are always irrelevant, but it does mean that the determining cause is not crucial to the judicial administration of matrimonial affairs.

1979—*Joy v. Joy*, 178 Conn. 254, 423 A.2d 895.

The legislature could rationally conclude that public policy requires an accommodation to the unfortunate reality that a marital relationship may terminate in fact without regard to the fault of either marital partner, and that such a relationship should therefore be dissoluble in law upon a judicial determination of irretrievable breakdown.

§ 7.02 Fault and Cause of Breakdown

2020—*Al-Fikey v. Obaiah*, 196 Conn. App. 13, 228 A.3d 668.

Trial court did not err in finding that defendant husband was at fault for the marriage breakdown because he left the family home without explanation to live with his mother in another country and ultimately lived separately from plaintiff wife and their children.

2018—*Conroy v. Idlibi*, 183 Conn. App. 460, 193 A.3d 663.

Trial court properly balanced evidence of the plaintiff's alleged affair with evidence of the defendant's controlling nature and allegations of physical abuse in finding that neither party was more at fault for the marital breakdown.

2003—*DiVito v. DiVito*, 77 Conn. App. 124, 822 A.2d 294.

Trial court properly considered husband's fault for breakdown of marriage due to his affair.

1989—*Lawler v. Lawler*, 16 Conn. App. 193, 547 A.2d 89.

Despite the defendant's belief that the marriage could be saved, the plaintiff was continually deceitful to her and was contemptuous of her ambitions, endeavors and emotional state.

1987—*Cuneo v. Cuneo*, 12 Conn. App. 702, 533 A.2d 1226.

The husband's physical and mental abuse of the wife led to the marital breakdown.

1987—*Debowsky v. Debowsky*, 12 Conn. App. 525, 532 A.2d 591.

Plaintiff made no financial or moral contribution and was sole cause for dissolution.

1986—*Carter v. Carter*, 8 Conn. App. 356, 512 A.2d 979.

In fixing the nature and value of the property, if any, to be assigned, the court shall consider the cause for the dissolution of the marriage.

1984—*Vaiuso v. Vaiuso*, 2 Conn. App. 141, 477 A.2d 678.

Husband's refusal to have children ground for divorce.

1983—*Sands v. Sands*, 188 Conn. 98, 448 A.2d 822.

Relative fault of parties was factor in breakdown.

1983—*Devino v. Devino*, 190 Conn. 36, 458 A.2d 692.

Finding that it was the plaintiff, because of his indifference and lack of cooperation and affection, who caused the marriage to break down irretrievably.

1982—*Robinson v. Robinson*, 187 Conn. 70, 444 A.2d 234.

A spouse whose conduct has contributed substantially to the breakdown of the marriage should not expect to receive financial kudos for his or her misconduct.

1982—*Beede v. Beede*, 186 Conn. 191, 440 A.2d 283.

Court found that the marriage had broken down irretrievably because the defendant committed adultery. There was nothing in the record to suggest that the trial court's awards were punitive because of the husband's adultery.

1981—*Venuti v. Venuti*, 185 Conn. 156, 440 A.2d 878.

The trial court did not err in finding that adultery was not the cause of the breakdown of the marriage. The court concluded that there was no basis for the trial court to have considered any adultery by the wife in making its award of alimony and counsel fees.

§ 7.03 Willful Desertion for One Year

1939—*McCurry v. McCurry*, 126 Conn. 175, 10 A.2d 365.

The elements of a cause of action on the ground of desertion are (1) cessation from cohabitation; (2) an intention on the part of the absenting party not to resume it; (3) the absence of the other party's consent; and (4) the absence of justification.

§ 7.04 Intolerable Cruelty

2023—*Buchenholz v. Buchenholz*, 221 Conn. App. 132, 300 A.3d 1233.

Trial court did not amend Plaintiff's complaint to allege intolerable cruelty as the ground for dissolution. Based on the evidence in the record, the court dissolved the parties' marriage pursuant to Conn. Gen. Stat. § 46b-40(c)(1) because the marriage had broken down irretrievably as result of Defendant's abusive behavior toward Plaintiff. Defendant's behavior was the primary cause of the breakdown. Nothing in the court's decision demonstrates that the court amended the complaint to allege intolerable cruelty pursuant to Conn. Gen. Stat. § 46b-40(c)(8). The court did not state that it dissolved the parties' marriage on the ground of intolerable cruelty.

1990—*Stephens v. Stephens*, 22 Conn. App. 337, 577 A.2d 303.

Emotional and physical abuse found as a cause of the breakdown.

1984—*Russo v. Russo*, 1 Conn. App. 604, 474 A.2d 473.

Where a defendant engages in acts of cruelty, making the continuance of the marital relationship unbearable, the court may conclude that the cause of the irretrievable breakdown of the marriage was the intolerable cruelty of the defendant.

1983—*Garrison v. Garrison*, 190 Conn. 173, 460 A.2d 945.

Trial court reasonably concluded that the husband's actions constituted intolerable cruelty because the trial court's finding that the husband's behavior constituted a continuing course of conduct was clearly supported by the record.

1980—*Koizim v. Koizim*, 181 Conn. 492, 435 A.2d 1030.

Court rendered a judgment dissolving the marriage based on intolerable cruelty on the part of the husband.

1980—*Hollingsworth v. Hollingsworth*, 180 Conn. 212, 429 A.2d 463.

Wife failed to establish a cause of action based on intolerable cruelty.

§ 7.05 Mental Illness

2011—*Corriveau v. Corriveau*, 126 Conn. App. 231, 11 A.3d 176.

Trial court has no authority sua sponte to address the competency of a self-represented party during dissolution proceedings.

1992—*Henin v. Henin*, 26 Conn. App. 386, 601 A.2d 550.

Spouse's failure to seek help for her mental illness caused the breakdown of the marriage.

1983—*Wolk v. Wolk*, 191 Conn. 328, 464 A.2d 780.

Emotional instability was cause of breakdown.

CHAPTER 8

ALIMONY

SYNOPSIS

§ 8.01 Alimony Generally

2024—*Hallock v. Hallock*, 228 Conn. App. 81, 324 A.3d 193.

Trial court did not apply an improper legal standard to the defendant's claim for alimony and the division of the marital property. The court properly cited and applied Conn. Gen. Stat. § 46b-81 and Conn. Gen. Stat. § 46b-82 in issuing its financial orders regarding alimony and the distribution of property.

2023—*Renstrup v. Renstrup*, 217 Conn. App. 252, 287 A.3d 1095.

The trial court failed to consider the criteria for alimony set forth in Conn. Gen. Stat. § 46b-82(a). Instead it improperly ordered an open-ended, uncapped percentage based supplemental alimony award to the wife that was based at least in part on the court's clearly erroneous findings of fact regarding the husband's annual salary and bonus. The appellate court reversed the supplemental alimony order and remanded the issue for a new trial.

2018—*Cohen v. Cohen*, 327 Conn. 485, 176 A.3d 92.

It may be a legitimate purpose of an alimony order to permit a supported spouse to share in the supporting spouse's standard of living after the divorce pursuant to *Dan v. Dan.*

Trial court was not required to presume the exclusive purpose of the original award was to permit the supported spouse to maintain the same standard of living she enjoyed during the marriage where the supported spouse was trying to reinstate a percentage provision of alimony.

Trial court properly considered extrinsic evidence and took judicial notice of the defendant's financial affidavit in the court file from the time of the divorce to shed light on the underlying purpose of the original alimony order.

2016—*Keller v. Keller*, 167 Conn. App. 138, 142 A.3d 1197.

Trial court properly used net income in determining financial orders.

2005—*Greco v. Greco*, 275 Conn. 348, 880 A.2d 872.

It was abuse of discretion and an incorrect application of law by the trial to court to base financial orders on the gross income rather than net income.

2003—*Kiniry v. Kiniry*, 79 Conn. App. 378, 830 A.2d 364.

Appellate court affirmed award of $40,000 per month for five years and $20,000 per month plus percentage of income for five years noting that, although the trial court made no specific finding that Husband had significant borrowing power, there was ample evidence from which the trial court could infer, and imply in its memorandum of decision, that the husband had significant borrowing power.

2002—*Clements v. Jones*, 71 Conn. App. 688, 803 A.2d 378.

Periodic payments are not automatically alimony unless the court specifically says they are.

2001—*Solomon v. Solomon*, 67 Conn. App. 91, 787 A.2d 4.

Ex-husband's claim for alimony properly denied.

2001—*Tevolini v. Tevolini*, 66 Conn. App. 16, 783 A.2d 1157.

Where alimony is in issue, trial court cannot deny plaintiff's right to be heard.

1998—*Sands v. Sands*, 188 Conn. 98, 448 A.2d 822.

Alimony can be awarded even if one party does not seek it and parties had an agreement to the contrary.

1997—*Wiegand v. Wiegand*, 129 Conn. App. 526, 21 A.3d 489.

Failure to award "some form of alimony" was an abuse of discretion when party was 55 years old, unemployed, ill, possessed few assets, and had expired unemployment benefits.

1991—*Berg v. Berg*, 24 Conn. App. 509, 589 A.2d 885.

Obligations to maintain house expenses are by way of support and not a property assignment.

1990—*Cabrera v. Cabrera*, 23 Conn. App. 330, 580 A.2d 1227.

Court has the duty to shape its orders so that those who are economically at risk are given protection.

1989—*Kronholm v. Kronholm*, 16 Conn. App. 124, 547 A.2d 61.

An award which is indefinite as to both amount and duration is alimony.

1988—*Pasqua v. Pasqua*, 16 Conn. App. 278, 547 A.2d 556.

Order, which defendant could not pay, on assumption defendant might be able to pay someday, was error.

1986—*Carter v. Carter*, 8 Conn. App. 356, 512 A.2d 979.

Financial orders are not to be a reward or a punishment.

1984—*Phares v. Phares*, 1 Conn. App. 172, 469 A.2d 791.

Court has the authority to order security for payment of alimony.

1983—*Brown v. Brown*, 190 Conn. 345, 460 A.2d 1287.

Child support award may not be used to disguise alimony awards to the custodial parent.

1983—*Sweet v. Sweet*, 190 Conn. 657, 462 A.2d 1031.

Court has the duty to shape its orders so that those who are economically at risk are given protection.

1982—*Weiman v. Weiman*, 188 Conn. 232, 449 A.2d 151.

The purpose of alimony is to meet one's continuing duty to support.

1982—*Tutalo v. Tutalo*, 187 Conn. 249, 445 A.2d 598.

Trial court was not required to show what importance it had assigned to the various statutory factors in making its award.

1981—*Scherr v. Scherr*, 183 Conn. 366, 439 A.2d 375.

Trial court which sees and hears the parties has broad discretion in making financial awards arising out of marital dissolutions.

1981—*McGinn v. McGinn*, 183 Conn. 512, 441 A.2d 8.

It was within the trial court's discretion to determine issues concerning alimony and child support.

§ 8.02 Pendente Lite Alimony

2016—*Dumbauld v. Dumbauld*, 163 Conn. App. 517, 136 A.3d 669.

The court's alimony order, which ordered that a party pay expenses in excess of his net income and thus required that the party pay alimony out of assets, was an impermissible distribution of marital assets, pendente lite. In this case, the parties had previously used assets to pay their expenses prior to the divorce.

2012—*Lynch v. Lynch*, 135 Conn. App. 40, 43 A.3d 667.

Trial court did not improperly grant retroactive relief on pendente lite motion for modification of alimony.

2011—*Gray v. Gray*, 131 Conn. App. 404, 27 A.3d 1102.

A contempt finding for failure to pay a pendente lite support arrearage which survived an earlier dissolution decree was not an abuse of discretion.

2011—*Bruno v. Bruno*, 31 A.3d 860.

Pendente lite orders terminate upon entry of a decree of dissolution and do not remain in effect during the pendency of the stay resulting from an appeal.

2011—*Gong v. Huang*, 129 Conn. App. 141, 21 A.3d 474.

Resolution of pendent lite motions to modify alimony delayed until dissolution of parties' marriage.

1999—*Milbauer v. Milbauer*, 54 Conn. App. 304, 733 A.2d 907.

Trial court did not abuse discretion in modifying pendente lite award back to date of motion to modify.

1999—*Papa v. Papa*, 55 Conn. App. 47, 737 A.2d 953.

Pendente lite order requiring defendant to pay mortgage payments did not merge with final order.

1998—*Elliott v. Elliott*, 14 Conn. App. 541, 541 A.2d 905.

Alimony pendente lite cannot be modified retroactively.

1995—*Wolf v. Wolf*, 39 Conn. App. 162, 664 A.2d 315.

Order reimbursing spouse for mortgage payments made under a pendente lite, order was an impermissible retroactive modification.

1993—*Dooley v. Dooley*, 32 Conn. App. 863, 632 A.2d 712.

Pendente lite modification of alimony must be based on a substantial change in circumstances.

1990—*Febbroriello v. Febbroriello*, 21 Conn. App. 200, 572 A.2d 1032.

Pendent elite orders terminate once a final judgment is rendered.

1989—*Weinstein v. Weinstein*, 18 Conn. App. 622, 561 A.2d 443.

Court cannot retroactively modify a pendente lite alimony award.

1987—*Seaver v. Seaver*, 10 Conn. App. 134, 521 A.2d 1053.

Trial court is not mandated to consider federal tax implications of its pendente lite financial orders.

1984—*Szilagyi v. Szilagyi*, 3 Conn. App. 25, 484 A.2d 469.

Connecticut unequivocally follows the widely established rule that no modification of alimony or support is to be granted unless there has been a showing of a substantial change in the circumstances of either party thus court denied plaintiff's request to modify pendente lite award.

1983—*Lyddan v. United States*, 721 F.2d 873.

The relevant Department of Treasury regulations permitting a deduction for alimony only apply where the husband and wife are separated and living apart.

§ 8.03 Factors and Evidence Considered by Court

[1] Age

1990—*Watson v. Watson*, 20 Conn. App. 551, 568 A.2d 1044.

Time limited alimony award was an abuse of discretion when recipient was 60 years old and had not worked for 10 years.

[2] Cause of Breakdown

2021—*Carten v. Carten*, 203 Conn. App. 598, 248 A.3d 808.

The trial court ruled within its broad discretion in declining to award alimony to the defendant when it found that the parties were able to continue to enjoy the standard of living they had during the marriage, the defendant was at fault for the breakdown of the marriage, the parties were in good health, and both were well-educated with significant employment experience, work history, and employability. The parties had grown their estate together during the marriage with steady income, ample employment, and financial acumen in spite of the defendant's spending, hoarding, and lack of accountability for monies spent after the plaintiff filed for divorce. The trial court found that with the division of property and other assets, and the agreed upon parenting plan, no alimony award was warranted. The defendant challenged none of these findings in asserting that the trial court should have at least awarded nominal alimony but was focused on her bad behavior.

2021—*Fronsaglia v. Fronsaglia*, 202 Conn. App. 769, 246 A.3d 1083.

The trial court did not abuse its discretion when it considered the defendant's extramarital affair with his twenty-two year old employee (including evidence that he paid all of her bills as well as evidence that he went on vacations with her, bought her expensive gifts, and paid all of her expenses in violation of the court's pendente lite orders) and his poor business decisions in fashioning the alimony award. The court is permitted to consider all causes for the dissolution of the marriage in determining whether to award alimony.

2002—*Greco v. Greco*, 70 Conn. App. 735, 799 A.2d 331.

Award upheld of only 33-1/3% of assets to husband found at fault for breakdown of marriage.

2001—*Clark v. Clark*, 66 Conn. App. 657, 785 A.2d 1162.

Alimony recipient's failure to plead Conn. Gen. Stat. § 46b-86(a) as basis for seeking upward modification of alimony, instead relying solely on terms of judgment, is proper basis for court's refusal to consider Conn. Gen. Stat. § 46b-82 factors, including causes for breakdown of marriage.

1992—*Martone v. Martone*, 28 Conn. App. 208, 611 A.2d 896.

Alimony award of $15,000 was awarded because defendant's conduct caused breakdown was appropriate.

1987—*Debowsky v. Debowsky*, 12 Conn. App. 525, 532 A.2d 591.

No alimony or property awarded to plaintiff who was sole cause for dissolution and made no financial or moral contribution.

1985—*Pavel v. Pavel*, 4 Conn. App. 575, 495 A.2d 1113.

When the parties choose to litigate the issues of alimony or division of property the causes of the dissolution must be considered by the court.

1983—*Sands v. Sands*, 188 Conn. 98, 448 A.2d 822.

Relative fault of parties was factor in breakdown.

1981—*Venuti v. Venuti*, 185 Conn. 156, 440 A.2d 878.

Trial court did not err in finding that adultery was not the cause of the breakdown of the marriage.

[3] Earning Capacity

2024—*Marshall v. Marshall*, 224 Conn. App. 45, 311 A.3d 235.

Because the trial court properly relied on the plaintiff's February 2022 financial affidavit in making alimony and child support orders, it properly exercised its discretion in declining to determine and rely on the plaintiff's earning capacity.

2021—*Oudheusden v. Oudheusden*, 338 Conn. 761, 259 A.3d 598.

It was not double counting for the trial court to award the wife a lump sum representing a portion of the value of a business and also award the wife alimony that was based on the husband's actual income from that business.

2021—*Fronsaglia v. Fronsaglia*, 202 Conn. App. 769, 246 A.3d 1083.

The trial court did not err in finding the defendant's actual earnings to be $160,000 per year when there was ample evidence in the record. His past earnings and spending habits, evidenced by his bank statements and credit card accounts, supported this finding. The record reflects that the trial court did not solely rely on the defendant's gross income as the basis of the alimony award. Although the trial court did not expressly state that it considered the defendant's net income in determining alimony, the Appellate Court inferred that it had considered the relevant statutory factors and all of the evidence from the parties.

2019—*Buxenbaum v. Jones*, 189 Conn. App. 790, 209 A.3d 664.

Although a court can base its financial orders on the parties' earning capacities, it is not required to do so, and the court did not abuse its discretion in making its financial orders, taking into consideration all facts and balancing the equities in the case.

2018—*Merk-Gould v. Gould*, 184 Conn. App. 512, 195 A.3d 458.

Earning capacity finding on the basis of defendant's investment income was clearly erroneous where court awarded 60 percent of those investment assets to the plaintiff at the time of dissolution.

2016—*Zilkha v. Zilkha*, 167 Conn. App. 480, 144 A.3d 447.

No abuse of discretion where the court denied a motion to modify alimony in which the ex-husband failed to demonstrate a substantial change in circumstances where the deterioration in earning capacity had been from his own making.

2015—*Callahan v. Callahan*, 157 Conn. App. 78, 116 A.3d 317.

There is no impermissible "double dipping" where a court determines earning capacity of a party independent of their employment at companies in which they have an ownership interest, which is an asset to be divided.

2013—*Traystman v. Traystman*, 141 Conn. App. 789, 62 A.3d 1149.

Computational errors in calculating earning capacity required a new trial on all financial issues.

2013—*Tanzman v. Meurer*, 309 Conn. 105, 70 A.3d 13.

Trial court may find an earning capacity within a range of amounts, but a broad range may constitute failure to provide the required specific earning capacity. When the court bases a financial support order on a party's earning capacity, the court must determine the specific dollar amount of that party's earning capacity.

2013—*Morrone v. Morrone*, 142 Conn. App. 345, 64 A.3d 803.

Financial orders were based on the earning capacity.

2012—*McRae v. McRae*, 139 Conn. App. 75, 54 A.3d 1049.

Court permissibly used actual earnings to determine alimony on a post-judgment motion where the court had previously used earning capacity at the time of trial.

2011—*Bruno v. Bruno*, 31 A.3d 860.

Trial court abused its discretion when it found a substantial change in circumstances based on a decline in the plaintiff's earning capacity when plaintiff's employment situation was unchanged since the date of dissolution.

2011—*McKechnie v. McKechnie*, 130 Conn. App. 411, 23 A.3d 779.

Court's finding of no earning capacity was not an implicit finding of disability.

2010—*Kovalsick v. Kovalsick*, 125 Conn. App. 265, 7 A.3d 924.

Trial court abused its discretion when it failed to award the plaintiff alimony and appeared to equate the parties' "equal standing in their education" to earning capacity.

2009—*Boyne v. Boyne*, 112 Conn. App. 279, 962 A.2d 818.

Earning capacity finding based on historical earnings was not clearly erroneous.

2009—*Rozsa v. Rozsa*, 117 Conn. App. 1, 977 A.2d 722.

Court did not abuse its discretion by basing net income finding on combination of actual income and earning capacity and there was no requirement to find plaintiff had willfully diminished income before imputing income.

2009—*Danehy v. Danehy*, 118 Conn. App. 29, 982 A.2d 273.

Trial court improperly denied a post-judgment motion to modify after finding no substantial change of payor's earning capacity where separation agreement did not mention earning capacity.

2007—*Elia v. Elia*, 99 Conn. App. 829, 916 A.2d 845.

The court has authority to establish earning capacity at a level less as well as more than parent's current income level.

2007—*Milazzo-Panico v. Panico*, 103 Conn. App. 464, 929 A.2d 351.

Award based on earning capacity was not an abuse of discretion where the parties' lifestyle exceeded their income and each were underemployed.

2006—*Dees v. Dees*, 92 Conn. App. 812, 887 A.2d 429.

The court did not abuse its discretion in imputing an earning capacity of $15,000 per year to the wife despite her claim that she was child's primary caretaker.

2003—*Carasso v. Carasso*, 80 Conn. App. 299, 834 A.2d 793.

Court did not rely on conventional methods in determining income or earning capacity.

1995—*Wolf v. Wolf*, 39 Conn. App. 162, 664 A.2d 315.

Time limited alimony can be based on a projected earning capacity. Court held that three years of alimony would allow the wife to complete residency and realize a standard of living similar to that achieved during the marriage.

1993—*Vandal v. Vandal*, 31 Conn. App. 561, 626 A.2d 784.

Alimony based on earning capacity based upon evidence from tax returns, and testimony regarding, among other things, perks and depreciation allowances.

1992—*Wolfburg v. Wolfburg*, 27 Conn. App. 396, 606 A.2d 48.

The length of time of alimony can sometimes be established by predicting when future earnings based on earning capacity as known at time of dissolution will be sufficient for self-sufficiency.

1992—*Ippolito v. Ippolito*, 28 Conn. App. 745, 612 A.2d 131.

"Self-sufficient" means that the spouse has developed an earning capacity that would allow her to maintain her previous lifestyle.

1989—*Hart v. Hart*, 19 Conn. App. 91, 561 A.2d 151.

Alimony and child support order was based on defendant's earning capacity rather than on his actual income when he voluntarily quit or avoided obtaining employment in his field.

1989—*Broderick v. Broderick*, 20 Conn. App. 145, 565 A.2d 3.

Trial court may base its finding on the earning capacity of a spouse entering a new business.

1985—*Stearns v. Stearns*, 4 Conn. App. 323, 494 A.2d 595.

The court determined that under the facts of the case, it was appropriate for the superior court to base its award for alimony and child support on the ex-husband's earning capacity rather than actual earned income.

1980—*Koizim v. Koizim*, 181 Conn. 492, 435 A.2d 1030.

Trial court's order of periodic alimony and lump sum assignment of property was fair and equitable in light of the financial circumstances of the parties and the husband's capacity to generate substantial income.

1980—*Miller v. Miller*, 181 Conn. 610, 436 A.2d 279.

Evidence that husband has been employed for more than 20 years and at the time of the action formed a sufficient basis for using the husband's earning capacity in determining the appropriate financial awards.

1980—*Schmidt v. Schmidt*, 180 Conn. 184, 429 A.2d 470.

The court held that the alimony and support order based on earning capacity was improper because the award was based on speculation and conjecture that could not stand because there was no evidence of the husband's past salary, or evidence of a salary that was typical for someone with the husband's ability and experience.

1980—*Miller v. Miller*, 181 Conn. 610, 436 A.2d 279.

Earning capacity is a factor to be considered when awarding support.

[4] Employability

2020—*Al-Fikey v. Obaiah*, 196 Conn. App. 13, 228 A.3d 668.

Trial court did not err in finding that for support purposes, the defendant husband was intentionally underemployed because he could pursue employment in his area of expertise and had recently worked in that field but he has done little since to improve his qualifications or pursue further employment therein.

1980—*Schmidt v. Schmidt*, 180 Conn. 184, 429 A.2d 470.

The court held that the alimony and support order was improper because the award was based on speculation and conjecture that could not stand because there was no evidence of the husband's past salary, or evidence of a salary that was typical for someone with the husband's ability and experience.

[5] Estate

2014—*Coleman v. Coleman*, 151 Conn. App. 613, 95 A.3d 569.

An inheritance received by one of the parties before the dissolution of marriage constitutes part of that person's estate subject to assignment under Conn. Gen. Stat. § 46b-81.

1996—*Tyc v. Tyc*, 40 Conn. App. 562, 672 A.2d 526.

Future workers' compensation benefits should be part of the marital estate as a presently existing interest.

1995—*Tremaine v. Tremaine*, 235 Conn. 45, 663 A.2d 387.

Trust principal is not part of plaintiff's estate because he has no control over its distribution.

1991—*Simms v. Simms*, 25 Conn. App. 231, 593 A.2d 161.

While court may not order the sale of an asset to pay alimony, conversion or depletion of assets is allowed.

1989—*Jackson v. Jackson*, 17 Conn. App. 431, 553 A.2d 631.

Inherited property is part of the marital estate for the purposes of equitable distribution.

1987—*Rubin v. Rubin*, 204 Conn. 224, 527 A.2d 1184.

Estate and property refer to present not future interests and evidence. Evidence of prospective inheritance is inadmissible.

1985—*Pavel v. Pavel*, 4 Conn. App. 575, 495 A.2d 1113.

Court concluded that evidence offered as to the wife's contribution to the acquisition, preservation, or appreciation in value of the husband's estate was also admissible pursuant to § 46b-81.

[6] Health

1990—*Watson v. Watson*, 20 Conn. App. 551, 568 A.2d 1044.

Time limited alimony was inappropriate when wife had a permanent disability.

1987—*Wanatowicz v. Wanatowicz*, 12 Conn. App. 616, 533 A.2d 239.

When payor suffers impairment of health resulting in decrease in income, payments can be modified.

1984—*Bronson v. Bronson*, 1 Conn. App. 337, 471 A.2d 977.

A substantial change in circumstances arising following the entry of a decree of dissolution can consist of the subsequent ill health of a party.

1983—*Misinonile v. Misinonile*, 190 Conn. 132, 459 A.2d 518.

The court affirmed the denial of the husband's motion and held that the express terms of the judgment clearly showed that the alimony award was within the trial court's power to hear and determine and court would not decide whether the trial court could consider the economic impact on the wife of providing care and comfort for her mentally disabled child after she had attained her majority when determining the issue of alimony.

1981—*Luttrell v. Luttrell*, 184 Conn. 307, 439 A.2d 981.

Wife stipulated that she would pay the state on a weekly basis for the expense of providing care for her mentally ill former husband.

1981—*McGuinness v. McGuinness*, 185 Conn. 7, 440 A.2d 804.

Health is a material factor in awarding alimony. Trial court modified alimony by extending the payment for two years because the ex-wife was unable to meet her medical expenses resulting from her substantially deteriorated health.

[7] Contributions

1988—*O'Neill v. O'Neill*, 13 Conn. App. 300, 536 A.2d 978.

Court must consider spouse's non-monetary contribution as a homemaker and responsibilities as the primary caretaker.

1987—*Debowsky v. Debowsky*, 12 Conn. App. 525, 532 A.2d 591.

No alimony or property awarded to plaintiff who was sole cause for dissolution and made no financial or moral contribution.

[8] Income of Parties

2024—*Marshall v. Marshall*, 224 Conn. App. 45, 311 A.3d 235.

Trial court soundly exercised its discretion in making alimony and child support orders based on the 2020 income the plaintiff earned as an equity partner in an investment banking firm, despite evidence of her distributions in 2021 and 2022 and the defendant's claim that the plaintiff had intentionally reduced her 2020 income. The court's decision to base the support orders on the plaintiff's February 2022 financial affidavit which reflected her 2020 K-1—her latest K-1 available at the time of trial—was reasonable in light of the evidence before it.

The court was unable to determine the plaintiff's current income based solely on her distributions from 2021 and year to date for 2022 based on the evidence presented. She had not received her 2021 K-1 by the time of trial and accordingly she based her February 2022 financial affidavit on the last K-1 she had received, the 2020 K-1. The distributions that the plaintiff received thus far in 2022 did not reflect her actual net income. She testified that her distributions were completely separate from what ultimately was shown on her K-1 for income and that she needed her K-1 and the tax return to determine what her income was. The court also considered other factors regarding the income reduction, including effects of the pandemic and the plaintiff's decreased economic participation in the investment banking firm.

2023—*Mitchell v. Bogonos*, 218 Conn. App. 59, 290 A.3d 825.

The trial court did not err in failing to impute $150,000 annual income to the husband as asserted by the wife, who had not presented compelling evidence from which the court could conclude that the husband had consistently earned more than $150,000 in each year of the marriage. In determining alimony, the trial court properly relied on the husband's actual income during marriage which had been ascertained from the evidence before the court. There was no requirement for the trial court to make a finding of the husband's earning capacity.

2023—*Onyilogwu v. Onyilogwu*, 217 Conn. App. 647, 289 A.3d 1214.

The trial court abused its discretion in fashioning a 10-year alimony award to the wife by including the temporary pandemic unemployment assistance benefits received by the husband as part of his income. While the definition of income under Conn. Gen. Stat. § 46b-82 is generally expansive, not every receipt of funds is considered income. The temporary pandemic unemployment assistance benefits did not occur with regularity due to their temporary nature and could not form the basis for determining the amount of income available for support.

2021—*O'Neill v. O'Neill*, 209 Conn. App. 165, 268 A.3d 79.

It was not an abuse of discretion for the trial court to base alimony and child support on its finding that the defendant had a $101,000 per year net earning capacity. The trial court's finding was not clearly erroneous because it was supported by the evidence. The defendant's tax returns and a summary prepared by his accountant substantiated a net earning capacity of $101,000 per year. He was in good health and had operated his own business for almost 25 years. He also testified that he had bids for construction work that, if accepted, would be worth $100,000 in profit for him.

2021—*L.W. v. M.W.*, 208 Conn. App. 497, 266 A.3d 189, *aff'g Winthrop v. Winthrop*, 189 Conn. App. 576, 207 A.3d 1109 (2019).

According to the parties' agreement, the defendant's "earned income" was to be the amount reflected on his W-2 and/or 1099 form. This definition of "earned income" contained no reference to business deductions for tax purposes. Therefore, under the terms of the agreement, any deductions made by the defendant for tax reasons was not included.

2020—*Leonova v. Leonov*, 201 Conn. App. 285, 242 A.3d 713.

Because the trial court had ample evidence at its disposal to adequately inform it about the defendant's financial status with respect to his net bonus income, the court did not abuse its discretion in making its supplemental alimony order a function of the defendant's future gross bonus income.

2020—*Halperin v. Halperin*, 196 Conn. App. 603, 230 A.3d 757.

Appellate court affirmed the trial court judgment resolving an ex-wife's motion for contempt in her favor. The trial did not clearly err in determining that the parties intended to include income from the ex-husband's ownership interests in two medical ventures in his total income for purposes of determining his unallocated support obligation because that income was reflected in the income tax form line the parties had designated to be used to determine his obligation. The trial court properly found that the ex-husband's income received from the medical ventures was not a conversion of marital assets and was not excluded from total income under the parties' separation agreement. It was something more and different from the original asset, the converted asset, interest, dividends or capital gains.

2019—*Nappo v. Nappo*, 188 Conn. App. 574, 205 A.3d 723.

Court correctly considered the income of ex-husband's current wife because it was relevant to his current expenses, a material factor in determining his current net income and, therefore, his ability to pay increased alimony. There was no evidence that the money was given as a loan, rather than as a gift.

2016—*Ferraro v. Ferraro*, 168 Conn. App. 723, 147 A.3d 188.

There was nothing in the underlying evidence to support the trial court's determination of father's weekly net income.

2016—*Keller v. Keller*, 167 Conn. App. 138, 142 A.3d 1197.

Trial court properly used net income in determining financial orders.

2015—*Salzbrunn v. Salzbrunn*, 155 Conn. App. 305, 109 A.3d 937.

A spouse with personal knowledge of the other party's finances can testify about that knowledge. If a spouse's testimony about the other party's finances is credited, that testimony can be used by the court to adjust the other party's income.

2014—*Keenan v. Casillo*, 149 Conn. App. 642, 89 A.3d 912.

Permanent alimony to the defendant was appropriate where there was significant disparity between the husband's income and the wife's income.

2014—*Harlow v. Stickels*, 151 Conn. App. 204, 94 A.3d 706.

Auto allowance should have been included in the calculation of income.

2014—*Marshall v. Marshall*, 151 Conn. App. 638, 97 A.3d 1.

Court should have included employer's payment of medical insurance premium in calculating the plaintiff's pre-tax income from employment as the premiums constituted a direct payment benefit to the plaintiff.

2014—*Mekrut v. Suits*, 147 Conn. App. 794, 84 A.3d 466.

Finding that the defendant willfully chose to prioritize payment of other financial obligations over alimony after receiving a severance payment was not clearly erroneous; the defendant should have budgeted his severance payment in order to comply with his alimony obligation.

2013—*Tuckman v. Tuckman*, 308 Conn. 194, 61 A.3d 449, *aff'g* 127 Conn. App. 417, 14 A.3d 428 (2010).

Court improperly considered all of the defendant's taxable income from an S corporation when entering alimony and child support orders. As the trial court did not make any findings as to the particular facts or circumstances of the S corporation, the Court remanded the case for a determination of what portion of the defendant's income was available income for purposes of fashioning alimony and child support orders.

2012—*Hirschfeld v. Machinist*, 137 Conn. App. 690, 50 A.3d 324.

Trial court improperly interpreted a provision in the separation agreement to restrict the plaintiff's ability to obtain documents relating to the defendant's earned income, where the purpose of the contract language was to require disclosure of documents to corroborate earned income, which formed the basis of a percentage-based support order.

2008—*Guarascio v. Guarascio*, 105 Conn. App. 418, 937 A.2d 1267.

Scaled alimony order can anticipate increases of income after the close of evidence, and can award a percentage of that income as alimony.

2007—*Lusa v. Grunberg*, 101 Conn. App. 739, 923 A.2d 795.

Income includes: (1) recurring gifts from parents and (2) proceeds from sale of personal property.

2006—*Cushman v. Cushman*, 93 Conn. App. 186, 888 A.2d 156.

Court rejected plaintiff's claim that court ordered alimony in excess of income where court correctly included $431,000 in loan forgiveness per year as part of income.

2004—*Medvey v. Medvey*, 83 Conn. App. 567, 850 A.2d 1092.

Funds due defendant by former employer paid to the limited liability company of which defendant had become a partner constituted income to defendant to be included in calculation of alimony.

2004—*Hartney v. Hartney*, 83 Conn. App. 553, 850 A.2d 1098.

Trial court considered gross and net income when determining alimony.

2003—*Carasso v. Carasso*, 80 Conn. App. 299, 834 A.2d 793.

Court did not rely on conventional methods but used defendant's spending level as factor in determining income or earning capacity.

2003—*Morris v. Morris*, 262 Conn. 299, 811 A.2d 1283.

Trial court applied incorrect legal standard when it utilized the gross income of the parties' base in order to determine child support and alimony rather than on net income.

2001—*Ludgin v. McGowan*, 64 Conn. App. 355, 780 A.2d 198.

Court must base orders of periodic alimony and child support on the net incomes of parties.

1999—*Schorsch v. Schorsch*, 53 Conn. App. 378, 731 A.2d 330.

Inclusion of principal payments of purchase money mortgage as part of income was improper.

1998—*Simmons v. Simmons*, 244 Conn. 158, 708 A.2d 949.

The marriage unit is an actual economic partnership.

1996—*Burns v. Burns*, 41 Conn. App. 716, 677 A.2d 971.

Percentage share of spouse's earned income may be awarded.

1994—*Misinonile v. Misinonile*, 35 Conn. App. 228, 645 A.2d 1024.

Alimony was reduced even though payor's income was greater in retirement than at the time of dissolution of marriage.

1993—*Fahy v. Fahy*, 227 Conn. 505, 630 A.2d 1328.

Net income not gross income is the criterion upon which the court must fix alimony.

1991—*Graham v. Graham*, 25 Conn. App. 41, 592 A.2d 424.

Amount of alimony and support can be in excess of income thereby necessitating depletion of assets to meet the order.

1991—*Simms v. Simms*, 25 Conn. App. 231, 593 A.2d 161.

Capital account was an asset representing husband's interest in the company and not income.

1990—*Paddock v. Paddock*, 22 Conn. App. 367, 577 A.2d 1087.

No evidence that the defendant had the time or ability to supplement his income with a part-time job to pay the alimony.

1990—*Febbroriello v. Febbroriello*, 21 Conn. App. 200, 572 A.2d 1032.

Trial court must base periodic alimony and child support order on net income.

1989—*Baldwin v. Baldwin*, 19 Conn. App. 420, 562 A.2d 581.

Separation agreement was ambiguous on issue of whether stock options were income from employment for purpose of escalation clause, court looks to intent of parties.

1987—*Misiorski v. Misiorski*, 11 Conn. App. 463, 528 A.2d 829.

What a spouse can afford to pay for alimony is a material consideration in court's determination of a proper order.

1987—*Wanatowicz v. Wanatowicz*, 12 Conn. App. 616, 533 A.2d 239.

Net income not gross income is the criterion upon which the court must fix alimony.

1985—*Harlan v. Harlan*, 5 Conn. App. 355, 498 A.2d 129.

Inflationary increases in income are foreseeable.

1985—*Tomanelli v. Tomanelli*, 5 Conn. App. 149, 497 A.2d 91.

Temporary reduction in payments due to fluctuating income.

1981—*Fattibene v. Fattibene*, 183 Conn. 433, 441 A.2d 3.

Given the assets and earnings of the parties, the trial court did not abuse its discretion in awarding periodic alimony or counsel fees.

1980—*Koizim v. Koizim*, 181 Conn. 492, 435 A.2d 1030.

Trial court's order of periodic alimony and lump sum assignment of property was fair and equitable in light of the financial circumstances of the parties and the husband's capacity to generate substantial income.

1980—*Schmidt v. Schmidt*, 180 Conn. 184, 429 A.2d 470.

Appellate court held that the alimony and support order was improper because the award was based on speculation and conjecture that could not stand because there was no evidence of the husband's past salary, or evidence of a salary that was typical for someone with the husband's ability and experience.

1979—*Collette v. Collette*, 177 Conn. 465, 418 A.2d 891.

Net income not gross income is the criterion upon which the court must fix alimony.

[9] Length of Marriage

2016—*Mensah v. Mensah*, 167 Conn. App. 219, 143 A.3d 622.

The length of a parties' marriage is only one factor to be considered and is not in itself necessarily dispositive in determining. It was not an abuse of discretion for the trial court to decline to award the plaintiff alimony solely on the basis of the marriage's duration.

2012—*Langley v. Langley*, 137 Conn. App. 588, 49 A.3d 272.

Length of the marriage in parties' second marriage to each other considered.

2009—*McMellon v. McMellon*, 116 Conn. App. 393, 976 A.2d 1.

Court did not abuse its discretion in awarding lifetime alimony in six year, childless marriage. Appellate Court would not adopt a bright line rule for how long a marriage must last before a trial court can award lifetime alimony.

2003—*DeMartino v. DeMartino*, 79 Conn. App. 488, 830 A.2d 394.

Trial court should not have considered fact that plaintiff paid alimony to defendant for 25 years following a marriage that lasted 20 years as that was not a proper equitable consideration to determine the modification of alimony and not a factor pursuant to Conn. Gen. Stat. § 46b-82.

1998—*Bornemann v. Bornemann*, 245 Conn. 508, 752 A.2d 978.

Time limited alimony order upheld even though wife spent most of seven-year marriage raising child.

1994—*Collucci v. Collucci*, 33 Conn. App. 536, 636 A.2d 1364.

Time limited alimony of seven years for a 17-year marriage was upheld.

1993—*Mathis v. Mathis*, 30 Conn. App. 292, 620 A.2d 174.

There was insufficient evidence to support order of 18 months of alimony with a 15-year marriage.

1987—*Cohen v. Cohen*, 11 Conn. App. 241, 527 A.2d 245.

Permanent alimony awarded to disabled spouse with a 10-year marriage.

[10] Education

1998—*Simmons v. Simmons*, 244 Conn. 158, 708 A.2d 949.

Medical degree may be used by court as primary factor in deciding to award alimony, even though degree is not property.

1991—*Eslami v. Eslami*, 218 Conn. 801, 591 A.2d 411.

Goodwill may constitute an element of value distinct from the tangible assets of a medical practice.

[11] Station

1998—*Simmons v. Simmons*, 244 Conn. 158, 708 A.2d 949.

Wife's need is not sole criterion for alimony.

1988—*Blake v. Blake*, 207 Conn. 217, 541 A.2d 1201.

Station is defined as social standing or standard of living.

[12] Lifestyle

2012—*Brody v. Brody*, 136 Conn. App. 773, 51 A.3d 1121.

Defendant's refusal to produce financial records hampered the trial court's ability to calculate net income and therefore the trial court properly looked to the defendant's expenses and lifestyle when calculating the alimony award.

2011—*Brown v. Brown*, 130 Conn. App. 522, 24 A.3d 1261.

Trial court's alimony award was not an abuse of discretion when court heard evidence regarding the parties' lifestyle and personal expenses.

1992—*Ippolito v. Ippolito*, 28 Conn. App. 745, 612 A.2d 131.

Self-sufficient means that the spouse has developed an earning capacity that would allow her to maintain her previous lifestyle.

[13] Statutory Factors Generally

2023—*Walker v. Walker*, 222 Conn. App. 192, 304 A.3d 523.

Trial court did not abuse its discretion in ordering alimony. While it was clear that the parties' respective financial circumstances were a critical consideration in making the award, it was not necessary to determine the precise amount of weight given to fault. Because it was evident from the decision that the trial court had considered all of the relevant statutory criteria in Conn. Gen. Stat. § 46b-82, the court had broad discretion to determine how much weight to give each factor. Its careful reasoning for the financial orders had a reasonable basis in the facts and reflected no abuse of its broad discretion to assign the weight to be given to each statutory factor. The Appellate Court will not disturb a trial court's financial orders in domestic relations cases unless the court has abused its discretion or could not reasonably reach its conclusions based on the facts presented.

1994—*Askinazi v. Askinazi*, 34 Conn. App. 328, 641 A.2d 413.

Court properly considered all of the relevant statutory factors.

1994—*Borkowski v. Borkowski*, 228 Conn. 729, 638 A.2d 1060.

Statutory factors of Conn. Gen. Stat. § 46b-82 must be considered in determining whether a modification of alimony is appropriate.

1989—*Koper v. Koper*, 17 Conn. App. 480, 553 A.2d 1162.

Motion for articulation is proper to seek elucidation from the trial court of its considered evaluation of statutory criteria.

1987—*Sweeny v. Sweeny*, 9 Conn. App. 498, 519 A.2d 1237.

Clause in agreement calling for a reduction in alimony does not require court to apply statutory criteria, but to infer parties' intent.

1982—*Tutalo v. Tutalo*, 187 Conn. 249, 445 A.2d 598.

Trial court was not required to show what importance it had assigned to the various statutory factors in making its award.

1981—*McGinn v. McGinn*, 183 Conn. 512, 441 A.2d 8.

Taken as a whole the record furnished a sufficient basis for the orders of alimony and property distribution and the court was not obligated to spell out each of the statutory criteria that it had taken into account.

1980—*Corbin v. Corbin*, 179 Conn. 622, 241 A.2d 878.

Trial court followed the statutory provisions in determining what awards of alimony and property distribution to make thus no abuse of discretion.

[14] Miscellaneous Factors

2016—*Hornung v. Hornung*, 323 Conn. 144, 146 A.3d 912.

Alimony and child support payments awarded in excess of wife's claimed expenses did not make the lump sum alimony award a functional property distribution.

2015—*Hammel v. Hammel*, 158 Conn. App. 827, 120 A.3d 1259.

Mistake regarding wife's education necessitated remand for new hearing on financial orders.

2008—*Picton v. Picton*, 111 Conn. App. 143, 958 A.2d 763.

Trial court gave properly considered recurring gifts from wife's mother in alimony award.

2003—*Zahringer v. Zahringer*, 262 Conn. 360, 815 A.2d 75.

Financial assistance provided by spouse's parent to be considered in establishing alimony and support obligation. Trial court's finding that payments from parents were loans, not gifts, was not clearly erroneous.

2003—*Carasso v. Carasso*, 80 Conn. App. 299, 834 A.2d 793.

Court reasonably could have decided to modify one aspect of defendant's alimony obligations without modifying other aspects.

2003—*DeMartino v. DeMartino*, 79 Conn. App. 488, 830 A.2d 394.

Trial court should not have considered fact that plaintiff paid alimony to defendant for 25 years following a marriage that lasted 20 years as that was not a proper equitable consideration to determine the modification of alimony and not a factor pursuant to Conn. Gen. Stat. § 46b-82.

2003—*Kiniry v. Kiniry*, 79 Conn. App. 378, 830 A.2d 364.

Trial court properly relied on defendant's significant borrowing power in fashioning its financial award.

1994—*Askinazi v. Askinazi*, 34 Conn. App. 328, 641 A.2d 413.

Evidence of periodic gifts to defendant from her family was properly relied on by the court.

1987—*Wanatowicz v. Wanatowicz*, 12 Conn. App. 616, 533 A.2d 239.

An inability to pay alimony due to indebtedness must not be brought about by defendant's own fault.

1986—*Tirado v. Tirado*, 7 Conn. App. 41, 507 A.2d 470.

The trial court's award of lump sum alimony was within its discretion as set forth in Conn. Gen. Stat. § 46b-82, and that the trial court properly considered and weighed all relevant factors.

1984—*Russo v. Russo*, 1 Conn. App. 604, 474 A.2d 473.

Findings regarding the use of the wife's income to maintain the family home and pay for the husband's medical expenses were not inconsistent with the evidence.

1983—*Sands v. Sands*, 188 Conn. 98, 448 A.2d 822.

Trial court did not abuse its discretion when it determined the stipulation agreement providing for child custody and support in lieu of alimony to be inequitable to the wife and that it inadequately protected a valid state interest arising from the wife's receipt of state benefits.

1982—*Lane v. Lane*, 187 Conn. 144, 444 A.2d 1377.

In fixing the nature and value of the property, the court shall consider the length of the marriage, the causes for the annulment, dissolution of the marriage or legal separation, the age, health, station, occupation, amount and sources of income, vocational skills, employability, estate, liabilities and needs of each of the parties, and the opportunity of each for future acquisition of capital assets and income as well as the contribution of each of the parties in the acquisition, preservation or appreciation in value of their respective estates.

1982—*Robinson v. Robinson*, 187 Conn. 70, 444 A.2d 234.

Following wife's affair, trial court properly considered factors such as husband's humiliation and mental anguish in the division of property.

1981—*Scherr v. Scherr*, 183 Conn. 366, 439 A.2d 375.

Court declined to create a rule that places more weight upon the duration of the marriage than upon the financial and personal circumstances of the parties.

1981—*McGinn v. McGinn*, 183 Conn. 512, 441 A.2d 8.

Taken as a whole the record furnished a sufficient basis for the orders of alimony and property distribution and the court was not obligated to spell out each of the statutory criteria that it had taken into account.

§ 8.04 Arrearages

[1] Generally

2020—*Marshall v. Marshall*, 200 Conn. App. 688, 241 A.3d 189.

The trial court acted within the scope of the Appellate Court's remand order when it used the methodology of reasonable compensation to determine the plaintiff's pre-tax income to calculate alimony arrearages and effectuate the terms of the parties' separation agreement, the relevant provisions of which had been determined to be ambiguous. How to calculate the plaintiff's income was relevant to the issues and purposes of the remand. The trial court's prior calculations did not constitute the law of the case on remand. The trial court reasonably found that the parties had negotiated and adopted the reasonable compensation calculation in their separation agreement and it properly carried that methodology forward.

2020—*Wells v. Wells*, 196 Conn. App. 309, 229 A.3d 1194.

Appellate court reversed a trial court order denying an ex-wife's motion seeking payment of unallocated support. Because their separation agreement clearly defined annual income and was structured to provide for the payment of certain percentages of such annual income according to three tiers, the language of the provision providing that the ex-husband would pay to the ex-wife certain sums as unallocated support was clear and unambiguous. The trial court improperly denied the ex-wife's motion for an order seeking payment of unallocated support owed by the husband because the plain language of the separation agreement required that the percentages stated in the second and third tiers be applied to the husband's gross income, not solely to his bonus as ex-husband argued. Given that the parties did not dispute the amount of the ex-wife's claim, the appellate court concluded that the ex-husband underpaid her. Judgment reversed and remanded with direction to grant the ex-wife's motion and render judgment for her.

2014—*Grasso v. Grasso*, 153 Conn. App. 252, 100 A.3d 996.

Trial court acted within its discretion in dissolution of marriage proceedings in declining to enter an order requiring husband to make payments on his alimony arrearage, where trial court found that husband was unable to pay more than the amount he was currently paying, but noted that the arrearage would continue to accrue and was to be paid at some point.

2011—*Gray v. Gray*, 131 Conn. App. 404, 27 A.3d 1102.

A contempt finding for failure to pay a pendente lite support arrearage which survived an earlier dissolution decree was not an abuse of discretion.

2009—*Barber v. Barber*, 114 Conn. App. 164, 968 A.2d 981.

Court properly dismissed an enforcement action because the plaintiff did not introduce any evidence of unpaid child support and alimony arrearages.

1994—*Evans v. Evans*, 35 Conn. App. 246, 644 A.2d 1317.

By failure of court to include unpaid temporary alimony arrearage in its final dissolution order, even though alimony recipient never requested it, court effectively stripped recipient's vested property right and impermissibly retroactively modified pendent lite order.

1991—*Moore v. Moore*, 187 Conn. 589, 447 A.2d 733.

Payment of arrearages as retroactive modification.

1988—*Elliott v. Elliott*, 14 Conn. App. 541, 541 A.2d 905.

Court cannot waive alimony arrearage at time of final judgment.

1982—*Moore v. Moore*, 187 Conn. 589, 447 A.2d 733.

Husband's motion to reduce the alimony arrearage was denied.

1981—*Johnson v. Johnson*, 185 Conn. 573, 441 A.2d 578.

Court ordered a reduction in husband's support obligations when he lost his job but gave the ex-wife an arrearage for the difference.

1981—*Hayes v. Beresford*, 184 Conn. 558, 440 A.2d 224.

Public policy does not require non-enforcement of arrearages long overdue under a separation agreement on which both parties have relied for more than 10 years.

1980—*Papcun v. Papcun*, 181 Conn. 618, 436 A.2d 282.

Husband's motion to waive his unpaid alimony and child support arrearages denied as wife was not guilty of laches although contempt application for arrears was made nine years after husband stopped making payments.

1977—*Sanchione v. Sanchione*, 173 Conn. 397, 378 A.2d 522.

Court cannot retroactively modify an alimony award by relieving payor of obligation to pay arrears.

[2] Contempt

2020—*Giordano v. Giordano*, 200 Conn. App. 130, 238 A.3d 113.

In the absence of a clear and unambiguous order underpinning the trial court's finding of contempt, and on the basis of the trial court's own finding of ambiguity within the alimony order, the trial court improperly concluded that the defendant's failure to pay the then existing alimony order was willful. The standard for a finding of contempt was not satisfied.

2015—*Parisi v. Parisi*, 315 Conn. 370, 107 A.3d 920.

Alimony buyout provision of separation agreement was ambiguous, and therefore, precluded a finding of contempt against husband for failing to comply with the agreement.

2014—*Mekrut v. Suits*, 147 Conn. App. 794, 84 A.3d 466.

Finding that the defendant wilfully chose to prioritize payment of other financial obligations over alimony after receiving a severance payment was not clearly erroneous; the defendant should have budgeted his severance payment in order to comply with his alimony obligation.

2013—*Hammond v. Hammond*, 145 Conn. App. 607, 76 A.3d 688.

Court improperly construed a post judgment stipulation and failed to include court ordered obligations in an arrearage calculation where the party was to pay expenses in lieu of support and failed to do so.

2011—*Gray v. Gray*, 131 Conn. App. 404, 27 A.3d 1102.

Contempt finding for failure to pay a *pendente lite* support arrearage which survived an earlier dissolution decree was not an abuse of discretion.

2011—*Oldani v. Oldani*, 132 Conn. App. 609, 34 A.3d 407.

Contempt order proper for deducting funds from alimony.

2009—*Kennedy v. Kennedy*, 114 Conn. App. 143, 968 A.2d 1002.

A party who was subject to "no contact" protective and restraining orders should not have been held in contempt for failure to comply with an obligation that he notify his former wife of a change in his employment.

2004—*Lamacchia v. Chilinsky*, 85 Conn. App. 1, 856 A.2d 459.

Contempt order proper for failure to pay alimony.

2001—*Bowers v. Bowers*, 61 Conn. App. 75, 762 A.2d 515.

Attorney fees awarded during contempt proceedings.

1998—*LaBow v. LaBow*, 13 Conn. App. 330, 537 A.2d 157.

Finding of arrearage can be made without a motion of contempt.

1997—*Dobozy v. Dobozy*, 241 Conn. 490, 697 A.2d 1117.

Attorney fees may be awarded even without contempt finding, but party paying fees has right to evidentiary hearing.

1984—*Mays v. Mays*, 193 Conn. 261, 476 A.2d 562.

Upon an application for a modification of an award of support of minor children, filed by a person who is in arrears under the terms of an award, a court shall, upon hearing, ascertain whether such arrearage has accrued without sufficient excuse so as to constitute a contempt of court.

[3] Defenses

2013—*Kasowitz v. Kasowitz*, 140 Conn. App. 507, 59 A.3d 347.

Trial court rejected a claim of laches and found the payee's delay in filing motions reasonable where the payor claimed he was unaware of a $100,000 arrearage which had accumulated over 10 years.

2008—*Fromm v. Fromm*, 108 Conn. App. 376, 948 A.2d 328.

Laches barred collection of a decade old alimony and child support arrearage.

2000—*Burrier v. Burrier*, 59 Conn. App. 593, 758 A.2d 373.

Laches defense was unsuccessful.

1990—*Paddock v. Paddock*, 22 Conn. App. 367, 577 A.2d 1087.

An alimony decree that can be modified retroactively is not entitled to full faith and credit in a foreign state unless it has been reduced to a money judgment for an arrearage.

1984—*Brock v. Cavanaugh*, 1 Conn. App. 138, 468 A.2d 1242.

Absent a finding of prejudice to the defendant, a trial court does not err in concluding that the plaintiff is not guilty of laches by virtue of her eight year delay in seeking payments.

1980—*Papcun v. Papcun*, 181 Conn. 618, 436 A.2d 282.

Trial court denied former husband's motion to dismiss the wife's application for alimony and child support arrearages brought nine years after the marriage ended, finding that the wife was not guilty of laches.

[4] Dischargeability in Bankruptcy

1999—*Newton v. Raymond*, 230 B.R. 234 (Bankr. D. Conn.).

Lump sum alimony is non-dischargeable in bankruptcy.

1996—*Celani v. Celani (In re Celani)*, 36 C.B.C.2d 58, 194 B.R. 719 (Bankr. D. Conn.).

Issue involved balancing benefit to debtor of discharging debt arising out of divorce decree against detrimental consequences to debtor's former spouse for purposes of discharge exception.

1993—*Cook v. Bieluch*, 32 Conn. App. 537, 629 A.2d 1175.

Award of counsel fees is in the nature of alimony and not dischargeable in bankruptcy.

1989—*Lesser v. Lesser*, 16 Conn. App. 513, 548 A.2d 6.

Bankruptcy does not discharge obligation for alimony and child support, however, obligations assumed as a property settlement are dischargeable in bankruptcy.

1987—*Forsdick v. Turgeon*, 812 F.2d 801, 16 C.B.C.2d 452.

Bankruptcy court must determine whether debtor's obligation is in the nature of alimony or support in determining which debts to discharge.

1984—*Soderholm v. Solderholm*, 33 B.R. 83 (Bankr. D. Conn.).

Bankruptcy, not state, law determines whether debt is in nature of support.

[5] Interest Award

2011—*Sosin v. Sosin*, 300 Conn. 205, 14 A.3d 307.

Court could award interest on unpaid lump sum, even though it had found that the plaintiff was not in contempt.

2011—*Dougan v. Dougan*, 301 Conn. 361, 21 A.3d 791, *aff'g* 114 Conn. App. 379, 970 A.2d 131 (2009).

A default provision in a separation agreement, requiring payment of interest from the date of the stipulated judgment until the date of payment in full, was enforceable despite established law that contract term imposing penalty for breach is contrary to public policy and invalid. The Supreme Court affirmed, concluding that the facts of the case satisfied the conditions for application of the doctrine of judicial estoppel to bar the plaintiff from now claiming that the provision was unenforceable.

1997—*Crowley v. Crowley*, 46 Conn. App. 87, 699 A.2d 1029.

Interest in retroactive modification of alimony improper.

1990—*DeMatteo v. DeMatteo*, 21 Conn. App. 582, 575 A.2d 243.

Absence of reference to interest in a separation agreement does not undermine the authority of the court to make an award of interest which can be awarded if retention of money was wrongful.

1989—*Buchetto v. Haggquist*, 17 Conn. App. 544, 554 A.2d 763.

Allowance of prejudgment interest on alimony and child support awards is within the discretion of the court.

1989—*Blake v. Blake*, 211 Conn. 485, 560 A.2d 396.

Interest can be obtained on delinquent property awards and not alimony.

1988—*LaBow v. LaBow*, 13 Conn. App. 330, 537 A.2d 157.

Interest on arrearage was proper when retention was wrongful.

1988—*Kronholm v. Kronholm*, 16 Conn. App. 124, 547 A.2d 61.

Interest on a judgment in a domestic relations case is permissible.

§ 8.05 Lump Sum Alimony

2016—*Hornung v. Hornung*, 323 Conn. 144, 146 A.3d 912.

Trial court's consideration of factors from property distribution statute did not demonstrate that the lump sum alimony award of $7.5 million was essentially a property distribution.

2015—*Brody v. Brody*, 315 Conn. 300, 105 A.3d 887.

Court may properly justify an award of alimony on one party's responsibility for the breakdown of the marriage and general lack of credibility.

2015—*Wood v. Wood*, 160 Conn. App. 708, 125 A.3d 1040.

No abuse of discretion in award of and payment schedule for lump sum settlement of $750,000.

2011—*Giordano v. Giordano*, 127 Conn. App. 498, 14 A.3d 1058.

Contempt found when husband failed to make yearly lump sum property settlement payments to wife.

2010—*Brooks v. Brooks*, 121 Conn. App. 659, 997 A.2d 504.

Lump sum alimony award was based on trial court's flawed asset valuation process, requiring new trial on all financial issues.

2006—*Pacchiana v. McAree*, 94 Conn. App. 61, 891 A.2d 86.

Order that husband pay lump sum alimony to wife and pay wife's counsel fees not an abuse of discretion.

1999—*Newton v. Raymond*, 230 B.R. 234 (Bankr. D. Conn.).

Lump sum alimony is non-dischargeable in bankruptcy.

1998—*Lord v. Lord*, 44 Conn. App. 370, 689 A.2d 509.

Court concluded that the trial court had equitable jurisdiction to award lump sum alimony and that the award was not unreasonable under the circumstances.

1989—*Kronholm v. Kronholm*, 16 Conn. App. 124, 547 A.2d 61.

If alimony award is payable in full regardless of future events such as death or remarriage it is lump sum alimony and cannot be modified.

1989—*Blake v. Blake*, 211 Conn. 485, 560 A.2d 396.

Change of characterization of lump sum alimony to property award was not a substantive change and could be made at any time.

1987—*Costa v. Costa*, 11 Conn. App. 74, 526 A.2d 4.

Lump sum and periodic alimony award is within trial court's discretion.

1986—*Tirado v. Tirado*, 7 Conn. App. 41, 507 A.2d 470.

The trial court's award of lump sum alimony was within its discretion as set forth in Conn. Gen. Stat. § 46b-82, and that the trial court properly considered and weighed all relevant factors.

1983—*Turgeon v. Turgeon*, 190 Conn. 269, 460 A.2d 1260.

Defendant was ordered to pay the plaintiff $100,000 in lump sum alimony, payable in installments over a period of seven years.

1980—*Koizim v. Koizim*, 181 Conn. 492, 435 A.2d 1030.

Trial court's order of periodic alimony and lump sum assignment of property was fair and equitable in light of the financial circumstances of the parties and the husband's capacity to generate substantial income.

§ 8.06 Time Limited Alimony

2022—*Ingles v. Ingles*, 216 Conn. App. 782, 286 A.3d 908.

Trial court did not abuse its discretion by awarding time limited alimony to Wife. The time limited alimony was for the permitted purpose of providing Wife with interim support until she was able either to refinance the mortgage on the marital home or list the marital home for sale. The two-year duration on alimony was not arbitrary because that time frame was requested.

2021—*O'Neill v. O'Neill*, 209 Conn. App. 165, 268 A.3d 79.

The trial court did not abuse its discretion in ordering the defendant to pay the plaintiff $280 per week in alimony until she vacated the family residence and $1,000 per week in alimony beginning after she vacated family residence. The court structured the award so that the plaintiff would receive a reduced amount for the period of time she remained in the marital residence with no mortgage or rental expense. In light of findings that the plaintiff would require a large residence to accommodate her five children and her father, and the court order granting her permission to relocate, it was reasonable to conclude the plaintiff would need additional support during the period after she vacated the marital residence and incurred additional housing expenses.

2017—*Horey v. Horey*, 172 Conn. App. 735, 161 A.3d 579.

Alimony terminating upon sale of husband's LLC was not an abuse of discretion.

2015—*Anderson v. Anderson*, 160 Conn. App. 341, 125 A.3d 606.

Evidence insufficient to support claim that spousal support was required for self-sufficiency.

2013—*Cunningham v. Cunningham*, 140 Conn. App. 676, 59 A.3d 874.

Seven years of time limited alimony after a 22-year marriage was not an abuse of discretion where payments would end several months before the payee would receive pension benefits.

2012—*Langley v. Langley*, 137 Conn. App. 588, 49 A.3d 272.

No abuse of discretion where the court ordered five years of alimony to the defendant based, in part, on her limited command of the English language.

2012—*Pite v. Pite*, 135 Conn. App. 819, 43 A.3d 229.

No abuse of discretion where the trial court modified and extended the duration of a time limited alimony award, making it a lifetime award, where modification effectuated the intent of the dissolution judgment.

2011—*Marmo v. Marmo*, 131 Conn. App. 43, 26 A.3d 652.

Four years of time limited alimony in a 17-year marriage was not an abuse of discretion where recipient had an employment history and was six months away from earning a BA degree.

1999—*Milbauer v. Milbauer*, 54 Conn. App. 304, 733 A.2d 907.

Court awarded time-limited alimony for 10 years having considered Conn. Gen. Stat. § 46b-82 criteria.

1998—*Bornemann v. Bornemann*, 245 Conn. 508, 752 A.2d 978.

Time limited alimony order upheld even though wife spent most of seven-year marriage raising child.

1995—*Wolf v. Wolf*, 39 Conn. App. 162, 664 A.2d 315.

Time limited alimony can be based on a projected earning capacity. Court held that three years of alimony would allow the wife to complete residency and realize a standard of living similar to that achieved during the marriage.

1994—*Collucci v. Collucci*, 33 Conn. App. 536, 636 A.2d 1364.

Time limited alimony of seven years for a 17-year marriage was upheld.

1993—*Ashton v. Ashton*, 31 Conn. App. 736, 627 A.2d 943.

Time limited alimony may be awarded to give the recipient incentive to procure training to attain self-sufficiency. The factual findings must support an award of time limited alimony.

1993—*Mathis v. Mathis*, 30 Conn. App. 292, 620 A.2d 174.

Court must identify a reason for awarding time limited alimony.

1992—*Ippolito v. Ippolito*, 28 Conn. App. 745, 612 A.2d 131.

The court need not make a detailed finding justifying time limited alimony. The evidence must support time limited alimony such as a time period enabling the spouse to obtain training to be employed in a chosen field.

1992—*Wolfburg v. Wolfburg*, 27 Conn. App. 396, 606 A.2d 48.

Time limited alimony is usually rehabilitative in purpose and must be based on sufficient evidence that the spouse should receive it for the particular duration. The purpose of time-limited alimony is to provide interim support until a future event occurs which makes support less necessary or unnecessary If the caretaker's ability to maximize self-sufficiency during the child's minority is impaired, alimony until child attains 18 is justified.

1992—*Henin v. Henin*, 26 Conn. App. 386, 601 A.2d 550.

One purpose of time limited alimony is to provide interim support until a future event.

1990—*Watson v. Watson*, 20 Conn. App. 551, 568 A.2d 1044.

Trial court's award of nonmodifiable limited periodic alimony was inappropriate and logically inconsistent with the facts where the wife had a permanent disability.

1990—*Roach v. Roach*, 20 Conn. App. 500, 568 A.2d 1037.

Time limited alimony award was an abuse of discretion when recipient was 60 years old and had not worked for 10 years but is appropriate for reasons other than rehabilitation.

1989—*Breen v. Breen*, 18 Conn. App. 166, 557 A.2d 140.

Court ordered $100 per week non-modifiable rehabilitative alimony for one year in a 23-year marriage.

1988—*O'Neill v. O'Neill*, 13 Conn. App. 300, 536 A.2d 978.

Purpose of rehabilitative alimony is to allow the recipient to attain self-sufficiency. Court held that rehabilitative alimony awarded was for an insufficient duration.

1988—*Louney v. Louney*, 13 Conn. App. 270, 535 A.2d 1318.

The concept of time limited alimony is to provide an incentive for self-sufficiency.

1987—*In re Rayna M.*, 13 Conn. App. 23, 534 A.2d 897.

Rehabilitation must be "within a reasonable time" and not "at some future date."

1984—*Markarian v. Markarian*, 2 Conn. App. 14, 475 A.2d 337.

Underlying the concept of time limited alimony is the sound policy that such awards may provide an incentive for the spouse receiving support to use diligence in procuring training or skills necessary to attain self-sufficiency.

§ 8.07 Modification of Alimony

[1] Generally

2024—*LeNczewski v. LeNczewski*, 229 Conn. App. 752.

The trial court did not abuse its discretion in denying defendant's motion to modify alimony. The defendant alleged factual circumstances in his appeal, which he did not allege or argue in his motion and which the trial court did not address in making its order. With respect to the claims the trial court did address, the defendant did not contend that any of the court's factual findings were clearly erroneous.

2022—*Bialik v. Bialik*, 215 Conn. App. 559, 283 A.3d 1062.

Trial court erred when it did not include funds received by Husband's dental practice from the federal Paycheck Protection Program (PPP) and Economic Injury and Disaster Loan program (EIDL) when it determined that modification of his alimony obligation under Conn. Gen. Stat. § 46b-86(a) was warranted. Under the parties' separation agreement, Husband's alimony obligation could not be adjusted downward unless he earned less than $350,000 adjusted gross earnings. The agreement defined "adjusted gross earnings" as gross business receipts less business expenses, less straight-line depreciation of business equipment, with certain add-backs. The PPP and EIDL funds were virtually indistinguishable from ordinary business receipts, differing primarily in their extraordinary dual tax favored status. These funds constituted cash flow transferred into Husband's business. That these funds were disbursed by the federal government for target purposes or were intended to be one-time or emergency disbursements was not a sufficient basis to exclude them. The PPP and EIDL funds should be included in the calculation of Husband's adjusted gross income. Trial court's judgment modifying the alimony obligation was reversed and remanded for a new hearing on Husband's motion for modification.

2021—*Berman v. Berman*, 203 Conn. App. 300, 248 A.3d 49.

At the hearing on the plaintiff's motion to modify alimony, the trial court's finding that the defendant gave up equity in certain marital assets in exchange for alimony was erroneous when there was no language in the parties' separation agreement that supported the court's finding and the defendant offered no evidence at the hearing that the parties had made such an exchange. Statements the self-represented defendant made while she questioned the plaintiff and in her closing argument did not constitute evidence. Therefore, the trial court abused its discretion when it denied plaintiff's motion based on its finding that the defendant had given up her claims to marital assets.

2018—*Peixoto v. Peixoto*, 185 Conn. App. 272, 196 A.3d 1229.

Trial court did not abuse its discretion in determining that additional exceptional circumstances existed, so as to distinguish from *Dan v. Dan*, 315 Conn. 1, 105 A.3d 118, and granting plaintiff's motion for upward modification of alimony.

2018—*Steller v. Steller*, 181 Conn. App. 581, 187 A.3d 1184.

Modification of alimony during a "second look" hearing must be based on evidence rather than speculation.

2018—*Cohen v. Cohen*, 327 Conn. 485, 176 A.3d 92.

The underlying purpose of the original order was properly considered once the court determined that the changed circumstances justifying the prior modification had ceased to exist.

Motion for modification was sufficient on its face; the motion need not cite the reasons why the substantial change in circumstances justified a modification or to cite case law supporting the motion.

2017—*Puff v. Puff*, 177 Conn. App. 103, 171 A.3d 1076.

In reducing the parties' oral agreement on the record to a written decision, the court did not improperly modify the agreement of the parties, where the terms included in the written decision simply memorialized the terms agreed upon by the parties.

2015—*Coury v. Coury*, 161 Conn. App. 271, 128 A.3d 517.

Trial court not required to set forth findings to support elimination of supplemental bonus alimony.

2013—*Shamitz v. Taffler*, 145 Conn. App. 132, 75 A.3d 62.

Trial court's silence on evidence presented regarding a motion to modify support does not mean that the court has not considered the evidence.

2012—*McRae v. McRae*, 139 Conn. App. 75, 54 A.3d 1049.

Trial court was not required to maintain income parity when rendering a modified alimony award.

2009—*Auerbach v. Auerbach*, 113 Conn. App. 318, 966 A.2d 292.

Alleged condition precedent in separation agreement did not deprive trial court of authority to modify alimony and child support. Agreement stated payor could seek to modify if annual income fell below $475,000.

2008—*Sutherland v. Sutherland*, 107 Conn. App. 1, 944 A.2d 395.

A clause that precluded oral modification of the separation agreement did not preclude modification of support under Conn. Gen. Stat. § 46b-86.

2003—*DeMartino v. DeMartino*, 79 Conn. App. 488, 830 A.2d 394.

Trial court should not have considered fact that plaintiff paid alimony to defendant for 25 years following a marriage that lasted 20 years as that was not a proper equitable consideration to determine the modification of alimony and not a factor pursuant to Conn. Gen. Stat. § 46b-82.

2001—*Clark v. Clark*, 66 Conn. App. 657, 785 A.2d 1162.

Alimony recipient's failure to plead Gen. Stat. § 46b-86(a) as basis for seeking upward modification of alimony, instead relying solely on terms of judgment, is proper basis for court's refusal to consider Gen. Stat. § 46b-82 factors, including causes for breakdown of marriage.

1999—*Amodio v. Amodio*, 247 Conn. 724, 724 A.2d 1084.

Trial court always has subject matter jurisdiction over modification of child support and alimony orders; proper inquiry is whether court has power to act under decree.

1996—*Cashman v. Cashman*, 41 Conn. App. 382, 676 A.2d 427.

Once a divorce judgment is granted by a court with personal jurisdiction, neither party can escape jurisdiction in future proceedings that attempt to modify the judgment.

1995—*Rau v. Rau*, 37 Conn. App. 209, 655 A.2d 800.

Statute suggests a legislative preference favoring the modifiability of alimony.

1994—*Borkowski v. Borkowski*, 228 Conn. 729, 638 A.2d 1060.

Statutory factors of Conn. Gen. Stat. § 46b-82 must be considered in determining whether a modification of alimony is appropriate. Only changes in circumstances that arise subsequent to the last modification can be considered.

1991—*Eslami v. Eslami*, 218 Conn. 801, 591 A.2d 411.

When periodic alimony has been ordered, a substantial change in the financial need or ability of a party provides a basis for modification of such an award, unless such a change was contemplated at the time of the marriage dissolution.

1986—*Neal v. Neal*, 7 Conn. App. 624, 510 A.2d 210.

There is a presumption of modifiability. Alimony is modifiable unless the judgment precludes it.

1984—*Guss v. Guss*, 1 Conn. App. 356, 472 A.2d 790.

A trial court cannot on its own initiative modify alimony or child support orders.

1983—*Connolly v. Connolly*, 191 Conn. 468, 464 A.2d 837.

Trial court's termination of the wife's alimony was unauthorized in that the parties conceded that no motion was submitted thus notice to wife was deficient.

1982—*Cummock v. Cummock*, 188 Conn. 30, 448 A.2d 204.

In an appeal from a modification of alimony, every reasonable presumption will be made in favor of the correctness of the trial court's exercise of discretion.

1982—*Moore v. Moore*, 187 Conn. 589, 447 A.2d 733.

The judgment of the trial court setting alimony arrearages, modifying the alimony award, and adjudging the husband in contempt was affirmed.

1980—*Krueger v. Krueger*, 179 Conn. 488, 427 A.2d 400.

The judgment rendered in one state is entitled to full faith and credit only if it is a final judgment, and the judgment is final only if it is not subject to modification in the state in which it was rendered.

1980—*Noce v. Noce*, 181 Conn. 145, 434 A.2d 345.

A modification of alimony is not warranted unless there has been a substantial change in the circumstances of either party, occurring subsequent to the entry of the original decree, and not contemplated by the parties at that time.

1980—*Theonnes v. Theonnes*, 181 Conn. 111, 434 A.2d 343.

A motion for modification of a child support or alimony judgment is not a substitute for an appeal.

[2] Automatic Modification

1989—*Fitzgerald v. Fitzgerald*, 16 Conn. App. 548, 547 A.2d 1287.

Appellate court upheld trial court's denial of husband's motion for modification of alimony in light of the wife's receipt of substantial income from the rental of the marital home.

[3] Change in Circumstances

2024—*Yanavich v. Yanavich*, 228 Conn. App. 444, 325 A.3d 1149.

Trial court's finding that the defendant's draws constituted income for purposes of setting his alimony and child support obligations was not clearly erroneous. The court correctly determined that there had been no substantial change in circumstances to warrant a modification of alimony and child support. The amounts reported as income by the defendant in 2018 when the support orders were entered and the flow of funds to him in 2022 were not meaningfully different. Although his company was nowhere near as healthy as it had been in 2018, the defendant's individual earnings, except for 2021, had remained the same.

2022—*Simms v. Zucco*, 214 Conn. App. 525, 280 A.3d 1226.

Trial court did not abuse its discretion by increasing Husband's alimony obligation under Conn. Gen. Stat. § 46b-86 and ordering him to pay retroactive alimony because the court fully considered the change in the parties' respective financial circumstances since the judgment of dissolution.

2020—*Budrawich v. Budrawich*, 200 Conn. App. 229, 240 A.3d 688.

Where the alimony provision of the parties' separation agreement expressed the intention to preclude modification as to the term of the alimony and to permit modification as to the amount, but only if the plaintiff's earnings fall below $100,000 per year, the plaintiff is not relieved of her burden to demonstrate a substantial change in circumstances on a motion for modification.

2019—*Callahan v. Callahan*, 192 Conn. App. 634, 218 A.3d 655.

Trial court did not abuse its discretion in granting defendant's motion to modify alimony and finding that defendant had shown his earning capacity had decreased with evidence and testimony regarding his companies' decreased profits, his inability to obtain comparable work with a Wall Street bank or hedge fund, and his inability to sell his companies due to plaintiff's failure to transfer her interest to him as previously ordered. Trial court used the same formula dissolution court had used to calculate defendant's earning capacity; it was not required to determine defendant's earning capacity based on what he might earn if he sold his companies and pursued employment.

2019—*Mountain v. Mountain*, 189 Conn. App. 228, 206 A.3d 802.

Where alleged changes in circumstances had previously been addressed by the trial court and rejected as not substantial, the court did not err in finding that there had been no substantial change in circumstances to support a modification of the unallocated alimony and child support obligation under Conn. Gen. Stat. § 46b-86(a).

2018—*LeSueur v. LeSueur*, 186 Conn. App. 431, 199 A.3d 1082.

Trial court, which found that plaintiff's decreased salary constituted a substantial change in circumstances, did not abuse its discretion in denying plaintiff's motion to modify unallocated alimony and child support after considering all of the factors enumerated by General Statutes § 46b-82.

2017—*Rubenstein v. Rubenstein*, 172 Conn. App. 370, 160 A.3d 419.

Change in circumstances was not solely plaintiffs increase in income due to inheritance, but was the worsening circumstances of the defendant (thus *Dan v. Dan* was inapposite).

2016—*Zilkha v. Zilkha*, 167 Conn. App. 480, 144 A.3d 447.

No abuse of discretion where the court denied a motion to modify alimony in which the ex-husband failed to demonstrate a substantial change in circumstances where the deterioration in earning capacity had been from his own making.

2016—*Juma v. Aomo*, 168 Conn. App. 845, 148 A.3d 255.

Order reinstating original financial orders after payor became reemployed was affirmed.

2016—*Ceddia v. Ceddia*, 164 Conn. App. 266, 137 A.3d 830.

The court was permitted to decrease an alimony order based upon, in part, the vesting of a contingent trust interest, even when the trust was awarded to the party in the separation agreement as an asset. The vesting of the trust and a change in the value of an asset is a substantial change in circumstances which the court may consider.

2014—*Dan v. Dan*, 315 Conn. 1, 105 A.3d 118.

Absent certain exceptional circumstances, an increase in income alone does not justify the modification of an alimony award in post-judgment motion to modify.

2014—*Altraide v. Altraide*, 153 Conn. App. 327, 101 A.3d 317.

Husband failed to establish a substantial change in circumstances that warranted modification of child support or alimony; husband's recent engagement and his change in tax filing status did not provide grounds for modifying child support or alimony, and husband's increased mortgage expense could not be considered because it was part of the property settlement in the judgment of dissolution.

2014—*Talbot v. Talbot*, 148 Conn. App. 279, 85 A.3d 40.

No modification where the payor's net income dropped from $245,000 to $204,000 and the payor was 65.

2013—*Malpeso v. Malpeso*, 140 Conn. App. 783, 60 A.3d 380.

Conn. Gen. Stat. § 46b-86(a) permits the court to modify alimony if the circumstances demonstrate that either of the parties' circumstances have substantially changed.

2013—*Olson v. Mohammadu*, 310 Conn. 665, 81 A.3d 215.

Reasons for payor's relocation should have been considered when assessing whether there was a substantial change in circumstances for purposes of post-judgment modification of alimony and child support.

2012—*McRae v. McRae*, 139 Conn. App. 75, 54 A.3d 1049.

Trial court was not required to maintain income parity when rendering a modified alimony award.

2012—*Pace v. Pace*, 134 Conn. App. 212, 39 A.3d 756.

Trial court properly denied two post-judgment motions for modification of alimony and child support and properly granted two motions for contempt where the court found that the movant's bank accounts held over $28,000, and that gross sales for his business had increased substantially.

2011—*Sargent v. Sargent*, 125 Conn. App. 824, 9 A.3d 799.

There was no basis for reduction of alimony where there was no change in cost of medical insurance for payor.

2010—*Schwarz v. Schwarz*, 124 Conn. App. 472, 5 A.3d 548.

Gross income increase of 20% constituted a substantial change in circumstances under Conn. Gen. Stat. § 46b-86(a).

2005—*Lucas v. Lucas*, 88 Conn. App. 246, 869 A.2d 239.

Modification of alimony based on change in circumstances may be retroactive to original application even though application was amended asserting additional grounds.

2003—*DeMartino v. DeMartino*, 79 Conn. App. 488, 830 A.2d 394.

Order ending future termination of alimony in 2005 ruled speculative.

2003—*Gay v. Gay*, 70 Conn. App. 772, 800 A.2d 1231, *cert. granted in part*, 261 Conn. 930, 806 A.2d 1064, *aff'd on other grounds*, 266 Conn. 641, 835 A.2d 1.

While capital gains cannot be considered income for purposes of modification, trial courts may consider changing value of property regardless of whether property was acquired before or after dissolution of marriage and regardless of whether change in value has been realized in justifying modification of alimony. This would be in consideration of substantial change in circumstances justifying modification of an alimony award.

1999—*Schorsch v. Schorsch*, 53 Conn. App. 378, 731 A.2d 330.

Alimony order remained the same despite fact that court found "substantial change in circumstance."

1994—*Borkowski v. Borkowski*, 228 Conn. 729, 638 A.2d 1060.

Only changes in circumstances that arise subsequent to the last modification can be considered.

1993—*Dooley v. Dooley*, 32 Conn. App. 863, 632 A.2d 712.

Pendente lite modification of alimony and child support must be based on a substantial change in circumstances.

1993—*Fahy v. Fahy*, 227 Conn. 505, 630 A.2d 1328.

Alimony is modifiable without a showing that the change of circumstances was not contemplated.

1991—*Bartlett v. Bartlett*, 220 Conn. 372, 599 A.2d 14.

Vesting of inheritance at mother's death was admissible evidence in hearing sufficient to support motion to modify alimony.

1991—*Simms v. Simms*, 25 Conn. App. 231, 593 A.2d 161.

Conn. Gen. Stat. § 46b-86(a) provides that the plaintiff, to obtain a court ordered modification of alimony, must show a substantial change in circumstances that must not have been contemplated by the parties at the time the decree was entered.

1990—*Curzi v. Curzi*, 21 Conn. App. 5, 570 A.2d 1134.

Increased income by plaintiff of 150% was not a substantial change in circumstances because she still had unmet expenses of $122 per week.

1990—*Richard v. Richard*, 23 Conn. App. 58, 579 A.2d 110.

Inability to pay does not automatically entitle a party to a decrease of an alimony order. It must be excusable and not brought about by the defendant's own fault.

1989—*Darak v. Darak*, 210 Conn. 462, 556 A.2d 145.

Unless and to the extent that the decree precludes modification, any final order for the periodic payment of permanent alimony or support or an order for alimony or support pendente lite may at any time thereafter be continued, set aside, altered or modified upon a showing of a substantial change in the circumstances of either party, whether or not such change of circumstances was contemplated at the time of dissolution.

1988—*Gleason v. Gleason*, 16 Conn. App. 134, 546 A.2d 966.

Inability to pay does not automatically entitle a party to a decrease of an alimony order.

1988—*Vonaa v. Vonaa*, 15 Conn. App. 745, 546 A.2d 923.

Movant must make a clear and convincing showing of a change in circumstances.

1987—*Rubin v. Rubin*, 7 Conn. App. 735, 510 A.2d 1000, *rev'd*, 204 Conn. 224, 527 A.2d 1184.

Payments of alimony may be contingent on a future event thus spouse's future inheritance when received can warrant an increase in alimony. Alimony cannot be awarded in the form of a share of the assets a spouse may receive upon fulfillment of an expectancy in absence of some necessity.

1986—*Pickman v. Pickman*, 6 Conn. App. 271, 505 A.2d 4.

In seeking a modification, a party must "clearly and definitely" demonstrate a substantial change of circumstances that had not been contemplated at the time of the order. A substantial change in circumstances demonstrates that continued operation of the original order would be unfair and improper.

1986—*Matles v. Matles*, 8 Conn. App. 76, 511 A.2d 363.

Unallocated alimony and child support order is modifiable when child attains age 18.

1985—*Wingerd v. Wingerd*, 3 Conn. App. 261, 487 A.2d 212.

A party seeking modification must show a substantial change in the circumstances of either party, occurring subsequent to the entry of the original decree.

1984—*Szilagyi v. Szilagyi*, 3 Conn. App. 25, 484 A.2d 469.

Connecticut unequivocally follows the widely established rule that no modification of alimony or support is to be granted unless there has been a showing of a substantial change in the circumstances of either party thus court denied plaintiff's request to modify pendente lite award.

1983—*Connolly v. Connolly*, 191 Conn. 468, 464 A.2d 837.

It is fundamental in proper judicial administration that no matter shall be decided unless the parties have fair notice that it will be presented in sufficient time to prepare themselves upon the issue thus wife's alimony could not be terminated without proper notice.

1983—*Walsh v. Walsh*, 190 Conn. 126, 459 A.2d 515.

Evidentiary hearing waived when neither party offers testimony or objects to the lack of testimony on motion for modification.

1981—*Hardisty v. Hardisty*, 183 Conn. 253, 439 A.2d 307.

Under Connecticut statutes and cases, modification may be premised upon a showing of substantial change in the circumstances of either party to the original decree.

1981—*McGuinness v. McGuinness*, 185 Conn. 7, 440 A.2d 804.

Trial court modified alimony by extending the payment for two years because the ex-wife was unable to meet her medical expenses resulting from her substantially deteriorated health.

[4] Change in Custody (Re: Unallocated Alimony and Support)

2015—*Coury v. Coury*, 161 Conn. App. 271, 128 A.3d 517.

No abuse of discretion in modifying supplemental bonus alimony based on change in physical custody.

2012—*Tomlinson v. Tomlinson*, 305 Conn. 539, 46 A.3d 112.

Court may modify the child support obligation of an unallocated alimony and child support based upon post-judgment change of custody where separation agreement provided that award was non-modifiable except upon "death, remarriage, or cohabitation."

[5] Cost of Living Increase

1989—*Lawler v. Lawler*, 16 Conn. App. 193, 547 A.2d 89, *app. dismissed*, 212 Conn. 117, 561 A.2d 128.

Cost of living adjustments automatically increasing alimony each year are permissible.

[6] Escalation Clause

1989—*Fitzgerald v. Fitzgerald*, 16 Conn. App. 548, 547 A.2d 1387.

Court based escalation on percentage of increased income.

1989—*Baldwin v. Baldwin*, 19 Conn. App. 420, 562 A.2d 581.

Separation agreement was ambiguous on issue of whether stock options were income from employment for purpose of escalation clause, court looks to intent of parties.

1987—*Rubin v. Rubin*, 7 Conn. App. 735, 510 A.2d 1000, *rev'd*, 204 Conn. 224, 527 A.2d 1184.

Automatic escalation of alimony based on future increases in husband's income is permissible.

1982—*Cogan v. Cogan*, 186 Conn. 592, 442 A.2d 1342.

The language contained in a contract is to be given its ordinary meaning unless a technical or special meaning is clearly intended. The word "annual" means continuing for the period of a year and connotes actual rather than hypothesized events.

[7] Inflation

2005—*Izard v. Izard*, 88 Conn. App. 506, 869 A.2d 1278.

In a dissolution context, although the mere fact of inflation may be judicially noticed without affording the parties an opportunity to be heard, the extent of that inflation and its effect on the necessary expenses of the parties is open to dispute.

1994—*Misinonile v. Misinonile*, 35 Conn. App. 228, 645 A.2d 1024.

Increases in salary due to normal inflation will not prevent a reduction in alimony under certain circumstances.

1985—*Harlan v. Harlan*, 5 Conn. App. 355, 498 A.2d 129.

Former wife's motion to modify alimony was denied where court determined that the increase in the former husband's salary was due to normal increments in salary and due to normal inflation. The trial court concluded that the change in circumstances was not outside the contemplation of the parties, therefore, was not unreasonable or an abuse of discretion.

1983—*Cariseo v. Cariseo*, 190 Conn. 141, 459 A.2d 523.

Trial court judgment granting the wife an increase in alimony due to inflation was set aside on appeal and the case was remanded with direction to render judgment for the husband.

[8] Loss of Employment

2018—*Thomasi v. Thomasi*, 181 Conn. App. 822, 188 A.3d 743.

To prove a substantial change in circumstances, the moving party must prove a loss of employment was not brought up by his own fault.

2017—*Bauer v. Bauer*, 173 Conn. App. 595, 164 A.3d 796.

Husband demonstrated adequate factual basis for failure to pay alimony; conduct following termination of employment was not culpable.

2016—*Juma v. Aomo*, 168 Conn. App. 845, 148 A.3d 255.

Order reinstating original financial orders after payor became reemployed was affirmed.

2009—*Danehy v. Danehy*, 118 Conn. App. 29, 982 A.2d 273.

Trial court improperly denied a post-judgment motion to modify after finding no substantial change of payor's earning capacity where separation agreement did not mention earning capacity.

2008—*Schade v. Schade*, 110 Conn. App. 57, 954 A.2d 846.

Ex-husband's motion to modify alimony was denied after he was discharged from his employment and court found him to be in contempt based on his failure to make alimony payments. The court found that his earning capacity was far in excess of his present earnings and that he did not pursue any of the considerable potential avenues to remedy his financial situation.

[9] Retirement

2012—*Jansen v. Jansen*, 136 Conn. App. 210, 46 A.3d 201.

Alimony obligor's forced retirement did not constitute a substantial change in circumstances.

1995—*Burns v. Burns*, 41 Conn. App. 716, 677 A.2d 971.

Remarriage, cohabitation or defendant's retirement are not grounds for terminating alimony.

1994—*Misinonile v. Misinonile*, 35 Conn. App. 228, 645 A.2d 1024.

Retirement at age 68 did not prevent a court from reducing the alimony.

1988—*Lawler v. Lawler*, 16 Conn. App. 193, 547 A.2d 89.

Alimony can be made nonmodifiable in the event of the payor's early retirement.

[10] Nonmodifiability

2021—*Oudheusden v. Oudheusden*, 338 Conn. 761, 259 A.3d 598.

The trial court erred when it awarded awarding alimony that was both permanent and nonmodifiable as to duration and amount. It constitutes an abuse of discretion for the trial court to have failed to contemplate the realistic possibility of the defendant's illness, disability, or the loss of income through no fault of his own.

2021—*O'Neill v. O'Neill*, 209 Conn. App. 165, 268 A.3d 79.

The trial court's order that the periodic alimony awarded to the plaintiff would not be modifiable was not an abuse of discretion. The trial court has statutory authority under Conn. Gen. Stat. § 46b-86 to award nonmodifiable alimony and the record supported its decision here.

2018—*Keusch v. Keusch*, 184 Conn. App. 822, 195 A.3d 1136.

Trial court erred in awarding unallocated alimony and child support that was not modifiable upon each child attaining the age of majority.

2011—*Tomlinson v. Tomlinson*, 305 Conn. 539, 46 A.3d 112.

Court may modify the child support obligation of an unallocated alimony and child support based upon post-judgment change of custody where separation agreement provided that award was non-modifiable except upon "death, remarriage, or cohabitation."

2006—*Burke v. Burke*, 94 Conn. App. 416, 892 A.2d 964.

Judgment lacked clear statement of non-modifiability thus alimony was modifiable.

1998—*Sheehan v. Balasic*, 46 Conn. App. 327, 699 A.2d 1036.

Order that husband "shall continue [alimony] for 24 months, nonmodifiable as to amount" construed to mean nonmodifiable as to amount and duration.

1998—*Wichman v. Wichman*, 49 Conn. App. 529, 714 A.2d 1274.

Judgment providing nonmodifiable alimony until death or remarriage is not modifiable based upon cohabitation.

1995—*Rau v. Rau*, 37 Conn. App. 209, 655 A.2d 800.

Nonmodifiability of alimony must be clear and unambiguous.

1990—*Brash v. Brash*, 20 Conn. App. 609, 569 A.2d 44.

Nonmodifiable alimony awarded for three years when there were two children ages nine and seven.

1986—*Lilley v. Lilley*, 6 Conn. App. 253, 504 A.2d 563.

Court erred in finding that the original decree of dissolution was nonmodifiable.

1985—*Calorossi v. Calorossi*, 4 Conn. App. 165, 493 A.2d 257.

Stipulation for nonmodification of alimony award must be approved by court to be binding.

[11] Remarriage or Cohabitation

2021—*Schott v. Schott*, 205 Conn. App. 237, 256 A.3d 732.

The trial court erred by failing to enforce the plain terms of the parties' separation agreement as it unambiguously provided that defendant's alimony obligation was to terminate when plaintiff was cohabitating with another person; once the court found that plaintiff had been living with another man and had experienced a change in circumstances, it was required to grant defendant's motion to modify his alimony obligation in accordance with the plain mandate of the separation agreement.

2019—*Boreen v. Boreen*, 192 Conn. App. 303, 217 A.3d 1040.

Trial court did not err in finding that plaintiff was living with another. Although plaintiff did not live with her boyfriend full time, her living arrangements had changed such that she no longer needed the same financial support she needed at the time of the original order. Trial court properly relied on the fact that plaintiff and her boyfriend had held themselves out as domestic partners when he added her to his health insurance policy, and properly considered the financial benefits plaintiff received as a result of the free health insurance when determining whether her financial needs had changed.

Upon finding that plaintiff had been living with another, trial court did not err in finding that termination of alimony was the only remedy available under the parties' separation agreement, which provided that alimony shall terminate when plaintiff commenced living with another person. Their agreement treated cohabitation as akin to death or remarriage, both of which are events that ordinarily terminate alimony. Finding that alimony should be modified upon plaintiff's cohabitation would be inconsistent with the structure of the separation agreement which contained provisions about the specific circumstances in which one or both parties could seek to modify alimony.

2018—*Murphy v. Murphy*, 181 Conn. App. 716, 188 A.3d 144.

The trial court erred in focusing on the lack of a boyfriend's financial contributions rather than the defendant's savings as a result of the cohabitation in denying the plaintiff's motion to modify alimony.

2016—*Gabriel v. Gabriel*, 324 Conn. 324, 152 A.3d 1230.

Error to focus on cohabitation in modifying alimony portion of unallocated alimony and child support because that violated the clear and unambiguous terms of the parties' separation agreement, which precluded consideration of that issue for modification purposes.

2016—*Norberg-Hurlburt v. Hurlburt*, 162 Conn. App. 661, 133 A.3d 482.

A court may terminate alimony based upon cohabitation where the moving party offered evidence of cohabitation, and the cohabitating party failed to appear (and thus failed to offer rebuttal evidence).

2016—*Fazio v. Fazio*, 162 Conn. App. 236, 131 A.3d 1162.

The court erred in not finding the cohabitation language ambiguous where the agreement provided that alimony would be payable to the wife until cohabitation "pursuant to" Conn. Gen. Stat. § 46b-85(b).

2015—*Nation-Bailey v. Bailey*, 316 Conn. 182, 112 A.3d 144.

Provision of separation agreement that was incorporated into divorce decree, requiring payment of unallocated alimony and child support by ex-husband "until" the death of either party, ex-wife's remarriage, or cohabitation as defined in statute governing payment of periodic alimony, required permanent termination of ex-husband's unallocated support obligation immediately upon ex-wife's cohabitation, rather than affording trial court discretion to suspend obligation only for cohabitation period.

2010—*Lehan v. Lehan*, 118 Conn. App. 685, 985 A.2d 378.

Modification of alimony was improper based on cohabitation where no demonstration that living arrangements had altered defendant's financial needs and without evidence of measurable and quantifiable change.

2010—*Marshall v. Marshall*, 119 Conn. App. 120, 988 A.2d 314.

No abuse of discretion in awarding alimony only modifiable upon cohabitation and terminable upon death or remarriage. Award did not improperly preclude future court from considering income.

2010—*Remillard v. Remillard*, 297 Conn. 345, 999 A.2d 713.

Trial court did not abuse its discretion by interpreting the term "cohabitation" to require proof of a romantic or sexual relationship.

2010—*Schwarz v. Schwarz*, 124 Conn. App. 472, 5 A.3d 548.

Upward modification of alimony was proper because the ex-wife had increased financial needs, arising from her health insurance costs, that were not being met by her cohabitation.

2008—*Krichko v. Krichko*, 108 Conn. App. 644, 948 A.2d 1092.

Agreement provision regarding termination of alimony upon cohabitation was automatic and self-executing and retroactivity under these circumstances was not limited by the statute.

2008—*Blum v. Blum*, 109 Conn. App. 316, 951 A.2d 587.

Court correctly denied a post-judgment motion for modification of alimony based on cohabitation where an unrelated male moved into the plaintiff's house before plaintiff gave birth to his child. Though he paid for household groceries and performed chores, there was no change in plaintiff's financial condition.

2005—*Williams v. Williams*, 276 Conn. 491, 886 A.2d 817.

Payor moving for modification of alimony based on payee's remarriage under an order of the court expressly providing for modification in the event of remarriage, nonetheless has the burden to establish that remarriage has altered the payee's financial needs.

2004—*Knapp v. Knapp*, 270 Conn. 815, 856 A.2d 358.

Plaintiff wife was not "cohabitating" at the time of entry of judgment because the man who had moved in with her was not contributing to her financial support.

2002—*DiStefano v. DiStefano*, 67 Conn. App. 628, 787 A.2d 675.

Cohabitation will not lead to alimony modification until financial needs of recipient are altered.

1999—*Smith v. Smith*, 249 Conn. 265, 752 A.2d 1023.

Proper for court to award both dual alimony and non-termination of alimony in event of remarriage.

1998—*Wichman v. Wichman*, 49 Conn. App. 529, 714 A.2d 1274.

Judgment providing nonmodifiable alimony until death or remarriage is not modifiable based upon cohabitation.

1996—*Burns v. Burns*, 41 Conn. App. 716, 677 A.2d 971.

Need for support does not automatically terminate with remarriage, cohabitation or retirement.

1996—*D'Ascanio v. D'Ascanio*, 237 Conn. 481, 678 A.2d 469.

Trial court erred in refusing to apply the terms of the modification agreement because the parties had previously agreed that once a finding of cohabitation was made, the alimony award would be reduced by one-half. Thus, wife's alimony award was reduced where wife was cohabitating with another man.

1996—*Draper v. Draper*, 40 Conn. App. 570, 672 A.2d 522.

Cohabitation can be a condition to automatically terminate alimony.

1993—*Vandal v. Vandal*, 31 Conn. App. 561, 626 A.2d 784.

Nonmodifiable alimony upheld even in the event of remarriage or cohabitation.

1993—*Mihalyak v. Mihalyak*, 30 Conn. App. 516, 620 A.2d 1327.

Alimony automatically terminated retroactive to the date of cohabitation per the express provisions of the judgment.

1991—*Battersby v. Battersby*, 218 Conn. 467, 590 A.2d 427.

Financial hardships that result from remarriage may be considered on a motion for modification.

1989—*Taylor v. Taylor*, 17 Conn. App. 291, 551 A.2d 1285.

Two women sharing household expenses do not constitute cohabitation.

1987—*O'Bymachow v. O'Bymachow*, 12 Conn. App. 113, 529 A.2d 747.

Spending three nights a week with an alimony recipient is insufficient to establish cohabitation.

1986—*Duhl v. Duhl*, 7 Conn. App. 92, 507 A.2d 523.

Court properly terminated alimony where ex-wife was cohabiting.

1986—*Warwick v. Warwick*, 7 Conn. App. 361, 508 A.2d 828.

Based upon the evidence that the defendant was living with someone, the court believes this living arrangement has caused sufficient change of circumstances of the plaintiff as to alter her financial needs.

1985— *Klein v. Klein*, 3 Conn. App. 421, 488 A.2d 1288.

Separation agreement provided that remarriage constituted cohabitation with an unrelated male for a period of four continuous months in the same residence.

1984—*Lupien v. Lupien*, 192 Conn. 443, 472 A.2d 18.

Cohabitation is a change in circumstances altering financial needs.

1981—*Kaplan v. Kaplan*, 185 Conn. 42, 440 A.2d 252.

The Superior Court may, in its discretion and after notice and hearing, modify an alimony award upon a showing that the party receiving the periodic alimony is living with another person under circumstances which the court finds should result in the modification, suspension, reduction or termination of alimony because the living arrangements cause such a change of circumstances as to alter the financial needs of that party.

[12] Retroactivity

2019—*Callahan v. Callahan*, 192 Conn. App. 634, 218 A.3d 655.

Trial court did not abuse its discretion in ordering that modification of alimony retroactive three years and ordering plaintiff to repay defendant. Appellate court affirmed trial court finding that it was equitable and appropriate under the circumstances to make the order retroactive to the date defendant's motion was served on plaintiff because there had been a substantial delay in hearing the motion. The original motion was pending for three years until the court, which treated defendant's amended motion as a continuation of the original motion, issued its memorandum of decision. Under Conn. Gen. Stat. § 46b-86(a), any retroactive relief would relate back to the date of service of the original motion.

2012—*Lynch v. Lynch*, 135 Conn. App. 40, 43 A.3d 667.

Trial court did not improperly grant retroactive relief on pendente lite motion for modification of alimony.

2008—*Cannon v. Cannon*, 109 Conn. App. 844, 953 A.2d 694.

It was not an abuse of discretion by modifying an unallocated alimony and child support order retroactive to service of a post-judgment motion to modify three years prior.

2008—*Rubenstein v. Rubenstein*, 107 Conn. App. 488, 945 A.2d 1043.

Trial court did not abuse its discretion when fashioning *de novo* alimony orders dating back nine years. Defendant-mother had removed parties' minor child from Connecticut and had hidden the child from 1997 to 2002. Dissolution judgment entered three months after the mother disappeared and alimony order in favor of father was without prejudice.

2005—*Lucas v. Lucas*, 88 Conn. App. 246, 869 A.2d 239.

Modification of alimony based on change in circumstances may be retroactive to original application even though application was amended asserting additional grounds.

1999—*Milbauer v. Milbauer*, 54 Conn. App. 304, 733 A.2d 907.

Trial court did not abuse discretion in modifying pendente lite award back to date of motion to modify.

1998—*Elliott v. Elliott*, 14 Conn. App. 541, 541 A.2d 905.

Alimony pendente lite cannot be modified retroactively.

1998—*Stein v. Stein*, 49 Conn. App. 536, 714 A.2d 1272.

Court erred in terminating alimony retroactive to date husband's motion to reopen was served on wife.

1997—*Crowley v. Crowley*, 46 Conn. App. 87, 699 A.2d 1029.

Award of interest in retroactive modification of alimony improper.

1995—*Wolf v. Wolf*, 39 Conn. App. 162, 664 A.2d 315.

Order reimbursing spouse for mortgage payments made under a pendente lite, order was an impermissible retroactive modification.

1993—*Shedrick v. Shedrick*, 32 Conn. App. 147, 627 A.2d 1387.

Retroactive modification permitted only if motion is served on opposing party.

1991—*Bartlett v. Bartlett*, 220 Conn. 372, 599 A.2d 14.

Modification of alimony was made retroactive to date motion was filed.

1991—*Trella v. Trella*, 24 Conn. App. 219, 587 A.2d 162.

In the absence of express legislative authorization for retroactive modification of unallocated alimony and support pendente lite, the trial court had no authority to order such modification.

1991—*Vickery v. Vickery*, 25 Conn. App. 555, 595 A.2d 905.

Modification is retroactive to the date of service of the notice of motion.

1990—*Febbroriello v. Febbroriello*, 21 Conn. App. 200, 572 A.2d 1032.

Failure to provide reasonable support for the family is actionable retroactively under Conn. Gen. Stat. § 46b-37.

1990—*Paddock v. Paddock*, 22 Conn. App. 367, 577 A.2d 1087.

An alimony decree that can be modified retroactively is not entitled to full faith and credit in a foreign state unless it has been reduced to a money judgment for an arrearage.

1989—*Weinstein v. Weinstein*, 18 Conn. App. 622, 561 A.2d 443.

Court cannot retroactively modify a pendente lite alimony award.

1977—*Sanchione v. Sanchione*, 173 Conn. 397, 378 A.2d 522.

No retroactive modification of alimony.

[13] Termination

2022—*Fogel v. Fogel*, 212 Conn. App. 784, 276 A.3d 1037.

Wife's contention that the trial court failed to consider the statutory criteria in Conn. Gen. Stat. § 46b-82 when it granted Husband's motion to modify alimony is belied by the trial court's memorandum of decision, in which the court specifically referenced the statutory factors and discussed many of them, including the age, health and education of the parties and their respective incomes. Judgment affirmed.

1985—*Wingerd v. Wingerd*, 3 Conn. App. 261, 487 A.2d 212.

Husband's motion to terminate alimony was denied on the basis that, while the circumstances had changed for each party, the changes were not substantial.

1985—*Ammirata v. Ammirata*, 5 Conn. App. 198, 497 A.2d 768.

The superior court may, in its discretion and upon notice and hearing, terminate the payment of periodic alimony upon a showing that the party receiving the periodic alimony is living with another person and living arrangements cause such a change of circumstances as to alter the financial needs of that party.

1984—*Guss v. Guss*, 1 Conn. App. 356, 472 A.2d 790.

Without written notice, court has no authority to terminate periodic alimony.

1983—*Connolly v. Connolly*, 191 Conn. 468, 464 A.2d 837.

Trial court's termination of the wife's alimony was unauthorized in that the parties conceded that no motion was submitted thus notice to wife was deficient.

§ 8.08 Abuse of Discretion

2023—*Anderson-Harris v. Harris*, 221 Conn. App. 222, 301 A.3d 1090.

Trial court did not abuse its discretion in making financial orders without addressing Defendant's earning capacity, his vocational skills, his present earnings, and the inconsistencies between the two financial affidavits he filed. The trial court was statutorily required to consider these factors but there was no requirement that the court specifically state how it weighed these factors or explain in detail the importance it assigned to these factors.

2023—*Buchenholz v. Buchenholz*, 221 Conn. App. 132, 300 A.3d 1233.

Trial court did not abuse its discretion in ordering Defendant pay Plaintiff $425 per week in alimony for nine years. The court expressly considered the factors enumerated in Conn. Gen. Stat. § 46b-82(a) in fashioning its alimony award, including that (1) Plaintiff was married to Defendant for fifteen years; (2) she was not at fault for the irretrievable breakdown of the marriage; (3) she was in poor health; (4) she was unable to perform her former jobs as a result of her health issues; (5) she would lose her health insurance upon dissolution of the marriage; (6) she had not been employed since November 2011; (7) she has no current source of income; and (8) she has a minimum wage earning capacity of $390 in gross weekly income. The court expressly found that Defendant had not credibly accounted for the for the reduction in his personal bank accounts and that his net weekly earnings are substantially more than his weekly expenses and weekly liabilities. It also concluded that Defendant could earn and has earned more than he had reported at the time of trial.

2021—*M.S. v. P.S.*, 203 Conn. App. 377, 248 A.3d 778.

The trial court did not abuse its discretion by issuing support orders that left the defendant with only 10% of his net income for his basic needs. The support orders were not excessive considering that alimony was limited to a six-year period and could not be extended, and the defendant had received substantial assets in the property distribution which he could use to pay support and sustain his basic welfare. The trial court expressly recognized that the parties had a history of using assets to meet their expenses as the defendant's income was never enough to pay all of the household expenses.

2019—*Wilson v. Di Iulio*, 192 Conn. App. 101, 217 A.3d 3.

Trial court did not abuse its discretion by deciding, based on the statutory factors, not to award husband more than nominal alimony but effectively creating an equal division of parties' marital assets by ordering wife to discharge the mortgage on the marital residence in which husband continued to live and ordering wife to convey additional funds from her 457 retirement plan to husband by designating him as a beneficiary pursuant to a domestic relations order.

Trial court did not err by awarding husband $1 per year in alimony modifiable only to enforce his rights to wife's retirement plan as security for his property award to account for the fact that the plan requires that wife's future spouse consent to the designation of husband as the survivor beneficiary. The purpose of modifiable alimony was to protect husband's interest, not to modify his property award in the future.

2019—*Zaniewski v. Zaniewski*, 190 Conn. App. 386, 210 A.3d 620.

The husband was entitled to a new trial regarding the financial orders for child support and alimony because the trial court's memorandum of decision failed to set forth the factual basis for its financial orders. Generally, an inadequate record would foreclose appellate review; however, here the inadequacy of the record arose from the trial court's issuance of a memorandum of decision that contained virtually no factual findings that would permit review of defendant's appellate claims.

2017—*Wood v. Wood*, 170 Conn. App. 724, 155 A.3d 816.

The court did not abuse its discretion in choosing to consider husband's stock options part of the property distribution mosaic and not in its alimony award.

2015—*Parisi v. Parisi*, 315 Conn. 370, 107 A.3d 920.

Superior Court's failure to clarify ambiguous alimony buyout provision of the parties' separation agreement, and to enter a concomitant order of compliance, constituted an abuse of discretion.

2014—*Mekrut v. Suits*, 147 Conn. App. 794, 84 A.3d 466.

No abuse of discretion by holding the defendant in contempt for not paying alimony from his severance, and by denying a motion to modify.

2014—*O'Donnell v. Bozzuti*, 148 Conn. App. 80, 84 A.3d 479.

No abuse of discretion where the court modified alimony and child support orders.

2013—*Cunningham v. Cunningham*, 140 Conn. App. 676, 59 A.3d 874.

Seven years of time limited alimony after a 22-year marriage was not an abuse of discretion where payments would end several months before the payee would receive pension benefits.

2013—*Tow v. Tow*, 142 Conn. App. 45, 64 A.3d 128.

No abuse of discretion where the court denied a motion for contempt and where the parties lived together post judgment and the separation agreement called for direct payments of alimony and child support to the wife but the husband made deposits to a joint account to which the wife had free access.

2012—*Langley v. Langley*, 137 Conn. App. 588, 49 A.2d 272.

No abuse of discretion where the court ordered five years of alimony to the defendant based, in part, on her limited command of the English language.

2012—*Larson v. Larson*, 138 Conn. App. 272, 51 A.3d 411.

No abuse of discretion where the court ordered a small reduction in alimony and child support on a post-judgment motion to modify.

2012—*Pite v. Pite*, 135 Conn. App. 819, 43 A.3d 229.

No abuse of discretion where the trial court modified and extended the duration of a time limited alimony award, making it a lifetime award, where modification effectuated the intent of the dissolution judgment.

2011—*Brown v. Brown*, 130 Conn. App. 522, 24 A.3d 1261.

Trial court's alimony award was not an abuse of discretion when court heard evidence regarding the parties' lifestyle and personal expenses.

2011—*Marmo v. Marmo*, 131 Conn. App. 43, 26 A.3d 652.

Four years of time limited alimony in a 17-year marriage was not an abuse of discretion where recipient had an employment history and was six months away from earning a BA degree.

2011—*Gray v. Gray*, 131 Conn. App. 404, 27 A.3d 1102.

A contempt finding for failure to pay a pendente lite support arrearage which survived an earlier dissolution decree was not an abuse of discretion.

2011—*Von Kohorn v. Von Kohorn*, 132 Conn. App. 709, 33 A.3d 809.

Abuse of discretion where the trial court changed the duration of a lifetime alimony award to an eight-year award by way of a motion for clarification.

2010—*Kovalsick v. Kovalsick*, 125 Conn. App. 265, 7 A.3d 924.

Trial court abused its discretion when it failed to award the plaintiff alimony and appeared to equate the parties' "equal standing in their education" to earning capacity.

2010—*Marshall v. Marshall*, 119 Conn. App. 120, 988 A.2d 314.

No abuse of discretion in awarding alimony only modifiable upon cohabitation and terminable upon death or remarriage. Award did not improperly preclude future court from considering income.

2009—*Utz v. Utz*, 112 Conn. App. 631, 963 A.2d 1049.

Court did not abuse its discretion by awarding alimony of $1 per year, modifiable until there is compliance with the property award. Award of alimony exceeding needs not abuse of discretion as alimony may be awarded for purpose other than rehabilitation.

2009—*Pellow v. Pellow*, 113 Conn. App. 122, 964 A.2d 1252.

Court's financial orders were excessive and abuse of discretion: alimony, child support, health insurance and unreimbursed medical expense awards would consume more than 90% of the defendant's gross income.

2008—*Cannon v. Cannon*, 109 Conn. App. 844, 953 A.2d 694.

It was not an abuse of discretion by modifying an unallocated alimony and child support order retroactive to service of a post-judgment motion to modify three years prior.

2008—*Radcliffe v. Radcliffe*, 109 Conn. App. 21, 951 A.2d 575.

Court did not abuse its discretion by awarding two years of alimony, nonmodifiable as to term, after 13-year marriage where recipient was *summa cum laude*, and had an MBA.

2007—*Milazzo-Panico v. Panico*, 103 Conn. App. 464, 929 A.2d 351.

Award based on earning capacity not abuse of discretion where parties lifestyle exceeded income and each were underemployed.

2006—*Pacchiana v. McAree*, 94 Conn. App. 61, 891 A.2d 86.

Order that husband pay lump sum alimony to wife and pay wife's counsel fees not an abuse of discretion.

2004—*Greco v. Greco*, 82 Conn. App. 768, 847 A.2d 1017.

It was abuse of discretion and an incorrect application of law by the trial to court to base financial orders on the gross income rather than net income.

1993—*Siracusa v. Siracusa*, 30 Conn. App. 560, 621 A.2d 309.

Seven year payout to wife for her interest in the family business plus alimony in excess of husband's income was not an abuse of discretion.

1990—*Watson v. Watson*, 20 Conn. App. 551, 568 A.2d 1044.

Time limited alimony award was an abuse of discretion when recipient was 60 years old and had not worked for 10 years.

1990—*Roach v. Roach*, 20 Conn. App. 500, 568 A.2d 1037.

Time limited alimony award was an abuse of discretion when recipient was 60 years old and had not worked for 10 years but is appropriate for reasons other than rehabilitation.

1983—*LaCroix v. LaCroix*, 189 Conn. 685, 457 A.2d 1076.

Husband could not challenge the unequal distribution of the sale of proceeds unless it was an abuse of discretion and he never claimed abuse of discretion.

1982—*Sands v. Sands*, 188 Conn. 98, 448 A.2d 822.

In determining whether there has been an abuse of discretion, the ultimate issue is whether the court could reasonably conclude as it did.

1981—*Powers v. Powers*, 183 Conn. 124, 438 A.2d 845.

The failure of the trial court to file a memorandum of decision or state on the record any basis for its order effectively prevents appellate review of the defendant's claim of an abuse of discretion.

1981—*Scherr v. Scherr*, 183 Conn. 366, 439 A.2d 375.

Appellate court held that the trial court had broad discretion in making its financial awards and when the awards were supported by ample evidence, the awards remained undisturbed thus there was no abuse of discretion.

1981—*McGinn v. McGinn*, 183 Conn. 512, 441 A.2d 8.

It was within the trial court's discretion to determine issues concerning alimony and where the trial court did not abuse its discretion, the financial orders were upheld accordingly.

1980—*Corbin v. Corbin*, 179 Conn. 622, 241 A.2d 878.

Trial court followed the statutory provisions in determining what awards of alimony and property distribution to make thus no abuse of discretion.

§ 8.09 Unallocated Award

2024—*De Almeida-Kennedy v. Kennedy*, 224 Conn. App. 19, 312 A.3d 150.

The trial court's finding that the defendant failed to demonstrate a substantial change in circumstances in his motion to modify unallocated alimony is clearly erroneous and not supported by the evidence. Under Conn. Gen. Stat. § 46b-86(a), a final order for alimony may be modified by the trial court upon a showing of a substantial change in the circumstances of either party. Based on the wholly undisputed evidence in the record, the change in residence of the parties' older child from plaintiff's home to defendant's home amounted to a substantial change in circumstances.

The trial court applied the wrong standard of law and consequently abused its discretion in denying the defendant's motion for modification of the alimony component of his unallocated support obligation. Contrary to the court's remarks during the hearing, the parties' separation agreement did not provide that the unallocated support obligation was nonmodifiable as to amount or term. The court incorrectly stated cohabitation could not form a basis for modification of alimony, refused to allow the defendant's son to testify without providing an evidentiary basis for that decision, and wholly discredited the testimony of a licensed private investigator without explanation.

Judgment reversed in part as to the order denying modification of the unallocated alimony and child support order. Case remanded for a new hearing on the defendant's motion for modification.

2019—*Mountain v. Mountain*, 189 Conn. App. 228, 206 A.3d 802.

Where alleged changes in circumstances had previously been addressed by the trial court and rejected as not substantial, the court did not err in finding that there had been no substantial change in circumstances to support a modification of the unallocated alimony and child support obligation under Conn. Gen. Stat. § 46b-86(a).

2018—*Keusch v. Keusch*, 184 Conn. App. 822, 195 A.3d 1136.

Trial court erred in awarding unallocated alimony and child support that was not modifiable upon each child attaining the age of majority.

2016—*Malpeso v. Malpeso*, 165 Conn. App. 151, 138 A.3d 1069.

When adjudicating a motion to modify unallocated alimony and support, the court must determine the proper child support number at the time of the original order (even if it is part of an unallocated order) and then compare the circumstances at the time of trial or agreement against the present circumstances.

2013—*Malpeso v. Malpeso*, 140 Conn. App. 783, 60 A.3d 380.

Trial court improperly determined that a separation agreement precluded modification of child support where agreement provided for unallocated support and precluded modification of "alimony" unless certain circumstances occurred.

2012—*Tomlinson v. Tomlinson*, 305 Conn. 539, 46 A.3d 112.

Trial court had authority to modify unallocated alimony and child support payments based on a change in primary residential custody, where the dissolution decree provided that unallocated payments would be non-modifiable.

2012—*Allen v. Allen*, 134 Conn. App. 486, 39 A.3d 1190.

Trial court improperly awarded the defendant a $52,000 "credit" against his unallocated alimony and support obligation as a sanction, based on the theory of unjust enrichment.

2008—*Cannon v. Cannon*, 109 Conn. App. 844, 953 A.2d 694.

It was not an abuse of discretion by modifying an unallocated alimony and child support order retroactive to service of a post-judgment motion to modify three years prior.

2003—*Zahringer v. Zahringer*, 262 Conn. 360, 815 A.2d 75.

Court adopted the parties' separation agreement and ordered the husband to pay his wife $25,000 per month as unallocated alimony and child support.

2002—*Kiniry v. Kiniry*, 71 Conn. App. 614, 803 A.2d 352.

Trial court's unallocated alimony and child support award did not require depletion of an asset awarded to husband.

1994—*Borkowski v. Borkowski*, 228 Conn. 729, 638 A.2d 1060.

Court reduced unallocated alimony and child support order when child turned age 18 and increased it due to wife's ill health.

1991—*Trella v. Trella*, 24 Conn. App. 219, 587 A.2d 162.

In the absence of express legislative authorization for retroactive modification of unallocated alimony and support pendente lite, the trial court had no authority to order such modification.

1986—*Matles v. Matles*, 8 Conn. App. 76, 511 A.2d 363.

Unallocated alimony and child support order is modifiable when child attains age 18.

1980—*Miller v. Miller*, 181 Conn. 610, 436 A.2d 279.

Orders for unallocated alimony and child support are severable and adjustments may be made when circumstances require.

§ 8.10 Taxes

2021—*Overley v. Overley*, 209 Conn. App. 504, 268 A.3d 691.

Where the parties' prenuptial agreement provides that in the event of marital dissolution, alimony payments are to be taxable as income to the plaintiff and deductible from the defendant's income, the trial court improperly ordered that the defendant may not, under any circumstances, deduct alimony payments from his income for tax purposes. Under the Tax Cuts and Jobs, Pub. L. No. 115–97, 131 Stat. 2054 (2017), alimony payments currently are no longer considered taxable income of the recipient and may not be deducted from income by the payor. However, as written, the trial court's unconditional order precludes the defendant from taking such deductions if his income tax obligations are governed by the laws of a jurisdiction that permits such deductions and precludes either party from seeking to enforce their agreement in the future if the federal tax laws are amended in a manner that permits enforcement of the agreement. Without justification, the trial court has prevented the defendant from ever exercising his contractual right to deduct alimony payments in accordance with the prenuptial agreement, even if his income tax obligations are governed by a jurisdiction that would permit such deductions.

1982—*Powers v. Powers*, 186 Conn. 8, 438 A.2d 846.

For income tax purposes an unallocated award of alimony and support is deductible by the payor-husband and taxable to the payee-wife.

§ 8.11 Payments

2010—*Campbell v. Campbell*, 120 Conn. App. 760, 993 A.2d 984.

No abuse of discretion by finding plaintiff not in contempt of the alimony order where evidence of plaintiff's cash payments was presented.

CHAPTER 9

PROPERTY DISTRIBUTION

SYNOPSIS

§ 9.01 Distribution of Property

2024—*K.S. v. R.S.*, 350 Conn. 692, 326 A.2d 187.

The trial court did not abuse its discretion in its treatment of the defendant's liability from New Jersey judgment the parties' property division. The court was not required to value the defendant's liability but to more generally consider the liabilities of both the plaintiff and the defendant in its equitable division of the marital estate. The court clearly considered the defendant's liability as a result of the New Jersey judgment in making its financial orders because it specifically ordered amounts that would go toward paying off the defendant's debt.

2024—*Hallock v. Hallock*, 228 Conn. App. 81, 324 A.3d 193.

Trial court did not apply an improper legal standard to the defendant's claim for alimony and the division of the marital property. The court properly cited and applied

Conn. Gen. Stat. § 46b-81 and Conn. Gen. Stat. § 46b-82 in issuing its financial orders regarding alimony and the distribution of property.

2024—*Briggs v. Briggs*, 227 Conn. App. 531, 322 A.3d 475.

Trial court did not abuse its discretion in awarding the defendant the entire interest in the Sunriver Fund, which consisted primarily of bonuses from the defendant's previous employment paid as carried interests, because the court expressly stated that it had considered the factors listed in Conn. Gen. Stat. § 46b-81 and expressly explained its consideration of several of those factors in dividing the marital property.

2024—*Nedder v. Nedder*, 320 A.3d 180.

It was legally and logically correct for the trial court to equitably divide the parties' property and order certain accounts to be used for their originally intended and historical purposes. Under Conn. Gen. Stat. § 46b-81, the court had authority to order that the plaintiff would retain accounts to be used, respectively, (1) solely for their children's medical expenses, (2) solely for their children's postsecondary educational expenses, and (3) solely for tax payments in 2022.

2024—*M.C. v. A.W.*, 226 Conn. App. 444, 319 A.3d 183.

Trial court did not abuse its discretion in allocating the parties' assets because its findings were supported by the record. It is not the function of the Appellate Court to review the evidence to determine whether a conclusion different from the one reached by the trial court could have been reached. 226 Conn. App. at 466, citing *Anderson-Harris v. Harris*, 221 Conn. App. 222, 251, 301 A.3d 1090 (2023).

2023—*Walker v. Walker*, 222 Conn. App. 192, 304 A.3d 523.

Trial court did not abuse its discretion in distributing the parties' marital property. Its memorandum of decision reflected that it had considered all statutory criteria for the distribution set out in Conn. Gen. Stat. § 46b-81. While it was clear that fault was one factor the trial court considered distributing property, it was not necessary to discern the precise weight given to fault. Because it was evident from the decision that the trial court had considered all of the relevant statutory criteria, the court had broad discretion to determine how much weight to give each factor. Its careful reasoning for the financial orders had a reasonable basis in the facts and reflected no abuse of its broad discretion to assign the weight to be given to each statutory factor.

2023—*Anderson-Harris v. Harris*, 221 Conn. App. 222, 301 A.3d 1090.

Trial court did not abuse its discretion in distributing the parties' assets. The court must consider the factors delineated by Conn. Gen. Stat. § 46b-81 when distributing assets but no single criterion is preferred over others. The court had wide latitude in varying the weight of each item under the circumstances of the case. It did not have to give each factor equal weight, or recite the statutory criteria it considered in making its decision, or make express findings on each statutory factor. 221 Conn. App. at 248, citing *Kent v. DiPaola*, 178 Conn. App. 424, 431–32, 175 A.3d 601 (2017).

2023—*Pencheva-Hasse v. Hasse*, 221 Conn. App. 113, 300 A.3d 1175.

Trial court did not abuse its discretion in rendering its property distribution orders because the distribution was not grossly disproportionate, particularly in light of the finding that Defendant had violated the automatic orders by withdrawing $342,000 from marital assets. There is no set formula that the court is obligated to apply when dividing the parties' assets. The court has broad discretion in fashioning financial orders.

2021—*Anketell v. Kulldorff*, 207 Conn. App. 807, 263 A.3d 972.

The trial court did not abuse its discretion when it awarded the plaintiff a lump sum property settlement of $52,500 for her share of the parties' house in Nicaragua plus her interest in funds the defendant unilaterally decided to transfer to their children's education trust accounts and to make overpayments on the mortgage on the marital home. The trial court's order was not based on a finding that the defendant had engaged in financial misconduct or intentionally wasted marital assets, but on its finding that the defendant unilaterally allotted portions of the marital estate solely in accordance with his own financial priorities.

2021—*Mecca v. Mecca*, 203 Conn. App. 541, 248 A.3d 772.

Where the defendant alleged that the judgment of dissolution had been obtained as a result of fraudulent misrepresentations by the plaintiff, the trial court applied the proper legal standard and was well within its discretion in denying the defendant's motion to open the judgment. The applicable law requires a continuing duty to disclose pertinent financial information until the judgment of dissolution is final. The trial court's finding is clearly supported by the record because the plaintiff timely disclosed the potential asset and it was appropriately classified as an intangible asset. The plaintiff met her continuing duty to disclose pertinent financial information. The defendant's waiver of any right to the potential asset in the separation agreement and in the final judgment of dissolution was not the result of fraud.

The trial court was also well within its discretion in finding that there was no fraud on the part of the plaintiff. She had clearly disclosed her intangible, potential interest to the defendant with ample time for him to review the disclosure but he simply failed to do so. By focusing on whether the plaintiff disclosed and characterized the asset in the documents provided to the defendant, the court applied the appropriate legal standard in addressing the defendant's claim of fraud. The court correctly applied the elements of fraud and correctly found that there was no fraud by the plaintiff.

2021—*Fronsaglia v. Fronsaglia*, 202 Conn. App. 769, 246 A.3d 1083.

The trial court did not abuse its discretion in issuing financial orders by ordering a disproportionate property distribution in the plaintiff's favor and assigning most of the marital debt to the defendant. This distribution was not grossly disproportionate because the trial court found the defendant misappropriated and dissipated $550,000 of marital assets in violation of the automatic orders, and the trial court merely reattributed those assets to him. *See O'Brien v. O'Brien*, 326 Conn. 81, 102–104, 161 A.3d 1236 (2017); *Shaulson v. Shaulson*, 125 Conn. App. 734, 736, 739–742, 9 A.3d 782 (2010); Conn. Gen. Stat. § 46b-81.

2020—*Bevilacqua v. Bevilacqua*, 201 Conn. App. 261, 242 A.3d 542.

The trial court properly determined the ownership and value of the properties in dispute on the basis of the evidence that was available to it. The defendant did not provide evidence of a transfer of ownership of the properties or appear at trial to contradict the plaintiff's evidence or otherwise challenge his ownership of the properties. He did not provide his own financial affidavit as to the value of the properties, leaving the trial court to rely on testimony and other financial affidavits to determine the value of the properties.

2020—*Kammili v. Kammili*, 197 Conn. App. 656, 232 A.3d 102.

Trial court did not abuse its discretion in distributing marital property under Conn. Gen. Stat. § 46b-81(c). It was not required to divide the parties' property equally. The evidence reasonably allowed the trial court to find that a withdrawal of funds from joint bank accounts did not violate automatic orders, that a home needed to be sold to provide the parties with cash to satisfy their liabilities, and that the plaintiff husband should either return jewelry to defendant wife or have a sum of money deducted from his share of the proceeds from the sale of the home to compensate her for the jewelry. Judgment affirmed.

2019—*Bilbao v. Goodwin*, 333 Conn. 599, 217 A.3d 977.

Pre-embryos created through in vitro fertilization during the parties' marriage are not marital property to be distributed under Conn. Gen. Stat. § 46b-81 when there is an enforceable agreement regarding their disposition. In the absence of formal legislative guidance, the contractual approach is the best first step in determining the disposition of pre-embryos upon divorce.

The trial court incorrectly determined that the parties had not entered an enforceable agreement to discard the pre-embryos upon divorce. The parties' storage agreement, in which they opted to have the pre-embryos discarded upon their divorce, initialed their selection and signed in full, acknowledged that they had discussed the agreement with a physician, and agreed they could modify their selection through written consent signed by both parties, is enforceable.

2019—*Callahan v. Callahan*, 192 Conn. App. 634, 218 A.3d 655.

Trial court did not err in ordering plaintiff to execute defendant's proposed transfer documents, amended to correct inconsistencies identified during hearing. This order effectuated rather than modified the existing judgment that required plaintiff to transfer her interests in certain companies to defendant.

2018—*Forgione v. Forgione*, 186 Conn. App. 525, 200 A.3d 190.

Trial court, upon reopening of judgment, did not err in dividing parties' assets and properly considered plaintiff's payment of $60,000 to the defendant as an advance against the defendant's equitable distribution.

2018—*Varoglu v. Sciarrino*, 185 Conn. App. 84, 196 A.3d 856.

Trial court properly considered plaintiff's contribution to the preservation of real property when dividing the equity in the parties' marital residence.

2017—*Kent v. DiPaola*, 178 Conn. App. 424, 175 A.3d 601.

Trial court did not abuse discretion in awarding the plaintiff 33% of the marital home, instead of 50%, where the court found that the defendant purchased the home prior to the marriage, made the down payment, had been solely responsible for major home improvements, and had made greater economic and non-economic contributions during the marriage.

Trial court did not abuse discretion in awarding the plaintiff 33% of the marital estate where the plaintiff failed to cite any authority for his claim that the court should have awarded more.

2017—*Powell-Ferri v. Ferri*, 326 Conn. 457, 165 A.3d 1124.

Although a chose in action existing at the time of dissolution can be considered an intangible property interest subject to distribution, the defendant-husband did not possess a chose in action because the trustees acted lawfully in decanting the trust.

2017—*Wood v. Wood*, 170 Conn. App. 724, 155 A.3d 816.

The court did not abuse its discretion in choosing to consider husband's stock options part of the property distribution mosaic and not in its alimony award.

2016—*Hornung v. Hornung*, 323 Conn. 144, 146 A.3d 912.

Trial court's consideration of factors from property distribution statute did not demonstrate that the lump sum alimony award of $7.5 million was essentially a property distribution.

Where alimony and child support payments were awarded in excess of wife's claimed expenses did not make the lump sum alimony award a functional property distribution.

2016—*Valentine v. Valentine*, 164 Conn. App. 354, 141 A.3d 884.

The court did not abuse its discretion where a party was ordered to attempt a refinance on a home every eight years, where the refinancing party allegedly had bad credit.

2015—*Wood v. Wood*, 160 Conn. App. 708, 125 A.3d 1040.

No abuse of discretion in award of and payment schedule for lump sum settlement of $750,000. Husband's interest in LLC was distributable property.

2015—*Perry v. Perry*, 156 Conn. App. 587, 113 A.3d 132.

Where the judgment of dissolution ordered the marital residence to be sold, the orders prohibited husband from paying wife the value of her equitable share in their marital home in exchange for exclusive possession.

2015—*Hammel v. Hammel*, 158 Conn. App. 827, 120 A.3d 1259.

Mistake regarding wife's education necessitated remand for new hearing on financial orders.

2014—*Brady-Kinsella v. Kinsella*, 154 Conn. App. 413, 106 A.3d 956.

Three stages of analysis regarding the equitable distribution of each resource in a dissolution proceeding: first, whether the resource is property within the estate to be equitably distributed; second, what is the appropriate method for determining the value of the property; and third, what is the most equitable distribution of the property between the parties.

2014—*Lynch v. Lynch*, 153 Conn. App. 208, 100 A.3d 968.

On remand, a trial court must craft property distribution orders in accordance with the facts as they existed at the time of the dissolution judgment, not at the time of remand.

2014—*Rousseau v. Perricone*, 148 Conn. App. 837, 88 A.3d 559.

Pending civil action was marital property for purposes of Conn. Gen. Stat. § 46b-81.

2011—*Dougan v. Dougan*, 301 Conn. 361, 21 A.3d 791.

Judicial estoppel applies if: (1) a party's later position is clearly inconsistent with its earlier position; (2) the party's former position has been adopted by the court in the earlier proceeding; and (3) the party asserting the two positions would derive an unfair advantage against the party seeking estoppel.

2005—*Dombrowski v. Noyes-Dombrowski*, 273 Conn. 127, 869 A.2d 164.

Court held it would be within its discretion to treat wife's lottery winnings as marital property, and also within court's discretion to treat winnings as an income stream and the wife's payments as alimony.

2001—*Wendt v. Wendt*, 59 Conn. App. 656, 757 A.2d 1225.

Equitable principles do not require that the marital estate be divided equally.

1993—*Passamano v. Passamano*, 228 Conn. 85, 634 A.2d 891.

Difference between an alimony order and a property distribution is that the latter alters the parties' respective ownership interests.

1993—*Roberts v. Roberts*, 32 Conn. App. 465, 629 A.2d 1160.

Court had subject matter jurisdiction to enter orders post-dissolution to carry out its decision to sell marital home.

1993—*Tessitore v. Tessitore*, 31 Conn. App. 40, 623 A.2d 496.

Trial court can employ equitable powers to order an accounting of rental properties to protect a party's interest pending appeal.

1989—*Fitzgerald v. Fitzgerald*, 16 Conn. App. 548, 547 A.2d 1387.

Court could order the sharing of rent on marital home post-dissolution pursuant to its equitable powers.

1988—*Mauro v. Mauro*, 16 Conn. App. 680, 548 A.2d 471.

Award of life insurance is within the court's equitable powers.

1985—*Bratz v. Bratz*, 4 Conn. App. 504, 495 A.2d 292.

The power to act equitably is the keystone to fashion relief.

§ 9.02 Valuation of Assets

2023—*Mitchell v. Bogonos*, 218 Conn. App. 59, 290 A.3d 825.

The trial court did not abuse its discretion in awarding the husband his comic book collection without hearing evidence from an appraiser as to its value. The trial court applied the factors in Conn. Gen. Stat. § 46b-81, concluding that the parties' five-year marriage was of a short duration and the wife had not contributed to the acquisition, preservation, or appreciation in value of any of the husband's assets. Because this decision was not related to the value of the comic book collection, the wife could not establish that the absence of an appraisal affected the ultimate disposition.

2019—*LaBorne v. LaBorne*, 189 Conn. App. 353, 207 A.3d 58.

The appellate court held that the trial court erred in its conclusion that a post-dissolution dissipation of an accrued pension benefit constituted an "exceptional intervening circumstance." Connecticut courts have previously held that a post-dissolution diminution of assets caused by market forces is not an exceptional circumstance and the court failed to see how an intentional reduction of the asset could qualify.

2018—*Merk-Gould v. Gould*, 184 Conn. App. 512, 195 A.3d 458.

Trial court abused its discretion by valuing defendant's interests in private equity companies as of the date of purchase rather than the date of dissolution.

2017—*Kent v. DiPaola*, 178 Conn. App. 424, 175 A.3d 601.

Court valued pension using a modified present division method and awarded all income from the pension to defendant in lieu of child support, thus, plaintiff's claim that the court improperly failed to include the defendant's pension in its division of the parties' marital property was without merit.

2016—*Britto v. Britto*, 166 Conn. App. 240, 141 A.3d 907.

The court exceeded its authority by disregarding a stipulation of the parties regarding the value of certain property, but the error was severable from other financial orders.

2016—*Antonucci v. Antonucci*, 164 Conn. App. 95, 138 A.3d 297.

Reopening evidence to obtain additional information regarding a discount rate was not an abuse of discretion.

2015—*Oldani v. Oldani*, 154 Conn. App. 766, 108 A.3d 272.

Although the proper time to value property is at the time of divorce, the trial court's valuing of the marital home at the time of the hearing on remand was harmless because the parties owned the property in equal shares at both points in time.

2015—*Cimino v. Cimino*, 155 Conn. App. 298, 109 A.3d 546.

Trial court may credit an appraisal of real property over contradictory testimony of the parties.

2010—*Brooks v. Brooks*, 121 Conn. App. 659, 997 A.2d 504.

Lump sum alimony award was based on trial court's flawed asset valuation process, requiring new trial on all financial issues.

2009—*Hannon v. Redler*, 117 Conn. App. 403, 979 A.2d 558.

Sufficient evidence to support the trial court's valuation of a medical practice was presented.

2005—*Brycki v. Brycki*, 91 Conn. App. 579, 881 A.2d 1056.

The trial court's valuation of property was not clearly erroneous.

1995—*Krafick v. Krafick*, 234 Conn. 783, 663 A.2d 365.

The court has the discretion to choose the method of valuation for pension benefits. The court may not reject present value or any value for vested pension benefits merely because asset is nonliquid.

1993—*Ashton v. Ashton*, 31 Conn. App. 736, 627 A.2d 943.

Estimates on financial affidavit were properly relied on by court.

1993—*Siracusa v. Siracusa*, 30 Conn. App. 560, 621 A.2d 309.

Court can order sale of family business to facilitate division of marital assets. Minority discount rejected in valuing spouse's interest in closely-held corporation.

1991—*Eslami v. Eslami*, 218 Conn. 801, 591 A.2d 411.

Capitalization of excess income is a permissible method for determining the value of the goodwill of a professional practice. Goodwill has no value if it cannot be detached from the personal reputation and ability of the practitioner through a sale. It is determined on the basis of the price that a willing buyer would pay in excess of the tangible assets to acquire the practice. Goodwill may constitute an element of value distinct from the tangible assets of a medical practice.

1990—*Sunbury v. Sunbury*, 216 Conn. 673, 583 A.2d 636.

The date of dissolution, rather than date of hearing on remand, is the appropriate time to value the parties' assets.

1990—*Sachs v. Sachs*, 22 Conn. App. 410, 578 A.2d 649.

Testimony as to the value of personal property is proper even if no qualification other than ownership is shown.

1990—*Brash v. Brash*, 20 Conn. App. 609, 569 A.2d 44.

Evidence regarding valuation of a business is admissible.

1989—*Kinderman v. Kinderman*, 19 Conn. App. 534, 562 A.2d 1151.

Case remanded because value for marital home accepted by court was taken from an outdated financial affidavit.

1987—*O'Bymachow v. O'Bymachow*, 12 Conn. App. 113, 529 A.2d 747.

Business valued at "amount unknown" at time of dissolution interpreted to mean "no value" for purpose of modification hearing.

1987—*Ferrucci v. Ferrucci*, 11 Conn. App. 369, 527 A.2d 1207.

Future appreciation of spouse's corporation can be one element of its value.

1986—*Ellsworth v. Ellsworth*, 6 Conn. App. 617, 506 A.2d 1080.

Value of closely held corporation by capitalization of income approach was made without an expert.

1985—*Stearns v. Stearns*, 4 Conn. App. 323, 494 A.2d 595.

Closely held corporate stock cannot be valued reasonably by the application of any inflexible formula.

1983—*Turgeon v. Turgeon*, 190 Conn. 269, 460 A.2d 1260.

In assessing the value of property the trier arrives at his own conclusions by weighing the opinions of the appraisers, the claims of the parties, and his own general knowledge of the elements going to establish value, and then employs the most appropriate method of determining valuation.

1983—*Wolk v. Wolk*, 191 Conn. 328, 464 A.2d 780.

Court permitted the defendant husband to testify to the value of ex-wife's personal jewelry.

§ 9.03 Property Rights of Spouses

[1] Dissipation of Assets

2024—*K.S. v. R.S.*, 350 Conn. 692, 326 A.2d 187.

The defendant's claim regarding dissipation was not moot. Whether the defendant dissipated the parties' Greenwich property and investment accounts by pledging them as security in his New Jersey litigation and then forfeiting them had to be considered in order to determine whether the trial court equitably distributed the marital estate.

The trial court correctly ruled on the elements of dissipation and determined that the defendant's pledge of the parties' Greenwich property and investment accounts constituted dissipation of the marital estate. The defendant's wilful, deceitful and misleading financial disclosures, in which he failed to disclose his transfer of millions of dollars overseas, violated the New Jersey trial court's orders, which resulted in the forfeiture of the Greenwich property and investment accounts. His conduct constituted financial misconduct involving marital assets. His pledge of the Greenwich property and its subsequent forfeiture were for his sole benefit and for the purpose of his lawsuit in New Jersey. The marriage was undergoing an irretrievable breakdown prior to the pledge or loss of the property; thus it was appropriate for the trial court to consider the actions taken by the defendant prior to the separation of the parties.

Because the Connecticut trial court was required to give full faith and credit to the New Jersey orders, the Greenwich property and the investment accounts had been removed from the marital estate prior to the trial court's judgment and, as a result, were not subject to equitable distribution in the dissolution action. The Connecticut trial court's inclusion of the Greenwich property and the investment accounts in the marital estate when it equitably distributed the assets was therefore improper.

2020—*Al-Fikey v. Obaiah*, 196 Conn. App. 13, 228 A.3d 668.

Appellate court found that the trial court had properly divided the marital property.

After finding the marital home had been foreclosed due to the defendant husband's misconduct, it was reasonable for the trial court to award the plaintiff wife another property and award the defendant his current residence and his interests in seven other properties.

2019—*LaBorne v. LaBorne*, 189 Conn. App. 353, 207 A.3d 58.

The appellate court held that the trial court erred in its conclusion that a post-dissolution dissipation of an accrued pension benefit constituted an "exceptional intervening circumstance." Connecticut courts have previously held that a post-dissolution diminution of assets caused by market forces is not an exceptional circumstance and the court failed to see how an intentional reduction of the asset could qualify.

2017—*O'Brien v. O'Brien*, 326 Conn. 81, 161 A.3d 1236.

The Court found that, although the trial court could not punish the husband because it had not found him in contempt, it nevertheless properly determined that it could compensate the wife for any losses caused by the husband's violations of the automatic orders. The trial court in the present case properly exercised its discretion by adjusting the property distribution to account for the loss caused by the plaintiff's violation of the automatic orders.

2008—*Sapper v. Sapper*, 109 Conn. App. 99, 951 A.2d 5.

Court did not abuse its discretion by using proceeds from the future sale of the marital home to replenish college education funds where defendant had withdrawn from the college funds, and the plaintiff-appellant had been aware of the invasions.

[2] Fraudulent Transfers

2012—*Cottrell v. Cottrell*, 133 Conn. App. 52, 33 A.3d 839.

Determination that the defendant had fraudulently conveyed four properties to the minor children was not clearly erroneous where the court found that deeds were executed in anticipation of the dissolution action.

2008—*Kaczynski v. Kaczynski*, 109 Conn. App. 381, 951 A.2d 690.

Absent an explicit or implicit finding of fraud by clear and convincing evidence, the trial court could not properly consider the values of the allegedly fraudulent transfers when fashioning its financial orders.

2007—*Jacobowitz v. Jacobowitz*, 102 Conn. App. 332, 925 A.2d 424.

Conveyance of parcels of real estate between first and second dissolution actions properly found to be fraudulent due to impending nature of second action.

2003—*Weinstein v. Weinstein*, 266 Conn. 933, 837 A.2d 807.

Trial court abused its discretion in denying motion to open judgment where wife learned that husband had a pending offer for the sale of his business during the divorce proceedings, which offer came to fruition. Husband fraudulently concealed his assets during the dissolution proceeding and if the court had known his true financial status, the outcome of the trial would likely be different. Offer clear proof that defendant had fraudulently concealed sale.

1999—*Dietter v. Dietter*, 54 Conn. App. 481, 737 A.2d 926.

Trial court improperly included as fraudulent transfer value of unsecured loan and other assets as assets included in marital estate.

1994—*Farrell v. Farrell*, 36 Conn. App. 305, 650 A.2d 608.

Fraudulent conveyance of real estate found by clear and convincing evidence.

1993—*Tessitore v. Tessitore*, 31 Conn. App. 40, 623 A.2d 496.

Clear and convincing standard of proof must be used for a finding of fraudulent conveyance.

1992—*Watson v. Watson*, 221 Conn. 698, 607 A.2d 383.

Transferees were made co-defendants in a claim of fraudulent conveyance; value of fraudulently conveyed property must be included in the estate for equitable distribution even if conveyance is not set aside.

1990—*Miller v. Miller*, 22 Conn. App. 310, 577 A.2d 297.

Husband's brother made a defendant on claim of fraudulent conveyance.

1990—*Gaudio v. Gaudio*, 23 Conn. App. 287, 580 A.2d 1212.

Fraudulent conveyance of stock in husband's corporation was found when transfer occurred during dissolution proceeding for less than adequate consideration; fraudulent transfer issue must be decided in order for the plaintiff to obtain complete relief; transaction is fraudulent if it removed property from the marital estate that would otherwise have been subject to claims of equitable distribution and transferee of alleged fraudulent conveyance may be joined as a party in a dissolution action.

1987—*Gelinas v. Gelinas*, 10 Conn. App. 167, 522 A.2d 295.

Diligence must be used to expose fraud.

1981—*Molitor v. Molitor*, 184 Conn. 530, 440 A.2d 215.

Conveyance was made with the knowledge of the divorce.

[3] Real Property

2020—*Moyher v. Moyher*, 198 Conn. App. 334, 232 A.3d 1212.

Trial court properly determined under Conn. Gen. Stat. § 46b-81(c) that real property in New Hampshire the husband had purchased prior marriage was marital property after considering the contributions, financial and otherwise, that both parties had made to designing, building and maintaining the house. The trial court particularly noted the substantial financial contributions the wife made that allowed the husband to make triple payments on his construction mortgage. However, in light of the husband's lack of employment, assets or other sources of income, including his inability to mortgage the property, and his sporadic employment history, the trial court's order under Conn. Gen. Stat. § 46b-81 that the husband must pay the wife on the award of her share of the New Hampshire property within five months of the dissolution judgment was an abuse of discretion. Judgment reversed in part and remanded for further proceedings in accordance with the opinion of the appellate court.

2017—*Kent v. DiPaola*, 178 Conn. App. 424, 175 A.3d 601.

Trial court did not abuse discretion in awarding the plaintiff 33% of the marital home, instead of 50%, where the court found that the defendant purchased the home prior to the marriage, made the down payment, had been solely responsible for major home improvements, and had made greater economic and non-economic contributions during the marriage.

2015—*Lawrence v. Cords*, 159 Conn. App. 194, 122 A.3d 713.

No contempt for failure to pay mortgage or list property for sale where defendant's failure to comply with the court's orders could not have been wilful because the dissolution judgment did not clearly require that he pay the mortgage, and the judgment placed the burden on both parties to list the property for sale.

2014—*Lewis v. Lewis*, 154 Conn. App. 233, 105 A.3d 344.

Wife solely responsible for the refinanced mortgages she acquired after the divorce upon the sale of marital home, where dissolution and supplemental memorandum of decision referenced only those mortgages that existed at the time of dissolution.

2007—*McGuire v. McGuire*, 102 Conn. App. 79, 924 A.2d 886.

It is within the court's power to award a "credit" to a party due to the other party's delay of sale of marital residence as an alternative to holding the delaying party in contempt and/or entering sanctions.

1993—*Roberts v. Roberts*, 32 Conn. App. 465, 629 A.2d 1160.

Court cannot order sale by auction of marital home without first holding an evidentiary hearing.

§ 9.04 Qualified Domestic Relations Order (QDRO)

2018—*Thomasi v. Thomasi*, 181 Conn. App. 822, 188 A.3d 743.

The term "marital portion" of the husband's pension contains a latent ambiguity because it can be determined using the "coverture method" or the "subtraction option" thereby requiring a hearing on the parties' intent.

2010—*Ranfone v. Ranfone*, 119 Conn. App. 341, 987 A.2d 1088.

Pension administrator rejected proposed QDRO and parties returned to Superior Court to reexamine pension order. Court did not impermissibly modify property division, but rather clarified an ambiguity in dissolution decree.

2009—*Cifaldi v. Cifaldi*, 118 Conn. App. 325, 983 A.2d 293.

Trial court should have fashioned a post-judgment order to effectuate division of pension benefits in accordance with parties' separation agreement, even though two QDROs had not been implemented.

§ 9.05 Pensions

2021—*Cunningham v. Cunningham*, 204 Conn. App. 366, 254 A.3d 330.

The trial court's domestic relations order regarding the defendant's nonqualified pension benefit did not impermissibly modify the property division in the dissolution judgment that awarded the plaintiff 50% of that portion of the defendant's pension that had vested and accrued as of the date of the memorandum of decision. The domestic relations order merely protected the integrity of that judgment, made sure the plaintiff did not receive an unintended windfall, and confirmed that the election of the survivor annuity resulted in a cost to both parties in the form of a lesser current pension benefit. The trial court's interpretation of its own order was not unreasonable. It clarified any ambiguity that could result from the employer's reduction or termination of the benefit by requiring the parties to share equally in any future reductions implemented by the employer.

2018—*Dinunzio v. Dinunzio*, 180 Conn. App. 64, 182 A.3d 706.

Trial Court improperly characterized the husband's pension in pay status as income rather than properly subject to equitable distribution.

2017—*Kent v. DiPaola*, 178 Conn. App. 424, 175 A.3d 601.

Court valued pension using a modified present division method and awarded all income from the pension to defendant in lieu of child support, thus, plaintiff's claim that the court improperly failed to include the defendant's pension in its division of the parties' marital property was without merit.

2014—*Reville v. Reville*, 312 Conn. 428, 93 A.3d 1076.

Trial court improperly concluded that unvested pension plan of the husband was not distributable marital property pursuant to Conn. Gen. Stat. § 46b-81.

2014—*Brady-Kinsella v. Kinsella*, 154 Conn. App. 413, 106 A.3d 956.

Financial order awarding husband's entire pension to husband in dissolution proceeding was equitable, even though husband had significant earning capacity, where pension was husband's only source of income at trial.

2013—*Bauer v. Bauer*, 308 Conn. 124, 60 A.3d 950.

Court properly clarified and did not improperly modify the judgment by equally dividing pensions where the memorandum of decision indicated in the factual findings that the parties agreed to equally split the defendant's pensions but the orders section did not divide or refer to the pensions.

2010—*Stechel v. Foster*, 125 Conn. App. 441, 8 A.3d 545.

Trial court improperly modified the property division, rather than merely effectuate the division of a defined benefit pension plan.

2007—*Martin v. Martin*, 101 Conn. App. 106, 920 A.2d 340.

Court permitted to consider husband's pensions when distributing property, despite the fact that he had acquired right to them prior to marriage. Finding that pensions had appreciated during the marriage not clearly erroneous.

2007—*O'Connell v. O'Connell*, 101 Conn. App. 516, 922 A.2d 293.

Federal and state pensions are exempt from attachment to enforce a child support order.

2003—*Rosato v. Rosato*, 77 Conn. App. 9, 822 A.2d 974.

Trial court did not abuse discretion in dividing the pension as of date of dissolution.

2001—*Bender v. Bender*, 258 Conn. 733, 785 A.2d 197.

Court-ordered equitable division of pension contributions made after dissolution upheld due to broad language. Unvested pensions are property subject to equitable distribution.

1999—*Perritt v. Perritt*, 54 Conn. App. 95, 730 A.2d 1234.

Provision in dissolution decree dividing pension does not apply to disability retirement payments to which owner of pension may become entitled under pension.

1996—*Durkin v. Durkin*, 43 Conn. App. 659, 685 A.2d 344.

Order splitting pension was upheld even though there was no evidence pension was vested.

1995—*Krafick v. Krafick*, 234 Conn. 783, 663 A.2d 365.

Pension benefits subject to equitable distribution.

1994—*Askinazi v. Askinazi*, 34 Conn. App. 328, 641 A.2d 413.

Connecticut courts have not classified pension as alimony or property and can view a pension as a potential source of future alimony rather than as property.

1993—*Kenny v. Kenny*, 226 Conn. 219, 627 A.2d 426.

Court cannot open judgment after four months to divide military pension because of a new federal law allowing the division.

1981—*Thompson v. Thompson*, 183 Conn. 96, 438 A.2d 839.

Pension benefits represent a form of deferred compensation for services rendered and as such they are conceptually similar to wages.

§ 9.06 Retirement Assets

2019—*Casablanca v. Casablanca*, 190 Conn. App. 606, 212 A.3d 1278.

Trial court erred in its determination that a retirement asset provision in proposed QDRO was unambiguous, as there were at least three possible interpretations of the provision. The court remanded for the trial court to determine the intent of the parties after consideration of "all available extrinsic evidence" and the circumstances surrounding the entering of the agreement.

2015—*Anderson v. Anderson*, 160 Conn. App. 341, 125 A.3d 606.

Evidence sufficient to support award from husband's retirement account of $43,158.

2013—*Cunningham v. Cunningham*, 140 Conn. App. 676, 59 A.3d 874.

Court's division of a nonqualified retirement plan on a percentage basis according to a coverture fraction and the court's subsequent reservation of jurisdiction was proper use of the present division method of deferred distribution in a case where the parties agreed that the defendant's interest in the plan constituted property and neither party offered evidence of present value.

2003—*Bijur v. Bijur*, 79 Conn. App. 752, 831 A.2d 824.

Trial court improperly concluded that certain moneys distributed to the defendant from a company retirement plan, which defendant had rolled over to an IRA, did not constitute a retirement distribution and thus improperly ordered him to resume making alimony payments.

2001—*Wendt v. Wendt*, 59 Conn. App. 656, 757 A.2d 1225.

Coverture is defined as the status and rights of the wife arising from the marriage relationship and has a long history of use regarding marital assets. In modern times, a coverture factor has reemerged as a mechanism for apportioning between spouses the benefit or value of unvested stock options, retirement plans or other benefits that were earned partially during and partially after the marriage.

1991—*Eslami v. Eslami*, 218 Conn. 801, 591 A.2d 411.

Valuation of retirement account without allowing for taxes was appropriate.

1990—*Caristia v. Caristia*, 22 Conn. App. 392, 577 A.2d 1096.

Fifty percent of retirement benefits payable to wife.

§ 9.07 Deferred Compensation

2016—*Nadel v. Luttinger*, 168 Conn. App. 689, 147 A.3d 1075.

Wife was entitled to one-half of net contingent cash award where separation agreement was clear and unambiguous and non-vested awards made prior to dissolution were considered property.

2007—*Czarzasty v. Czarzasty*, 101 Conn. App. 583, 922 A.2d 272.

In considering unvested interest in employer's performance based deferred compensation plan, whether an "interest" constitutes property under Conn. Gen. Stat. § 46b-81 depends on case by case "probabilistic assessment" of the degree of certainty that the litigant will eventually receive the asset.

§ 9.08 Inheritance

2014—*Coleman v. Coleman*, 151 Conn. App. 613, 95 A.3d 569.

An inheritance received by one of the parties before the dissolution of marriage constitutes part of that person's estate subject to assignment under Conn. Gen. Stat. § 46b-81.

1996—*Karen v. Parciak-Karen*, 40 Conn. App. 697, 673 A.2d 581.

Inherited property is subject to equitable distribution.

1991—*Eslami v. Eslami*, 218 Conn. 801, 591 A.2d 411.

Court did not consider wife's potential inheritance because the will was contested.

1991—*Bartlett v. Bartlett*, 220 Conn. 372, 599 A.2d 14.

Fact that inheritance would not be received until all inheritance taxes were paid did not prevent admissibility of evidence of inheritance.

1990—*Bonelli v. Bonelli*, 22 Conn. App. 248, 576 A.2d 587.

In a case where the parties were married 17 years, with no children, where all the assets were inherited by the husband, the wife was given 13% of total and no alimony.

1990—*Rostain v. Rostain*, 213 Conn. 686, 569 A.2d 1126.

Remand by Supreme Court requesting trial judge to articulate specific questions regarding inherited asset.

1987—*Rubin v. Rubin*, 7 Conn. App. 735, 510 A.2d 1000, *rev'd*, 204 Conn. 224, 527 A.2d 1184.

Future inheritance subject to equitable distribution.

§ 9.09 Trusts

2017—*Powell-Ferri v. Ferri*, 326 Conn. 457, 165 A.3d 1124.

The court did not need to consider plaintiff-wife's contributions to trust in light of the court's decision in *Ferri v. Powell-Ferri* that the first trust could not be considered in the marital distribution.

Court did not abuse discretion in failing to consider the entire value of a spendthrift trust where no chose in action existed at the time of dissolution.

2017—*Ferri v. Powell-Ferri*, 326 Conn. 438, 165 A.3d 1137.

Court did not abuse discretion in failing to consider the entire value of a spendthrift trust where no chose in action existed at the time of dissolution.

§ 9.10 Modification Prohibited

2022—*Walzer v. Walzer*, 209 Conn. App. 604, 268 A.3d 1187.

Trial court's decision on plaintiff's motion for contempt was not a modification of the property assignment in the dissolution judgment incorporating the parties' separation agreement. Instead, the trial court fashioned a remedy appropriate to protect the integrity of its original judgement. Defendant had been awarded the former marital home and ordered pay plaintiff $2,580,000 in periodic payments secured by a mortgage in plaintiff's favor against the former marital home. When defendant failed to make the payments, despite evidence that he had the ability to do so, the trial court's order that he sell the former marital home to ensure he makes the payments due to plaintiff was not a modification of its original judgment, but a postjudgment order to effectuate its original judgment.

2020—*Silver v. Silver*, 200 Conn. App. 505, 238 A.3d 823.

Under Conn. Gen. Stat. § 52-212a, a judgment may not be opened unless the motion is made within four months following the date it was rendered. The trial court properly exercised its authority to open and modify a property assignment made pursuant to Conn. Gen. Stat. § 46b-81 because the motion was timely filed within four months, its title as a motion for clarification was not determinative, and its substance sufficiently apprised the opposing party of the requested relief and made clear that the dissolution judgment would be modified if the trial court granted the motion.

2018—*Shirley P. v. Norman P.*, 329 Conn. 648, 189 A.3d 89.

The trial court's property division award, which was based on the defendant's criminal conviction, was reversed following the reversal of the defendant's criminal conviction.

2016—*Lawrence v. Cords*, 165 Conn. App. 473, 139 A.3d 778.

The court crafted an appropriate remedy to effectuate the terms of a judgement. The remedy was not an impermissible modification of a property settlement.

2011—*Perry v. Perry*, 130 Conn. App. 720, 24 A.3d 1269.

Post-judgment order that each party would be responsible for the liabilities listed on their respective financial affidavits was an improper modification of equitable division.

1985—*Ammirata v. Ammirata*, 5 Conn. App. 198, 497 A.2d 768.

The trial court had no jurisdiction to alter the terms of the property assignment.

CHAPTER 10

CHILD SUPPORT

SYNOPSIS

§ 10.01 Uniform Interstate Family Support Act (UIFSA)

2014—*Hornblower v. Hornblower*, 151 Conn. App. 332, 94 A.3d 1218.

The language of the Uniform Interstate Family Support Act (UIFSA), is clear and unambiguous as to personal jurisdiction over the parties involved in such a dispute. Under the UIFSA, only a tribunal of the state that issues a support order may modify that order.

2005—*Segal v. Segal*, 86 Conn. App. 617, 863 A.2d 221.

Uniform Enforcement of Foreign Judgments Act—modification of a previously domesticated foreign judgment in Nevada must be refiled only if change is substantial.

§ 10.02 Pendente Lite Child Support

1999—*W. v. W.*, 248 Conn. 487, 728 A.2d 1076.

Trial court had subject matter jurisdiction to order pendente lite child support regardless of whether child at issue was considered "child of marriage."

1994—*Thomas v. Thomas*, 34 Conn. App. 926, 644 A.2d 980.

An award of child support based on financial circumstances at time of pendente lite orders was improper.

1993—*Dooley v. Dooley*, 32 Conn. App. 863, 632 A.2d 712.

Pendente lite modification of child support must be based on a substantial change in circumstances.

§ 10.03 Child Support Guidelines

[1] Income

2024—*Y.H. v. J.B.*, 224 Conn. App. 793, 313 A.3d 1245.

The trial court abused its discretion by declining to award child support on the ground that it was not requested by either party. The record revealed that the defendant consistently had requested child support. Even if he had not requested it, the trial court improperly declined to order child support without considering the applicable statutes and child support guidelines.

2024—*Marshall v. Marshall*, 224 Conn. App. 45, 311 A.3d 235.

Trial court soundly exercised its discretion in making alimony and child support orders based on the 2020 income the plaintiff earned as an equity partner in an investment banking firm, despite evidence of her distributions in 2021 and 2022 and the defendant's claim that the plaintiff had intentionally reduced her 2020 income. The court's decision to base the support orders on the plaintiff's February 2022 financial affidavit which reflected her 2020 K-1—her latest K-1 available at the time of trial—was reasonable in light of the evidence before it.

The court was unable to determine the plaintiff's current income based solely on her distributions from 2021 and year to date for 2022 based on the evidence presented. She had not received her 2021 K-1 by the time of trial and accordingly she based her February 2022 financial affidavit on the last K-1 she had received, the 2020 K-1. The distributions that the plaintiff received thus far in 2022 did not reflect her actual net income. She testified that her distributions were completely separate from what ultimately was shown on her K-1 for income and that she needed her K-1 and the tax return to determine what her income was. The court also considered other factors regarding the income reduction, including effects of the pandemic and the plaintiff's decreased economic participation in the investment banking firm.

Because the trial court properly relied on the plaintiff's February 2022 financial affidavit in making alimony and child support orders, it properly exercised its discretion in declining to determine and rely on the plaintiff's earning capacity.

2019—*Thunelius v. Posacki*, 193 Conn. App. 666, 220 A.3d 194.

Trial court did not abuse its discretion in relying on net income figures in child support guidelines worksheet when issuing its child support orders because the evidence supports the figures enumerated in the court's guidelines worksheet.

2018—*LeSueur v. LeSueur*, 186 Conn. App. 431, 199 A.3d 1082.

Trial court's findings underlying its granting of defendant's motion to modify child support were clearly erroneous where plaintiff's income was inclusive of alimony.

2018—*Kirwan v. Kirwan*, 185 Conn. App. 713, 197 A.3d 1000.

Trial court, in making income findings for purposes of child support, was not bound by arbitrator's income findings made for purposes of alimony.

2016—*McKeon v. Lennon*, 321 Conn. 323, 138 A.3d 242.

The exercise of stock options and income received from vested restricted stock should be considered part of a party's gross income for the purposes of child support calculations.

2015—*Hendricks v. Haydu*, 160 Conn. App. 103, 124 A.3d 554.

Abuse of discretion for trial court to modify child support without addressing bonuses.

2014—*Fox v. Fox*, 152 Conn. App. 611, 99 A.3d 1206.

Trial court improperly based Child Support Guidelines on the husband's imputed income, and not his actual income, in violation of the principles set forth in *Maturo v. Maturo*, 296 Conn. 80, 995 A.2d 1 (2010).

2013—*Dowling v. Szymczak*, 309 Conn. 390, 72 A.3d 1.

Child support award based on the highest percentage in the guidelines was proper, even though the parties' net income exceeded the maximum in the guidelines.

2013—*Tuckman v. Tuckman*, 308 Conn. 194, 61 A.3d 449.

Court improperly considered all of the defendant's taxable income from an S corporation when entering alimony and child support orders. As the trial court did not make any findings as to the particular facts or circumstances of the S corporation, the Court remanded the case for a determination of what portion of the defendant's income was available income for purposes of fashioning alimony and child support orders.

2013—*Winters v. Winters*, 140 Conn. App. 816, 60 A.3d 351.

Court's determination that the defendant had not proven a substantial change in circumstances was based on a flawed income calculation and the court improperly did not consider the increase in value of the defendant's assets.

2010—*Misthopoulos v. Misthopoulos*, 297 Conn. 358, 999 A.2d 721.

Trial court improperly ordered defendant to pay 20% of his annual net cash bonus as child support.

2010—*Maturo v. Maturo*, 296 Conn. 80, 995 A.2d 1.

Child support guidelines apply to high income cases.

2005—*Arena v. Arena*, 92 Conn. App. 463, 885 A.2d 765.

Child support modification granted where ex-husband's salary, bonus, and total income had decreased while ex-wife's had increased.

2004—*Nunez v. Nunez*, 85 Conn. App. 735, 858 A.2d 873.

Defendant father properly held in contempt where he intentionally produced less reported income in order to avoid alimony and child support obligations.

2003—*Morris v. Morris*, 262 Conn. 299, 811 A.2d 1283.

Trial court applied incorrect legal standard when it utilized the gross income of the parties' base in order to determine child support and alimony rather than on net income.

2001—*Ludgin v. McGowan*, 64 Conn. App. 355, 780 A.2d 198.

Court must base orders of periodic alimony and child support on the net incomes of parties.

1999—*Hayward v. Hayward*, 53 Conn. App. 1, 752 A.2d 1087.

Deducting the value of motor vehicle provided by his employer when determining gross income for purposes of child support guidelines was improper.

1996—*Hill v. Hill*, 39 Conn. App. 258, 664 A.2d 812.

Retroactive increase was proper in child support when original order was based on incorrect net income of the payor who took too many deductions.

1994—*Evans v. Evans*, 35 Conn. App. 246, 644 A.2d 1317.

Child support modified to $900 per week for two children when father made $320,000 per year.

1993—*Diamond v. Diamond*, 32 Conn. App. 733, 631 A.2d 1157.

Retroactive modification of child support for father's failure to report the increase in his income inappropriate with a contempt motion.

1992—*Mulholland v. Mulholland*, 26 Conn. App. 585, 602 A.2d 1054.

Child support award for the express purpose of balancing the income of the divorced parents is error.

1991—*Battersby v. Battersby*, 218 Conn. 467, 590 A.2d 427.

Purpose of a child support order is to provide for the care and wellbeing of minor children and not to equalize the available income; child support guidelines do not apply to income levels above the guidelines.

1989—*Main v. Main*, 17 Conn. App. 670, 555 A.2d 997.

Abuse of discretion found when court ordered $25 per week child support where payor's income was $1,410 per week.

[2] Additional Sources of Income Other Than Salary and Wages

2021—*R.A. v. R.A.*, 209 Conn. App. 327, 268 A.3d 685.

The defendant could not prevail on her allegation that the trial court relied on inaccurate financial information in determining child support because it did not consider the plaintiff's receipt of certain government benefits. In determining whether the trial court has abused its broad discretion, every reasonable presumption in favor of the correctness of its action is allowed. An appellant would be entitled to relief from the court's ruling only if it is harmful. The defendant did not demonstrate any harm suffered as a result of the court's allegedly improper order. Moreover, given the plain mandate of that order, it is clear that the court's reliance on even inaccurate information did not harm the defendant because that order completely absolved her of any child support obligations.

2013—*Tuckman v. Tuckman*, 308 Conn. 194, 61 A.3d 449.

Court improperly considered all of the defendant's taxable income from an S corporation when entering alimony and child support orders. As the trial court did not make any findings as to the particular facts or circumstances of the S corporation, the Court remanded the case for a determination of what portion of the defendant's income was available income for purposes of fashioning alimony and child support orders.

2012—*Pace v. Pace*, 134 Conn. App. 212, 39 A.3d 756.

Trial court properly denied two post-judgment motions for modification of alimony and child support and properly granted two motions for contempt where the court found that the movant's bank accounts held over $28,000, and that gross sales for his business had increased substantially.

2010—*Misthopoulos v. Misthopoulos*, 297 Conn. 358, 999 A.2d 721.

Trial court improperly ordered defendant to pay 20% of his annual net cash bonus as child support.

2005—*Weinstein v. Weinstein*, 87 Conn. App. 699, 867 A.2d 111.

Abuse of discretion to impute an amount of investment income not supported in the record in modification of child support proceeding.

2003—*Syragakis v. Syragakis*, 79 Conn. App. 170, 829 A.2d 885.

Court based modification of child support in part on fact that defendant had substantial assets, income producing and non-income producing and substantial financial resources not included in the definition of net income.

2001—*Marrocco v. Giardino*, 255 Conn. 617, 767 A.2d 720.

Public assistance may not be considered in a determination of child support.

1998—*Jenkins v. Jenkins*, 243 Conn. 584, 704 A.2d 231.

Social Security dependency benefits paid directly to minor children because of father's disability are to be included in father's gross income for purposes of determining his child support obligations under guidelines.

1996—*Feliciano v. Feliciano*, 37 Conn. App. 856, 658 A.2d 141, *aff'd*, 236 Conn. 719, 674 A.2d 1311.

AFDC benefits should not be included in income under the guidelines.

1996—*Tyc v. Tyc*, 40 Conn. App. 562, 672 A.2d 526.

Future workers' compensation benefits should be part of the marital estate as a presently existing interest.

1980—*Remkiewicz v. Remkiewicz*, 180 Conn. 114, 429 A.2d 833.

The State became a party to the wife's dissolution action against the husband because the wife was receiving assistance from the State for herself and her child from a previous relationship. The State sought support from the husband on behalf of the child but the trial court properly concluded that it did not have jurisdiction to enter an order for her support. No statutory formalities had been observed to allow the husband to acquire parental status over the child even though the husband had signed the parentage affidavit and claimed tax benefits, the husband was permitted to deny paternity.

[3] Deviation from Child Support Guidelines

2024—*K.S. v. R.S.*, 350 Conn. 692, 326 A.2d 187.

Trial court failed to make a finding of the presumptive amount of child support and failed to make a finding that the presumptive amount, as found by applying the child support guidelines, was inequitable or inappropriate before it issued a child support order that deviated from the guidelines. The trial court's lack of findings makes it impossible to review whether such a deviation was justified.

2024—*Wald v. Cortland-Wald*, 226 Conn. App. 752, 319 A.3d 769.

The trial court improperly deviated from the presumptive amount of child support with its order for a reduced amount during the time period while both parties continue to live in the same residence because the court did not make the findings required by Conn. Gen. Stat. § 46b-215b(a). Without the specific findings that would support a deviation based on the parties' shared physical custody of their minor child, it is impossible to ascertain how the court determined that application of the child support guidelines was inequitable and inappropriate due to this criterion.

The trial court also improperly ordered that the plaintiff's child support obligation did not commence until the sale of the parties' residence and that until the sale of their residence, the plaintiff's support to the defendant was being paid by way of the household expenses where the parties both reside. Again, the court did not make findings on the record that the application of the guidelines would be inequitable or inappropriate as required by § 46b-215b(a).

2023—*Gainty v. Infantino*, 222 Conn. App. 785, 306 A.3d 1171.

Trial court did not abuse its discretion in modifying the child support orders to extend support for the parties adult daughter who has mental disabilities without first considering the child support guidelines. Under Conn. Gen. Stat. § 46b-84(c), the court may make appropriate orders of support for any child with a mental disability who resides with a parent and is principally dependent upon that parent for maintenance until such child reaches age twenty-one. The child support guidelines in Conn. Gen. Stat. § 46b-215a do not apply to orders entered under § 46b-84(c). Defendant did not raise with the trial court his claim that it lacked statutory authority to increase the amount of support previously ordered. Defendant did not provide any basis for the Appellate Court to conclude that the trial court had abused its discretion in determining his daughter's needs would be met by a $300 weekly contribution and that he had the ability to make that contribution.

2023—*Pencheva-Hasse v. Hasse*, 221 Conn. App. 113, 300 A.3d 1175.

Trial court properly determined the presumptive child support amount based on the parties' stated weekly incomes and used its broad discretion to deviate from that presumptive amount based on recognized deviation criteria established by the child support guidelines. The court specifically found presumptive amount was inequitable and inappropriate because of the parties' shared parenting schedule pursuant to Conn. Agencies Regs. § 46b-215a-5c(b)(6) and because it found Defendant's income disclosures to be not credible and understated.

2023—*Renstrup v. Renstrup*, 217 Conn. App. 252, 287 A.3d 1095.

The trial court abused its discretion in issuing a supplemental child support order that deviated from the child support guidelines and was based on erroneous findings. The trial court made the order without making an explicit finding connecting the supplemental support to the characteristics or needs of the children as required by Conn. Gen. Stat. § 46b-84(d). The appellate court reversed the order and remanded the issue for a new trial.

2021—*Anketell v. Kulldorff*, 207 Conn. App. 807, 263 A.3d 972.

The trial court properly calculated the presumptive amount of child support based on the defendant's actual income, found that the presumptive amount was determined to be unfair and inequitable, and, using the deviation criteria, deviated upward on the basis of the defendant's earning capacity then deviated downward based on the parties' shared custody, the defendant's variability of income, and his increased commuting expenses to arrive at the child support amount. The Appellate Court disagreed with all of the defendant's claims that the trial court had not based the presumptive amount on his actual income, the trial court had not articulated why the amount calculated using his actual income would be inequitable and inappropriate, and the trial court had erred in basing the child support award on improper incomes for both parties.

2021—*Zhe Zheng v. FeifeiXia*, 204 Conn. App. 302, 253 A.3d 69.

The trial court improperly considered the disparity between the parties' incomes when it granted the defendant's motion to modify child support and ordered the plaintiff to pay her 13% of his net bonus income as supplemental child support. Income disparity may be considered only when the custodial parent has the higher income and deviation from the guidelines would enhance the noncustodial parent's ability to foster a relationship with the child.

2020—*Flood v. Flood*, 199 Conn. App. 67, 234 A.3d 1076.

The trial court did not err in determining the amount of modified child support under the guidelines. It conducted an extensive evidentiary hearing and expressly noted in its order that it had considered the statutory criteria of Conn. Gen. Stat. § 46b-84(d), the parties' respective gross and after tax incomes, and their respective assets. The trial court was not required to cite additional reasons for increasing the child support obligation because the order was consistent with statutory criteria and within the range between the minimum and maximum support amounts established by the guidelines. A finding in support of a deviation from the guidelines was not necessary.

2019—*Cyganovich v. Cyganovich*, 189 Conn. App. 164, 206 A.3d 797.

The trial court did not abuse its discretion by ordering the defendant to pay child support despite the parties' shared custody arrangement, since the record showed that the parties did not spend equal amounts of money to support their child.

2018—*Keusch v. Keusch*, 184 Conn. App. 822, 195 A.3d 1136.

Trial court erroneously calculated the defendant's presumptive child support obligation on the basis of defendant's earning capacity and not actual earnings.

2018—*Battistotti v. Suzanne A.*, 182 Conn. App. 40, 188 A.3d 798.

Trial Court must consider whether significant visitation expenses justified a deviation from the child support guidelines.

2017—*Righi v. Righi*, 172 Conn. App. 427, 160 A.3d 1094.

Finding that an agreement is fair and equitable is not sufficient for a deviation from the Child Support Guidelines; the language of Conn. Gen. Stat. §§ 46b-215b and 46b-86 require an explicit finding that application of the guidelines would be "inequitable or inappropriate."

2016—*McKeon v. Lennon*, 321 Conn. 323, 138 A.3d 242.

The appellate court incorrectly relied on case law in determining that both alimony and child support orders were subject to the same modification requirements under Conn. Gen. Stat. § 46b-86(a). The plaintiff was not required to show additional circumstances, beyond an increase in defendant's income, to justify an upward modification of the child support award issued in connection with the parties' judgment of dissolution. Also, the appellate court incorrectly determined that the trial court had not abused its discretion in excluding income defendant derived from certain exercised stock options and restricted stock that vested following the dissolution judgment in calculating his gross income for the purpose of determining whether it should grant the plaintiff's 2008 motion for an upward modification of child support.

2015—*Berger v. Finkel*, 161 Conn. App. 416, 128 A.3d 508.

Remand for rehearing on motion to modify child support was warranted because the trial court viewed the husband's evidence under an inapplicable legal standard.

2015—*Chowdhury v. Masiat*, 161 Conn. App. 314, 128 A.3d 545.

Abuse of discretion when trial court deviated from requirements of child support guidelines.

2014—*Rostad v. Hirsch*, 148 Conn. App. 441, 85 A.3d 1212.

Refusal to apply Child Support Guidelines for three years prior to commencement of action pursuant to Conn. Gen. Stat. § 46b-215(a)(7)(A) was not an abuse of discretion where the payor made voluntary payments and the payee accepted.

2013—*Dowling v. Szymczak*, 309 Conn. 390, 72 A.3d 1.

Child support award between the presumptive minimum amount and the corresponding percentage does not require deviation from the child support guidelines.

2013—*Deshpande v. Deshpande*, 142 Conn. App. 471, 65 A.3d 12.

Abuse of discretion where the court awarded child support without finding the presumptive amount due under the guidelines or deviating from the guidelines.

2013—*Kavanah v. Kavanah*, 142 Conn. App. 775, 66 A.3d 922.

Court misapplied the child support guidelines by deviating based on family obligations where no evidence supported the deviation.

2011—*Tuckman v. Tuckman*, 127 Conn. App. 417, 14 A.3d 428, *aff'd*, 308 Conn. 194, 61 A.3d 449 (2013).

Trial court must require child support guidelines worksheets before entering child support orders.

2011—*Budrawich v. Budrawich*, 132 Conn. App. 291, 32 A.3d 328.

Trial court abused its discretion by modifying child support post-judgment where the court failed to find the presumptive amount of child support under the guidelines, and did not justify its deviation from the guidelines.

2010—*Maturo v. Maturo*, 296 Conn. 80, 995 A.2d 1.

Open-ended, variable child support award was inconsistent with Conn. Gen. Stat. § 46b-84 and child support guidelines; child support payments for cases presumptively "off the child support guidelines" should nonetheless not exceed 15.89% of net income in a high-income case.

2008—*Korsgren v. Jones*, 108 Conn. App. 521, 948 A.2d 358.

Court properly declined to deviate from the child support guidelines in hearing on motion to set child support; court properly relied on *Lefebvre* regarding deviation in the context of shared physical custody.

2007—*Weinstein v. Weinstein*, 104 Conn. App. 482, 934 A.2d 306.

An order based on a deviation from the child support guidelines is not modifiable on the ground that it substantially deviates from the guidelines but rather if there is a substantial change of circumstances under Conn. Gen. Stat. § 46b-86(a).

2003—*Pagliaro v. Jones*, 75 Conn. App. 625, 817 A.2d 756.

Trial court did not abuse its discretion in ordering a downward deviation from child support guidelines during period of time when plaintiff lived with her former husband.

2003—*Lefebvre v. Lefebvre*, 75 Conn. App. 662, 817 A.2d 750.

Change in children's visitation schedule did not warrant a finding of shared physical custody and thus deviation from the child support guidelines.

2000—*Russack v. Russack*, 58 Conn. App. 517, 753 A.2d 950.

Appellate court found trial court properly deviated from child support guidelines.

2000—*Amodio v. Amodio*, 56 Conn. App. 459, 743 A.2d 1135.

Modification was permissible based upon substantial deviation from child support guidelines.

1999—*Unkelbach v. McNary*, 244 Conn. 350, 710 A.2d 717.

Earning capacity of a party may not be used to justify deviation from child support guidelines where evidence introduced showed that party was employed at full capacity. Court may include domestic partner's regular contributions in husband's income for child support purposes.

1998—*Baker v. Baker*, 47 Conn. App. 672, 707 A.2d 300.

In deviating from child support guidelines, court must justify its decision to deviate on one of the deviation criteria set forth in the guidelines.

1993—*Castro v. Castro*, 31 Conn. App. 761, 627 A.2d 452.

Deviation from the guidelines was proper when wife of 20 years received no alimony.

1991—*O'Brien v. O'Brien*, 138 Conn. App. 544, 53 A.3d 1039.

Abuse of discretion was found where the court entered an unallocated alimony and child support order without considering and applying the child support guidelines and failed to explain a basis for deviation.

§ 10.04 Additional Factors to be Considered

[1] Age of Child

2013—*McKeon v. Lennon*, 147 Conn. App. 366, 83 A.3d 639.

Post judgment stipulation for payment of a child's automobile insurance expenses terminated upon the child's eighteenth birthday, when child support terminated, as a matter of law. Termination was self-executing as a matter of law because there was written agreement for payment of post majority support.

2008—*Sutherland v. Sutherland*, 107 Conn. App. 1, 944 A.2d 395.

Child support order terminating on the younger of two children's 18th birthday is not post majority support order. Separation agreement clearly and unambiguously provided for support of minor children.

2003—*O'Bryan v. O'Bryan*, 262 Conn. 355, 813 A.2d 1001.

Trial court had improperly modified plaintiff's obligation to pay post-majority child support because parties did not have written agreement that provided that court could modify post-majority child support as required by Conn. Gen. Stat. § 46b-66.

1999—*Pina v. Pina*, 55 Conn. App. 42, 737 A.2d 961.

Oral agreement regarding post-majority child support may be enforceable based on traditional contract principles in a separate civil action.

1998—*Miner v. Miner*, 48 Conn. App. 409, 709 A.2d 605.

Post-majority support agreement nonmodifiable by court.

1997—*Lowe v. Lowe*, 47 Conn. App. 354, 704 A.2d 236.

Oral stipulation on record regarding post-majority education of children not enforceable because statute requires such an agreement to be in writing.

1992—*Irizzary v. Irizzary*, 29 Conn. App. 368, 614 A.2d 868.

When one of two children attained majority, there was a substantial change in circumstances supporting a modification of child support.

1989—*Albrecht v. Albrecht*, 19 Conn. App. 146, 562 A.2d 528.

Trial court does not have jurisdiction to modify post majority support provisions without written agreement of parties regarding modification.

1986—*Matles v. Matles*, 8 Conn. App. 76, 511 A.2d 363.

Unallocated alimony and child support order is modifiable when child attains age 18.

1984—*Van Wagner v. Van Wagner*, 1 Conn. App. 578, 474 A.2d 110.

Connecticut public policy does not prohibit the enforcement of a foreign contempt order, requiring a defendant to pay for support of a child beyond the age of 18 years pursuant to an agreement which is incorporated in a dissolution decree executed in another state and which agreement, as to support payments, is consonant with the laws of that state both as of the date of the dissolution and as of the date of the contempt order.

[2] Child Care Expenses

2005—*Irizarry v. Irizarry*, 90 Conn. App. 340, 876 A.2d 593.

Trial court's finding of weekly childcare costs was not supported by evidence.

[3] Earning Capacity

2019—*Buxenbaum v. Jones*, 189 Conn. App. 790, 209 A.3d 664.

Although a court can base its financial orders on the parties' earning capacities, it is not required to do so, and the court did not abuse its discretion in making its financial orders, taking into consideration all facts and balancing the equities in the case.

2013—*Schoenborn v. Schoenborn*, 144 Conn. App. 846, 74 A.3d 482.

Although a court is obligated under Connecticut law to consider earning capacity, the decision whether to deviate from the guidelines on the basis of that criterion is left to the court's sound discretion.

2008—*Gentile v. Carneiro*, 107 Conn. App. 630, 946 A.2d 871.

Trial court's finding of earning capacity for purposes of child support was not clearly erroneous because commission income is within the definition of gross income insofar as it has a reasonably ascertainable value.

2007—*Rosier v. Rosier*, 103 Conn. App. 338, 928 A.2d 1228.

Party may introduce evidence of earnings prior to last child support order, which was issued at time of dissolution, to support earning capacity argument.

1999—*Unkelbach v. McNary*, 244 Conn. 350, 710 A.2d 717.

Earning capacity of a party may not be used to justify deviation from child support guidelines where evidence introduced showed that party was employed at full capacity.

1992—*Carey v. Carey*, 29 Conn. App. 436, 615 A.2d 516.

Child support can be based on earning capacity when payor voluntarily terminates employment.

1981—*Lucy v. Lucy*, 183 Conn. 230, 439 A.2d 302.

The trial court may under appropriate circumstances in a marital dissolution proceeding base financial awards on the earning capacity of the parties rather than on actual earned income.

1980—*Schmidt v. Schmidt*, 180 Conn. 184, 429 A.2d 470.

It is appropriate to enter an award of alimony and child support based on demonstrated earning capacity where the actual income of the party charged with that order is not shown.

[4] Emancipation

1996—*In re Thomas C.*, 691 A.2d 1140, 44 Conn. Supp. 437.

Emancipation of a 16-year old requested by his parents was denied.

1985—*Mills v. Theriault*, 499 A.2d 89, 40 Conn. Supp. 349.

Under Conn. Gen. Stat. § 46b-150d(l), the parent of a minor who is emancipated by court order is relieved of the obligation of support.

1983—*Town v. Anonymous*, 467 A.2d 687, 39 Conn. Supp. 35.

Parents are not compelled to pay the bill for whatever lifestyle a minor may select when he or she lawfully moves out of her parents' home. Parents who offer a home, food, shelter, medical care, and other necessities of life to their minor child have adequately discharged their obligation of support under and are not subject to orders of support.

1982—*State v. Clark*, 452 A.2d 316, 38 Conn. Supp. 503.

Any minor who has reached his sixteenth birthday and is residing in this state, or any parent or guardian of such minor, may petition the superior court for a determination that the minor named in the petition be emancipated. An order that a minor is emancipated shall relieve the parents of all obligation to support the minor.

[5] Health of Child

2014—*Talbot v. Talbot*, 148 Conn. App. 279, 85 A.3d 40.

No abuse of discretion where the court denied a motion for modification and noted that the payee spouse was caring for a special-needs child, but did not base its decision on that fact.

2011—*Clark v. Clark*, 130 Conn. App. 786, 26 A.3d 640.

Court properly allocated special needs expenses based on child support guidelines.

1990—*Bucy v. Bucy*, 23 Conn. App. 98, 579 A.2d 117.

Father ordered to reimburse the mother for the cost of psychological services rendered in the treatment of the daughter's bulimia and anorexia.

[6] Incarceration of Obligor

1992—*Comm'r of Human Resources v. Bridgeforth*, 604 A.2d 836, 42 Conn. Supp. 126.

Child support was suspended during incarceration.

[7] Needs of the Child

2013—*Dowling v. Szymczak*, 309 Conn. 390, 72 A.3d 1.

Purpose of the guidelines is to promote equity, uniformity and consistency for children at all income levels; retroactive award that exceeded the child's actual expenditures during the relevant time period was not improper.

2011—*Clark v. Clark*, 130 Conn. App. 786, 26 A.3d 640.

Court properly allocated special needs expenses based on child support guidelines.

1985—*Rempt v. Rempt*, 5 Conn. App. 85, 496 A.2d 988.

Evidence must be presented regarding the child's needs.

1985—*Pascal v. Pascal*, 2 Conn. App. 472, 481 A.2d 68.

Child support may be modified to satisfy unmet or continuing needs of child.

1984—*Guille v. Guille*, 196 Conn. 260, 492 A.2d 175.

Children have an independent right to support.

1981—*Hardisty v. Hardisty*, 183 Conn. 253, 439 A.2d 307.

The parents of a minor child of the marriage, shall maintain the child according to their respective abilities, if the child is in need of maintenance.

[8] Station

2013—*Dowling v. Szymczak*, 309 Conn. 390, 72 A.3d 1.

Reasonable to infer that a child was more likely to attend private school, travel, attend a major university, and pursue other opportunities beyond the reach of many children based on family history.

[9] Extracurricular Activities

2020—*Powers v. Hiranandani*, 197 Conn. App. 384, 232 A.3d 116.

The trial court did not abuse its discretion by ordering defendant to pay for 53% of the child's extracurricular activities as the cost listed on plaintiff's financial affidavit was de minimus ($1 per week). The defendant failed to demonstrate how he is harmed by the order now or would be harmed by the order in the future. The trial court did not speculate on what the child's future interests or activities would be. It simply provided a means for the parties to pay for them in the present.

§ 10.05 Health Insurance Coverage

[1] Generally

2015—*Ciottone v. Ciottone*, 154 Conn. App. 780, 107 A.3d 1004.

Evidence supported finding that mother willfully failed to utilize father's health insurance as secondary coverage for child.

1996—*Keeys v. Keeys*, 43 Conn. App. 575, 684 A.2d 1214.

As the trial court had an evidentiary basis for its factual determination that dental insurance was available and affordable, its order requiring the husband to obtain and to maintain such insurance for the minor children did not constitute an abuse of discretion.

[2] Unreimbursed Medical Expenses

2016—*Schull v. Schull*, 163 Conn. App. 83, 134 A.3d 686.

The trial court was permitted to provide a party with an additional opportunity to demonstrate that certain costs were "unreimbursed medical expenses," and did not improperly add a new condition to the parties' separation agreement. A party should not receive a windfall by obtaining reimbursement for expenses that were not actually incurred.

2014—*Doyle v. Doyle*, 150 Conn. App. 312, 90 A.3d 1024.

Trial court did not abuse its discretion in applying legal principals of contract construction, rather than relying upon child support guidelines, in determining intent of parties as to payment of children's medical expenses under separation agreement.

1996—*Keeys v. Keeys*, 43 Conn. App. 575, 684 A.2d 1214.

Medical expenses payable beyond a child's majority is an improper order.

1992—*Calway v. Calway*, 26 Conn. App. 737, 603 A.2d 434.

A former husband did not have a continuing obligation to pay a portion of the cost of unreimbursed medical expenses of his minor children where the dissolution judgment was silent on the issue.

1990—*Bucy v. Bucy*, 23 Conn. App. 98, 579 A.2d 117.

Father ordered to reimburse the mother for the cost of psychological services rendered in the treatment of the daughter's bulimia and anorexia.

§ 10.06 Life Insurance Coverage

2014—*Torla v. Torla*, 152 Conn. App. 241, 101 A.3d 275.

Upon entry of default against named beneficiary of former husband's life insurance policy on claim brought by former wife under terms of divorce decree that former husband maintain life insurance for benefit of minor children, and beneficiary's failure to file notice of defense or appear at wife's subsequent hearing on damages, allegations in wife's complaint were deemed admitted, and beneficiary's liability was conclusively established.

2013—*Szynkowicz v. Szynkowicz*, 140 Conn. App. 525, 59 A.3d 1194.

Trial court could reasonably have found that defendant had not met his burden to show that he was unable to secure life insurance.

2013—*Sagalyn v. Pederson*, 140 Conn. App. 792, 60 A.3d 367.

Court properly found that a life insurance order was not a property order and thus could be modified.

1999—*Billings v. Billings*, 54 Conn. App. 142, 732 A.2d 814.

Trial court has statutory authority to decide life insurance obligations.

1999—*Papa v. Papa*, 55 Conn. App. 47, 737 A.2d 953.

Trial court improperly ordered defendant to pay life insurance without any evidence of defendant's insurability.

1999—*Cordone v. Cordone*, 51 Conn. App. 530, 752 A.2d 1082.

Trial court is not required to secure alimony order with life insurance.

1999—*Carroll v. Carroll*, 55 Conn. App. 18, 737 A.2d 963.

Trial court properly ordered defendant to provide $100,000 life insurance policy.

1998—*Lake v. Lake*, 49 Conn. App. 89, 712 A.2d 989.

Court cannot order life or medical insurance in absence of evidence of availability or cost.

1997—*Crowley v. Crowley*, 46 Conn. App. 87, 699 A.2d 1029.

Life insurance order is nonmodifiable.

1995—*Wolf v. Wolf*, 39 Conn. App. 162, 664 A.2d 315.

Court cannot order additional life insurance without evidence of cost and availability.

1993—*Michel v. Michel*, 31 Conn. App. 338, 624 A.2d 914.

Life insurance cannot be ordered to be purchased by a party without evidence of insurability, availability of the insurance, its cost, or whether party was insurable.

1988—*Mauro v. Mauro*, 16 Conn. App. 680, 548 A.2d 471.

Award of life insurance is within the court's equitable powers.

1984—*Arseniadis v. Arseniadis*, 2 Conn. App. 239, 477 A.2d 152.

Support for a minor child extends to age 18 years only and, absent a written agreement, a court had no jurisdiction to render orders that require the supporting spouse to name adult children as the irrevocable beneficiaries of life insurance policies.

1980—*Broaca v. Broaca*, 181 Conn. 463, 435 A.2d 1016.

A court order requiring a parent with the duty of child support to name his child as beneficiary of an insurance policy on his life is an appropriate order for the maintenance of that child, however, any order of child support purporting to extend beyond a child's 18th birthday is outside the jurisdiction of the superior court and of no force and effect.

§ 10.07 Modification of Child Support

2024—*Yanavich v. Yanavich*, 228 Conn. App. 444, 325 A.3d 1149.

Trial court's finding that the defendant's draws constituted income for purposes of setting his alimony and child support obligations was not clearly erroneous. The court correctly determined that there had been no substantial change in circumstances to warrant a modification of alimony and child support. The amounts reported as income by the defendant in 2018 when the support orders were entered and the flow of funds to him in 2022 were not meaningfully different. Although his company was nowhere near as healthy as it had been in 2018, the defendant's individual earnings, except for 2021, had remained the same.

2024—*Trent v. Trent*, 321 A.3d 454.

Trial court improperly denied the plaintiff's motion to modify child support because it did not determine whether he had demonstrated a substantial change in circumstances to warrant the modification. There is no authority for the court making its ruling on the sole basis that the plaintiff requested to reduce only his child care and health care contributions instead of requesting to modify the entire order.

2024—*Czunas v. Mancini*, 226 Conn. App. 256, 317 A.3d 843.

The trial court did not err when it denied the defendant's motion to modify child support, holding that a minimal change in custody, without more, did not constitute a substantial change circumstances warranting a modification of the child support order or a determination that there had been a change in custody. The extension of the defendant's alternate weekends extended his time with the child by little more than 12 hours every other week, including when the child was sleeping between Sunday evening and Monday morning. Although a change in custody warrants a modification of child support, there was no change in custody in this case that would have triggered Conn. Gen. Stat. § 46b-224, requiring child support to be redirected to a new custodial parent so that it followed the minor child.

2024—*L.K. v. K.K.*, 226 Conn. App. 279, 318 A.3d 243.

The trial court properly denied the defendant's motion to modify his unallocated alimony and child support obligation based on a change in circumstances because he failed to show there had been a change in circumstances. At the hearing, the trial court properly declined to address the defendant's subsequently filed motion to modify his unallocated alimony and child support obligation on the ground that one of his children had reached the age of majority because the defendant had not raised that claim in the motion then before the court and he had not presented any testimony concerning the issue of one of the children reaching the age of majority. Also, proceeding on the defendant's second motion to modify just three days after it was filed would have deprived the plaintiff of the opportunity to prepare a defense to allegations raised in that motion.

The fact that a child has attained the age of majority does not automatically entitle a parent to a reduction in his alimony and support obligation; it provides a basis for seeking a modification. *Hughes v. Hughes*, 95 Conn. App. 200, 209, 895 A.2d 274 (2006). The defendant had already filed another motion to modify asserting this ground as a basis for modification. At the hearing on that motion, the parties could litigate the issue of whether they considered their children reaching the age of majority when they crafted their agreement regarding financial matters.

2023—*Marcus v. Cassara*, 223 Conn. App. 69, 308 A.3d 39.

The trial court exceeded its authority in modifying a child support order when it improperly considered whether an order regarding costs for extracurricular activities was a deviation from the child support guidelines and modified that order on a ground not contained in the motion for modification. Plaintiff filed the motion on the ground that there had been material changes in circumstances as a result of Defendant unilaterally signing up their children for extracurricular activities to which he had not agreed and which he could not afford. However, the trial court modified the extracurricular activities order on the ground that it was an unjustified deviation from the child support guidelines. A substantial change in the financial circumstances of the parties and a substantial deviation from the child support guidelines are two alternative, independent grounds for granting a motion for modification. The trial court improperly used Plaintiff's motion as an opportunity to evaluate, sua sponte, the propriety of the extracurricular activities order years after it was imposed.

Further, the trial court incorrectly concluded that the extracurricular activities order constituted a deviation from the child support guidelines, as that order had been issued separate from and independent of the order regarding Plaintiff's presumptive guideline child support obligation. It was not modifiable on the basis that it was a substantial deviation from the guidelines. On remand the trial court should consider the motion for modification on the basis of a substantial change in the circumstances of either party and the financial reasons Plaintiff alleged.

2022—*Moore v. Moore*, 216 Conn. App. 179, 283 A.3d 994.

Trial court erred when it denied Father's motion to modify child support pursuant to Conn. Gen. Stat. § 46b-86 because the court denied the motion solely on the basis that it did not find a substantial change in circumstances. Trial court failed to address the motion with respect to the propriety of child support in this case relative to the child support guidelines.

2022—*Swain v. Swain*, 213 Conn. App. 411, 277 A.3d 895.

On Wife's post-trial motion to modify, the trial court did not improperly modify existing orders as to visitation, the parental access plan, and child support because the plain language of Wife's motion to modify placed before the court the issues of custody, visitation, and the parental access schedule, not just child support as Husband had argued. Wife also testified about these issues at the hearing but Husband declined to present any rebuttal witnesses. None of the requests for clarification presented by Husband's counsel after the trial court's oral ruling contested the scope of the ruling.

2020—*Ross v. Ross*, 200 Conn. App. 720, 239 A.3d 1280.

After the parties' children had all reached the age of majority and the unallocated alimony and child support order could be modified pursuant to Conn. Gen. Stat. § 46b-86, the trial court erred in modifying the unallocated support award without unbundling child support from alimony and in failing to consider and to apply the child support guidelines to determine how much of the unallocated award constituted child support.

2020—*Brown v. Brown*, 199 Conn. App. 134, 235 A.3d 555.

The trial court did not abuse its discretion by denying a father's motion for modification of child support under Conn. Gen. Stat. § 46b-86 because he failed to show a substantial change in circumstances. Although he had been unemployed for a period of time and his salary had declined, he had maintained his lifestyle and his expenses and liabilities were unchanged. Thus, he failed to establish the threshold requirement of a substantial change in his financial circumstances.

2020—*Flood v. Flood*, 199 Conn. App. 67, 234 A.3d 1076.

Child support was properly modified under Conn. Gen. Stat. § 46b-86 because the savings resulting from the termination of the husband's court ordered obligation to pay 100% of private school tuition and costs when his child began attending public school was a material improvement in the husband's financial situation that represented a substantial change in circumstances entitling the mother to a modification in child support.

2019—*Bolat v. Bolat*, 293 Conn. 397, 215 A.3d 736.

Trial court did not abuse its discretion in denying father's motion modify child support due to substantial change in circumstances, alleging a nearly 50% reduction in his gross income. A party seeking modification bears burden of showing the existence of substantial change in circumstances. While father provided testimony and documentary evidence, trial court as fact finder was free to discredit his testimony. It found that father's first exhibit specified he had been laid off due to company reorganization but it was not a document from the company itself and was not supported by testimony explaining the exhibit or what it was supposed to detail. Trial court could not determine what actual changes had been made to father's compensation or that no income could be assigned to him. The second exhibit lacked credibility as father had prepared it in preparation for the hearing and provided no supporting documents. Appellate court found that in absence of any credible evidence that father's income had declined, trial court could have reasonably found that father failed to prove substantial change in circumstances.

2019—*Cyganovich v. Cyganovich*, 189 Conn. App. 164, 206 A.3d 797.

The trial court did not abuse its discretion by ordering the defendant to pay child support despite the parties' shared custody arrangement, since the record showed that the parties did not spend equal amounts of money to support their child.

2017—*Mason v. Ford*, 176 Conn. App. 658, 168 A.3d 525.

Trial court's determination that the defendant had failed to pay the plaintiff child support since the middle of November 2015 was not clearly erroneous where the court implicitly credited the plaintiff's testimony that the payments had ended during the middle to end of November 2015.

Trial court abused discretion in ordering a modification of alimony and child support retroactive to March 2016 when the operative motion was filed in June of 2016.

2017—*LeSueur v. LeSueur*, 172 Conn. App. 767, 162 A.3d 32.

Trial court did not err in declining to grant a child support overpayment credit retroactively to date of service.

2017—*Righi v. Righi*, 172 Conn. App. 427, 160 A.3d 1094.

A motion to modify child support may be granted, absent a substantial change in circumstances; where the initial trial court order deviated from the Child Support Guidelines but failed to make a finding that application of the Child Support Guidelines would be inappropriate or inequitable.

2017—*Robinson v. Robinson*, 172 Conn. App. 393, 160 A.3d 376.

Only alimony received from a nonparty to the support determination is included in gross income for determination of child support under the Child Support Guidelines. Court did not err in denying reduction of child support where doing so would have left the receiving parent unable to meet the basic needs of the children.

2016—*Gabriel v. Gabriel*, 324 Conn. 324, 152 A.3d 1230.

The trial court properly denied the former wife's motion for contempt, as the support order was not sufficiently clear or unambiguous when the husband unilaterally reduced his support payments because the unspecified portion of the preexisting unallocated support order attributable to child support was suspended automatically under Conn. Gen. Stat. § 46b-224 by a change in primary physical custody of the parties' children to the husband without the trial court's determination on the support issue.

2016—*Olson v. Mohammadu*, 169 Conn. App. 243, 149 A.3d 198.

Trial court's rejection of deductions from gross income and denial of motion to modify child support was not an abuse of discretion.

2016—*McKeon v. Lennon*, 321 Conn. 323, 138 A.3d 242.

The reasoning set forth in *Dan v. Dan* does not apply to modifications of child support orders.

2016—*Studer v. Studer*, 320 Conn. 483, 131 A.3d 240.

The modification of a child support order is governed by the law of the state which originally issued the order.

2016—*Malpeso v. Malpeso*, 165 Conn. App. 151, 138 A.3d 1069.

When adjudicating a motion to modify unallocated alimony and support, the court must determine the proper child support number at the time of the original order (even if it is part of an unallocated order) and then compare the circumstances at the time of trial or agreement against the present circumstances.

2016—*Farmassony v. Farmassony*, 164 Conn. App. 665, 138 A.3d 417.

Retroactive modification of child care costs, which were an element of child support, was an abuse of discretion.

2015—*Coury v. Coury*, 161 Conn. App. 271, 128 A.3d 517.

Failure to comply with service of process requirements did not prevent retroactive modification of child support portion of unallocated award. Statute requiring modification of child support on transfer of custody (Conn. Gen. Stat. § 46b-224) controls over statute precluding retroactive modification of child support (Conn. Gen. Stat. § 46b-86(a)).

2014—*Altraide v. Altraide*, 153 Conn. App. 327, 101 A.3d 317.

Husband failed to establish a substantial change in circumstances that warranted modification of child support or alimony; husband's recent engagement and his change in tax filing status did not provide grounds for modifying child support or alimony, and husband's increased mortgage expense could not be considered because it was part of the property settlement in the judgment of dissolution.

2013—*Malpeso v. Malpeso*, 140 Conn. App. 783, 60 A.3d 380.

Trial court improperly determined that a separation agreement precluded modification of child support where agreement provided for unallocated support and precluded modification of "alimony" unless certain circumstances occurred.

2008—*Sutherland v. Sutherland*, 107 Conn. App. 1, 944 A.2d 395.

A clause that precluded oral modification of the separation agreement did not preclude modification of support under Conn. Gen. Stat. § 46b-86.

2003—*Fusco v. Fusco*, 266 Conn. 649, 835 A.2d 6.

Trial courts always have subject matter jurisdiction over motions for modification of post-majority child support.

1999—*Amodio v. Amodio*, 247 Conn. 724, 724 A.2d 1084.

Trial court always has subject matter jurisdiction over modification of child support and alimony orders; proper inquiry is whether court has power to act under decree.

1994—*Evans v. Evans*, 35 Conn. App. 246, 644 A.2d 1317.

Child support was modified to $900 per week for two children when father made $320,000 per year.

1986—*Kaplan v. Kaplan*, 8 Conn. App. 114, 510 A.2d 1024.

An order for support of children may not be modified unless there has been a substantial change of circumstances after the issuance of the original order.

§ 10.08 Arrearages

2024—*M.S. v. M.S.*, 226 Conn. App. 482, 319 A.3d 223.

In denying the defendant's motion for contempt, the trial court erred by failing to determine the amount of the arrearage attributable to the plaintiff's noncompliance with the parties' June 2017 child support order. The terms of that order provided that the plaintiff would pay $2,600 per month until June 30, 2019 and expressly contemplated that after that date, child support would be modified based on the support guidelines. The plaintiff's unilateral decision to self-calculate and thereby reduce the amount of his obligation based on his understanding of the child support guidelines was inconsistent with the plain language of the order referencing modification. The only fair and reasonable construction of the June 2017 order was that it contemplated a judicial determination of the plaintiff's child support obligation following consideration of the child support guidelines, as required by statute. However, the plaintiff did not file his motion to modify until September 2020; and the trial court did not rule on that motion until March 2021. Judgment reversed in part as to the defendant's motion for contempt. Matter remanded for further proceedings limited to a new hearing to identify properly any arrearage owed to the defendant for the period of July 1, 2019 through March 24, 2021 and to establish the terms for payment of that arrearage.

2020—*Davis v. Davis*, 200 Conn. App. 180, 238 A.3d 46.

The trial court abused its discretion under Conn. Gen. Stat. § 46b-224 by calculating the defendant's outstanding child support obligations without deducting from the arrearage the amount for the time that the minor child was in the defendant's custody because the defendant had not filed a motion for modification of child support. The statute plainly requires that a court order changing custody shall operate to suspend a child support order if custody is transferred to the obligor.

2018—*Kirwan v. Kirwan*, 185 Conn. App. 713, 197 A.3d 1000.

Trial court did not abuse its discretion in ordering the defendant to make a lump sum payment in satisfaction of his child support arrearage where the defendant had the ability to pay.

2017—*Pressley v. Johnson*, 173 Conn. App. 402, 162 A.3d 751.

Trial court erred in denying plaintiff's motion for contempt and finding that the defendant did not owe her an arrearage for the work-related child care expenses she had incurred.

2015—*Tavani v. Riley*, 160 Conn. App. 669, 124 A.3d 1009.

Father's complaint, seeking an accounting that he owed no child support arrearage, was justiciable.

2015—*Lisko v. Lisko*, 158 Conn. App. 734, 121 A.3d 722.

Arrearage owed to plaintiff was not satisfied by the social security dependency benefits paid directly to plaintiff.

2013—*Carpender v. Sigel*, 142 Conn. App. 379, 67 A.3d 1011.

Court improperly found that laches, waiver and estoppel applied to reimbursement of expenses for extracurricular activities where the party incurred expenses seven to eight years before filing a motion for contempt and the court made no factual findings with respect to the holding.

1984—*Brock v. Cavanaugh*, 1 Conn. App. 138, 468 A.2d 1242.

Equitable estoppel is the effect of the voluntary conduct of a party whereby he is absolutely precluded, both at law and in equity, from asserting rights which might perhaps have otherwise existed as against another person, who has in good faith relied upon such conduct, and has been led thereby to change his position for the worse.

1981—*Hayes v. Beresford*, 184 Conn. 558, 440 A.2d 244.

Separation agreement was properly considered a contract under seal thus support arrearages were enforceable.

§ 10.09 Duration of Support Obligation

2013—*McKeon v. Lennon*, 147 Conn. App. 366, 83 A.3d 639.

Post-judgment stipulation for payment of a child's automobile insurance expenses terminated upon the child's eighteenth birthday, when child support terminated, as a matter of law. Termination was self-executing as a matter of law because there was written agreement for payment of post-majority support.

2008—*Sutherland v. Sutherland*, 107 Conn. App. 1, 944 A.2d 395.

Child support order terminating on the younger of two children's 18th birthday is not post majority support order where separation agreement clearly and unambiguously provided for support of minor children.

1991—*Hirtle v. Hirtle*, 217 Conn. 394, 586 A.2d 578.

Written agreement is a jurisdictional prerequisite to the valid modification of an order for post-majority support thus where there is a post age 18 order, it is presumed there was a written agreement.

1989—*Albrecht v. Albrecht*, 19 Conn. App. 146, 562 A.2d 528.

Trial court does not have jurisdiction to modify post majority support provisions without written agreement of parties regarding modification.

§ 10.10 Educational Support

[1] In General

2020—*Leonova v. Leonov*, 201 Conn. App. 285, 242 A.3d 713.

The trial court's order to establish two § 529 plans to secure any future educational support order for the parties' children was eminently fair because both parties were ordered to contribute equally to the creation of the § 529 plans after they had used their children's gift money to renovate a home that the children will never occupy. The trial court properly exercised its authority to secure the contemplated future educational support orders by requiring each party to restore one half of the children's gift money and to protect it for their future educational needs.

2020—*Longbottom v. Longbottom*, 197 Conn. App. 64, 231 A.3d 310.

The trial court did not abuse its discretion in denying the plaintiff ex-wife's motion to open and to modify the trial court's previous judgment modifying an existing educational support order for the parties' daughter, alleging fraudulent nondisclosure on the defendant ex-husband's part. The trial court determined that the plaintiff failed to establish probable cause of fraudulent nondisclosure. Although the defendant's stock sale income and proceeds were in different places on his financial affidavit, they were listed on his financial affidavit and had not been omitted or concealed. The court had the ex-husband's W-2 and tax returns, which showed the stock options he received as income. Judgment affirmed.

2019—*Kirwan v. Kirwan*, 187 Conn. App. 375, 202 A.3d 458.

Plaintiff was not required to confer or consult with defendant regarding the children's continued enrollment at their private schools; it was not a decision governed by the parenting plan because it was the status quo—the children were already attending that school when the parties entered into the parenting plan.

1997—*Lowe v. Lowe*, 47 Conn. App. 354, 704 A.2d 236.

Oral stipulation on record regarding post-majority education of children not enforceable because statute requires such an agreement to be in writing.

1986—*Masters v. Masters*, 201 Conn. 50, 513 A.2d 104.

Conn. Gen. Stat. § 46b-56 grants the trial court continuing jurisdiction to make or modify any proper order regarding the education and support of the children.

1981—*Hardisty v. Hardisty*, 183 Conn. 253, 439 A.2d 307.

The right of the custodial parent to make educational choices is an insufficient basis, absent a showing of special need or some other compelling justification, for increasing the support obligation of the noncustodial parent who genuinely doubts the value of the program that he is being asked to underwrite.

1981—*Gallo v. Gallo*, 184 Conn. 36, 440 A.2d 782.

Decree ordering the husband to contribute to an educational fund for his son was proper because the husband had agreed to make such payments, and the order did not go past the child's 18th birthday.

[2] College Expenses

2023—*Simpson v. Simpson*, 222 Conn. App. 466, 306 A.3d 477.

Trial court improperly ordered Defendant to pay 90% of college expenses for the parties' older child to attend Clemson University. Their separation agreement specifically provided that the court would retain jurisdiction under the Connecticut Educational Support Act to enter an order regarding each child's four-year undergraduate college education as provided for in Conn. Gen. Stat.§ 46b-56c if the parties were unable to reach an agreement by themselves. The trial court's finding that the parties had agreed that educational support for their older child would exceed the cost of attendance at University of Connecticut was clearly erroneous. While they had agreed their child would attend Clemson, their agreement as to school selection did not amount to an agreement to provide educational support in excess of the statutory cap. Remanded for new hearing on Plaintiff's motion for order regarding college education costs.

2022—*Buehler v. Buehler*, 211 Conn. App. 357, 272 A.3d 736.

Trial did not abuse its discretion in granting a mother's motion for order re: postsecondary education support, postjudgment where the dissolution court had reserved jurisdiction regarding orders for postsecondary education for the parties' three children. The mother sent the father an email about their daughter's interest in attending college during the child's junior year of high school. She also sent him communications throughout the following summer and into their daughter's senior year. Father did not participate in the college selection process, provide information for financial aid, nor contribute to tuition. The court's finding that the mother had attempted to include the father in the college selection process was not clearly erroneous and was supported by evidence in the record.

2019—*Malpeso v. Malpeso*, 189 Conn. App. 486, 207 A.3d 1085.

The trial court did not err in finding that defendant's payment of the children's college expenses constituted a substantial change in circumstances warranting modification of alimony where the magnitude of the expense was not anticipated by the parties. The cost included $40,000 to $60,000 per year for each of the parties' three children, plus miscellaneous expenses of $130,000 over just a two-year period.

2016—*Dumbauld v. Dumbauld*, 163 Conn. App. 517, 136 A.3d 669.

A party cannot be ordered to pay all educational costs, in excess of the UCONN cap, where the parties have not provided a waiver of the college education statute.

2015—*Barbour v. Barbour*, 156 Conn. App. 383, 113 A.3d 77.

Expenses for restaurant meals, lodging and transportation are not within the scope of statute governing educational support orders pursuant to Conn. Gen. Stat. § 46b-56c.

2013—*Carpender v. Sigel*, 142 Conn. App. 379, 67 A.3d 1011.

No abuse of discretion where the court found that the plaintiff had not unreasonably withheld consent to pay for college when the plaintiff objected to the child's choice of college based on the child's academic history.

2012—*Glenn v. Glenn*, 133 Conn. App. 397, 35 A.3d 376.

Trial court did not improperly order payment of college expenses under Conn. Gen. Stat. § 46b-56c where court retained jurisdiction to enter orders, but failed to state that the parents more likely than not would have provided for higher education if the family were intact.

2012—*Hopson v. Hopson*, 135 Conn. App. 690, 42 A.3d 528.

Trial court did not unreasonably order defendant to reimburse the plaintiff for one half of son's college tuition, where the university credited plaintiff with payment because she was an employee.

2011—*Bock v. Bock*, 127 Conn. App. 553, 14 A.3d 479.

Court lacked jurisdiction to address a motion to modify educational support orders under Conn. Gen. Stat. § 46b-56c.

2011—*Loso v. Loso*, 132 Conn. App. 257, 31 A.3d 830.

Educational support provision in the parties' separation agreement was clear and unambiguous.

2011—*Kleinman v. Chapnick*, 131 Conn. App. 812, 30 A.3d 3.

Court did not create an ambiguity when it ordered that each party be responsible for liabilities on their respective financial affidavits and plaintiff's financial affidavit listed "anticipated" future educational expenses. Trial court did not abuse its discretion when it did not order the plaintiff to pay several months of educational support under Conn. Gen. Stat. § 46b-56c after annual cap had already been met under Conn. Gen. Stat. § 46b-56c(f).

2010—*Creatura v. Creatura*, 122 Conn. App. 47, 998 A.2d 798.

Appellate Court rejected defendant's reading of a college education provision in separation agreement and found provision unambiguous.

2010—*Tobet v. Tobet*, 119 Conn. App. 63, 986 A.2d 329.

Finding by the trial court that cost of annual tuition and board at University of Connecticut was "roughly $16,000 or $17,000" without evidence was improper.

2010—*Flaherty v. Flaherty*, 120 Conn. App. 266, 990 A.2d 1274.

Trial court incorrectly determined it lacked authority to order plaintiff to contribute specific sums toward postsecondary educational expenses where separation agreement provided plaintiff would "contribute towards" such expenses but did not specify amount or a percentage.

2004—*Kelman v. Kelman*, 86 Conn. App. 120, 860 A.2d 292.

Trial court exceeded its authority under Conn. Gen. Stat. § 46b-56c in fashioning its educational support order since it failed to limit the ex-husband's obligation to pay for the children's education to a period of four academic years or until the children reached the age of 23, at a cost equivalent to that charged by the University of Connecticut for a full-time in-state student.

2001—*BonHotel v. BonHotel*, 64 Conn. App. 561, 781 A.2d 318.

Obligation to pay the cost of "room and board of any undergraduate college" is not limited to college providing room and board and does not include the cost of living with the other parent while attending college.

1997—*Lowe v. Lowe*, 47 Conn. App. 354, 704 A.2d 236.

Oral stipulation on record regarding post-majority education of children not enforceable because statute requires such an agreement to be in writing.

1997—*Legg v. Legg*, 44 Conn. App. 303, 688 A.2d 1354.

Spirit and intent of separation agreement required father to pay one-half of child's room and board when he lived with mother and commuted to college.

1992—*Greenburg v. Greenburg*, 26 Conn. App. 591, 602 A.2d 1056.

Nothing in the separation agreement gave the father sole decision making power over college choice.

1989—*Albrecht v. Albrecht*, 19 Conn. App. 146, 562 A.2d 528.

Parents' agreement to pay the cost of the college and professional education of the children in proportion to their adjusted gross incomes after deducting the first $25,000 therefrom must be strictly construed and trial court properly followed that formula, which omitted use of the parties' earning abilities.

1989—*Buchetto v. Haggquist*, 17 Conn. App. 544, 554 A.2d 763.

"Financially able" language regarding the payment of college may be an expression of intent and not a binding obligation.

1989—*Breen v. Breen*, 18 Conn. App. 166, 557 A.2d 140.

Court may consider one party's payment of college expenses in making other financial orders.

1989—*Cattaneo v. Cattaneo*, 19 Conn. App. 161, 561 A.2d 967.

Where plaintiff brought a motion asking court to state the extent to which defendant must contribute to college, court held that contribution to college expenses "in accordance with respective financial abilities" implies a court must set the amount if the parties cannot agree.

1987—*Gallagher v. Gallagher*, 11 Conn. App. 509, 528 A.2d 379.

Trial court did not err in setting the father's college tuition payment dates based on when he received his salary, commissions, and bonuses.

1986—*Pickman v. Pickman*, 6 Conn. App. 271, 505 A.2d 4.

Court held that the husband freely and voluntarily, after caution by the trial court and consultation with his attorney, agreed to be responsible for the children's college education.

1985—*Trubowitz v. Trubowitz*, 5 Conn. App. 681, 502 A.2d 940.

Payment of college education expenses cannot be a factor in award of property.

1985—*LaVigne v. LaVigne*, 3 Conn. App. 423, 488 A.2d 1290.

Language in agreement contemplated father would pay college expenses but did not obligate him thus father's obligation in pre-1977 agreement was not enforceable by contempt.

[3] Private School

2019—*Thunelius v. Posacki*, 193 Conn. App. 666, 220 A.3d 194.

Trial court abused its discretion in ordering the parties divide private school tuition past eighth grade when there was no evidence that the parties had agreed on their child attending private high school and the court lacked sufficient evidence to make such an order.

2019—*Kirwan v. Kirwan*, 187 Conn. App. 375, 202 A.3d 458.

Plaintiff was not required to confer or consult with defendant regarding the children's continued enrollment at their private schools; it was not a decision governed by the parenting plan because it was the status quo—the children were already attending that school when the parties entered into the parenting plan.

2011—*Culver v. Culver*, 127 Conn. App. 236, 17 A.3d 1048.

Father not given credit for private school expenses paid when based on disputed oral agreement.

2009—*Afkari-Ahmadi v. Fotovat-Ahmadi*, 294 Conn. 384, 985 A.2d 319.

Failure of the parties' minor child to achieve a C average in public school triggered the private school enrollment provision in post-judgment stipulation when contract defined the academic goal as C average.

2005—*Scott v. Scott*, 90 Conn. App. 883, 879 A.2d 540.

Private school charges identified as "therapeutic services" constitute "medical or therapy expenses" within meaning of child support clause of dissolution decree.

1999—*Carroll v. Carroll*, 55 Conn. App. 18, 737 A.2d 963.

Trial court properly ordered defendant to contribute to child's private school tuition.

1986—*Flynn v. Flynn*, 7 Conn. App. 745, 510 A.2d 1005.

A trial court has the power to direct one or both parents to pay for private schooling, if the circumstances warrant, and may exercise that power in its sound discretion, giving consideration to all of the circumstances, including the financial ability of the parties, the availability of public schools, the schools attended by the children prior to the divorce and the special needs and general welfare of the children.

CHAPTER 11

CHILD CUSTODY AND VISITATION

SYNOPSIS

§ 11.01 Best Interests of the Child Standard

[1] Generally

2024—*K.S. v. R.S.*, 350 Conn. 692, 326 A.3d 187.

Trial court did not abuse its discretion in ordering that the mother could relocate to the Czech Republic with the parties' children. The custody order indicated that the court considered many of the statutory factors set forth in Conn. Gen. Stat. § 46b-56(c) and Con. Gen. Stat. § 46b-56d(b), insofar as the court articulated the basis for its decision. There could be no conclusion that the court abused its discretion when it based its decision on the application of the various statutory factors and considered the testimony of two experts.

2024—*Labieniec v. Megna*, 228 Conn. App. 127, 324 A.3d 181.

Trial court did not abuse its discretion in denying the defendant's motion for an order regarding a passport for the parties' child. There was evidence to support the court's findings that granting the order was not in the child's best interest in light of her age and development.

2024—*N.R. v. M.P.*, 227 Conn. App. 698, 323 A.3d 1142.

Trial court did not abuse its discretion in awarding the mother sole legal and physical custody of the parties' children because the court appropriately made its custody orders pursuant to the best interests of the children standard set out in Conn. Gen.

Stat. § 46b-56. The court was not required to apply the test in Conn. Gen. Stat. § 46b-56d, which applies only to relocation matters arising after the entry of judgment awarding custody; the father's claim that the court had not applied this test did not provide a legal basis for challenging the custody order. Further, the father failed to demonstrate any abuse of discretion by the court in relying on the testimony of the guardian ad litem in making its determination of the best interests of the children.

2024—*F.S. v. J.S.*, 223 Conn. App. 763, 310 A.3d 961.

Trial court did not abuse its discretion in granting sole legal and physical custody of the parties' son to the plaintiff, setting conditions on the defendant's supervised visitation, and limiting the defendant's ability to seek modification or expansion of his parenting access because the court had considered the evidence presented in making a custody determination that was in the best interests of the child as required by Conn. Gen. Stat. § 46b-56(c). Contrary to the defendant's claim, the court did not render its decision solely on the basis of his mental health diagnosis as prohibited by § 46b-56(c)(13). Instead the court was concerned by the defendant's failure to make reasonable progress to address its harmful effect on his parenting as set forth in the decision.

The defendant did not demonstrate that the court made any clearly erroneous findings regarding his mental health. The court did not abuse its discretion by considering the 2019 custody evaluation. To the extent the evaluation may have had some limitations because of the delay while the courts were closed due to COVID-19, that went solely to its weight rather than its admissibility. There was ample more current evidence of the defendant's present inability to parent presented at trial that supported the court's custody determination.

2023—*Pencheva-Hasse v. Hasse*, 221 Conn. App. 113, 300 A.3d 1175.

Trial court did not abuse its discretion in issuing child custody orders as its memorandum of decision noted that it had fully considered the criteria of Conn. Gen. Stat. § 46b-56 and § 46b-56c, evidence, applicable case law, and the demeanor and credibility of the witnesses in making the orders. The court found it to be in the best interests of the parties' child to order them to share joint legal custody and to order parenting plan that provided equal parenting time with each party.

2023—*In re Paulo T.*, 347 Conn. 311, 297 A.3d 194.

Trial court did not apply a presumption in favor of a mother when it determined that reinstatement of her guardianship rights was in the best interests of the parties' child. Although the trial court had stated in its oral decision that parents are entitled to a presumption that reinstatement of guardianship rights is in the best interests of the child, Supreme Court accepted the trial court's unequivocal response to its articulation order that the trial court did not apply the presumption. The trial court had not precisely stated the law but confirmed that it had appropriately applied the law. The remainder of trial court's decision demonstrated that the court determined reinstatement of guardianship was in the best interests of the child by considering and applying the statutory factors set forth in Conn. Gen. Stat. § 46b-56(c). The judgment of the Appellate Court concluded that the trial court had applied the proper, best interests balancing test and had not applied the presumption was affirmed.

2023—*Prioleau v. Agosta*, 220 Conn. App. 248, 297 A.3d 1012.

In ruling on Mother's motion for reconsideration, the trial court did not abuse its discretion in adjusting the parties' parenting schedule to give her some weekend parenting time instead of awarding Father parenting time every weekend as ordered in the initial judgment. Pursuant to Conn. Gen. Stat. § 46b-56, the trial court determined it was in their child's best interests to allow both parties to enjoy roughly equal amounts of parenting time and attempted to apportion the visitation accordingly. While it was understandable that Father was dissatisfied with his reduced number of overnights, the trial court's attempt to balance the parties' competing desires for quality time with their child did not constitute an abuse of its broad discretion.

2022—*J.Y. v. M.R.*, 215 Conn. App. 648, 283 A.3d 520.

Trial court did not err by transferring the child's primary residence for school purposes from Mother to Father because it properly considered the child's best interests and did not engage in speculation. Although the child was not scheduled to begin kindergarten until 2021, trial court found that issuing the residence order immediately was proper considering the parties' history of litigation.

2021—*R.A. v. R.A.*, 209 Conn. App. 327, 268 A.3d 685.

The trial court did not abuse its discretion by crafting a visitation order which adopted the recommendations of the family relations counselor and granted plaintiff the right to facilitate visitation. The court appropriately weighed the counselor's input against that of other witnesses and evidence before issuing the order.

2021—*Coleman v. Bembridge*, 207 Conn. App. 28, 263 A.3d 403.

Under Conn. Gen. Stat. § 46b-56a, the trial court had the authority to order joint physical custody notwithstanding that both parties requested only sole custody.

The trial court did not violate the plaintiff's rights to due process in ordering joint physical custody because the plaintiff sought broad relief and custody was the primary contested issue at trial where the plaintiff testified, elicited testimony from a family relations counselor, cross-examined the defendant, and offered exhibits into evidence. On the basis of the evidence before it, the trial court concluded joint physical custody was in the best interests of the parties' child. Under these circumstances, particularly where the plaintiff herself requested broad relief from the court, the Appellate Court was not convinced she did not have fair notice and a reasonable opportunity to be heard as to the court's award of joint physical custody.

There was no inconsistency in the trial court making the reasonable determination that, although the plaintiff had communicated with the defendant about the child following his birth and maintained regular video contact, the totality of the evidence established that without court intervention, the plaintiff was unlikely to foster a relationship between the defendant and the child. There was substantial evidence that the plaintiff was unable to be an adequate gatekeeper promoting a relationship between the defendant and their child.

2020—*Nietupski v. Del Castillo*, 196 Conn. App. 31, 228 A.3d 1053.

Trial court did not abuse its discretion in permitting the parties' son to remain enrolled at his school. The trial court made findings, including giving credit to testimony from the child's guardian ad litem, that provided an adequate basis to conclude that attending the school was in the child's best interest. Similarly, the trial court did not abuse its discretion in permitting the child to travel outside the United States on vacations with either party, again crediting the recommendation of the guardian ad litem, who was in favor of permitting the child to travel internationally. Judgment affirmed.

2016—*Petrov v. Gueorguieva*, 167 Conn. App. 505, 146 A.3d 26.

Trial court assessed the present best interests of the child when it considered the mother's past conduct to give context to the mother's more recent actions.

2016—*D'Amato v. Hart-D'Amato*, 169 Conn. App. 669, 152 A.3d 546.

Evidence supported trial court's award of sole custody to father where the mother had consumed large amounts of vodka daily, children did not want contact with the mother, and mother minimized the nature and extent of her alcohol difficulties.

2015—*In re Nevaeh W et al.*, 317 Conn. 723, 120 A.3d 1177.

Determination about best interests of the child would not be overturned based on one factor. Statutory findings about child's feelings and emotions are required.

2014—*Keenan v. Casillo*, 149 Conn. App. 642, 89 A.3d 912.

Trial court had statutory authority to enter an order granting joint custody of the children, so long as it found that it was in the best interests of the children and at least one party had filed a pleading requesting joint custody.

2012—*In re Zowie*, 135 Conn. App. 470, 41 A.3d 1056.

Trial court can order either parent to participate in counseling if participation is in the best interests of the minor child.

2011—*McKechnie v. McKechnie*, 130 Conn. App. 411, 23 A.3d 779.

Case law makes it abundantly clear that the best interests of a child control a custody determination.

2008—*Watrous v. Watrous*, 108 Conn. App. 813, 949 A.2d 557.

The court is not required to consider all the factors in Conn. Gen. Stat. § 46b-56(c) when determining best interests of a child, just the factors that most appropriate in a particular case.

2006—*Stahl v. Bayliss*, 98 Conn. App. 63, 907 A.2d 139.

Custody determination must be based on the present best interests of the minor children.

2001—*McGinty v. McGinty*, 66 Conn. App. 35, 783 A.2d 1170.

Best interests of child properly utilized when modifying visitation schedule.

2000—*Ignacio v. Montana-Ignacio*, 57 Conn. App. 647, 750 A.2d 491.

Motion for modification of custody and child support denied where appellate court found trial court could have reasonably determined that plaintiff looked out for children's best interests.

1999—*Kelly v. Kelly*, 54 Conn. App. 50, 732 A.2d 808.

Court must find material change of circumstances or that order that is sought to be modified was not in best interest of children in order to modify custody award.

1999—*In re Charles A.*, 55 Conn. App. 293, 738 A.2d 222.

Mother's parental rights' termination was in best interest of the children.

1998—*Temple v. Meyer*, 208 Conn. 404, 544 A.2d 629.

The burden of proof on plaintiff to show that visitation is in the child's best interest.

1996—*Brubeck v. Burns-Brubeck*, 42 Conn. App. 583, 680 A.2d 327.

Material change in circumstances plus best interest test must be satisfied before a court can modify custody.

1995—*Fiddelman v. Redmon*, 37 Conn. App. 397, 656 A.2d 234.

The court has an independent duty to determine best interest of child, and court isn't bound by claims of one or both of the parents.

1985—*Cappetta v. Cappetta*, 196 Conn. 10, 490 A.2d 996.

The court found that the plaintiff had violated a court order prohibiting visits of male friends and that, because the plaintiff "is immature, lacks judgment and has no respect for authority," she should not be awarded custody.

1981—*Yontef v. Yontef*, 185 Conn. 275, 440 A.2d 899.

Inquiries into psychological parenting and into life style are relevant insofar as they shed light upon the effect that a parent's behavior is having on a child's well-being.

1980—*Seymour v. Seymour*, 180 Conn. 705, 433 A.2d 1005.

Trial court did not err when it looked to other factors, such as the child's psychological relationship with her parents, in determining who should retain custody of the minor child.

1980—*Presutti v. Presutti*, 181 Conn. 622, 436 A.2d 299.

The controlling principle in a determination respecting custody is that the court shall be guided by the best interests of the child.

[2] Abuse

2023—*C.D. v. CD.*, 218 Conn. App. 818, 293 A.3d 86.

The trial court had broad discretion to make orders limiting the husband's visitation with the parties' children after finding he did not have the ability to take care of them and to act in their best interests by putting their welfare first and foremost. The visitation orders tracked the recommendations of the children's guardian ad litem who testified she had significant concerns about the husband's ability to care for the children because of his unrelenting desire to be vindicated and to see the wife punished for purportedly falsifying the details of an alleged domestic violence incident between the parties, the husband's unwillingness to shield the children from that incident (of which they were so far unaware), and his unsubstantiated belief that the wife sought to cause him serious harm. The testimony of the guardian ad litem, as well as the husband's own testimony buttressing her concerns, adequately supported the finding upon which the trial court based its orders.

2015—*In re Quidanny L.*, 159 Conn. App. 363, 122 A.3d 1281.

Termination of parental rights based on "severe physical abuse" does not require proof of severe physical injury. Evidence sufficient to terminate parental rights based on parental commission.

1993—*Knock v. Knock*, 224 Conn. 776, 621 A.2d 267.

Battered woman's syndrome testimony was relevant to the best interests of the child.

1981—*In re Juvenile Appeal*, 183 Conn. 11, 438 A.2d 801.

Factual evidence did not support the judicial truth of sexual abuse.

[3] Presumptions

1988—*Hurtado v. Hurtado*, 14 Conn. App. 296, 541 A.2d 873.

There is no presumption in favor of a mother having custody.

1982—*Schaffer v. Schaffer*, 187 Conn. 224, 445 A.2d 589.

There is a presumption that a child born during marriage is the husband's child.

[4] Religion

1991—*Tatro v. Tatro*, 24 Conn. App. 180, 587 A.2d 154.

Court cannot order that child participate in religious ceremonies and changes in religious affiliation implicate fundamental personal rights that cannot be subject to a court order.

[5] Drug and Alcohol Testing

2014—*Greenan v. Greenan*, 150 Conn. App. 289, 91 A.3d 909.

Adverse inference may be drawn by court as to husband's drug use based on his refusal to testify regarding his prior drug related arrest.

[6] Death of Parent

1986—*Evans v. Santoro*, 6 Conn. App. 707, 507 A.2d 1007.

After father who had custody of daughter died, paternal grandparents continued to care for child until mother was awarded custody. The appellate court affirmed holding that, upon the death of the father, the mother became the sole legal guardian of the person of the child and, as such, she had a prima facie right to the physical custody, however, she still had the burden of proving that changing her daughter's physical custody would be in the child's best interest. Based on the evidence, the trial court found that the mother was a fit custodial parent who enjoyed a positive relationship with her child.

1984—*McGaffin v. Roberts*, 193 Conn. 393, 479 A.2d 176.

After the mother of the child died suddenly, both the father and the grandmother sought custody and the trial court awarded custody to the grandmother. The court found that it was in the best interests of the child to remain with the grandmother insofar as the father only had visitation with the child, and there was evidence that the child was injured, abused, and not well cared for while she was in the father's care.

§ 11.02 Types of Custody Orders

[1] Joint Custody

2020—*Chang v. Chang*, 197 Conn. App. 733, 232 A.3d 1186.

Appellate reversed the trial court's judgment on parents' mutual motions for contempt regarding the joint custody of their children. (1) The trial court improperly granted the mother's parenting access schedule adjustment motion for contempt because the language of the underlying order was not clear and unambiguous. The father's lengthy telephone conversation with the guardian ad litem, in which he stated his reasons for not wanting to adjust the parenting access schedule, could reasonably have been interpreted as "working with the guardian ad litem" as required by the order because of the imprecision in the language used in the order. (2) Because the order requiring the mother to engage in good faith consultation with the father prior to making decisions about the children's health and the order prohibiting her from unreasonably withholding consent were two separate components of the judge's order, the father was required to plead in his motion for contempt that the mother had refused to consult in good faith with him concerning their daughter's physical therapy before the court could make a ruling that the mother had violated that order. The father's motion did not allege that the mother refused to consult in good faith.

Appellate court upheld the trial court's ruling denying a third motion for contempt regarding the father returning the minor son to the mother at the end of the school day. The underlying stipulation did not specify a time for return and the father's timing was reasonable considering that their son had stayed after school to meet with his teachers and tutors on each of the days in question.

2019—*Lopes v. Ferrari*, 188 Conn. App. 387, 204 A.3d 1254.

Father's motion for a psychological evaluation of the mother was properly denied by the court, which found that the father was "engaged in a fishing expedition" and properly awarded the parties joint custody.

2017—*Baronio v. Stubbs et al.*, 178 Conn. App. 769, 177 A.3d 600.

Trial court properly concluded that joint legal custody and shared physical custody was in the best interest of the child; defendant did not object to joint legal custody and did not file any contrary proposed orders.

Defendant's claim that the court committed plain error by expressing preconceived notions to increase plaintiff's parenting time and to award joint legal custody was unavailing and unsupported by the record.

2014—*Keenan v. Casillo*, 149 Conn. App. 642, 89 A.3d 912.

Trial court had statutory authority to enter an order granting joint custody of the children, so long as it found that it was in the best interests of the children and at least one party had filed a pleading requesting joint custody.

2012—*Hibbard v. Hibbard*, 139 Conn. App. 10, 55 A.3d 301.

Mother found in contempt where the separation agreement provided for joint legal custody and the mother unilaterally had cancelled numerous visits with the father because of unsubstantiated claims; Court modified the joint legal custody order and awarded sole custody to the father.

2011—*Gillespie v. Jenkins*, 127 Conn. App. 228, 14 A.3d 1019.

Primary decision making authority awarded to mother based on court's personal observations, court file, and statements for counsel that parties had difficulty making joint decisions.

2010—*Desai v. Desai*, 119 Conn. App. 224, 987 A.2d 362.

Awarding joint legal custody under which one parent had ultimate decision-making power was not error.

1999—*Carroll v. Carroll*, 55 Conn. App. 18, 737 A.2d 963.

Trial court did not give plaintiff sole authority to make decisions regarding child's welfare in a joint custody case.

1999—*Papa v. Papa*, 55 Conn. App. 47, 737 A.2d 953.

No authority to find a "de facto joint custody arrangement" where court orders sole custody but children spend equal time at each parent's home.

1991—*Tabackman v. Tabackman*, 25 Conn. App. 366, 593 A.2d 526.

The court cannot award joint custody if no party sought it in the pleadings or by motion.

1990—*Cabrera v. Cabrera*, 23 Conn. App. 330, 580 A.2d 1227.

The court cannot grant joint custody in the absence of either an agreement for joint custody or a motion for conciliation.

1988—*Blake v. Blake*, 207 Conn. 217, 541 A.2d 1201.

Joint legal custody can be awarded when parents live in different states.

1987—*Giordano v. Giordano*, 9 Conn. App. 641, 520 A.2d 1290.

Joint custody can be awarded even if parents have "no meeting of the mind."

1986—*Emerick v. Emerick*, 5 Conn. App. 649, 502 A.2d 933.

The court may award joint legal custody, with or without joint physical custody, if the parties agree to joint custody or if one party seeks joint custody and files a motion for conciliation.

1985—*Timm v. Timm*, 195 Conn. 202, 487 A.2d 191.

The ultimate decision as to joint custody rests with the trier of fact and must be based on all of the testimony and factors that are properly brought before the court, including the ability of the trier to observe the demeanor and manner in which the witnesses answer pertinent questions.

1980—*Adams v. Adams*, 180 Conn. 498, 430 A.2d 19.

Plaintiff father retained his right of joint custody with ample visitation rights.

[2] Shared Custody

2019—*Cyganovich v. Cyganovich*, 189 Conn. App. 164, 206 A.3d 797.

The trial court did not abuse its discretion by ordering the defendant to pay child support despite the parties' shared custody arrangement, since the record showed that the parties did not spend equal amounts of money to support their child.

2017—*Baronio v. Stubbs et al.*, 178 Conn. App. 769, 177 A.3d 600.

Trial court properly concluded that joint legal custody and shared physical custody was in the best interest of the child; defendant did not object to joint legal custody and did not file any contrary proposed orders.

2010—*Kiniry v. Kiniry*, 299 Conn. 308, 9 A.3d 708.

Shared custody is a deviation criterion, but the court is required to establish the presumptive support amount before deviation criteria may be applied.

2003—*Lefebvre v. Lefebvre*, 75 Conn. App. 662, 817 A.2d 750.

Change in children's visitation schedule did not warrant a finding of shared physical custody and thus deviation from the child support guidelines.

1999—*Papa v. Papa*, 55 Conn. App. 47, 737 A.2d 953.

No authority to find a "de facto joint custody arrangement" where court orders sole custody but children spend equal time at each parent's home.

1995—*Fiddelman v. Redmon*, 37 Conn. App. 397, 656 A.2d 234.

Possession of a home in a "bird nesting" arrangement is not a property assignment but is part of a shared custody award.

1993—*Fiddelman v. Redmon*, 31 Conn. App. 201, 623 A.2d 1064.

Child custody arrangement gave each party exclusive use of the home during their respective period of shared physical custody.

[3] Sole Custody

2017—*Lugo v. Lugo*, 176 Conn. App. 149, 168 A.3d 592.

Trial court did not err in awarding the plaintiff sole legal custody where the defendant had notice that a change in custody was being contemplated because the plaintiff's motion for modification requested a broader role for the plaintiff, and the plaintiff's proposed orders requested the plaintiff have sole legal custody of the minor child.

2012—*Eisenlohr v. Eisenlohr*, 135 Conn. App. 337, 43 A.3d 694.

Post-judgment custody modification from joint legal with child residing primarily with defendant to sole legal and physical custody to plaintiff was appropriate where defendant habitually denied plaintiff parenting access and filed baseless DCF reports.

2010—*Stancuna v. Schaffer*, 122 Conn. App. 484, 998 A.2d 1221.

No abuse of discretion where the court allowed plaintiff, a Russian citizen, to travel to Russia without giving prior notice to defendant where the plaintiff had sole custody and did not pose a flight risk.

2002—*Crockett v. Pastore*, 259 Conn. 240, 789 A.2d 453.

Court has subject matter jurisdiction to consider maternal grandmother's petition for sole custody.

1987—*Giordano v. Giordano*, 9 Conn. App. 641, 520 A.2d 1290.

Trial court's conclusion after third day of six day trial, that sole custody was not possible for defendant, did not justify his disqualification.

[4] Primary Decision Making

2021—*McNamara v. McNamara*, 207 Conn. App. 849, 263 A.3d 899.

After a hearing on a postjudgment motion to modify custody, the trial court did not abuse its discretion in determining that it was in the best interests of the parties' children to award the plaintiff final decision-making authority on issues of health, treatment, and therapeutic providers of the children. The trial court made specific findings that the parties communicated poorly with each other and that their inability to agree on important issues resulted in their children being denied therapeutic services. It heard evidence that the children had not received in-home therapy for approximately one year due to the parties' inability to agree on a provider and that the defendant unilaterally terminated the children's relationship with their pediatrician. The trial court's ruling referenced the parties' disagreement about the children's pediatrician, and the defendant's disagreement with the school's educational plan for the parties' younger child and her objection to the continued participation of the parties' older child in an extended school year program. The trial court found that there were "serious problems in getting decisions made" and a "tiebreaker" was needed.

2020—*Yun Zhou v. Hao Zhang*, 334 Conn. 601, 223 A.3d 775.

Supreme Court held that the trial court did not abuse its discretion when it granted the defendant husband final decision making authority for the parties' children in situations in which the parties are unable to agree. Despite the plaintiff wife's claim that the trial court improperly based its custody orders on the testimony of the children's guardian ad litem, on the ground that the guardian ad litem testified that she had not seen the children in two years, there was nothing in the record to suggest that the guardian ad litem did not conduct an investigation into the best interests of the children. Even though she met with the children only once, shortly after her appointment, due to their tender years and to keep them removed from their parents' conflicts, the guardian ad litem was in regular communication with the parties, read the reports prepared by the court appointed psychologist, and consulted with him about his findings, and attended all court proceedings and depositions. The plaintiff had a full and fair opportunity to cross examine the guardian ad litem about any possible deficiencies concerning the time she spent with the children and how all, any such deficiencies may have impaired her ability to form a legitimate opinion as to their best interests. The plaintiff failed to demonstrate that she was prejudiced by the limited contact the guardian ad litem had with the children. The court appointed psychologist, who spent far more time evaluating the children, largely agreed with the observations and recommendations of the guardian ad litem. The trial court based granting final decision making authority to the defendant on its finding that he had more insight into the children's developmental needs, activities, education, and environment, which finding was based on the testimony of the guardian ad litem and other witnesses.

2011—*Gillespie v. Jenkins*, 127 Conn. App. 228, 14 A.3d 1019.

Primary decision making authority awarded to mother based on court's personal observations, court file, and statements for counsel that parties had difficulty making joint decisions.

2010—*Desai v. Desai*, 119 Conn. App. 224, 987 A.2d 362.

Awarding joint legal custody under which one parent had ultimate decision-making power was not error.

§ 11.03 Temporary Custody and Visitation

2019—*Thunelius v. Posacki*, 193 Conn. App. 666, 220 A.3d 194.

The trial court's sua sponte protective order pending any potential appeal was not an abuse of discretion considering it was in the child's best interest to provide as smooth a transition as possible during the immediate postjudgment period and considering the record of extraordinarily high level of conflict and mistrust between the parties, their willingness to disregard court orders and engage in self help, and the fact that the parties' behavior had the potential to do irreparable harm to the child.

2015—*In re J.R.*, 161 Conn. App. 563, 127 A.3d 1155.

Evidence of immediate physical danger supported order of temporary custody.

1986—*Cookson v. Cookson*, 201 Conn. 229, 514 A.2d 323.

The various interests in a temporary custody hearing are best served by applying the normal civil standard of proof which is a fair preponderance of the evidence.

1983—*In re Juvenile Appeal*, 189 Conn. 276, 455 A.2d 1313.

The deprivation of rights in a temporary custody adjudication is neither final nor irrevocable.

§ 11.04 Modification of Custody and Visitation

[1] Child's Preference

2022—*Lehane v. Murray*, 215 Conn. App. 307, 283 A.3d 62.

Trial court did not improperly delegate its judicial authority under Conn. Gen. Stat. § 46b-56(a) by ordering that Father may alter, change, or modify Mother's visitation schedule. The parties had a history of conflict in parenting their son and Mother had a consistent tendency to instigate that conflict.

2022—*Swain v. Swain*, 213 Conn. App. 411, 277 A.3d 895.

On Wife's post-trial motion to modify, trial court did not improperly modify existing orders as to visitation, the parental access plan, and child support because the plain language of Wife's motion to modify placed before the court the issues of custody, visitation, and the parental access schedule, not just child support as Husband had argued. Wife also testified about these issues at the hearing but Husband declined to present any rebuttal witnesses. None of the requests for clarification presented by Husband's counsel after the trial court's oral ruling contested the scope of the ruling.

2022—*Dolan v. Dolan*, 211 Conn. App. 390, 272 A.3d 768.

The trial court did not abuse its discretion in granting plaintiff's motion to modify the judgment which required her to move with the parties' minor child to Massachusetts, where defendant lived, not farther than one hour from her place of employment in West Hartford and required defendant to explore relocation in Massachusetts so that the parties would live within thirty minutes of each other. Plaintiff had been offered a promotion. She requested that the child and she be permitted to remain in West Hartford and requested a parenting plan that was in the best interests of the child. Finding that the promotion constituted a substantial increase in salary and potential career growth for plaintiff, the trial court determined that it would be in the child's best interests for plaintiff to accept the promotion to be better able to provide financially for the child and her, and that it would be in the child's best interests to continue residing with plaintiff in West Hartford. The trial court further found that maintaining financial independence was critical to plaintiff's financial stability and her stability was in the best interest of the child. Defendant had previously put plaintiff in a vulnerable financial position when he willfully failed to contribute monthly to the mortgage payment on the former marital home as required by their separation agreement, forcing her to file a contempt motion to resolve that issue. On the basis of the trial court's factual findings supported by the record, the court did not abuse its discretion in granting plaintiff's motion for modification.

2018—*Zilkha v. Zilkha*, 180 Conn. App. 143, 183 A.3d 64.

Trial court did not improperly delegate its judicial function by granting teenage children a considerable level of control over the extent of their father's access to them in connection with his motion to modify custody considering the difficult history of parenting since the parties' 2005 divorce.

1984—*Gennarini v. Gennarini*, 2 Conn. App. 132, 477 A.2d 674.

Whether the child's preferences and feelings as to custody and visitation are a significant factor in the court's ultimate determination of the best interest of the child depends on all the facts of the particular case, including the child's age and ability intelligently to form and express those preferences and feelings.

1981—*Gallo v. Gallo*, 184 Conn. 36, 440 A.2d 782.

In making or modifying any order with respect to custody or visitation, the court shall give consideration to the wishes of the child if he is of sufficient age and capable of forming an intelligent preference.

1980—*Friedman v. Friedman*, 180 Conn. 132, 429 A.2d 823.

In awarding custody, the trial court should consider the wishes of a child of a sufficient age.

[2] Generally

2024—*Thomas v. Cleary*, 229 Conn. App. 15, 326 A.3d 1109.

Trial court properly granted the father's motion to modify child custody and visitation. The court's finding that the mother had made yet another false accusation of sexual abuse against the father was supported by abundant evidence in the record and was not clearly erroneous. In finding the mother had ongoing struggles with substance abuse, the court relied on the prior finding of her substance abuse made in connection with the July 2022 judgment. The court's factual findings, all supported by the record, supported a determination that there was a material change in circumstances and that it was in the best interests of the parties' children to grant the father's motion for modification. The mother did not prove that the court's ruling reflected an abuse of its discretion.

2024—*Labieniec v. Megna*, 228 Conn. App. 127, 324 A.3d 181.

Trial court improperly granted the mother's motion for modification under Conn. Gen. Stat. § 46b-56, changing the child's primary residence for school purposes from the father's address to the mother's address. The court improperly determined that the language of the parties' agreement, which was incorporated into the judgment, was clear and unambiguous with respect to their intent concerning where their child would attend school. Concluding that the parties' agreement was ambiguous as to the child's schooling, the Appellate Court remanded the case so that the trial court can consider extrinsic evidence concerning the parties' intent.

2023—*Prioleau v. Agosta*, 220 Conn. App. 248, 297 A.3d 1012.

Trial court properly considered Mother's "motion for clarification, articulation, and reargument, postjudgment" seeking an alteration of the judgment as a motion for reconsideration, not as a motion for modification. Mother had filed her motion within days after the court rendered judgment, pursuant to Conn. Practice Book § 11-11, and requested that the court reconsider the judgment solely on the basis of the evidence presented at trial. The trial court did not consider any new evidence. It ruled on the motion in light of the evidence it had previously heard, concluding that its previous judgment was incorrect and making clear that upon reconsideration, the court had determined it was in the best interests of parties' minor child to amend the parenting schedule. The trial court did not abuse its discretion in granting Mother's request for weekend parenting time sought in her postjudgment motion. The court reasonably could have concluded on the basis of the evidence presented at trial that this change to the judgment was required. It also recognized that Father would have less parenting time due to its decision to grant Mother's request and attempted to offset some of that lost time by providing Father with additional parenting time during the fourth week of each month.

2023—*A.D. v. L.D.*, 220 Conn. App. 172, 297 A.3d 568.

The appellate court's standard of review regarding the trial court's decision on child custody and visitation is one of abuse of discretion. The controlling principle in determining child custody is that the trial court shall be guided by the best interests of the child; it has broad discretion in determining what is in the child's best interests. In this case, the father failed to demonstrate that the trial court had abused its discretion by making modifications to the child custody orders. The trial court found that he was distressed by his poor relationship with his children but unwilling to acknowledge his role in the circumstances.

2021—*Tannenbaum v. Tannenbaum*, 208 Conn. App. 16, 263 A.3d 998.

A 2019 judgment denying the defendant's motion for contempt did not improperly modify the underlying 2018 travel related child custody order by requiring the plaintiff to accompany his minor child on any airline travel, except in the case of emergency, because it did not alter the meaning or substantive terms of the 2018 order. Both orders contemplated the exception to parent supervised child air travel would apply only in the limited case of an emergency. The 2019 order made clear that the exception contained in the 2018 order was available to the plaintiff only "in the case of emergency, not his convenience" and did not broadly apply to all types of health, work, or other family commitments. The transcript of the 2019 hearing showed the plaintiff did not understand the limited nature of the visitation provisions contained in the 2018 order, requiring the trial court to clarify the terms of the order.

2021—*Batista v. Cortes*, 203 Conn. App. 365, 248 A.3d 763.

The trial court did not abuse its discretion in denying a father's motion to modify child custody by changing the child's primary residence because the record indicates that it properly assessed the relevant factors under Conn. Gen. Stat. § 46b-56(c) in finding it was in the child's best interest to remain in the primary custody of her mother. There was nothing in the record to indicate that the trial court failed to consider the referral it made to the Department of Children and Families after the father had accused the mother of using corporal punishment against the child or the mother's concession that she had struck the child. The Appellate Court would not second-guess the trial court's conclusion which was fully supported by its factual findings.

2020—*Weaver v. Sena*, 199 Conn. App. 852, 238 A.3d 103.

The trial court did not abuse its discretion in granting the father's motion to modify child custody under Conn. Gen. Stat. § 46b-56. There was ample evidence that the mother's efforts to embroil the minor child in the custody dispute and alienate him from the father had intensified, as alleged in the father's motion, constituting a material change in circumstances since the entry of the prior order. The record amply supports the trial court's determination that it was in the best interests of the minor child to transfer primary physical custody to the father. Because the trial court was entitled to accept or to reject all of part of a witness' testimony, it was not improper for it to agree with most of the findings of the psychologist who had conducted a court ordered child custody psychological evaluation but decline to follow his recommendation.

2019—*M.M. v. H. F.*, 194 Conn. App. 472, 221 A.3d 523.

Trial court properly denied defendant leave to file a motion to modify custody and visitation where defendant had failed to allege facts sufficient to constitute a substantial change in circumstances and reiterated allegations she had previously presented to the court.

2019—*Peters v. Senman*, 193 Conn. App. 766, 220 A.3d 114.

Trial court did not err in denying plaintiff's motion for modification of custody when it carefully considered and applied the criteria of Conn. Gen. Stat. § 46b-56 and made factual findings as to plaintiff's claims of changed circumstances.

2019—*Nahlawi v. Nahlawi*, 189 Conn. App. 825, 209 A.3d 723.

Trial court erred in entering a final child custody and visitation order that incorporated a pendente lite parenting plan stipulation that had been superseded by a subsequent pendente lite parenting plan that had been agreed to by the parties.

2017—*Lugo v. Lugo*, 176 Conn. App. 149, 168 A.3d 592.

Trial court did not err in awarding the plaintiff sole legal custody where the defendant had notice that a change in custody was being contemplated because the plaintiff's motion for modification requested a broader role for the plaintiff, and the plaintiff's proposed orders requested the plaintiff have sole legal custody of the minor child.

2016—*Petrov v. Gueorguieva*, 167 Conn. App. 505, 146 A.3d 26.

Father's failure to assert the start of full-time school for child as a ground for modification in his motion to modify primary custody did not unduly prejudice or surprise the mother.

2016—*Clougherty v. Clougherty*, 162 Conn. App. 857, 133 A.3d 886.

In order to modify custody, there must be a material change in circumstances which affects the best interests of the minor child. Not every change in circumstance is material, and not every material change impacts the best interests of the child.

2014—*Baker-Grenier v. Grenier*, 147 Conn. App. 516, 83 A.3d 698.

No abuse of discretion where the court granted a post-judgment motion to modify custody and the evidence supported the decision.

1999—*Kelly v. Kelly*, 54 Conn. App. 50, 732 A.2d 808.

Court must find material change of circumstances or that order that is sought to be modified was not in best interest of children in order to modify custody award.

1996—*Walshon v. Walshon*, 42 Conn. App. 651, 681 A.2d 376.

Judgment of dismissal of motion to modify custody granted for failure to make out a prima facie case.

1987—*Ferrucci v. Ferrucci*, 11 Conn. App. 369, 527 A.2d 1207.

Modification of joint custody to sole custody granted where parties could not effectively communicate regarding issues of school and medical treatment.

§ 11.05 Attorney for Child

2020—*In re Walker C.*, 195 Conn. App. 604, 226 A.3d 175.

Trial court's failure to accurately set forth the position of the child's attorney was a harmless error because there was clear and convincing evidence warranting termination of the mother's parental rights under Conn. Gen. Stat. § 17a-112(j)(3) for the mother's failure to rehabilitate. Judgment affirmed.

2014—*Perry v. Perry*, 312 Conn. 600, 95 A.3d 500.

Attorney for the minor children in a dissolution action may file an appeal only if the court determines that an appeal is in the best interests of the children.

2010—*Fennelly v. Norton*, 294 Conn. 484, 985 A.2d 1026.

An award of counsel fees against grandparents or other third parties petitioning for visitation is not authorized under Conn. Gen. Stat. § 46b-62 and appointing attorney for minor child for proceeding intended solely to address attorneys' fees was abuse of discretion.

2006—*Machado v. Statewide Grievance Comm.*, 93 Conn. App. 832, 890 A.2d 622.

Client's appointment of an agent to communicate with attorney does not relieve attorney of obligation to communicate directly with client.

2005—*Carrubba v. Moskowitz*, 274 Conn. 533, 877 A.2d 773.

Attorney for minor children is protected by quasi-judicial immunity.

2003—*Oliver v. Oliver*, 85 Conn. App. 57, 855 A.2d 1022.

The attorney for the minor child was allowed to offer his opinion on the ultimate issue of the child's best interests in relocation case and relocation was permitted to North Carolina.

2003—*In re Tayquon H.*, 76 Conn. App. 693, 821 A.2d 796.

The roles of attorney and guardian ad litem for minor child are discussed.

1998—*Lord v. Lord*, 44 Conn. App. 370, 689 A.2d 509.

Case discusses the grounds and standing for removing counsel for minor child.

1998—*Ireland v. Ireland*, 246 Conn. 413, 717 A.2d 676.

The attorney for the minor child was not permitted to submit opinions to the court.

1997—*Schult v. Schult*, 241 Conn. 767, 699 A.2d 134.

The attorney for children may advocate a position contrary to that of the guardian *ad litem* if court finds such conflicting advocacy to be in best interests of the children.

1997—*Taff v. Bettcher*, 243 Conn. 380, 703 A.2d 759.

A parent has no constitutional right to dictate how the best interests of her child should be legally represented and no standing to require counsel for minor child to be present at custody hearing.

1995—*Wolf v. Wolf*, 39 Conn. App. 162, 664 A.2d 315.

The attorney for the child is permitted to make a report post-judgment if the parents cannot agree about boarding school.

1995—*Newman v. Newman*, 35 Conn. App. 449, 646 A.2d 885, *rev'd*, 235 Conn. 82, 663 A.2d 980.

Counsel for minor children must pursue the child's interests even if he or she disagrees and may file an appeal if appellate court determines first it is in their best interest, among other factors.

1995—*Jaser v. Jaser*, 37 Conn. App. 194, 655 A.2d 790.

The attorney for children must be present at hearings for child support unless the appointment is limited.

1990—*G.S. v. T.S.*, 23 Conn. App. 509, 582 A.2d 467.

The trial court abused its discretion in failing to appoint counsel for the minor children.

1989—*Weinstein v. Weinstein*, 18 Conn. App. 622, 561 A.2d 443.

The court cannot delegate its authority to counsel for the minor child.

1987—*Cotton v. Cotton*, 11 Conn. App. 189, 526 A.2d 547.

The court is not mandated to appoint an attorney for the minor children.

1986—*Pisch v. Pisch*, 7 Conn. App. 720, 510 A.2d 455.

Failure to appoint counsel for minor child is not a clear abuse of discretion.

1985—*Emerick v. Emerick*, 5 Conn. App. 649, 502 A.2d 933.

The trial court is not bound to accept the opinion of the Family Relations Officer or the counsel for the minor child.

§ 11.06 Guardian ad Litem

2019—*Thunelius v. Posacki*, 193 Conn. App. 666, 220 A.3d 194.

Trial court did not improperly delegate its decision-making authority by defining the duties and responsibilities of the guardian ad litem.

However, trial court abused its discretion in ordering that the prevailing party in any dispute between the parties adjudicated by the court after unsuccessful mediation with the guardian ad litem be reimbursed by the other party for his or her share of the guardian ad litem's fees. The amount of any future fees and the parties' respective abilities to pay them are purely speculative. There is nothing in record to guarantee that if such guardian ad litem fees become due, the parties' respective financial situations will have remained unchanged.

2019—*In re Kadon M.*, 194 Conn. App. 100, 219 A.3d 985.

Trial court did not abuse its discretion in denying mother's oral motion to appoint guardian ad litem for minor child that had been neglected. The trial court has broad discretion to decide whether to appoint a guardian ad litem. The trial court did not require a guardian ad litem to determine the best interests of the child as there was ample evidence to assist the court in making that determination. Denying mother's motion did not prohibit her from presenting evidence for the court's best interest of the child analysis. Mother failed to show how the court's failure to appoint a guardian ad litem would have affected the trial.

2015—*Zilkha v. Zilkha*, 159 Conn. App. 167, 123 A.3d 439.

Superior court lacked authority to order distribution to pay the fees of the guardian ad litem from escrow account. Husband's opinion as to propriety of GAL's conduct was not admissible.

2015—*Sargent v. Sargent*, 156 Conn. App. 109, 113 A.3d 72.

Where the guardian ad litem had been removed by the trial court, orders allowing the guardian ad litem to meet with the minor children were moot, and were not appealable by the father.

2014—*Keenan v. Casillo*, 149 Conn. App. 642, 89 A.3d 912.

The court did not commit plain error by allowing the guardian ad litem to testify, even though they served for a period of time as both attorney for the minor children and as their guardian ad litem.

2013—*Schoenborn v. Schoenborn*, 144 Conn. App. 846, 74 A.3d 482.

No abuse of discretion where visitation was awarded pursuant to the guardian ad litem's recommendation.

2013—*Kavanah v. Kavanah*, 142 Conn. App. 775, 66 A.3d 922.

Sua sponte award of guardian ad litem fees was an abuse of discretion.

2011—*Clougherty v. Clougherty*, 131 Conn. App. 270, 26 A.3d 704.

No reversal under the plain error doctrine where father did not object to testimony by the guardian ad litem about child's purported failure to thrive.

2010—*Stancuna v. Schaffer*, 122 Conn. App. 484, 998 A.2d 1221.

Trial court properly struck a tort action against a former guardian ad litem.

2009—*Buehler v. Buehler*, 117 Conn. App. 304, 978 A.2d 1141.

Trial court did not abuse its discretion by ordering fees for guardian ad litem and counsel for guardian ad litem, even though neither attorney had signed a retainer agreement with the plaintiff.

2008—*Johnson v. Johnson*, 111 Conn. App. 413, 959 A.2d 637.

Court improperly allowed a guardian ad litem to act as a conduit for hearsay, and to testify about out of court statements and reports of a physician and a therapist where guardian ad litem stated no opinion related to hearsay comments.

2006—*Gil v. Gil*, 94 Conn. App. 306, 892 A.2d 318.

Guardian ad litem invokes child's psychologist/patient privilege.

2004—*Butler v. Butler*, 271 Conn. 657, 859 A.2d 26.

Trial court not required to adopt the recommendation of guardian ad litem and the court-appointed psychologist that sole custody be awarded to mother.

2003—*In re Tayquon H.*, 76 Conn. App. 693, 821 A.2d 796.

Grandmother's interest as natural guardian had been replaced by the powers of the guardian ad litem who had been appointed to protect the interests of the child; guardian is proper person to speak on behalf of the child. The roles of attorney and guardian ad litem for minor child are discussed.

2003—*Lamacchia v. Chilinsky*, 79 Conn. App. 372, 830 A.2d 329.

Court's order to have plaintiff pay guardian ad litem 80% of present and future legal fees was reversed as too speculative.

1994—*Favrow v. Vargas*, 231 Conn. 1, 647 A.2d 731.

Guardian has no legal obligation to support his or her ward.

§ 11.07 Family Relations

2019—*Dufresne v. Dufresne*, 191 Conn. App. 532, 215 A.3d 1259.

Trial court's failure to credit testimony of family relations counselor on the basis of her hearsay testimony was an abuse of discretion when father failed to object to the testimony on hearsay grounds. Substance of the testimony pertained to court ordered supervised visits and therefore was probative to issue before the court, father's motion to modify visitation.

2014—*Lineberry v. Estevam*, 151 Conn. App. 264, 95 A.3d 1132.

Parties shall have an opportunity to examine and refute the contents of a family relations report and argue that the court reconsider its rulings.

2013—*Barros v. Barros*, 309 Conn. 499, 72 A.3d 367.

A party's procedural due process rights are not violated by the family relations office's policy of barring counsel from its evaluations and interviews in child custody proceedings.

1986—*Emerick v. Emerick*, 5 Conn. App. 649, 502 A.2d 933.

The trial court is not bound to accept the opinion of the Family Relations Officer or the counsel for the minor child.

§ 11.08 Miscellaneous Child Custody Issues

[1] Supervised Visitation

2018—*Nassra v. Nassra*, 180 Conn. App. 421, 183 A.3d 1198.

Supervisor had standing to file an appearance in the divorce action and the trial court had subject matter jurisdiction to order the payment of delinquent supervisor fees.

2013—*Mirjavadi v. Vakilzadeh*, 310 Conn. 176, 74 A.3d 1278.

Trial court's flawed analysis of causation and foreseeability undermined its determination that a visitation supervisor had not been negligent when a minor child was abducted to Iran during a supervised visitation.

2010—*Stancuna v. Schaffer*, 122 Conn. App. 484, 998 A.2d 1221.

No abuse of discretion where the court ordered that defendant would have to disclose information from treating psychotherapists and psycho-pharmacologists if he sought to modify existing supervised visitation orders.

[2] Relocation of Custodial Parent

2022—*In re Delilah G.*, 214 Conn. App. 604, 280 A.3d 1168.

Appellate Court affirmed trial court order allowing Father, the custodial parent, to relocate with the parties' child. Mother failed to show under Conn. Gen. Stat. § 45a-717 that Father had made it inevitable that there would be no relationship between Mother and the child. Mother presented no evidence about the nature of her relationship with the child before Father allegedly sought to interfere with it. She also failed to follow through with scheduled visitations.

2021—*O'Neill v. O'Neill*, 209 Conn. App. 165, 268 A.3d 79.

The trial court did not abuse its discretion in granting the plaintiff's request to relocate with the minor children. The defendant did not claim that the trial court failed to consider the best interests of the children as required by Conn. Gen. Stat. § 46b-56 when it decided the relocation issue. There is sufficient evidence to support the court's decision.

2021—*M.S. v. P.S.*, 203 Conn. App. 377, 248 A.3d 778.

Trial court did not abuse its discretion by ordering that the plaintiff had the right to relocate to New York provided it was not more than thirty-five miles from her current residence, thereby modifying the parties' pendente lite parenting plan although neither party had requested a relocation order. It was in the children's best interests for the plaintiff to be able to relocate to New York to establish residency so that she could afford to pursue the doctorate program to which she had applied and been accepted. This professional degree would provide her with meaningful employment and income to become self-sufficient after the expiration of her nonmodifiable, six-year alimony award. For potential future relocations, the order did not alter the parties' agreement that it was in the best interests of their children that they live within thirty-five miles of each other, unless they agreed otherwise in writing.

2015—*Havis-Carbone v. Carbone*, 155 Conn. App. 848, 112 A.3d 779.

Trial court abused its discretion in granting mother permission to relocate with parties' minor child without considering all required statutory factors used to determine whether to approve relocation.

2013—*Nweeia v. Nweeia*, 142 Conn. App. 613, 64 A.3d 1251.

Appellate court refused to review the plaintiff's claim that a relocation from Kent to Greenwich was not a material change of circumstances when she had previously argued the opposite position at the trial court level.

2013—*Tow v. Tow*, 142 Conn. App. 45, 64 A.3d 128.

Court denied motion to relocate with minor child to France.

2011—*Emrich v. Emrich*, 127 Conn. App. 691, 15 A.3d 1104.

Relocation request granted with respect to youngest children and custody of older children awarded to non-relocating parent.

2009—*Lederle v. Spivey*, 113 Conn. App. 177, 965 A.2d 621.

Conn. Gen. Stat. § 46b-56 governs relocation at the time of dissolution, rather than post-judgment when Conn. Gen. Stat. § 46b-56d applies.

2005—*Racsko v. Racsko*, 91 Conn. App. 315, 881 A.2d 460.

Appellate court upheld trial court's judgment that denied the mother's request to relocate to another state since that would severely restrict the husband's parenting time with the children, who bonded with both parents and who needed regular contact from both parents.

2004—*Brennan v. Brennan*, 85 Conn. App. 172, 857 A.2d 927.

A custodial parent seeking permission to relocate bears the initial burden of demonstrating, by a preponderance of the evidence, that (1) the relocation is for a legitimate purpose, and (2) the proposed location is reasonable in light of that purpose. Once the custodial parent has made such a prima facie showing, the burden shifts to the noncustodial parent to prove, by a preponderance of the evidence, that the relocation would not be in the best interests of the child.

2002—*Ford v. Ford*, 68 Conn. App. 173, 789 A.2d 1104.

Relocation is a pertinent factor to consider in arriving at an initial custody determination. Postjudgment relocation matters differ and should be treated differently from relocation issues that arise at the time of marital dissolution.

2001—*Barzetti v. Marucci*, 66 Conn. App. 802, 786 A.2d 432.

Custodial parent seeking to relocate with child must make prima facie case by a fair preponderance of the evidence that the proposed relocation is for a legitimate purpose.

2001—*Azia v. DiLascia*, 64 Conn. App. 540, 780 A.2d 992.

Relocation was denied.

2001—*McGinty v. McGinty*, 66 Conn. App. 35, 783 A.2d 1170.

Relocation to New Jersey permitted.

1998—*Ireland v. Ireland*, 246 Conn. 413, 717 A.2d 676.

Initial burden of proof in relocation cases is on custodial parent to prove relocation is for a legitimate purpose, and that proposed relocation is reasonable in light of that purpose. Burden then shifts to noncustodial parent to prove that relocation is not in child's best interests.

1980—*Presutti v. Presutti*, 181 Conn. 622, 436 A.2d 299.

Where the non-custodial parent's visitation with his child will be infrequent as a result of the distance that separates them, the trial court should, when at all possible, set specific and usually substantial periods of visitation time if to do so is consistent with the child's best interests.

[3] New Romantic Partners

1988—*Charpentier v. Charpentier*, 206 Conn. 150, 536 A.2d 948.

Wife's paramour ordered not to be present during visitation with children.

[4] Habeas Corpus

2001—*In re Jonathan M.*, 255 Conn. 208, 764 A.2d 739, *aff'g* 26 Conn. L. Rptr. 215.

Biological parent cannot bring a writ of habeas corpus to challenge a termination of parental rights.

1995—*Weidenbacher v. Duclos*, 234 Conn. 51, 661 A.2d 988.

Person claiming to be father of child born to woman during marriage to another man has standing to seek habeas corpus relief.

1986—*Evans v. Santoro*, 6 Conn. App. 707, 507 A.2d 1007.

A habeas corpus petition concerning a minor child's custody is an equitable proceeding in which the trial court is called upon to decide, in the exercise of its sound discretion, the custodial placement that will be best for the child.

1986—*Franklin v. Dunham*, 8 Conn. App. 30, 510 A.2d 1007.

Matters within the jurisdiction of the superior court deemed to be family relations matters shall be matters affecting or involving habeas corpus and other proceedings to determine the custody and visitation of children. Thus, while habeas corpus is the usual method of bringing a custody and visitation claim before the court; it is not the exclusive method.

1984—*McGaffin v. Roberts*, 193 Conn. 393, 479 A.2d 176.

The time-honored function of habeas corpus in child custody cases is what is in the best interests of the child.

[5] Department of Children and Families

2024—*In re M. S.*, 226 Conn. App. 857, 319 A.3d 833, *appeal denied*, 320 A.3d 978.

Trial court did not apply an incorrect legal standard in sustaining an order of temporary custody and adjudicating a child neglected. Although the court did not recite the "immediate physical danger" standard as set out in Conn. Gen. Stat. § 46b-129, the record reflects that the court accurately set forth the relevant legal standard more than once and made several appropriate factual findings in support of that legal standard, which findings were not challenged on appeal. The court's use of the phrase "suitable and worthy" in issuing its decision did not lead to the conclusion that it improperly used that standard in sustaining the order of temporary custody.

2020—*In re Brooklyn O.*, 196 Conn. App. 543, 230 A.3d 895.

Appellate court affirmed trial court order denying a father's motion to revoke the commitment of his child to the custody of the Commissioner of Children and Families under Conn. Gen. Stat. § 46b-129. The trial court did not err in denying the father's motion because he did not claim that the decision to commit the minor child was not legally and logically correct and he failed to meet his burden of proving that the cause for commitment no longer existed. The father may not challenge the issue of whether there is a need for the commitment of the minor child and certain factual findings set forth in the trial court's April 5, 2018 adjudication of neglect because he did not appeal from that judgment.

2017—*In re Elianah T.-T., et al.*, 326 Conn. 614, 165 A.3d 1236.

Vaccinations are not "medical treatments" under Conn. Gen. Stat. 17a-10(c); thus Commissioner of Children and Families could not vaccinate children in its temporary custody without parental consent; trial court erred in granting Commissioner's motion where parents objected based on religious grounds.

[6] Improper Delegation of Court's Authority

2024—*R.H. v. M.H.*, 350 Conn. 432, 324 A.3d 720.

Trial court's order authorizing the father to exercise unilateral control over the mother's visitation with their son was an improper delegation of judicial authority because the court delegated to the father, in consultation with the child's therapist, the ultimate authority to suspend or terminate the mother's visitation altogether. Unlike the order in *Lehane v. Murray*, 215 Conn. App. 307, 283 A.3d 62 (2022), the order here was not limited to allowing the father to modify the visitation schedule; it permitted the father to unilaterally suspend the mother's right to visitation. When a governing statute squarely places the obligation on the trial courts to decide custody and visitation, a trial court may not impermissibly delegate that judicial authority. While it is critically important that trial judges have broad discretion when crafting visitation orders in order to best account for the interests of the parties and the children, trial judges may not delegate to the custodial parent the authority to suspend the visitation rights of the noncustodial parent.

2023—*C.D. v. CD.*, 218 Conn. App. 818, 293 A.3d 86.

The trial court improperly delegated its judicial authority to nonjudicial entities when it ordered that if the parties' children received of therapeutic counseling, the counselors would decide whether either parent shall have access to the children's private therapy records. Under the unambiguous language of Conn. Gen. Stat. § 46b-56(g), the father, as the noncustodial parent, was statutorily entitled to have access to the children's private therapy records, subject only to a court order denying him the right of access to the records for good cause shown. By giving the children's therapeutic counselors the authority to determine whether he would be allowed access to the children's private therapy records, the trial court improperly delegated its judicial authority set forth in § 46b-56(g).

2018—*Kyle S. v. Jayne K.*, 182 Conn. App. 353, 190 A.3d 68.

Trial Court improperly delegated to the minor child's psychologist the "scope, nature and duration" of parenting time with the father.

§ 11.09 Parental Abduction

[1] Custodial Interference

2022—*State v. Lori T.*, 345 Conn. 44, 282 A.3d 1233.

Defendant had visitation with her four children with her ex-husband. Father had sole physical and legal custody, but one child had been staying with Defendant for several months following a physical incident between him and his father. Defendant was charged with custodial interference after she refused to return the children to Father at the end of her visit with them over Memorial Day weekend in 2015. The children had decided they did not want to go home with their father, who had received emails from one of them telling him that she did not want to return to his home and wanted to stay at Defendant's home. When Father went to pick up the children on Memorial Day pursuant to the visitation and custody order, Defendant told him that she was not sending the children out, they did not want to come out, and she was going to do what the children wanted to do.

After the Appellate Court affirmed the trial court judgment of conviction on three counts of custodial interference, the Supreme Court granted Defendant's request for certification to appeal, limited to two issues: (1) whether the Appellate Court incorrectly concluded that Conn. Gen. Stat. § 53a-98(a)(3) was not unconstitutionally vague as applied to Defendant; and (2) whether the Appellate Court incorrectly concluded that the evidence presented was sufficient to prove that Defendant otherwise refused to return the children.

Judgment of the Appellate Court was affirmed. The evidence was sufficient to prove that Defendant otherwise refused to return the children to Father under Conn. Gen. Stat. § 53a-98(a)(3). Defendant told Father that she was not sending the children out because they did not want to go with him. She abdicated her parental responsibility by allowing the children to decide whether to comply with the custody and visitation order.

2013—*Mirjavadi v. Vakilzadeh*, 310 Conn. 176, 74 A.3d 1278.

Trial court's flawed analysis of causation and foreseeability undermined its determination that a visitation supervisor had not been negligent when a minor child was abducted to Iran during a supervised visitation.

1999—*State v. Vakilzaden*, 251 Conn. 656, 742 A.2d 767.

Joint custodians were held liable for abducting child.

[2] Parental Kidnapping Act of 1980

1985—*Brown v. Brown*, 195 Conn. 98, 486 A.2d 1116.

While the Parental Kidnapping Prevention Act creates a preference for the home state, it does not significantly disrupt the jurisdictional provisions of the Uniform Child Custody Prevention Act thus the argument of the mother who relocated children from Connecticut to Florida that Connecticut was an inconvenient forum was upheld.

§ 11.10 Third Party Intervention for Custody and Visitation

[1] In General

2024—*Hepburn v. Brill*, 348 Conn. 827, 312 A.3d 1.

The trial court improperly dismissed the plaintiff's petition for third-party visitation with her niece. The Superior Court has plenary jurisdiction over family relations matters under Conn. Gen. Stat. § 46b-1 and the 2012 amendments to the third-party visitation statute, Conn. Gen. Stat. § 46b-59(b), which provides that any person may submit a verified petition to the Superior Court for the right of visitation with any minor child. The plaintiff's amended petition alleged facts sufficient to warrant a hearing under § 46b-59.

2020—*Hunter v. Shrestha*, 195 Conn. App. 393, 225 A.3d 285.

Trial court properly dismissed a third party petition by relatives of child's mother who had abandoned the child. The petition failed to satisfy the jurisdictional requirements set out in *Roth v. Weston*, 259 Conn. 202, 789 A.2d 431 (2002) and Conn. Gen. Stat. § 46b-120. The petition must contain specific, good faith allegations that the petitioner has a relationship with the child similar to a parent child relationship. It must also contain specific, good faith allegations that denial of visitation will cause real and significant harm to the child. The degree of harm alleged must be more than a determination that visitation would be in the child's best interest. The petitioner has the burden to prove these allegations by clear and convincing evidence. Here, the petitioners' allegation that denial of visitation would cut the child off from the maternal side of the family is not commensurate with the level of harm contemplated by *Roth*. Their allegation that denying visitation would have the effect of the child feeling they had abandoned her does not rise to the level of harm cited in § 46b-120. Their claim that denying visitation would compound the child's early childhood trauma and harm her, without alleging how the child will be harmed, ignored the requirement that the facts must be pleaded with sufficient specificity to warrant the court's intrusion. Judgment for dismissal affirmed.

2017—*Fuller v. Baldino*, 176 Conn. App. 451, 168 A.3d 665.

Trial court properly dismissed the plaintiff's third-party petition for visitation for lack of subject matter jurisdiction where the plaintiff's petition failed to establish a parent-like relationship and that denial of visitation would result in real and substantial harm to the minor child.

2015—*In re Santiago G.*, 318 Conn. 449, 121 A.3d 708.

Joint motion to revoke commitment of minor child did not warrant revocation of neglect commitment.

2008—*Carrier v. King*, 105 Conn. App. 391, 939 A.2d 1.

Appellate court concluded that the trial court properly denied the great-aunt's visitation application because she offered no evidence of significant harm to the child and, absent such evidence, the mother had the right to raise the child free from state interference.

2008—*Fish v. Fish*, 285 Conn. 24, 939 A.2d 1040.

The proper standard of proof in third party custody cases is a fair preponderance of the evidence.

2002—*Roth v. Weston*, 259 Conn. 202, 789 A.2d 431.

The Supreme Court of Connecticut concluded that, in light of the presumption of parental fitness under *Troxel v. Granville*, parents should not be faced with unjustified intrusions into their decision-making in the absence of specific allegations and proof of a relationship of a parent-like relationship with the person with whom contact is desired.

2002—*Crockett v. Pastore*, 259 Conn. 240, 789 A.2d 453.

Third party seeking visitation with child under Conn. Gen. Stat. § 46b-59 must allege and prove by clear and convincing evidence that there exists a parent-like relationship and denial of visitation will cause real and significant harm to the child.

1995—*Weidenbacher v. Duclos*, 234 Conn. 51, 661 A.2d 988.

Person claiming to be father of child born to woman during marriage to another man has standing to seek habeas corpus relief.

1989—*In re Jennifer P.*, 17 Conn. App. 427, 553 A.2d 196.

Former foster parents have standing under Conn. Gen. Stat. § 46b-59 (third party visitation) to seek visitation privilege.

1981—*Manter v. Manter*, 185 Conn. 502, 441 A.2d 146.

Conn. Gen. Stat. § 46b-57 permits interested third parties to intervene in custody controversies before the superior court.

[2] Grandparents

2022—*Delena v. Grachitorena*, 216 Conn. App. 225, 283 A.3d 1090.

Trial court did not err in denying a grandmother's petition for visitation with her grandchildren pursuant to Conn. Gen. Stat. § 46b-59(d) because she did not satisfy her burden to show by clear and convincing evidence that she had a parent-like relationship with the children.

2020—*Igersheim v. Bezrutczyk*, 197 Conn. App. 412, 231 A.3d 1276.

Appellate court reversed at trial court judgment granting a grandmother's petition under Conn. Gen. Stat. § 46b-59(b) for visitation with her grandson. The trial court did not have subject matter jurisdiction over the grandmother's petition for visitation because the petition lacked the specific allegations necessary to meet the jurisdictional requirements of § 46b-59(b). The petition did not contain the required specific, good faith allegations of real and significant harm. Besides a general statement that denial of visitation would jeopardize the child's relationship with his grandparents, the petition contained no specific references to harm, much less the specific allegations of harm that the minor child would endure if visitation were denied. Judgment reversed and remanded with direction to render judgment dismissing the petition.

2020—*In re Brian P.*, 195 Conn. App. 582, 226 A.3d 152.

Appellate court dismissed the appeal brought by a paternal grandmother after her motion to intervene was in a child protection proceeding was denied. The trial court properly denied the grandmother's motion to intervene after the final judgment had been entered terminating parental rights because her motion was very untimely and the child was entitled to a determination as to his permanency. The opportunity had passed for the grandmother to present evidence concerning the viability of granting her permanent guardianship in lieu of terminating parental rights and by her delay, she had lost any colorable claim to intervene. The appellate court did not have subject matter jurisdiction over the grandmother's appeal because she was never a party to the underlying child protection proceeding and did not have standing to appeal it.

2020—*Romeo v. Bazow*, 195 Conn. App. 378, 225 A.3d 710.

Trial court properly dismissed the petition of maternal grandparents for visitation for lack of subject matter jurisdiction. A petition for visitation must contain specific, good faith allegations that the petitioner has a relationship with the child similar in nature to a parent child relationship and must also contain specific, good faith allegations that denial of the visitation will cause real and significant harm to the child, which harm must be more than a determination that visitation would be in the child's best interest. The grandparents' claim that the children were being harmed by "deracinating them from their extended family and family roots" failed to plead the level of harm required by the second jurisdictional element set forth in *Roth v. Weston*, 259 Conn. 202, 789 A.2d 431 (2002). The trial court properly did not consider their expert witness disclosure, which was not attached to the grandparents' petition and was not filed until months after briefing on the motion to dismiss was complete. This disclosure constituted an attempt to supplement their petition with additional allegations to satisfy the jurisdictional element. The grandparents' only allegations as to harm were general allegations that never rose to the level of neglect, abuse, or abandonment contemplated by *Roth* nor specified the type of harm the children would suffer if their maternal grandparents were denied visitation.

2019—*Boisvert v. Gavis*, 332 Conn. 115, 210 A.3d 1.

Maternal grandparents were entitled to child visitation, pursuant to Conn. Gen. Stat. § 46b-59 and the Due Process Clause, over the objection of the child's father. The father had requested a broad order requiring the maternal grandparents to abide by all of the father's parental decisions regarding the child's care during the course of the grandparents' visitation; the Court held that it was not required to order the grandparents to abide by all of the father's parental decisions.

2019—*Firstenberg v. Madigan*, 188 Conn. App. 724, 205 A.3d 716.

Petition for visitation by the maternal grandfather was dismissed for lack of subject matter jurisdiction because the grandfather's petition failed to include specific and good-faith allegations that parent-like relationship existed between himself and grandson and that denial of visitation would cause real and significant harm.

2009—*Collins v. Collins*, 117 Conn. App. 380, 979 A.2d 543.

Grandparent must initiate action for custody or visitation and cannot create statutory right to intervene.

2007—*Fennelly v. Norton*, 103 Conn. App. 125, 931 A.2d 269.

Application for grandparent visitation denied due to lack of "specific good faith allegations" as required by *Roth v. Weston*, 259 Conn. 202, 789 A.2d 431 (2002), despite applicants having filled out a judicial branch form alleging they had a parent-like relationship with the child and denial of access would result in harm to the child.

2005—*Denardo v. Bergamo*, 272 Conn. 500, 863 A.2d 686.

When a grandparent seeks to establish or maintain visitation rights with respect to a child over the opposition of that child's parent, the parent's rights necessarily carry greater weight because parenting remains a protected fundamental right.

2002—*Clements v. Jones*, 71 Conn. App. 688, 803 A.2d 378.

Paternal grandmother lacked standing to bring visitation action.

2000—*Troxel v. Granville*, 530 U.S. 57, 120 S. Ct. 2054, 147 L. Ed. 2d 49.

If a fit parent's decision regarding grandparent visitation becomes subject to judicial review, the court must accord at least some special weight to the parent's own determination thus the grandparents were denied visitation rights.

1990—*Lehrer v. Davis*, 214 Conn. 232, 571 A.2d 691.

Custodial rights of an intact family do not automatically preclude the visitation right of grandparents.

1986—*In re Cynthia A.*, 8 Conn. App. 656, 514 A.2d 360.

Child was committed to grandparents after adjudication of neglect.

§ 11.11 Trial

[1] Testimony of Child

2022—*In re Alizabeth L.-T.*, 213 Conn. App. 541, 278 A.3d 547.

Trial court abused its discretion in failing to sustain Husband's objections to the admission of hearsay statements of the children. Mother had the burden to show why it was not possible to have the children testify. Because the children were older, they should have been summoned to testify at the hearing.

2017—*Medeiros v. Medeiros*, 175 Conn. App. 174, 167 A.3d 967.

Trial court's preclusion of hearsay statements of the minor children was harmless error where defendant effectively conveyed the substance of the statements via other testimony.

2008—*Johnson v. Johnson*, 111 Conn. App. 413, 959 A.2d 637.

Court improperly allowed a guardian ad litem to act as a conduit for hearsay, and to testify about out of court statements and reports of a physician and a therapist where guardian ad litem stated no opinion related to said hearsay comments.

1990—*G.S. v. T.S.*, 23 Conn. App. 509, 582 A.2d 467.

Any child who is a victim of assault, sexual assault or abuse shall be competent to testify without prior qualification; parent cannot waive child's privilege not to reveal communications made to sexual abuse counselor if parent has an interest in the outcome of the proceeding.

1987—*Cotton v. Cotton*, 11 Conn. App. 189, 526 A.2d 547.

Child's hearsay statement through father can be given limited weight.

1985—*In re Juvenile Appeal*, 3 Conn. App. 184, 485 A.2d 1362.

Child's hearsay statement admitted as verbal act.

1984—*Gennarini v. Gennarini*, 2 Conn. App. 132, 477 A.2d 674.

Whether the child's preferences and feelings as to custody and visitation are a significant factor in the court's ultimate determination of the best interest of the child depends on all the facts of the particular case, including the child's age and ability intelligently to form and express those preferences and feelings.

[2] Testimony of Party

1997—*Gomeau v. Gomeau*, 242 Conn. 202, 698 A.2d 818.

Rebuttal testimony should be allowed by trial court after husband impeached during cross-examination.

1989—*Perez v. Perez*, 212 Conn. 63, 561 A.2d 907.

Absence at a hearing of a party seeking to retain custody allows the court to infer that his testimony would have been unfavorable to his cause.

1983—*Wolk v. Wolk*, 191 Conn. 328, 464 A.2d 780.

Spouse testified regarding the emotional instability of the other spouse.

[3] Testimony of Expert

2008—*Johnson v. Johnson*, 111 Conn. App. 413, 959 A.2d 637.

Court improperly allowed a guardian ad litem to act as a conduit for hearsay, and to testify about out of court statements and reports of a physician and a therapist where guardian ad litem stated no opinion related to said hearsay comments.

2003—*Sheppard v. Sheppard*, 80 Conn. App. 202, 834 A.2d 730.

Plaintiff neither prevailed in her claim that trial court improperly failed to find parties' child was autistic nor provided expert medical testimony to that effect.

1993—*Knock v. Knock*, 224 Conn. 776, 621 A.2d 267.

Expert testimony is relevant if her knowledge or experience is helpful to the fact finder in the determination of the ultimate issue.

1993—*Ashton v. Ashton*, 31 Conn. App. 736, 627 A.2d 943.

Expert witness disclosed two days before trial was precluded from testifying.

1990—*In re Barbara J.*, 215 Conn. 31, 574 A.2d 203.

Expert opinion that is partly derived from written sources is admissible.

1989—*Main v. Main*, 17 Conn. App. 670, 555 A.2d 997.

Physician who is consulted for professional treatment or advice may testify as to statements made to him by the patient.

1985—*Pascal v. Pascal*, 2 Conn. App. 472, 481 A.2d 68.

Court ordered psychiatric evaluation of child.

1982—*Dubicki v. Dubicki*, 186 Conn. 709, 443 A.2d 1268.

Communications that bear no relationship to the purpose for which the privilege was enacted do not obtain shelter under the statute and are admissible subject to the normal rules of evidence thus psychiatrist's testimony in child custody case is not privileged.

§ 11.12 Psychological Evaluations

2019—*Merkel v. Hill*, 189 Conn. App. 779, 207 A.3d 1115.

Trial court abused its discretion in a child custody matter by adopting custody and parental access plan recommendations contained in an outdated report. The expert explicitly stated she could not make any present recommendations because she would have nothing on which to base such recommendations, and that she "would be doing a disservice to the minor child to say that" her recommendations were still valid at the time of the hearing.

2019—*Lopes v. Ferrari*, 188 Conn. App. 387, 204 A.3d 1254.

Father's motion for a psychological evaluation of the mother was properly denied by the court, which found that the father was "engaged in a fishing expedition" and properly awarded the parties joint custody.

2014—*Martowska v. White*, 149 Conn. App. 314, 87 A.3d 1201.

Court-ordered psychological evaluation of plaintiff was not rendered moot by temporary visitation order of the court when the court still needs to establish if the final visitation schedule is in the best interest of the children.

§ 11.13 Termination of Parental Rights

2024—*In re A.H.*, 226 Conn. App. 1, 317 A.3d 197.

Judgment terminating a father's parental rights was affirmed. The trial court's reliance on social studies prepared by the Department of Children and Families in the adjudicatory phase of the trial was not improper and did not violate Conn. Gen. Stat. § 45a-717(e)(1) and Conn. Practice Book § 35a-9. The Appellate Court's decision in *In re Tabitha P.*, 39 Conn. App. 353, 664 A.2d 1168 (1995), authorized the court's use of a social study in the adjudicatory phase of a termination of parental rights proceeding, as well as in the dispositional phase. However, the decision in *In re Tabitha P.* should not be construed as tacitly allowing the admission of material that is otherwise inadmissible. The decision in *In re Tabitha P.* in no way created an exception to any evidentiary rule, including the rule against hearsay, nor did it prohibit counsel from objecting to the admission of hearsay. Therefore, counsel for a respondent parent may object to the admission of material contained within a social study on evidentiary or other grounds.

2022—*In re Amias I.*, 343 Conn. 816, 276 A.3d 955.

Judgments terminating a mother's parental rights as to each of her three children were affirmed. Trial court knew or should have known that a conflict existed between the goals of the two younger children, who wished to remain with their foster parents, and the older child, who wished to be reunited with her parents if they were together. However, it was apparent that even if it was assumed that the children's conflicting goals triggered the trial court's duty under Conn. Gen. Stat. § 46b-129a to inquire whether their attorney was able to advocate effectively on behalf of each child, the trial court's failure to make such an inquiry was harmless beyond a reasonable doubt. There was no possibility that the trial court would have allowed the children to return to their mother's care in light of its findings concerning her failure rehabilitate, her lack of candor regarding her relationship with the children's father, and the court's concern that she could not or would not protect them from him.

2022—*In re Annessa J.*, 343 Conn. 642, 284 A.3d 562.

Biological parents appealed trial court judgment terminating their parental rights and denying their posttermination motion for visitation. The trial had been held remotely because of the COVID-19 pandemic.

The appellate court properly found that the record was inadequate for review of the mother's claim that she had a right under article first, § 10, and article fifth, § 1 of the Connecticut Constitution to confront the witnesses against her at an in-person trial. The mother failed to establish that there is a fundamental right to an in person termination of parental rights trial under article first, § 10, and article fifth, § 1. During the trial, the mother never put the Commissioner and the trial court on notice that she objected to the virtual nature of the trial so that the court could make findings of fact regarding the threat posed by the COVID-19 pandemic and whether that threat was sufficiently compelling to curtail any constitutional right to in-person confrontation. In cases of unpreserved constitutional claims, the Supreme Court has consistently refused to order a new trial when it would be necessary to elicit additional evidence to determine whether the constitutional violation exists.

In its ruling regarding posttermination visitation, the appellate court incorrectly determined that the trial court held biological parents to a more exacting legal standard than the standard set forth in *In re Ava W*, 336 Conn. 545, 248 A.3d 675 (2020). The proper standard for deciding motions for posttermination visitation is the "necessary or appropriate" standard in Conn. Gen. Stat. § 46b-121(b)(1). The trial court's finding that posttermination visitation was "not required" merely reiterated its earlier conclusion that such visitation was not "necessary," consistent with the standard set forth in *In re Ava W.*, which requires trial courts to consider whether posttermination visitation is "necessary or appropriate" for the child's wellbeing.

2022—*In re Riley B.*, 342 Conn. 333, 269 A.3d 776.

Trial court properly denied a mother's motion for visitation brought after her parental rights were terminated. Once a judgment is entered terminating parental rights, a biological parent has no colorable right to intervene in the juvenile case to seek posttermination visitation. After a judgment terminating parental rights, the court is authorized to enter posttermination orders only to protect the child's interests, not the biological parents' interests. Conn. Gen. Stat. § 46b-121.

2021—*In re Amanda L.*, 209 Conn. App. 1, 267 A.3d 362.

Appellate Court affirmed judgment terminating the parental rights of both parents. The trial court made the required factual findings under Conn. Gen. Stat. § 17a-112, finding that the parents never participated in learning about the services their autistic child needed to thrive, their refusal was demonstrated to be profound and hostile to their child's well-being, they prioritized their apparent psychological need to defy authority over the child's welfare, and clear and convincing evidence showed that termination was in the child's best interests. Neither parent ever complied with the court-ordered specific steps issued for their rehabilitation so that they could care for their child. The parents' claim that the termination was unconstitutional, unlawful, and fraudulent was not supported by the facts or law.

2021—*In re Karter F.*, 207 Conn. App. 1, 262 A.3d 195.

Appellate Court affirmed the judgment terminating an incarcerated father's parental rights. The trial court did not err in finding that (1) the Department of Children and Family Services made reasonable efforts to reunify the father with his child and he was unable or unwilling to benefit from reunification services, (2) the father failed to rehabilitate, and (3) it was in the best interests of the child to terminate the father's parental rights. The department's efforts to provide visits and to refer the father to resources offered by the Department of Correction were in line with efforts the Appellate Court has found reasonable in other cases involving incarcerated parents. There were relevant factual findings regarding father's unresolved mental and emotional issues and his failure to take advantage of the opportunities that the department offered him to treat those issues or to bond with the child during his incarceration. Specifically, the trial court found he did not complete the therapeutic treatment required by the court-ordered specific steps provided to facilitate reunification.

2021—*State v. Felimon C.*, 206 Conn. App. 727, 261 A.3d 127.

Conn. Gen. Stat. § 45a-719 provides that no motion to open or set aside a judgment terminating parental rights and no petition for a new trial on the issue of termination of parental rights may be granted if a final decree of adoption was issued prior to filing the motion or petition. The defendant's appeal of the trial court's judgment denying his motion to correct an illegal sentence, claiming inter alia that the sentencing court lacked statutory authority to impose a condition of probation prohibiting him from contesting the adoption of the minor child conceived as a result of his sexual assault, was moot because the defendant's rights were terminated, his appeal of the termination of his parental rights had been dismissed, and the minor child had been adopted.

2021—*In re Sequoia G.*, 205 Conn. App. 222, 256 A.3d 195.

The trial court's judgment to terminate a mother's parental rights was affirmed. The court made findings on the factors in Conn. Gen. Stat. § 17a-112(k), including considering the bond between the children and their foster parents and the children's feelings and emotional ties with their mother. There was ample evidence to support the trial court's conclusions. With evidence that the mother had refused to allow the Department of Children and Families to conduct home visits, it was not clearly erroneous for the trial court to find she had not fulfilled her obligations under the court orders concerning visitation with the children. The trial court's findings as to what was in the children's best interests were factually supported and legally sound.

2021—*In re Jacob M.*, 204 Conn. App. 763, 255 A.3d 918.

The trial court's judgment terminating the parental rights of a mother and father were affirmed. The record was sufficient to conclude the Department of Children and Families had made reasonable efforts to reunify each parent with their respective children (the parents had a son together and the mother also had a daughter). The conclusion that it was in the best interest of their son to terminate of the father's parental rights was not clearly erroneous and was supported by the court's findings on the statutory factors in Conn. Gen. Stat. § 17a-112(k). The Appellate Court declined to review the mother's claim that the trial court improperly denied her post-termination motion to intervene in which she sought visitation with the children because the record was inadequate. Since the court did not file a memorandum of decision explaining its ruling, the mother should have filed a notice pursuant to Conn. Practice Book 64-1(b) to get a statement of decision or filed a motion asking the court to articulate the factual and legal basis for its ruling.

2021—*In re Kiara Liz V.*, 203 Conn. App. 613, 248 A.3d 813.

The trial court's decision that terminating the father's parental rights was in his child's best interests was not clearly erroneous. The trial court's conclusion was based on its findings related to the seven statutory factors in Conn. Gen. Stat. § 17a-112(k), including the father's difficulty accepting and understanding his mental illness, his inability to comply with mental health treatment, and his failure to make progress in his parenting abilities. The father did not challenge these findings on appeal.

2021—*In re Miyuki M.*, 202 Conn. App. 851, 246 A.3d 1113.

In proceedings to terminate parental rights, the trial court did not err in denying the mother's petition to transfer guardianship to the child's grandmother, concluding that the evidence was insufficient to prove that the grandmother was a suitable and worthy guardian for the child and also concluding that a transfer of guardianship to the grandmother was not in the child's best interests. Adjudicating a motion to transfer guardianship pursuant to Conn. Gen. Stat. § 46b-129(j)(2) requires a two-step analysis: (1) the court must determine whether it would be in the best interests of the child for guardianship to be transferred from the petitioner to the proposed guardian; and (2) the court must then find that the third party is a suitable and worthy guardian. Conn. Practice Book § 35a-12A(d) similarly provides the moving party has the burden of proof to show that the proposed guardian is suitable and worthy and that transfer of guardianship is in the child's best interests. *See In re Leo L.*, 191 Conn. App. 134, 139–140, 214 A.3d 430 (2019).

2021—*In re Phoenix A.*, 202 Conn. App. 827, 246 A.3d 1096.

The trial court's judgment terminating a father's parental rights was affirmed. His claim that the trial court improperly found he was unable or unwilling to benefit from reunification services was moot because his claim challenged only one of two separate and independent bases for the trial court's findings. Even if the Appellate

Court agreed with him on this point, it was unable to provide him relief on appeal. The trial court did not err in concluding that the father had failed to achieve a sufficient degree of personal rehabilitation. There was abundant evidence that he had been referred to the appropriate services but continued to struggle with substance abuse issues, had continuing involvement with the criminal justice system, and had difficulty implementing the skills he learned at the various programs he attended.

2021—*In re Kameron N.*, 202 Conn. App. 637, 264 A.3d 578.

The trial court's judgment terminating a mother's parental rights was affirmed. Her challenges to the adequacy of the notice to her tribe on the grounds that it did not comply with the Guidelines for Implementing the Indian Child Welfare Act and it was not sent by registered mail were unavailing. The trial court did not abuse its discretion in denying the mother's motion to introduce new evidence that the child's foster family was no longer an adoptive or long-term resource because questions of where the child should reside and with whom were not questions related to whether it was in the child's best interest to terminate his relationship with his parents. The purported new evidence was irrelevant to the issues before the trial court. The mother's claim that the decision to terminate her parental rights was clearly erroneous was not supported by the ample evidence of her shortcomings against which the trial court could weigh the benefit of the child's relationship with her. It is within the court's discretion to credit all, part or none of the testimony at trial, to weigh the evidence presented, and to determine the effect to be given to that evidence.

2021—*In re Kameron N.*, 202 Conn. App. 628, 246 A.3d 526.

The trial court's judgment terminating a father's parental rights was affirmed. The Appellate Court rejected his claim that his tribe did not receive adequate notice of the termination proceedings as required by the ICWA. The tribe had been notified of the termination proceedings and had filed a Notice of Intervention. The plain and unambiguous language of 25 U.S.C. § 1912(a) does not require that notice sent in any involuntary termination proceeding explicitly indicate the involuntary nature of the proceedings. Because a tribe is not entitled to intervene in voluntary proceedings, the fact that notice was sent to the father's tribe was indicative of the involuntary nature of the termination proceedings in this case.

2021—*In re Josiah D.*, 202 Conn. App. 234, 245 A.3d 898.

Trial court did not commit reversible error by not notifying a father that, pursuant to Conn. Practice Book § 35a-7A, it would draw an adverse inference from his failure to testify in the proceedings to terminate his parental rights. Prior to the presentation of evidence, the trial court properly notified the father of his rights, including an advisement that an adverse inference would be drawn from his failure to testify. The trial court was not required to inform the father again when it later learned of his decision not to testify. Even if the trial court were required to give such additional notice, not doing so would have been a harmless error because the trial court found that the father had failed to achieve the degree of rehabilitation that would encourage the belief that he could assume a responsible position in his sons' lives. The Appellate Court declined to exercise its supervisory authority to require notice beyond what is required by Conn. Practice Book § 35a-7A.

2020—*In re November H.*, 202 Conn. App. 106, 243 A.3d 839.

The trial court properly terminated a father's parental rights where it expressly found that the child was in need of a safe and permanent home with a proven competent caretaker because neither biological parent was capable of providing such a home for her within a reasonable time.

2020—*In re Miracle C.*, 201 Conn. App. 598, 243 A.3d 347.

The appeal of a judgment terminating a mother's parental rights is moot because she challenged only one of the two bases for the trial court's determination that Conn. Gen. Stat. § 17a-112(j)(1) had been satisfied. The trial court found that the Department of Children and Families had made reasonable efforts to reunify the mother with her child and that the mother was unable or unwilling to benefit from reunification efforts. The mother questioned the finding that the department had made reasonable efforts but she failed to challenge the court's finding that she was unable or unwilling to benefit from the department's attempts at reunification.

2020—*In re Ja'La L.*, 201 Conn. App. 586, 243 A.3d 358.

The trial court's judgment terminating a mother's parental rights was affirmed. The court had found her children uncared for in a prior proceeding and the mother failed to achieve the degree of personal rehabilitation that would encourage the belief that within a reasonable time, considering the age and the needs of the children, she could assume a responsible position in their lives. There was sufficient evidence in the record to support the trial court's conclusion that it was in the best interests of the children to terminate the mother's parental rights.

2020—*In re Ja'Maire M.*, 201 Conn. App. 498, 242 A.3d 747.

The trial court's judgment terminating a father's parental rights was affirmed. The father claimed that the trial court improperly relied on a finding that the child was neglected made at a previous proceeding at which he was not present. His appeal constitutes an impermissible collateral attack on the neglect judgment. The father's absence at the neglect hearing is not legally significant because the child's father was undetermined at the time the child was adjudicated neglected. The father was not legally required to be a party because that proceeding centered on the status of the child. Following the results of a paternity test, the trial court immediately joined the father into the case and ordered specific steps for the father and the Department of Children and Families amended its permanency plan to focus on reunification with the father. However, the father did not fulfill the court-ordered steps.

2020—*In re D'Andre T.*, 201 Conn. App. 396, 242 A.3d 766.

The Appellate Court declined to exercise its supervisory authority over the administration of justice to reverse the judgments terminating a mother's parental rights and denying her motion to transfer guardianship, to award her a new trial, and to obligate the trial court to apply a new procedural rule that would require the Superior Court to make certain written findings in all cases in which a court concurrently considers a transfer of guardianship motion and a petition to terminate parental rights. The mother's proposed procedural rule implicated a policy consideration best addressed by the legislature. There was no evidence of pervasive, significant problems or conduct that threatened the sound administration of justice.

2020—*In re Xavier H.*, 201 Conn. App. 81, 240 A.3d 1087.

The trial court properly terminated the father's parental rights under Conn. Gen. Stat. § 17a-112. He had a criminal history. The Department of Children and Families had attempted to engage him in services with little success. It took 10 attempts to engage him in substance abuse evaluations and screenings before he finally engaged. He had also been diagnosed with adjustment disorder and personality disorder.

The mother's parental rights were also properly terminated under Conn. Gen. Stat. § 17a-112. She had discharged herself from a recommended intensive outpatient program for opioid dependence. She resisted participating in any domestic violence counseling and was unwilling to engage in such counseling. She continued interactions with the father that were indicative of her ongoing inability to put the child's needs first. She was also angry and argumentative with the foster mother in the presence of the child, and repeatedly undermined the child's relationship with his foster mother.

2020—*In re Ava W.*, 336 Conn. 545, 248 A.3d 675.

A trial court has authority to issue a post termination visitation order that is requested within the context of a termination proceeding, so long as it is necessary or appropriate to secure the welfare, protection, proper care and suitable support of the child. That authority is derived from the court's broad common-law authority over juvenile matters and the legislature's enactment of Conn. Gen. Stat. § 46b-121(b)(1) codifying that authority. The trial court incorrectly determined that it lacked authority to consider a post termination visitation order on the basis of a mother's failure to satisfy the statutory requirements of Conn. Gen. Stat. § 17a-112(b)–(h), which governs cooperative post adoption agreements under which parents voluntarily relinquish their parental rights and the intended adoptive parents willingly enter into a post adoption contact agreement. The present case does not fall within those circumstances. The mother's failure to satisfy those requirements did not deprive the trial court of authority to consider post termination visitation pursuant to its broad authority under § 46b-121(b)(1).

2020—*In re Zakai F.*, 336 Conn. 272, 255 A.3d 767.

Where a mother had voluntarily given temporary guardianship of her son to her sister, the appellate court erred in affirming the trial court's decision to deny the mother's motion under Conn. Gen. Stat. § 45a-611 to reinstate her guardianship rights. Once a parent demonstrates that the factors that resulted in the removal of the parent as guardian have been resolved satisfactorily, the parent is entitled to a presumption that reinstatement of guardianship rights is in the best interests of the child. The party opposing reinstatement must rebut this presumption by clear and convincing evidence. Because it is unclear whether the trial court applied this presumption and because it did not determine that the mother's sister had rebutted that presumption by clear and convincing evidence, the trial court had improperly denied the mother's motion.

Due process requires the application of the clear and convincing evidence standard of proof to rebut the presumption that reinstatement of guardianship rights is in the best interests of the child. The trial court's application of the preponderance of the evidence standard was a violation of the mother's due process rights.

2020—*In re Corey C.*, 198 Conn. App. 41, 232 A.3d 1237.

Appellate court affirmed trial court order terminating a father's parental rights. The trial court correctly determined that the Department of Children and Families made reasonable efforts to reunify the child with the father as required by Conn. Gen. Stat. § 17a-112(j)(1). The agency monitored the father's engagement with his existing therapist, identified a couples counselor for the father and the mother, referred them to three separate parenting education services, and offered to provide the parents with an additional supervised visit every week but they declined. The trial court correctly determined that the father failed to rehabilitate because he did not have a reasonable plan as to who would care for the child, other than the mother, while he was at work, was unable or unwilling to change the mother's smoking habits to make the home environment safer for the child's asthmatic condition, and lacked sufficient insight into the negative effect the mother's mental health had on her parenting despite his substantial period of counseling.

2020—*In re Omar I.*, 197 Conn. App. 499, 231 A.3d 1196.

Appellate court affirmed trial court order terminating a father's parental rights and refusing to revoke the commitment of his children to the custody and care of the Commissioner of Children and Families. The trial court properly rejected the father's claim of judicial bias because he did not cite to any instance in which any of the several persons identified in his brief were precluded from testifying; the court considered their testimony in its evaluation of the evidence, and carefully explained its factual findings. The trial court properly found that the father failed to rehabilitate pursuant to Conn. Gen. Stat. § 17a-112 because, by the time of the trial, he had not recognized his role in the circumstances that led to the children's removal from the home, continued to undermine efforts to reunify the mother with the children, and continued his underlying pattern of exerting control in all matters concerning the mother to the detriment of his children. The trial court properly found that the father failed to recognize how those failures impacted the children.

2020—*In re Cataleya M., In re Isabella M., In re Savanah F.*, 196 Conn. App. 333, 229 A.3d 1073.

Appellate court affirmed judgments terminating a mother's parental rights with respect to her minor children. (1) The trial court did not abuse its discretion in denying the mother's motion to disqualify the guardian ad litem because the mother failed to meet her burden of demonstrating that the proceedings in which the attorney served as the mother's guardian ad litem in 2005 were substantially related to the issues addressed in the 2019 termination of parental rights trial. Rule 1.9 of the Rules of Professional Conduct was not implicated because information received by an attorney acting as a guardian ad litem for a minor child is not subject to attorney client confidentiality pursuant to the Judicial Branch's Code of Conduct for Counsel for the Minor Child and Guardian Ad Litem. (2) The mother could not prevail on her claim that the social studies were improperly admitted as they contained hearsay and had not been ordered by the court because she failed to specify to which hearsay statements contained in the social studies she objected, which denied the petitioner, the Commissioner of Children and Families, the opportunity to argue which hearsay exception applied to which statement. (3) The trial court properly found by clear and convincing evidence, on the basis of its factual findings and reasonable inferences drawn therefrom, that the mother failed to achieve sufficient rehabilitation that would have encouraged the belief that, within a reasonable time, she could have assumed a responsible position in the children's lives.

2020—*In re Walker C.*, 195 Conn. App. 604, 226 A.3d 175.

Trial court did not err by finding that the termination of the mother's parental rights was in her child's best interest because she had a history of alcohol and substance abuse and she did not cooperate with or benefit from multiple offers of therapeutic and rehabilitative services. Appellate court did not consider the mother's argument that the trial court had erred by not making a permanent transfer of guardianship the child's foster parent because that claim was contrary to the mother's position during trial that the petition to terminate her parental rights should be denied because she had rehabilitated. To allow the mother to reverse her trial court strategy and argue something completely different on appeal would amount to sanctioning a trial where representations to the court and other counsel do not count. Judgment affirmed.

2020—*In re Brian P.*, 195 Conn. App. 558, 226 A.3d 159.

Appellate court affirmed the trial court order terminating parental rights of a mother and father pursuant to Conn. Gen. Stat. § 17a-112. The trial court did not clearly err because even though the parents' drug use and arrests were not the sole basis for the termination, there was evidence that the parents had failed to rehabilitate, including positive urine screens and other instances of bad parental judgment. There was nothing improper with the trial court factoring the parents' credibility into its analysis because the parents testified on their own behalf and did so in ways that conflicted with the testimony presented by the Commissioner of Children and Families. While the parents did make efforts to address their addictions, there was sufficient evidence for the finding that they failed to achieve sufficient personal rehabilitation so as to encourage the belief that they could assume a responsible position in the life of their child within a reasonable time. The trial court did not clearly err in finding that termination of the mother's and father's parental rights was in their child's best interest because the court considered and made findings under each of the seven factors of Conn. Gen. Stat. § 17a-112(k) and it properly considered the child's need for a permanent, safe, and supportive home given his age and that the fact that he had spent more than half of his life in foster care.

2020—*In re Yolanda V.*, 195 Conn. App. 334, 224 A.3d 182.

Appellate court affirmed trial court ruling terminating a mother's parental rights. Appropriate standard of review is evidentiary sufficiency, whether the trial court could have concluded that the cumulative effect of the evidence was sufficient to justify its ultimate conclusions. If the trial court could reasonably have reached its conclusion, the judgment must stand. The mere existence of evidence in the record that would support a different conclusion, without more, is insufficient to undermine trial court ruling. Here, there was sufficient evidence for the trial court to conclude that the mother had not corrected several factors that led to the initial commitment of her minor children to the custody of the Commissioner of Children and Families and to support the trial court's determination that the mother had failed to attain a degree of rehabilitation sufficient to warrant the belief that sometime in the foreseeable future she would be capable of assuming a responsible position with respect to the care of her minor children, who needed permanency and consistency. Evidence also supported the trial court's determination that termination of the mother's parental rights was in the best interest of her minor children.

2019—*In re Tresin J.*, 334 Conn. 314, 222 A.3d 83.

Appellate court properly upheld trial court's termination of father's parental rights finding that there was clear and convincing evidence of a lack of an ongoing parent child relationship. The interference exception did not apply because it is like the equitable doctrine of "clean hands" and is triggered only by the conduct of the petitioner, not by a third party or some other external factor. Mother's inability to foster a relationship between father and their child while father was incarcerated is not relevant. The virtual intimacy exception did not apply because the child was six years old at the time of trial and was able to communicate that he did not have present memories of father as his parent.

2019—*In re Cameron W.*, 194 Conn. App. 633, 221 A.3d 885.

Trial court reasonably determined that petitioner, Commissioner of Children and Families, proved by clear and convincing evidence that respondent mother was unable or unwilling to benefit from reunification efforts. The appellate court did not need to reach merits of mother's claims that the Department of Children and Families had not made reasonable efforts to reunify her with her son because a finding that mother was unable or willing to benefit from reunification was sufficient to terminate parental rights under § 17a-112(j)(1).

2019—*In re Jacob W.*, 330 Conn. 744, 200 A.3d 1091.

The appellate court properly reversed the trial court's denial of a maternal grandmother's petitions to terminate a father's parental rights and remanded the matter for a new trial, as the trial court applied an incorrect legal test in determining that the grandmother had failed to prove the lack of an ongoing parent-child relationship for purposes of Conn. Gen. Stat. § 45a-717(g)(2)(C).

2019—*In re Anaishaly C.*, 190 Conn. App. 667, 213 A.3d 12.

The parents failed to achieve the requisite degree of personal rehabilitation required by Conn. Gen. Stat. § 17a-112 where the parents refused to submit to substance abuse testing; legalization of marijuana did not preclude trial court's consideration of parents' unresolved drug abuse.

2019—*In re Bianca K.*, 188 Conn. App. 259, 203 A.3d 1280.

Clear and convincing evidence justified the termination of the mother's parental rights for failing to achieve sufficient personal rehabilitation. Mother maintained relationship with an abusive boyfriend and failed to understand the harm of the continued relationship to the child and could not provide the child with a consistent, stable, safe and secure environment.

2018—*In re Egypt E. et al.*, 327 Conn. 506, 175 A.3d 21.

Filing of an amended petition to terminate parental rights established a new adjudicatory date and therefore the court properly considered harmful acts of parental omission that occurred after the removal of one child from the home as the basis for termination of parental rights.

Failure of both parents to acknowledge the father was the cause of injuries to one of the children constituted a failure to protect a child by acknowledging the existence of a dangerous situation.

Expert testimony from psychologists was afforded great weight in termination proceeding.

2017—*In re Elijah C.*, 326 Conn. 480, 165 A.3d 1149.

Americans with Disabilities Act cannot be relied on as a defense in parental termination or child neglect proceedings.

2017—*In re Harmony Q.*, 171 Conn. App. 568, 157 A.3d 137.

Court's ultimate conclusion that the respondent failed to achieve sufficient rehabilitation was not clearly erroneous.

2017—*In re Savannah Y.*, 172 Conn. App. 266, 158 A.3d 864.

Court did not err in ruling DCF had made reasonable efforts to reunify where multiple attempts were made by DCF but the respondent failed to respond or comply.

Court did err in determining that respondent had failed to achieve a significant degree of rehabilitation where, although respondent had made significant progress, her road to recovery would be a lengthy one.

2017—*In re Natalie S.*, 325 Conn. 833, 160 A.3d 1056.

Department of Children and Families was not required to provide reunification services to mother and child after father had been granted temporary custody and guardianship of the child.

2017—*In re Unique R.*, 170 Conn. App. 833, 156 A.3d 1.

Duty of the Department of Children and Families to make reasonable efforts to reunify child with her father did not require the Department to investigate possible relatives for placement of the child.

2017—*In re Luis N.*, 175 Conn. App. 271, 165 A.3d 1270; *related proceeding at In re Luis N.*, 175 Conn. App. 307, 167 A.3d 476.

Any errors by the court in permitting the Department of Children and Families to meet with the minor children ex parte was harmless and was not a violation of the respondent's constitutional rights under *State v. Golding*.

2016—*In re Glerisbeth C. et al.*, 162 Conn. App. 273, 130 A.3d 917.

No abuse of discretion in failing to *sua sponte* order a competency evaluation.

2015—*In re Gabriella A.*, 319 Conn. 775, 127 A.3d 948.

Termination of parental rights when mother was unable to benefit from reunification service.

2015—*In re Shane M.*, 318 Conn. 569, 122 A.3d 1247.

Parental rights terminated based on failure to complete court-ordered steps for reunification and prevention of termination. Procedural safeguards regarding "right to silence" did not apply to refusal to submit to court-ordered drug screenings; rights terminated.

2015—*In re Yasiel R. et al.*, 317 Conn. 773, 120 A.3d 1188.

Due process does not require a canvass of a represented party about decision to not contest exhibits and waive right to full trial. Supreme Court would exercise supervisory authority to require a trial court to canvass all parents immediately before termination hearing.

2015—*In re Nioshka A.N.*, 161 Conn. App. 627, 128 A.3d 619.

Termination of parental rights was in the child's best interests.

2015—*In re Victor D.*, 161 Conn. App. 604, 128 A.3d 608.

DCF efforts to reunify father with son were reasonable. Evidence sufficient to support finding that father had failed to rehabilitate in a reasonable time.

2015—*In re James O., Jr.*, 160 Conn. App. 506, 127 A.3d 375.

DCF made reasonable efforts to reunify mother and children. Mother failed to achieve sufficient degree of personal rehabilitation after finding of neglect.

2015—*In re Ariana S.*, 159 Conn. App. 513, 123 A.3d 463.

Denial of motion to reopen judgment terminating parental rights, based on insufficient notice, was not an abuse of discretion.

2015—*In re Joseph M., Jr.*, 158 Conn. App. 849, 120 A.3d 1271.

Termination of parental rights in best interests of child after father failed to rehabilitate.

2003—*In re Alexander C.*, 262 Conn. 308, 813 A.2d 87.

Termination of father's parental right granted where incarcerated father lacked relationship with son.

2001—*In re Jonathan M.*, 255 Conn. 208, 764 A.2d 739, *aff'g* 26 Conn. L. Rptr. 215.

Biological parent cannot bring a writ of habeas corpus to challenge a termination of parental rights.

2001—*In re Ashley E.*, 62 Conn. App. 307, 771 A.2d 160.

Appellate Court confirms abandonment, and that termination was in best interests of child.

1999—*In re Charles A.*, 55 Conn. App. 293, 738 A.2d 222.

Termination of mother's parental rights was in the best interest of the children.

1998—*In re Darlene C.*, 247 Conn. 1, 717 A.2d 1242.

DCF practice of filing papers in parental termination matters is not unauthorized practice of law.

1995—*In re Bruce R.*, 34 Conn. App. 176, 640 A.2d 643 (1994), *aff'd*, 234 Conn. 194, 662 A.2d 107.

Parent may petition to terminate his or her parental rights; financial condition of parent must be considered in parental rights termination decision.

1988—*In re Jason D.*, 13 Conn. App. 626, 538 A.2d 1073.

Neither probate court nor superior court can entertain petitions to terminate parental rights of child over fourteen who has not affirmatively joined in such petition.

1988—*In re Jessica M.*, 14 Conn. App. 805, 539 A.2d 1004.

Mother did not present sufficient evidence to justify termination of father's parental rights.

CHAPTER 12

ENFORCEMENT OF ORDERS

SYNOPSIS

§ 12.01 Motion for Contempt

[1] Procedure

2024—*Trent v. Trent*, 321 A.3d 454.

Trial court abused its discretion in issuing a contempt order regarding the child care costs ordered in accordance with the child support guidelines. The defendant failed to satisfy her burden to prove by clear and convincing evidence that the child care costs for which she sought reimbursement were qualifying costs that were reasonable and necessary for her to maintain employment. Consequently, the defendant failed to prove the plaintiff violated the child care order because he had no obligation to reimburse her for nonqualifying child care. Even if the defendant had met her burden to prove the child care costs were qualifying, there was not enough in the record to conclude there was clear and convincing evidence that the plaintiff wilfully violated the child care order.

2022—*Szymonik v. Szymonik*, 213 Conn. App. 421, 278 A.3d 41.

Husband failed to show the trial court committed any instance of reversible error when it found him in contempt on two separate occasions and sanctioned him for engaging in bad faith litigation. Trial court's factual findings were not clearly erroneous. It applied the proper legal standards and analyses.

2020—*Leonova v. Leonov*, 201 Conn. App. 285, 242 A.3d 713.

The trial court erred when it held the defendant in contempt for spending $10,000 for a ski lodge rental because there was no notice to the defendant that there was a motion for contempt pending on that issue. However, the court properly determined that the ski lodge rental was not in the usual course of business and that it therefore had the authority to fashion a remedial order to offset the defendant's violation of the automatic orders in Conn. Practice Book § 25-5.

2020—*Barr v. Barr*, 195 Conn. App. 479, 225 A.3d 972.

The trial court improperly granted plaintiff ex-wife's motion for contempt because she did not properly serve the defendant ex-husband with process. When the trial court held the hearing on the motion without the defendant being present, it made no findings as to whether the out of state defendant had been served in accordance with applicable long arm statutes. The defendant's claim on appeal that he had not been properly served was reviewable by the appellate court because his claim challenged personal jurisdiction. A post judgment motion for contempt to enforce an antecedent judicial order requires proper service of process in the manner required for the service of civil process. The record reflects that plaintiff's counsel certified he mailed a copy of the motion to an address on file for the defendant in Georgia and sent a copy to the defendant's email address on file. Whether or not this actually occurred, or whether the defendant was provided with actual notice, is immaterial because knowledge of the motion without proper service is insufficient to confer personal jurisdiction over the defendant. Appellate court reversed and remanded with direction to dismiss the motion for contempt.

2019—*Bolat v. Bolat*, 293 Conn. 397, 215 A.3d 736.

Trial court did not abuse its discretion in granting mother's motion for contempt and holding father in contempt for violating parties' stipulation stating that if the custodial parent cannot be with the children, it is the custodial parent's responsibility to make arrangements for them unless the noncustodial parent agrees in writing to take them. The stipulation, including the meaning of "custodial parent," is sufficiently clear and unambiguous as to support a judgment of contempt and trial court could have reasonably found that father had willfully violated the stipulation.

Trial court did not abuse its discretion in granting mother's motion for contempt and finding father in contempt for violating parties' stipulation to contribute to the purchase of a car for their children. Although father correctly asserted stipulation does not specify who would purchase the vehicle or when, he provided no legal authority the absence of those details made the stipulation ambiguous. The stipulation is sufficiently clear and unambiguous and trial court could have reasonably found that father had willfully violated the stipulation.

2017—*Puff v. Puff*, 177 Conn. App. 103, 171 A.3d 1076.

Trial court's finding of contempt was clearly erroneous where plaintiff's only obligation was to endeavor to secure an opinion letter and the record demonstrated the plaintiff made efforts to obtain such a letter.

2017—*Medeiros v. Medeiros*, 175 Conn. App. 174, 167 A.3d 967.

Where it was not clear what standard of proof the trial court used in determining contempt, the defendant could not prevail on his claim that the trial court used the improper standard of proof.

2017—*Dejana v. Dejana*, 176 Conn. App. 104, 168 A.3d 595.

Trial court did not abuse discretion in denying the plaintiff's motion for contempt where the separation agreement clearly and unambiguously stated the defendant had the right to apply any and all portions of his income received from his employer's long term stock incentive program to college expenses for the parties' son.

2017—*Powell-Ferri v. Ferri*, 326 Conn. 457, 165 A.3d 1124.

Court did not abuse discretion where it failed to find defendant-husband in contempt where husband had no affirmative duty to recover marital assets lawfully decanted from a trust and husband was unaware of decanting.

2017—*Watkins v. Demos*, 172 Conn. App. 730, 161 A.3d 655.

Denial of plaintiff's motion to open based on mutual mistake was not clearly erroneous.

2017—*DiGiuseppe v. DiGiuseppe*, 174 Conn. App. 855, 167 A.3d 411.

Defendant failed to preserve claims on appeal regarding payment of college expenses before the trial court; appellate court declined review ruling on contempt motion.

2017—*Pressley v. Johnson*, 173 Conn. App. 402, 162 A.3d 751.

Trial court erred in denying her motion for contempt and finding that the defendant did not owe her an arrearage for the work related child care expenses she had incurred.

2017—*Richman v. Wallman*, 172 Conn. App. 616, 161 A.3d 666.

The court did not erroneously hold the plaintiff in contempt where the court did not rule on the defendant's motion for contempt.

2016—*Valentine v. Valentine*, 164 Conn. App. 354, 141 A.3d 884.

The court abused its discretion by impermissibly ignoring a series of contempt findings and monetary sanction orders of another judge. The court declined to determine the amount of money due to the wife that had accumulated pursuant to those orders, and improperly shifted the burden of proving the husband's noncompliance with the wife's discovery requests back to the wife.

2016—*Norberg-Hurlburt v. Hurlburt*, 162 Conn. App. 661, 133 A.3d 482.

A party's failure to attend a hearing, after three prior failures to appear, does not prevent a court from finding the party in contempt.

2014—*Brody v. Brody*, 153 Conn. App. 625, 103 A.3d 981.

Court may order post-judgment discovery in regards to a pending motion for contempt pertaining to fraudulent conduct that allegedly transpired after the entry of judgment and involved noncompliance with the court's outstanding orders.

2009—*Dionne v. Dionne*, 115 Conn. App. 488, 972 A.2d 791.

Court did not abuse its discretion by granting a six week continuance of a contempt hearing, despite attorney's representation that check was in the mail. Obligor ultimately found in contempt for nonpayment during the previous six weeks.

2005—*Kennedy v. Kennedy*, 88 Conn. App. 442, 869 A.2d 1252.

Case discusses civil versus criminal contempt.

1999—*Kelly v. Kelly*, 54 Conn. App. 50, 732 A.2d 808.

Evidentiary hearing must be held before holding a party in civil contempt.

1995—*Avella v. Avella*, 39 Conn. App. 669, 666 A.2d 822.

Motion for contempt need not be heard prior to motion for modification.

1994—*Clement v. Clement*, 34 Conn. App. 641, 643 A.2d 874.

Court can fashion a remedy in a contempt action that preserves the integrity of the original order.

1994—*Bryant v. Bryant*, 228 Conn. 630, 637 A.2d 1111.

Due process of law requires that one charged with contempt of court be advised of the charges against him, have a reasonable opportunity to meet them by way of defense or explanation, have the right to be represented by counsel, and have a chance to testify and call other witnesses in his behalf, either by way of defense or explanation.

1991—*Duve v. Duve*, 25 Conn. App. 262, 594 A.2d 473.

Contempt may be direct or indirect depending on whether it occurred within or outside the presence of the court.

1989—*Broderick v. Broderick*, 20 Conn. App. 145, 565 A.2d 3.

An appeal may be dismissed if appellant is in contempt of court.

1988—*Fitzgerald v. Fitzgerald*, 16 Conn. App. 548, 547 A.2d 1387.

Civil contempt conduct is directed against some civil right of an opposing party.

1988—*Sgarellino v. Hightower*, 13 Conn. App. 591, 538 A.2d 1065.

Finding of contempt must be based on sworn testimony.

1988—*Nelson v. Nelson*, 13 Conn. App. 355, 536 A.2d 985.

Testimony must be presented with a motion for contempt.

1988—*Kronholm v. Kronholm*, 16 Conn. App. 124, 547 A.2d 61.

Despite a finding of contempt, trial court has broad discretion to make whole a party who has suffered as a result of another's failure to comply with the court order.

1987—*Gallagher v. Gallagher*, 11 Conn. App. 509, 528 A.2d 379.

Court can alter terms of payment with a motion for contempt without a motion to modify.

1983—*Greenwood v. Greenwood*, 191 Conn. 309, 464 A.2d 771.

The court will dismiss appeals for contemptuous conduct of an appellant not necessarily related to the merits of the appeal.

1983—*Friedlander v. Friedlander*, 191 Conn. 81, 463 A.2d 587.

An adjudication of contempt is final and may be reviewed only on questions of jurisdiction such as whether the court had authority to impose the punishment inflicted and whether the act or acts for which the penalty was imposed could constitute a contempt.

[2] Defenses

2024—*Wethington v. Wethington*, 223 Conn. App. 715, 309 A.3d 356.

Trial court improperly granted two of the plaintiff's motions for contempt because the court adjudicated the defendant in contempt of automatic orders pursuant to Conn. Practice Book § 25-5(b) for actions he committed before the automatic orders had become effective against him. The plaintiff commenced the dissolution action in October 2019 then filed several motions for contempt pendente lite alleging that the defendant had violated the automatic orders through his financial transactions in October 2019. As a matter of law, the defendant could not be adjudicated in contempt of the automatic orders for his actions in October 2019 because under the clear and unambiguous language of § 25-5, he was not subject to the automatic orders until they had been served on him, through counsel, in November 2019.

2021—*Boyd-Mullineaux v. Mullineaux*, 203 Conn. App. 664, 249 A.3d 759.

The trial court properly denied the plaintiff's postjudgment motion for contempt as to a claimed arrearage of unallocated alimony and child support based on distributions the defendant received but did not include in his earned income when calculating support. After the dissolution judgment, the defendant purchased a membership interest in an LLP associated with the LLC that employed him. The evidence presented supported the trial court's conclusion that the distributions the defendant received as a member of the LLP were not included in the clear and unambiguous definition of gross annual earned income from employment in the parties' separation agreement because the distributions were not related to services he rendered. Further, the separation agreement provided that all other income earned by the defendant due to his investment of assets distributed to him in the dissolution shall not be considered in the definition of earned income from employment. The trial court correctly concluded that the return on the defendant's investment of the purchased membership interest in the LLP was not related to his employment with the LLC, and, therefore, was excluded from the definition of his earned income from employment.

2020—*Casiraghi v. Casiraghi*, 200 Conn. App. 771, 241 A.3d 717.

The trial court improperly granted the former wife's motion for contempt because it failed to consider the former husband's inability to make unallocated support and lump sum property payments pursuant to their dissolution judgment. A party's conduct must be willful to constitute contempt. A party who is unable to comply with financial orders due to a demonstrable inability to pay has a defense to a claim of contempt.

2019—*Grogan v. Penza*, 194 Conn. App. 72, 220 A.3d 147.

Defendant's motion for contempt after plaintiff failed to true up alimony was properly denied where nonpayment was the result of a calculation pursuant to specific and plain language in the parties' separation agreement.

2018—*Hirschfeld v. Machinist*, 181 Conn. App. 309, 186 A.3d 771.

Contempt is not warranted when the order is vague and indefinite.

2014—*Aliano v. Aliano*, 148 Conn. App. 267, 85 A.3d 33.

Motion for contempt was properly denied where nonpayment was based on a good faith dispute or legitimate misunderstanding of the terms of the order.

2013—*Brody v. Brody*, 145 Conn. App. 654, 77 A.3d 156.

Contempt finding was an abuse of discretion where the party "not seeing the world in a reasonable way."

2013—*Bauer v. Bauer*, 308 Conn. 124, 60 A.3d 950.

Courts may exercise continuing jurisdiction to clarify a judgment when ambiguity in language arises as a result.

2003—*Behrns v. Behrns*, 80 Conn. App. 286, 835 A.2d 68.

Defendant was required to seek help in trial court rather than resort to self-help as subject provision was complex and ambiguous.

2003—*Detels v. Detels*, 79 Conn. App. 467, 830 A.2d 381.

Because the term "discharge" in parties' separation agreement was ambiguous, trial court properly determined that plaintiff's non-compliance was willful.

2001—*Sablosky v. Sablosky*, 258 Conn. 713, 784 A.2d 890.

Ambiguity in terms of judgment does not, as a matter of law, preclude finding of contempt for the willful failure to comply with judgment.

1996—*Meehan v. Meehan*, 40 Conn. App. 107, 669 A.2d 616.

Motion for contempt denied when there was an adequate basis to explain the failure to honor the order.

1995—*Jenks v. Jenks*, 39 Conn. App. 139, 663 A.2d 1123.

Payor who misread court's decision and agreed to make up missed alimony payments was not in willful contempt.

1991—*Zivic v. Zivic*, 26 Conn. App. 5, 596 A.2d 475.

The inability of a party to obey an order of the court, without fault on his part, is a good defense to the charge of contempt.

1989—*Blake v. Blake*, 211 Conn. 485, 560 A.2d 396.

There must be a good faith dispute over the amount owed before the doctrine is applied.

1988—*Mallory v. Mallory*, 207 Conn. 48, 539 A.2d 995.

Inability of a party to obey an order of the court, without fault on his part, is a good defense to a charge of contempt.

1986—*Niles v. Niles*, 9 Conn. App. 240, 518 A.2d 932.

Genuine controversy over judgment justifies court's failure to hold party in contempt.

1985—*Marcil v. Marcil*, 4 Conn. App. 403, 494 A.2d 620.

Unintentional violation does not justify contempt order.

1983—*Turgeon v. Turgeon*, 190 Conn. 269, 460 A.2d 1260.

Inability of a contemnor to obey a court order through no fault of her own is a defense to a claim for contempt.

[3] Penalties

2024—*LeNczewski v. LeNczewski*, 229 Conn. App. 752.

The trial court did not abuse its discretion by awarding attorney's fees to plaintiff after finding the defendant in contempt for not complying with the provision in the parties' separation agreement regarding their exchange of tax returns. Conn. Gen. Stat. § 46b-87 provides that a trial court may exercise its discretion to award attorney's fees to the prevailing party in a contempt proceeding. Also, the court stated that its attorney's fees award was made in accordance with paragraph 18.2 of the parties' separation agreement. The defendant's arguments did not support a conclusion that the trial court abused its discretion.

2024—*Yanavich v. Yanavich*, 228 Conn. App. 444, 325 A.3d 1149.

Trial court did not abuse its discretion by not imposing sanctions on the plaintiff after finding her in contempt for inappropriately involving two of the parties' children in their disagreements. Instead of a financial penalty, the court ordered the parties to reestablish their use of AppClose for all communications between them, including but not be limited to submission of unreimbursed medical expenses, notification of payments addressing the same, visitation with the children by either party, and notable school and health related events. This child-centered remedial response was well within the scope of the trial court's discretionary authority.

2022—*Walzer v. Walzer*, 209 Conn. App. 604, 268 A.3d 1187.

Where evidence showed that defendant had ample assets and the ability to make periodic payments to plaintiff, secured by a mortgage on the former marital home awarded to defendant, as additional property settlement pursuant to the parties' separation agreement, the trial court properly found that defendant's failure to pay was wilful. Trial court did not abuse its discretion in finding defendant in contempt, ordering him to bring all payments current by a date certain, and ordering the sale of the former marital home to ensure the payments are made.

2019—*Grogan v. Penza*, 194 Conn. App. 72, 220 A.3d 147.

Whether to award attorney's fees in contempt proceedings is within the trial court's discretion. Where the record did not reveal trial court's reason for denying plaintiff's request for attorney's fees incurred in successfully opposing defendant's motion for contempt, appellate court was unable to conclude that trial court had abused its discretion.

2019—*Barber v. Barber*, 193 Conn. App. 190, 219 A.3d 378.

The trial court did not err in not awarding plaintiff attorney's fees pursuant to the default provision in the parties' agreement because plaintiff's motion for contempt was not successful, she failed to prove that defendant was in willful and intentional violation of the agreement, the court found that there was a good faith dispute between the parties regarding the amount defendant owed plaintiff, neither party was in full compliance with the agreement, there was no evidence that defendant was unwilling to pay, and defendant made a settlement proposal. That defendant offered to pay what he owed rather than the amount plaintiff demanded should not result in him having to pay plaintiff's attorney's fees to have the court resolve disputes the parties should have been able to resolve by following their agreement.

2017—*O'Brien v. O'Brien*, 326 Conn. 81, 161 A.3d 1236.

Trial court did not abuse its discretion in adjusting asset distribution to remedy wife's loss; decision to value stocks as of date of new trial was not arbitrary or irrational.

2013—*Tow v. Tow*, 142 Conn. App. 45, 64 A.3d 128.

No abuse of discretion where the court denied a motion for contempt in a case in which the parties lived together post judgment and the separation agreement called for direct payments of alimony and child support to the wife but the husband instead made deposits into a joint account to which the wife had free access.

1992—*Emerick v. Emerick*, 28 Conn. App. 794, 613 A.2d 1351.

Remedy for contempt is confinement under Conn. Gen. Stat. § 46b-87.

1989—*Tufano v. Tufano*, 18 Conn. App. 119, 556 A.2d 1036.

Court can fine a person found in contempt and to force compliance through various sanctions in addition to awarding attorney fees.

1988—*Sardilli v. Sardilli*, 16 Conn. App. 114, 546 A.2d 926.

Court need not find a contempt of court to make other party whole, when court order was not followed.

1988—*Nelson v. Nelson*, 13 Conn. App. 355, 536 A.2d 985.

In a contempt proceeding, even in the absence of a finding of contempt, a trial court has broad discretion to make whole any party who has suffered as a result of another party's failure to comply with a court order.

1985—*Marcil v. Marcil*, 4 Conn. App. 403, 494 A.2d 620.

A contempt is considered civil when the punishment is wholly remedial, serves only the purposes of the complainant, and is not intended as a deterrent to offenses against the public.

1984—*Mays v. Mays*, 193 Conn. 261, 476 A.2d 562.

In civil contempt the punishment must be conditional and coercive, and may not be absolute. In criminal contempt the sanction is punitive in order to vindicate the authority of the court. However, indefinite incarceration exceeded the trial court's authority.

§ 12.02 Enforcement of Alimony and Child Support Order

2024—*K.S. v. R.S.*, 350 Conn. 692, 326 A.2d 187.

The trial court improperly granted the plaintiff's motion for contempt regarding the defendant's obligation to maintain insurance coverages for the family. The trial court made no finding that the insurance was actually canceled. It also failed to make an explicit finding of a wilful violation of its order with respect to the insurance coverages issue.

2024—*M.S. v. M.S.*, 226 Conn. App. 482, 319 A.3d 223.

In denying the defendant's motion for contempt, the trial court erred by failing to determine the amount of the arrearage attributable to the plaintiff's noncompliance with the parties' June 2017 child support order. The terms of that order provided that the plaintiff would pay $2,600 per month until June 30, 2019 and expressly contemplated that after that date, child support would be modified based on the support guidelines. The plaintiff's unilateral decision to self-calculate and thereby reduce the amount of his obligation based on his understanding of the child support guidelines was inconsistent with the plain language of the order referencing modification. The only fair and reasonable construction of the June 2017 order was that it contemplated a judicial determination of the plaintiff's child support obligation following consideration of the child support guidelines, as required by statute. However, the plaintiff did not file his motion to modify until September 2020; and the trial court did not rule on that motion until March 2021. Judgment reversed in part as to the defendant's motion for contempt. Matter remanded for further proceedings limited to a new hearing to identify properly any arrearage owed to the defendant for the period of July 1, 2019 through March 24, 2021 and to establish the terms for payment of that arrearage.

2023—*Simpson v. Simpson*, 222 Conn. App. 466, 306 A.3d 477.

The trial court improperly interpreted the parties' separation agreement, disregarding its clear and unambiguous language about the calculation of additional child support and alimony payments to be paid by Defendant. The Appellate court reversed the trial court's judgment denying Plaintiff's motion for contempt only with respect to the court's remedial orders, in particular its calculation of the arrearage Defendant owed to Plaintiff, and remanded for further proceedings consistent with its opinion. The scope of the new trial court proceedings must involve application of the clear and unambiguous language of the parties' agreement to calculate any additional alimony or child support obligation.

On January 23, 2024, the Connecticut Supreme Court granted an appeal on the following two questions:

"1. Did the Appellate Court err in reversing the trial court's remedial orders on the basis of its erroneous conclusion that the parties' separation agreement clearly and unambiguously relieved the defendant of the obligation to pay supplemental child support and alimony?

"2. Did the Appellate Court err in concluding that the parties' separation agreement clearly and unambiguously relieved the defendant of the obligation to pay supplemental child support and alimony when, inter alia, (a) both parties advanced reasonable and plausible interpretations of the relevant provisions, (b) the Appellate Court majority failed to give effect to the intent of the parties as expressed in the agreement, (c) the concurring and dissenting judge correctly concluded that the agreement was ambiguous and thus its meaning presented a question of fact for the trial court, and (d) both the majority and the concurring and dissenting judge noted the absence of extrinsic evidence on the issue of the parties' intent, as well as the need for such evidence in order to interpret the agreement?"

Simpson v. Simpson, 348 Conn. 942, 307 A.3d 909.

2023—*Graham v. Graham*, 222 Conn. App. 560, 306 A.3d 499.

Trial court did not abuse its discretion in granting the motion for contempt of the parties' postjudgment stipulation, which had been approved by the court and made into an order. The court properly found that the circumstances surrounding the execution of the postjudgment stipulation, which required Defendant to make lump sum payments in 2019 and 2020 to satisfy his outstanding unallocated alimony and child support obligations for the years 2018 and 2019, rendered its meaning clear and unambiguous and that Defendant willfully violated that stipulation when he refused to make the January and April 2020 payments to Plaintiff. The judgment of contempt was not improper because Defendant had not argued that he was unable to make those payments.

The trial court also properly found that Defendant willfully violated his obligation under the postjudgment stipulation to pay 100% of the children's medical expenses when he refused to reimburse Plaintiff for a $5,000 concierge fee for a physician treating their daughter. Because an email from the doctor clearly stated the concierge fee was based on a review of unreimbursed costs of the medical treatment provided to the parties' daughter during the prior year, Defendant's argument that he believed in good faith that the fee was merely an access fee was unfounded.

The trial court properly rejected Plaintiff offer of compromise to resolve her claim against Defendant for his alleged violation of the postjudgment stipulation requiring him to make two $504,000 payments to satisfy his 2019 alimony and child support obligation. Conn. Gen. Stat. § 52-192a did not apply to does not apply to marital dissolutions cases.

2021—*L.W. v. M.W.*, 208 Conn. App. 497, 266 A.3d 189.

In its judgment denying the plaintiff's motion for contempt, the trial court erred when it found the defendant's earned income for 2018 was $135,569 based on his tax return, instead of the $159,079 that was listed on his 1099 form and was also specifically identified in the parties' separation agreement incorporated into the dissolution judgment. The trial court also erred when it reduced the defendant's earned income to $102,363 by deducting his self-employment expenses from the amount of his 1099 form earned income. The unambiguous language of the parties' separation agreement provided that the defendant's 2018 earned income was $159,079, the amount listed on his 1099 form for that tax year. There was no need to resort to the Internal Revenue Code to determine what "earned income" means.

2021—*Bray v. Bray*, 206 Conn. App. 46, 259 A.3d 712.

Appellate Court vacated the trial court's remedial order issued after a postjudgment motion for contempt alleging that the defendant failed to comply with provisions of the parties' separation agreement regarding child support and alimony which had been incorporated into the dissolution judgment. The rationale underlying the remedial order—"that the separation agreement clearly and unambiguously did not contemplate the consideration of the defendant's net income because it did not provide for an annual reconciliation of the amount owed to the plaintiff based on the defendant's tax obligation"—was inconsistent with a 2015 order after a prior motion for contempt which required the parties to employ that exact procedure.

2021—*Schott v. Schott*, 205 Conn. App. 237, 256 A.3d 732.

The trial court improperly denied the defendant's postjudgment motion to modify his alimony obligation. The parties' separation agreement plainly and unambiguously provided that the defendant's alimony obligation shall be terminated upon cohabitation by the plaintiff. It was error for the trial court to apply Conn. Gen. Stat. § 46b-86(a) which permits modification of alimony upon a showing of a substantial change of circumstances, instead of Conn. Gen. Stat. § 46b-86(b) which requires only a change of circumstances. When the court found out the plaintiff was cohabiting, it was required to grant the defendant's motion to modify alimony in accordance with the plain mandate of parties' separation agreement.

[Conn. Gen. Stat. § 46b-86(b) specifically contemplates the change of circumstances caused when a party receiving periodic alimony lives with another person.]

2021—*Giordano v. Giordano*, 203 Conn. App. 652, 249 A.3d 363.

The trial court did not err in determining the defendant willfully violated the order requiring him to pay the plaintiff $300 per week until the $175,000 lump sum alimony award was paid in full. It was reasonable to extend the court's finding that the defendant was not credible to the contents of the letters he had mailed to plaintiff about support payments and to his accounting, all of which were crafted by the defendant. Thus, the trial court did not commit error granting the plaintiff's motion for contempt.

2021—*Bouffard v. Lewis*, 203 Conn. App. 116, 247 A.3d 667.

Pursuant to Conn. Practice Book § 61-11(c), orders requiring the defendant pay periodic alimony and child support were not automatically stayed by his filing an appeal of postjudgment orders denying his motion to modify alimony and child support and granting the plaintiff's motion to hold the defendant in contempt for failure to pay alimony and child support.

2020—*Giordano v. Giordano*, 200 Conn. App. 130, 238 A.3d 113.

The trial court properly interpreted the parties' separation agreement as including the defendant's supplemental pension within the definition of "gross annual compensation," from which the defendant was to pay alimony to the plaintiff. The fact that the defendant had crossed off the reference to the supplemental pension on his financial affidavit, removing it from the list of property to be considered assets, led to the conclusion that the supplemental pension had not been considered a marital asset nor distributed as an asset at the time of dissolution.

2019—*M.B. v. S.A.*, 194 Conn. App. 727, 222 A.3d 551.

Trial court did not abuse its discretion in granting the defendant's postjudgment motions for contempt for plaintiff's failure to make timely support payments. Plaintiff's filing of an appeal from the family support order did not automatically stay the order's payment requirements and Plaintiff never moved for a stay. Therefore, his support payments were still due as scheduled.

Trial court did not err in considering financial affidavits when ruling on defendant's motion for contempt as it had sole discretion to assign weight to evidence and also considered evidence presented by plaintiff.

Subsequent rulings on the support arrears did not vacate the contempt orders or eliminate the court's ability to impose attorney's fee sanctions as penalties for Plaintiff's contempt.

There was no requirement for the trial court to hear defendant's motion to modify the visitation schedule before the contempt motions The court has discretion to hear pending motions in the order it deems appropriate.

2019—*Barber v. Barber*, 193 Conn. App. 190, 219 A.3d 378.

The trial court properly sought to facilitate enforcement of the parties' New York separation agreement by providing the parties with a timeline for the exchange of information as required by their agreement. Pursuant to their agreement, the parties were to instruct their accountants to calculate support using the New York guidelines and illustrations in the agreement, then have the accountants meet to discuss the claimed arrears. The trial court's order was necessary to narrow the issues of dispute at any further hearing. It required the parties, who appeared unable or unwilling to comply with the terms of their agreement, to do what they should have done before plaintiff filed her motion. The trial court did not rewrite the agreement by including the term "adjusted gross income" in the order because that term had already been incorporated by means of an example of how to calculate defendant's child support obligation into the agreement that became part of the New York judgment.

2019—*Ayres v. Ayres*, 193 Conn. App. 224, 219 A.3d 894.

Appellate court reversed the trial court's order that defendant must include restricted stock units, performance stock units, and severance pay in his gross income for alimony purposes. The parties' separation agreement defined each party's gross income for the calculation of alimony as base pay and any performance based bonus received, and unambiguously excluded stock from the calculation. The trial court erred in ordering defendant to include his severance pay and all past and future RSUs in his income because his severance pay was distinct from both base pay and performance based bonuses, and the vested RSUs were designed to be and were in fact distributed as stock. However, the trial court properly concluded that defendant's PSUs were performance based bonuses that could be included his gross income because he had no shareholder rights with respect to the PSUs and they were paid in cash as part of a performance based long term incentive program.

2018—*Becue v. Becue*, 185 Conn. App. 812, 198 A.3d 601.

Trial court abused its discretion by not finding defendant in contempt for failure to pay child support where defendant engaged in "self-help" by unilaterally reducing his child support payments.

2018—*Brochard v. Brochard*, 185 Conn. App. 204, 196 A.3d 1171.

Plaintiff found not in contempt for failure to pay for child activity expenses where record unclear as to whether the defendant had complied with the parenting agreement regarding notice and prior agreement provision prior to incurring the extracurricular activity expenses.

2014—*Valentine v. Valentine*, 149 Conn. App. 799, 90 A.3d 300.

Financial orders were excessive where the defendant was left with little or no income to sustain his basic welfare. Financial orders were improper where the trial court failed to consider the defendant's ability to comply with the orders.

2013—*Hammond v. Hammond*, 145 Conn. App. 607, 76 A.3d 688.

Court improperly construed a post judgment stipulation and failed to include court ordered obligations in an arrearage calculation where the party was to pay expenses in lieu of support and failed to do so.

2013—*Guaragno v. Guaragno*, 141 Conn. App. 337, 61 A.3d 1119.

Defendant found in contempt when he reversed a credit card charge that the plaintiff permissibly made on a business credit card for the family business one day prior to dissolution.

2013—*Fox v. Fox*, 147 Conn. App. 44, 80 A.3d 916.

No abuse of discretion where a party was found in contempt for failing to make child support payments.

2013—*Kasowitz v. Kasowitz*, 140 Conn. App. 507, 59 A.3d 347.

No abuse of discretion where the court found the defendant in contempt for partial compliance with past court orders.

2011—*Gray v. Gray*, 131 Conn. App. 404, 27 A.3d 1102.

Finding of contempt for making support payments to the minor children's bank accounts, rather than directly to the plaintiff, was not an abuse of discretion.

2011—*Oldani v. Oldani*, 132 Conn. App. 609, 34 A.3d 407.

Contempt order proper for deducting funds from alimony.

2010—*Fuller v. Fuller*, 119 Conn. App. 105, 987 A.2d 1040.

Finding of $154,000 child support arrearage without making a contempt finding is not abuse of discretion in contempt proceeding.

2010—*DeFeo v. DeFeo*, 119 Conn. App. 30, 986 A.2d 1099.

No abuse of discretion in denying post-judgment contempt motion for non-payment of timeshare expenses.

2009—*LaBossiere v. Jones*, 117 Conn. App. 211, 979 A.2d 522.

Court did not abuse its discretion by finding plaintiff in contempt for failure to pay alimony where plaintiff had repeatedly been in contempt of alimony obligation and court rejected his "my secretary forgot to mail the check" defense.

2007—*O'Connell v. O'Connell*, 101 Conn. App. 516, 922 A.2d 293.

No abuse of discretion to hold pro se child support obligor in contempt for nonpayment despite his request for continuance in middle of hearing which was denied.

2004—*Lamacchia v. Chilinsky*, 85 Conn. App. 1, 856 A.2d 459.

Contempt order proper for failure to pay alimony.

2002—*Van Nest v. Kegg*, 70 Conn. App. 191, 800 A.2d 509.

Contempt finding upheld where father paid for his lawyers and vacation instead of wife's insurance premium.

2002—*Legnos v. Legnos*, 70 Conn. App. 349, 797 A.2d 1184.

Contempt finding upheld where father had "the ability to determine who and when and how much to pay to anybody."

2001—*Prial v. Prial*, 67 Conn. App. 7, 787 A.2d 50.

The ex-husband's action of voluntarily terminating his employment in a family owned business was willful and warranted imposition of a contempt order.

2000—*Bowers v. Bowers*, 61 Conn. App. 75, 762 A.2d 515.

When inheritance was available to him, plaintiff found in contempt of failure to pay child support.

1999—*Issler v. Issler*, 250 Conn. 226, 737 A.2d 383.

Both trial and appellate courts improperly found defendant in contempt of separation agreement.

1999—*Billings v. Billings*, 54 Conn. App. 142, 732 A.2d 814.

Court properly found party in indirect and willful contempt where party failed to maintain life insurance policy.

1995—*Wolf v. Wolf*, 39 Conn. App. 162, 664 A.2d 315.

Court cannot order marital property set aside in a trust for the benefit of the children unless it is for their support.

1994—*Mulholland v. Mulholland*, 229 Conn. 643, 643 A.2d 246.

Contempt order for failure to pay child support arrearage during the appeal period was proper even though the child support order was reversed on appeal before the contempt order was entered.

1994—*Bunche v. Bunche*, 36 Conn. App. 322, 650 A.2d 917.

Lack of any explanation why payment was not made is evidence that party has ability to pay.

1993—*Miller v. Kirshner*, 225 Conn. 185, 621 A.2d 1326.

Court can order interest bearing note and mortgage to secure child support arrearage.

1992—*Emerick v. Emerick*, 28 Conn. App. 794, 613 A.2d 1351.

Civil contempt is a remedy for failure to pay court ordered support.

1984—*Phares v. Phares*, 1 Conn. App. 172, 469 A.2d 791.

Court has the authority to order security for payment of alimony.

1983—*Morabito v. Wachsman*, 191 Conn. 92, 463 A.2d 593.

In a child support enforcement action, the issue of jurisdiction had been fully and fairly litigated when the husband specially appeared in Nevada to contest jurisdiction and was unsuccessful.

1982—*Schurman v. Schurman*, 188 Conn. 268, 449 A.2d 169.

In determining whether to hold the plaintiff in contempt for failure to pay child support, the trial court is entitled to take into account not only its knowledge of the out-of-state decree but also the serious nature of the sanctions that attend a finding of contempt.

§ 12.03 Enforcement of Property Division Order

2024—*Walton v. Walton*, 227 Conn. App. 251, 321 A.3d 1180.

Trial court did not abuse its discretion in finding the defendant in contempt for failing to pay the mortgage on the marital residence pursuant to the parties' pendente lite stipulation. The defendant knew she had lost her job when she agreed to assume responsibility for the mortgage. While the action was pending, she withdrew funds from her retirement accounts and received money from her parents, which she could have used to pay the mortgage, but she chose not to do so.

2020—*Davis v. Davis*, 200 Conn. App. 180, 238 A.3d 46.

Where the defendant who had been ordered to maintain the marital residence until it was sold and there was no dispute that the septic system required repairs due to recurring problems, the trial court did not abuse its discretion in ordering the defendant to reimburse plaintiff for septic system repairs and declining to apply the unclean hands doctrine despite the defendant's claims that the plaintiff had obstructed his effort to repair the septic system.

2012—*Allen v. Allen*, 134 Conn. App. 486, 39 A.3d 1190.

No abuse of discretion where plaintiff was found in contempt for failing to make any meaningful effort to refinance or sell the former marital home.

2011—*Giordano v. Giordano*, 127 Conn. App. 498, 14 A.3d 1058.

Contempt found when husband failed to make yearly lump sum property settlement payments to wife.

1985—*Croke v. Croke*, 4 Conn. App. 663, 496 A.2d 235.

Wife was held in contempt for failure to list the marital house for sale.

§ 12.04 Enforcement of Child Visitation Order

2005—*Kennedy v. Kennedy*, 88 Conn. App. 442, 869 A.2d 1252.

It was abuse of discretion to decide Motion for Contempt regarding visitation without hearing from Guardian ad litem.

2002—*Berglass v. Berglass*, 71 Conn. App. 771, 804 A.2d 889.

Court properly enforced judgment by ordering overnight visitation.

2001—*Lane v. Lane*, 64 Conn. App. 255, 779 A.2d 859.

Plaintiff found in contempt for not consulting on non-emergency health issues regarding children.

1995—*Wilson v. Wilson*, 38 Conn. App. 263, 661 A.2d 621.

Mother held in contempt for denying visitation.

1989—*Tufano v. Tufano*, 18 Conn. App. 119, 556 A.2d 1036.

Money judgment ordered plus fees for each violation of visitation order.

1988—*Fischer v. Goldstein*, 14 Conn. App. 487, 542 A.2d 731.

Duty of support is independent of the right of visitation.

§ 12.05 Uniform Reciprocal Enforcement of Support

1999—*Taravella v. Stanley*, 52 Conn. App. 431, 727 A.2d 727.

There is no right to a jury trial under URESA.

1988—*Fischer v. Goldstein*, 14 Conn. App. 487, 542 A.2d 731.

Connecticut enforces child support order issued by West Germany under URESA and Court sitting in a URESA proceeding has jurisdiction to determine paternity.

§ 12.06 Counsel Fees

2021—*Giordano v. Giordano*, 203 Conn. App. 652, 249 A.3d 363.

The trial court did not abuse its discretion in granting plaintiff's motion for appellate attorney fees. The award was necessary avoid undermining the judgment of contempt and its attendant orders regarding the defendant's obligation to pay plaintiff the outstanding balance of lump sum alimony.

2018—*Becue v. Becue*, 185 Conn. App. 812, 198 A.3d 601.

Trial court did not abuse discretion in awarding counsel fees to plaintiff where court found defendant in breach of the parties' separation agreement by engaging in self-help and separation agreement provided for payment of counsel fees by the breaching party.

2018—*Fredo v. Fredo*, 185 Conn. App. 252, 196 A.3d 1235.

Trial court abused its discretion in awarding attorney's fees pursuant to the bad faith exception where it failed to make express findings that the defendant's claims were entirely without color and made in bad faith.

2017—*Lederle v. Spivey*, 174 Conn. App. 592, 166 A.3d 636.

Court abused its discretion in awarding fees pursuant to the bad faith exception where it failed to delineate in its decision that the defendant's appeal lacked any indicia of colorability by clear and convincing evidence and a high degree of specificity.

Court failed to use the proper standard for colorability as it applies to the party, not the attorney.

2017—*Powell-Ferri v. Ferri*, 326 Conn. 457, 165 A.3d 1124.

Award of attorney's fees was not an abuse of discretion in absence of evidence that the defendant-husband failed to pay his attorneys or would fail to do so in the future.

Trial court did not abuse discretion in determining that the plaintiff's payment of some legal costs would not undermine the courts other financial orders.

2017—*Ferri v. Powell-Ferri*, 326 Conn. 438, 165 A.3d 1137.

Trial court abused discretion in awarding attorney's fees to the plaintiff where the plaintiff demonstrated no exception to the general rule that each party must bear his or her own litigation expenses.

2015—*Light v. Grimes*, 156 Conn. App. 53, 111 A.3d 551.

Orders for counsel fees must be based on statutory authority or conform to one of the established standards for such an award.

2013—*Colbert v. Carr*, 140 Conn. App. 229, 57 A.3d 878.

Request for attorney's fees properly denied in paternity action where father acknowledged paternity and had provided financial support for the child but had not followed all formal requirements for acknowledging paternity.

2011—*Hirschfeld v. Machinist*, 131 Conn. App. 364, 27 A.3d 395.

Trial court did not abuse its discretion by sanctioning plaintiff and awarding counsel fees when parties' separation agreement contained a merger clause and plaintiff filed a New York action seeking damages based on matters that occurred before the parties signed the separation agreement.

2007—*Ramin v. Ramin*, 281 Conn. 324, 915 A.2d 790.

Despite each party having ample liquid funds, court can award attorney's fees to address litigation misconduct, where not doing so would undermine other orders.

2005—*Kennedy v. Kennedy*, 88 Conn. App. 442, 869 A.2d 1252.

Father, who committed fraud upon court to get order permitting him to take minor child outside country, held in civil contempt and attorney fees and costs awarded to mother.

2001—*BonHotel v. BonHotel*, 64 Conn. App. 561, 781 A.2d 318.

Wife who filed 21 motions was barred from filing additional motions; motion for attorneys' fees denied although motion for sanctions was granted in that the court found all 21 motions to be frivolous.

1995—*Feuerman v. Feuerman*, 39 Conn. App. 775, 667 A.2d 802.

Counsel who failed to appear at a preargument conference ordered to pay opposing counsel's fees.

1993—*Miller v. Kirshner*, 225 Conn. 185, 621 A.2d 1326.

Attorney's fees to defend appeal of paternity judgment can be awarded after the appeal.

1993—*Diamond v. Diamond*, 32 Conn. App. 733, 631 A.2d 1157.

Counsel fees cannot be awarded by judge for a prior hearing before a different judge without evidence.

1993—*Castro v. Castro*, 31 Conn. App. 761, 627 A.2d 452.

Court cannot award counsel fees without first conducting a hearing to allow the opposing party to challenge the reasonableness of the fees or the services rendered.

1989—*Tufano v. Tufano*, 18 Conn. App. 119, 556 A.2d 1036.

Court can fine a person found in contempt and to force compliance through various sanctions in addition to awarding attorney fees.

1988—*Mallory v. Mallory*, 207 Conn. 48, 539 A.2d 995.

Counsel fees may be awarded when a person is properly found in contempt for failure to comply with child support orders.

1987—*Bielen v. Bielen*, 12 Conn. App. 513, 531 A.2d 941.

Evidentiary hearing waived if no party asks for it on issue of counsel fees.

1985—*Eldridge v. Eldridge*, 4 Conn. App. 489, 495 A.2d 283.

An award of attorney fees in contempt proceeding was vacated.

1984—*Lake v. Speziale*, 580 F. Supp. 1318.

An indigent has the right to appointed counsel in contempt proceeding.

1983—*Friedlander v. Friedlander*, 191 Conn. 81, 463 A.2d 587.

Ex-husband found to be in contempt numerous times and awarded the ex-wife attorney's fees.

CHAPTER 13

DOMESTIC VIOLENCE

SYNOPSIS

§ 13.01 "Family Member" Defined

2022—*L.L. v. M.B.*, 216 Conn. App. 731, 286 A.3d 489.

Trial court did not abuse its discretion by dismissing Plaintiff's application for relief from abuse under Conn. Gen. Stat. § 46b-15 on behalf of her minor daughter, N.R., on the basis that N.R. was not eligible for relief because she was not a family or household member as required by § 46b-15 and as defined in Conn. Gen. Stat. § 46b-38a(2). The parties, high school seniors, had a dating relationship for about a month in 2019 when they were sophomores. That relationship had ceased almost two years prior to Plaintiff filing the application.

The Appellate Court rejected Defendant's arguments that the appeal had become moot since: (1) the parties would be in different schools by the time the appeal was heard and (2) by the time the appeal was heard the events leading up to the application would be remote in time and there was no evidence of a continuing threat of present physical pain or physical injury. His proposed grounds for a determination of mootness did not implicate mootness. Instead they were arguments as to the merits of what would be decided at a potential new hearing. Because the court could grant Plaintiff practical relief, her appeal was not moot.

2011—*Krystyna W. v. Janusz W.*, 127 Conn. App. 586, 14 A.3d 483.

Court has authority under Conn. Gen. Stat. § 46b-15 to order alcohol counseling and extend order to an adult child living in home.

§ 13.02 Application for Relief From Abuse

2023—*R. H. v. M. S.,* 220 Conn. App. 212, 297 A.3d 592.

Trial court abused its discretion in extending the protection of an ex parte restraining order under Conn. Gen. Stat. § 46b-15(b) to the parties' children when Plaintiff's application for relief for himself did not also include a request for the protection for his minor children nor did it contain any statements that Defendant had engaged in any conduct related to those children. There was nothing in the application warranting the additional protection. For the order regarding the children to have been appropriate, it necessarily had to be supported by a statement in the application materials that related to those children, particularly because Plaintiff did not check the box on the judicial form to request that the order he sought would protect his minor children. However, the trial court did not abuse its discretion in finding sufficient evidence that Defendant had stalked Plaintiff. The ex parte restraining order was vacated to the extent it extended protection to the parties' children. The judgment issuing a one-year restraining order for Plaintiff's protection was affirmed.

2023—*V.V. v. V.V.*, 218 Conn. App. 157, 291 A.3d 109.

A child may bring a civil action only by means of a guardian or next friend, whose responsibility it is to ensure that the interests of the child are well represented. Here, the minor child's father (and the defendant's former husband) had standing to apply for a domestic violence restraining order against the defendant on the child's behalf, while acting in the capacity of the child's next friend. As the child's father, and the person to whom the court previously had granted sole physical custody of the child, the father's interests were not only *not* adverse to those of the child but were well aligned with her interests, as confirmed by the child's guardian ad litem, who opined at the hearing that the issuance of the restraining order was in the child's best interest. Thus, the father had standing to apply for the order as the child's next friend. The appellate court rejected the defendant's claim that the child's father lacked standing to bring the action and affirmed the trial court's judgment granting the requested relief.

2022—*K.D. v. D.D.*, 214 Conn. App. 821, 282 A.3d 528.

Trial court erred when it granted Wife's application under Conn. Gen. Stat. § 46b-15 for a civil restraining order against Husband by using a subjective standard to analyze the pattern of threatening instead of the objective standard required by the statute. By incorporating by reference the definition of threating in the second degree under Conn. Gen. Stat. § 53a-62 of the Penal Code in Conn. Gen. Stat. § 46b-15(a), the legislature indicated an intent that an objective standard should be used when assessing patterns of threatening under § 46b-15. Judgment was reversed and the case was remanded with direction to vacate the civil restraining order.

2022—*W.K. v. M.S.*, 212 Conn. App. 532, 275 A.3d 232.

Trial court abused its discretion in issuing an order of civil protection because it determined that defendant's absence from the hearing hurt the credibility of his position and improperly relied on the allegations in the summary process complaint to render its decision. Defendant's failure to appear was not evidence. Moreover, because he did not testify at the hearing, the court had no basis for making a determination as to his credibility. The trial court's reliance on unproven allegations in the complaint resulted in harm to defendant.

2022—*L.D. v. G.T.*, 210 Conn. App. 864, 271 A.3d 674.

In hearing on whether to extend an order granting plaintiff's ex parte application for relief from abuse, the trial court abused its discretion by prohibiting defendant from cross-examining plaintiff before entering a protective order. When the exercise of the trial court's discretion depends on issues of fact that are disputed, due process requires a trial-like hearing with an opportunity to present evidence and to cross-examine adverse witnesses. Judgment reversed and case remanded with order to vacate the domestic violence order of protection.

2021—*L. H.-S. v. N. B.*, 341 Conn. 483, 267 A.3d 178.

Supreme Court affirmed denial of civil protection order and clarified standard courts must apply to determine whether applicant for civil protection order under Gen. Stat. § 46b-16a has established the element of fear necessary for such an order. Plaintiff was required to establish that (1) she subjectively feared for her personal safety and (2) her fear was objectively reasonable. Gen. Stat. § 46b-16a unambiguously creates a subjective-objective standard for assessing fear. Trial court appropriately applied this standard in denying the protection order.

2019—*M.B. v. S.A.*, 194 Conn. App. 721, 222 A.3d 559.

Trial court did not abuse its discretion in denying plaintiff's request for relief from abuse where the court had considered plaintiff's evidence and made factual findings supported by testimony that the court alone had discretion to credit or disregard.

Trial court did not abuse its discretion in sanctioning plaintiff and awarding attorney's fees to defendant after considering plaintiff's actions throughout the litigation and in the context of Conn. Practice Book § 1-25(a), which prohibits bringing frivolous actions, and finding plaintiff's claims that he had a good faith basis for filing the application for relief unpersuasive.

2012—*Rosemarie B.-F v. Curtis P.*, 133 Conn. App. 472, 38 A.3d 138.

One incident is sufficient to satisfy Conn. Gen. Stat. § 46b-15 and trial court's finding that father posed a continuous threat of present physical pain or physical injury.

2011—*Krystyna W. v. Janusz W.*, 127 Conn. App. 586, 14 A.3d 483.

Application for relief from abuse granted based on threatening actions of husband.

§ 13.03 Enforcement of Order of Protection

2020—*D.S. v. R.S.*, 199 Conn. App. 11, 234 A.3d 1150.

The trial court did not err at a hearing pursuant to Conn. Gen. Stat. § 46b-15, when it found sufficient evidence to continue a domestic violence restraining order on application of abuse by a daughter against her father to protect herself, her mother, and her minor child and ordered the father not to harass, follow, interfere with, or stalk the daughter or her minor child. A broader standard of stalking is employed in the context of a civil protection order than in the criminal context. Although the trial court's reference to the statutory definition of criminal stalking set forth in Conn. Gen. Stat. § 53a-181d was incorrect, evidence establishing that the father's conduct met the criminal standard of stalking was more than sufficient to satisfy the civil standard. The narrower statutory definition of criminal stalking set forth is not inconsistent with the common understanding of stalking.

2013—*Eric S. v. Tiffany S.*, 143 Conn. App. 1, 68 A.3d 139.

Violation of a Conn. Gen. Stat. § 46b-15 restraining order was civil contempt, and not quasi-criminal contempt and therefore incarceration was in inappropriate penalty as incarceration would have been purely punitive rather than coercive.

2009—*Gail R. v. Bubbico*, 114 Conn. App. 43.

Application for restraining order denied; although the boyfriend's behavior was cause for concern, there was insufficient evidence before the trial court to prove that the boyfriend's behavior was a continuous threat of present physical pain or physical injury to the girlfriend or to her sons.

2005—*State v. Wright*, 273 Conn. 418, 870 A.2d 1039.

"Collateral Bar Rule" applied to violation of domestic violence protective order.

2004—*State v. Alexander*, 269 Conn. 107, 847 A.2d 970.

Restraining orders are not punitive in nature.

CHAPTER 14

PARENTAGE

SYNOPSIS

§ 14.01 Acknowledgment of Paternity and Agreement to Support

2018—*Doyle v. Chaplen*, 184 Conn. App. 278, 194 A.3d 1198.

Trial court properly found that mother and acknowledged father signed the acknowledgment of paternity on the basis of a material mistake where mother relied on ultrasounds and advice from medical technicians to calculate date of conception.

2018—*Asia A.M. v. Geoffrey M.*, 182 Conn. App. 22, 188 A.3d 762.

Plaintiff could not rescind his paternity acknowledgment without proving fraud, duress or mistake. Best interest of the child cannot be the sole criteria to open a judgment of paternity even with clear evidence the plaintiff was not the biological father.

2013—*Colbert v. Carr*, 140 Conn. App. 229, 57 A.3d 878.

Request for attorney's fees properly denied in paternity action where father acknowledged paternity and had provided financial support for the child but had not followed all formal requirements for acknowledging paternity.

2003—*Comm'r of Soc. Servs. v. Smith*, 265 Conn. 723, 830 A.2d 228.

Uncertified acknowledgment of paternity is inadmissible.

1989—*Bleidner v. Searles*, 19 Conn. App. 76, 561 A.2d 954.

Father who acknowledged paternity in judicial proceeding could not obtain a new trial three years later.

1980—*Remkiewicz v. Remkiewicz*, 180 Conn. 114, 429 A.2d 833.

No statutory formalities had been observed to allow the husband to acquire parental status over the wife's child from a previous relationship thus although the husband had signed the parentage affidavit and claimed tax benefits, the husband was permitted to deny paternity.

§ 14.02 Establishing Paternity

[1] Evidence; Admissibility of Evidence

2015—*DiMichele v. Perrella*, 158 Conn. App. 726, 120 A.3d 551.

Husband failed to establish fraud claim against biological father of children born during husband's marriage.

1989—*Blake v. Blake*, 211 Conn. 485, 560 A.2d 396.

Adverse inference may be drawn when potential witness not produced to testify.

1987—*Fortier v. Laviero*, 10 Conn. App. 181, 522 A.2d 313.

Resemblance of child to father is competent evidence.

1987—*DiMauro v. Natalino*, 11 Conn. App. 548, 528 A.2d 851.

Jury in paternity action was charged on issue of other sexual partners.

1986—*Durso v. Misiorek*, 9 Conn. App. 93, 526 A.2d 450.

Admissibility of evidence of nonaccess by husband in paternity action.

1985—*Perkins v. Perkins*, 3 Conn. App. 322, 487 A.2d 1117.

Paternity issue is waived if not raised at trial.

1979—*Remkiewicz v. Remkiewicz*, 180 Conn. 114, 429 A.2d 833.

No person shall acquire parental status unless certain formalities are observed.

[2] Genetic Testing

1986—*Moore v. McNamara*, 201 Conn. 16, 513 A.2d 660, *aff'g* 478 A.2d 634, 40 Conn. Supp. 6.

HLA test admissible to establish paternity.

1985—*DeMace v. Whittaker*, 196 Conn. 413, 493 A.2d 219.

Blood test was inadmissible.

[3] Timing

1984—*Hayes v. Smith*, 194 Conn. 52, 480 A.2d 425.

Paternity action must be brought during putative father's lifetime.

§ 14.03 Authority of Court

1999—*W. v. W.*, 248 Conn. 487, 728 A.2d 1076.

Trial court properly estopped party from denying parentage.

1987—*Boccuzzi v. Choquette*, 205 Conn. 411, 533 A.2d 567.

The superior court may, in proper cases, grant relief against decrees of the probate court procured by fraud, accident, mistake, and the like.

§ 14.04 Enforcement of Paternity Judgment

2011—*Rostad v. Hirsch*, 128 Conn. App. 119, 15 A.3d 1176.

Pendente lite counsel fee award under Conn. Gen. Stat. § 46b-171 was a final judgment for purposes of appeal in this paternity case.

1991—*Delgado v. Martinez*, 25 Conn. App. 155, 593 A.2d 518.

Three-year statute of limitation is unenforceable against a party who has not validly waived his procedural due process rights when judgment of paternity entered without notice and an opportunity to be heard.

1986—*Swett v. Martin*, 9 Conn. App. 327, 518 A.2d 678.

Because the father's obligation to support his minor legitimate child is created at common law; his similar obligation to support his minor illegitimate child is derivatively based upon common law.

§ 14.05 Assisted Reproduction

2019—*Bilbao v. Goodwin*, 333 Conn. 599, 217 A.3d 977.

Reversing the trial court and enforcing a contract entered into by the parties stating that any frozen pre-embryos stored at fertility clinic would be discarded if the parties ever divorced. The Court also made two holdings regarding the scope of its decision: (1) the decision applies only to contracts that, if enforced, will not result in procreation; and (2) the decision does not decide what court must do in the absence of an enforceable agreement.

§ 14.06 Surrogacy Agreements

2011—*Raftopol v. Ramey*, 299 Conn. 681, 12 A.3d 783.

The Supreme Court held that Conn. Gen. Stat. § 7-48a conferred parental status on a nongenetic, intended parent who was a party to a valid gestational agreement, without first adopting the children, because the intended parent acquired legal parent status by operation of law. The superior court properly ordered the Department of Health to issue a replacement birth certificate listing the nongenetic, intended parent as a legal parent to the children.

CHAPTER 15

APPEAL AND REVIEW

SYNOPSIS

§ 15.01 Pleading and Procedure

2023—*Gainty v. Infantino*, 222 Conn. App. 785, 306 A.3d 1171.

In his appeal of orders extending support for adult child with mental disabilities, Defendant contended that Plaintiff's entitlement for reimbursement for certain educational expenses had been addressed by two prior courts. Because examination of the record revealed that Defendant had not raised with the trial court any of the claims he asserted on appeal with respect to these expenses, those claims were not properly before the Appellate Court. Therefore, the Appellate Court declined to review them.

2023—*Anderson-Harris v. Harris*, 221 Conn. App. 222, 301 A.3d 1090.

Appellate Court declined to consider Plaintiff's claim that the trial court violated Conn. Gen. Stat. § 46b-7, the rules of Conn. Practice Book § 25-60, and her due process rights by entering custody and access orders before any court-ordered evaluations had been filed with the court. It would be manifestly unjust for Appellate Court to consider this claim when Plaintiff had failed to distinctly raise the issue before the trial court. As a general rule appellate courts will not review claims made for the first time on appeal. A party cannot present a case to the trial court on one theory then seek relief on appeal on a different theory.

2022—*Pishal v. Pishal*, 212 Conn. App. 607, 276 A.3d 434.

Trial court's oral ruling denying defendant's motion to modify alimony payments to plaintiff did not afford the appellate court with an adequate basis for review. Defendant did not comply with Practice Book § 64-1 by filing with the appellate clerk a notice that a statement of decision had not been filed so that the appellate clerk could notify the trial court and obtain a memorandum of the oral decision. Nor did Defendant fulfill his responsibility as the appellant to move for an articulation of the oral decision after the trial court did not specify the factual or legal basis for its ruling.

2022—*R.S. v. E.S.*, 210 Conn. App. 327, 269 A.3d 970.

After the trial court entered its memorandum of decision dissolving the parties' marriage, defendant challenged numerous decisions on appeal, including the trial court's pendente lite order imposing travel restrictions. Once a final judgment has been entered, an issue regarding a pendente lite order is moot because the appellate court cannot provide practical relief. *See Altraide v. Altraide*, 153 Conn. App. 327, 332, 101 A.3d 317 (2014). Thus, defendant's appeal regarding that order is moot. His remaining claims on appeal were unfounded and had no merit.

2021—*In re Yassell B.*, 208 Conn. App. 816, 267 A.3d 316.

The biological father's appeal of the trial court's determination of paternity in a neglect proceeding was moot because there was no actual controversy from which the Appellate Court could grant him any practical relief. The trial court had addressed the issue of paternity in order to determine which parties had a cognizable interest in that proceeding and determined that the biological father was not the legal father of the child. During the pendency of the biological father's appeal, the underlying neglect proceeding was resolved. Adjudicating the paternity in the context of this case would not afford the biological father practical relief because with the termination of the neglect proceeding, no orders would be issued that could affect his alleged interest in or relationship to the child.

Because the biological father did not cause his appeal to become moot through any voluntary action and because it would be unfair to bind him to a judgment he challenged but could not contest through no fault of his own, vacatur of the trial court's paternity decision was appropriate.

2021—*Batista v. Cortes*, 203 Conn. App. 365, 248 A.3d 763.

The Appellate Court declined to review a father's claim on appeal that he had overpaid child support. The trial court analyzed his allegations of overpayment only in the context of determining the best interests of the child for his motion to modify physical custody. It made no orders concerning the audits of previous payments the father questioned, only an order concerning his future child support obligations. Because the past child support payments were not before the trial court and it did not rule on the audits, there was nothing for the Appellate Court to review on appeal.

2021—*Ricketts v. Ricketts*, 203 Conn. App. 1, 247 A.3d 223.

The Appellate Court did not have jurisdiction to consider the plaintiff's appeal of trial court orders denying his postjudgment motions to transfer the matter and appointing a guardian ad litem for the parties' children because these orders were interlocutory and not immediately appealable. An interlocutory order is appealable (1) where it terminates a separate and distinct proceeding, or (2) where it so concludes the rights of the parties that further proceedings cannot affect them. *State v. Curcio*, 191 Conn. 27, 463 A.2d 566 (1983). Here, postjudgment motions to regarding custody, education, and visitation issues were still pending. The order denying the transfer motion was rendered during the course of continued litigation, did not terminate a separate and distinct proceeding, and did not in and of itself conclude any recognized right of the parties. The order appointing a guardian ad litem pursuant to Conn. Gen. Stat. § 46b-54 similarly was not appealable as it was a step toward a resolving the postjudgment issues, not a final judgment.

2020—*Kammili v. Kammili*, 197 Conn. App. 656, 232 A.3d 102.

Pursuant to Conn. Gen. Prac. Book § 61-10(a), it is the responsibility of the appellant to provide an adequate record for review. Self-represented litigants are not excused from this requirement. Here, the self-represented plaintiff's failure to request that exhibits be marked for identification rendered the record inadequate to review his claim of error in their exclusion.

2020—*Shear v. Shear*, 194 Conn. App. 351, 221 A.3d 450.

Appellate court reversed Superior Court ruling on an appeal from family court magistrate's decision. The family support magistrate's interlocutory order on ex-husband's post-dissolution motion to modify child support did not constitute a final judgment appealable to the Superior Court because the magistrate did not address one of the two issues raised in the motion. An interlocutory order is appealable if (1) it terminates a separate and distinct hearing or (2) it so concludes the rights of the parties that further proceedings cannot affect them. This final judgment requirement applies to appeals from the decisions of family support magistrates to the Superior Court. Because the magistrate's order did not fulfill either requirement, it was not appealable. Judgment reversed and remanded with direction to dismiss the appeal for lack of subject matter jurisdiction.

2019—*In re Anthony L.*, 194 Conn. App. 111, 219 A.3d 979.

Appellate court declined to review respondent's claim that her and her children's substantive due process rights were violated when the trial court granted the request of petitioner, Commissioner of Children and Families, to terminate her parental rights because respondent failed to raise her claim in the trial court and she did not provide an adequate record of evidence supporting alternatives to petitioner's plan for the court to review her claim.

2019—*In re Taijha H.-B.*, 333 Conn. 297, 216 A.3d 601.

Appellate court improperly dismissed mother's appeal of termination of her parental rights for failure to comply with Practice Book § 79a-3, which dictates procedure for appointed appellate review counsel. To preserve mother's rights, her appointed appellate review attorney filed the original appeal before he fully reviewed the merits because he was unable to fully review case before the filing deadline. The rule does not mandate dismissal under such circumstances.

2019—*Callahan v. Callahan*, 192 Conn. App. 634, 218 A.3d 655.

Appellate court's decision and remand order disposing of parties' prior appeals constituted a reversal of judgment, which commanded a new effective date for financial orders. The new effective date is the date on which the parties' appeals were finally determined.

2019—*Colby v. Colby*, 190 Conn. App. 140, 209 A.3d 1273.

No abuse of discretion where trial court denied relief to the husband from a 2007 California judgment as untimely where there was no evidence presented that the wife prevented him from timely seeking relief.

2018—*Forgione v. Forgione*, 186 Conn. App. 525, 200 A.3d 190.

Appellate court exercised its discretion in reviewing defendant's unpreserved and unavailing claim in.

2018—*Guddo v. Guddo*, 185 Conn. App. 283, 196 A.3d 1246.

Appellate court declined to review plaintiff's conflict of interest claim where plaintiff failed to raise that claim or any objection to counsel's representation of the defendant in the underlying hearing.

2018—*Fredo v. Fredo*, 185 Conn. App. 252, 196 A.3d 1235.

Appellate court determined that three of the defendant's claims were moot on that basis that there was no practical relief the court could afford.

2017—*Dejana v. Dejana*, 176 Conn. App. 104, 168 A.3d 595.

Plaintiff's claim was preserved and considered by the court and thus reviewable on appeal.

2017—*Lugo v. Lugo*, 176 Conn. App. 149, 168 A.3d 592.

Where the defendant failed to provide the appellate court with trial court transcripts, the appellate court could not find an abuse of discretion by the trial court.

2017—*Buehler v. Buehler*, 175 Conn. App. 375, 167 A.3d 1108.

Record was inadequate for review of a denial of a post-judgment contempt motion where only three transcripts of a four-day hearing were provided to the appellate court.

2017—*Ferri v. Powell-Ferri*, 326 Conn. 438, 165 A.3d 1137.

The defendant had standing to challenge the plaintiffs-trustees' actions as she had a demonstrated a claim of injury.

Standing is procedural and thus determined under Connecticut law.

2017—*Medeiros v. Medeiros*, 175 Conn. App. 174, 167 A.3d 967.

Defendant failed to raise an objection to the plaintiff's requests for attorney's and marshal's fees and thus the defendant could not prevail on that claim on appeal.

2017—*DiGiuseppe v. DiGiuseppe*, 174 Conn. App. 855, 167 A.3d 411.

Court need not consider a claim that was not raised at trial.

Defendant failed to preserve a claim regarding his liability for college expenses where he failed to distinctly raise it before the trial court.

2017—*In re Elijah C.*, 326 Conn. 480, 165 A.3d 1149.

Appellate court properly concluded that trial court issues were adequately briefed where argument could be discerned from the record in addition to briefs.

2017—*Cimino v. Cimino*, 174 Conn. App. 1, 164 A.3d 787.

Plaintiff's challenge to the improper valuation of a pension constituted and impermissible collateral attack; challenge should have been made within 20 days of the dissolution.

2017—*Watkins v. Demos*, 172 Conn. App. 730, 161 A.3d 655.

Denial of plaintiff's motion to open based on mutual mistake was not clearly erroneous.

2017—*Sousa v. Sousa*, 173 Conn. App. 755, 164 A.3d 702.

A party seeking to open a judgment beyond the passage of the four-month limitation period from its rendering provided by General Statutes § 52-212a under an exception for judgments procured by fraud, bears the burden of proving fraud in all of its elements by clear and convincing evidence.

2016—*Zilkha v. Zilkha*, 167 Conn. App. 480, 144 A.3d 447.

Trial court did not abuse discretion in denying ex-husband's motion to reopen based on duress filed eight years after the judgment.

2016—*D'Amato v. Hart-D'Amato*, 169 Conn. App. 669, 152 A.3d 546.

Wife was not entitled to an evidentiary hearing before the trial court denied her motion to reopen the judgment and for a new trial.

2016—*Ill v. Manzo-Ill*, 166 Conn. App. 809, 142 A.3d 1176.

Defendant's failure to pursue a post-judgment motion resulted in dismissal of the motion under Practice Book Sections 24-34(e) and 14-3 where ex-wife failed to show good cause for her failure to reclaim her motion.

2016—*Weyher v. Weyher*, 164 Conn. App. 734, 138 A.3d 969.

A party may not collaterally attack an order of the court, even if said order was impermissibly made, if the order was made under proper subject matter jurisdiction and the party failed to challenge the order in a timely manner.

2015—*Wendy V. v. Santiago*, 319 Conn. 540, 125 A.3d 983.

Ex-girlfriend's appeal was not within the mootness exception for issues capable of repetition yet evading review.

2015—*Forgione v. Forgione*, 162 Conn. App. 1, 129 A.3d 766.

Trial court lacked jurisdiction to reopen judgment of dissolution based on parties' stipulation.

2015—*Tittle v. Skipp-Tittle*, 161 Conn. App. 542, 128 A.3d 590.

Former wife's motion to reopen lacked subject matter jurisdiction.

2015—*Baker v. Whitnum-Baker*, 161 Conn. App. 227, 127 A.3d 330.

Denial of wife's motion for religious based conciliation was superseded by final judgment of dissolution.

2015—*In re Tiarra O.*, 160 Conn. App. 807, 125 A.3d 1094.

Appeal dismissed; GAL failed to demonstrate collateral consequences barred dismissal under mootness doctrine.

2015—*Sorrentino v. Sorrentino*, 160 Conn. App. 25, 123 A.3d 1287.

Subsequent order vesting sole custody with father rendered mother's appeal regarding visitation moot.

2015—*Zappola v. Zappola*, 159 Conn. App. 84, 122 A.3d 267.

Appellate court declined to review former husband's claims based on inadequate briefing.

2015—*Araujo v. Araujo*, 158 Conn. App. 429, 119 A.3d 22.

Judgment affirmed and appeal denied based on inadequate briefing.

2015—*Leftridge v. Wiggins*, 157 Conn. App. 213, 115 A.3d 1134.

In a case involving several appeals of plaintiff father's child support obligation, the father was not entitled to review of the claims on the merits because the father failed to address the issues in his brief and therefore had abandoned them.

2015—*Martocchio v. Savoir*, 156 Conn. App. 224, 112 A.3d 211.

A father's appeal of an order in a custody proceeding that dealt with grandparent visitation rights was dismissed as moot because no active controversy existed, and there was no form of practical, meaningful relief that could be provided to the father after the grandparents abandoned the motion for contempt they had filed against the father and conceded that were they to pursue their visitation rights in the future, they would be required to submit a new petition, at which time they would be evaluated for standing under *Roth* pursuant to the appellate court's decision on a previous appeal related to standing.

2015—*Sargent v. Sargent*, 156 Conn. App. 109, 113 A.3d 72.

Where the guardian ad litem had been removed by the trial court, orders allowing the guardian ad litem to meet with the minor children were moot, and were not appealable by the father.

2015—*McGuinness v. McGuinness*, 155 Conn. App. 273, 108 A.3d 1181.

Trial court's order that the income cap provision in parties' separation agreement was nonmodifiable was an interlocutory post-dissolution order, and did not constitute final order for purposes of appeal.

2014—*Tonghini v. Tonghini*, 152 Conn. App. 231, 98 A.3d 93.

Appellate court will not review lower court decision where moving party fails to provide the appellate court with an adequate record for review and fails to comply with several rules of appellate practice.

2014—*Clark v. Clark*, 150 Conn. App. 551, 91 A.3d 944.

Appeal was moot as there was no action that the court could take that would have any practical effect on the judgment under appeal.

2014—*O'Hara v. Mackie*, 151 Conn. App. 515, 97 A.3d 507.

Assenting to a court's decision to seal medical documents waives any claim to challenging that decision on appeal.

2014—*Perry v. Perry*, 312 Conn. 600, 95 A.3d 500.

Attorney for the minor children in a dissolution action may file an appeal only if the court determines that an appeal is in the best interests of the children.

2014—*Clelford v. Bristol*, 150 Conn. App. 229, 90 A.3d 998.

Appellate court refused to review husband's claim on appeal where husband provided the court with an inadequate appellate brief and inadequate appellate record.

2013—*Foley v. Foley*, 140 Conn. App. 490, 58 A.3d 977.

Court rejected request for a *de novo* review of the trial court's denial of motions for contempt.

2012—*Manzi v. Manzi*, 134 Conn. App. 333, 38 A.3d 1247.

Appeal from post-judgment contempt orders lacked merit, and the record was inadequate for review.

2012—*Liberti v. Liberti*, 132 Conn. App. 869, 37 A.3d 166.

Appellate court would not provide *Golding* review to due process claim because the issue had not been properly raised.

2012—*Morgan v. Morgan*, 136 Conn. App. 371, 46 A3d 255.

Appeal dismissed where the parties agreed at oral argument that appeal was not taken from a final judgment.

2011—*McKeon v. Lennon*, 131 Conn. App. 585, 37 A.3d 436.

Appeal dismissed for lack of subject matter jurisdiction.

2011—*Bubrosky v. Bubrosky*, 129 Conn. App. 338, 20 A.2d 79.

Appeal dismissed based on appellant's willful contempt and defiance of the court's authority and orders.

2010—*Bento v. Bento*, 125 Conn. App. 229, 8 A.3d 531.

The record was inadequate to review the trial court's orders relating to asset division, alimony, payment of carrying costs on the marital home, and counsel fees.

2010—*Kaczynski v. Kaczynski*, 294 Conn. 121, 981 A.2d 1068.

When a trial court in civil matter requiring proof by clear and convincing evidence fails to state what standard of proof it has applied, a reviewing court will presume that the correct standard was used. If a party believes trial court incorrectly applied the standard of proof, that party has the burden of seeking articulation or re-argument if impropriety is apparent.

2009—*Feinberg v. Feinberg*, 114 Conn. App. 589, 970 A.2d 776.

Appeal dismissed on the ground that certification was improvidently granted.

2008—*Kennedy v. Kennedy*, 109 Conn. App. 591, 952 A.2d 115.

Appeal from a visitation order which had been superseded by a subsequent expanded visitation schedule was dismissed as moot.

2008—*Moreira v. Moreira*, 105 Conn. App. 637, 938 A.2d 1289.

Pendente lite child support order entered "without prejudice" is a final judgment for appeal.

2008—*Sabanovic v. Haseljic*, 108 Conn. App. 89, 946 A.2d 1288.

Order revoking the court's earlier order to seal portions of the court file is a final judgment for purposes of appeal.

2004—*Calo-Turner v. Turner*, 83 Conn. App. 53, 847 A.2d 1085.

Court could not review the defendant's claim that the trial court was incorrect in determining fault where court did not articulate reasoning.

2002—*Wittman v. Krafick*, 67 Conn. App. 415, 787 A.2d 559.

Court declines to reach merits because appellant's brief is devoid of legal authority.

2001—*Mazzella v. Mazzella*, 67 Conn. App. 147, 786 A.2d 1113.

Appellate Court will not review claims when parties cite no law and provide no factual or legal analysis of their claims.

2001—*Strobel v. Strobel*, 64 Conn. App. 614, 781 A.2d 356.

Adequate record not presented on appeal.

2000—*Alder v. Alder*, 60 Conn. App. 612, 760 A.2d 1263.

Appellate court affirmed trial court's denial of motion to reargue.

2000—*Fitzgerald v. Fitzgerald*, 61 Conn. App. 162, 763 A.2d 669.

Supreme Court will assume lower courts acted properly without motion for articulation.

1999—*Lombardi v. Lombardi*, 55 Conn. App. 117, 737 A.2d 988.

Appellate court refused to review claim on appeal where defendant failed to provide adequate record.

1997—*Gardner v. Falvey*, 45 Conn. App. 699, 697 A.2d 711.

Appeal dismissed because no disposition of reargument.

1996—*Kane v. Kane*, 43 Conn. App. 508, 683 A.2d 1034.

Exception to a ruling must be taken to make it a ground for appeal.

1996—*Burns v. Burns*, 41 Conn. App. 716, 677 A.2d 971.

Claim not raised in statement of issues may be addressed if fully briefed.

1996—*Brubeck v. Burns-Brubeck*, 42 Conn. App. 583, 680 A.2d 327.

Constitutional claims do not have to be considered by the appellate court if they were not raised at trial.

1996—*White v. White*, 42 Conn. App. 747, 680 A.2d 1368.

Denial of motion to strike for failure to state a cause of action is not a final judgment and therefore appealable.

1995—*Cook v. Cook*, 38 Conn. App. 499, 661 A.2d 1043.

Appeal is dismissed as moot.

1995—*Cruz v. Gonzalez*, 40 Conn. App. 33, 668 A.2d 739.

Discovery orders are generally not appealable interlocutory.

1995—*Gallant v. Esposito*, 36 Conn. App. 794, 654 A.2d 380.

Appeal dismissed when appellant failed to provide an adequate record for review.

1995—*Newman v. Newman*, 235 Conn. 82, 663 A.2d 980.

Counsel for children may file an appeal if appellate court determines first it is in their best interest, among other factors.

1995—*Mark v. Mark*, 40 Conn. App. 171, 669 A.2d 579.

Appeal may be dismissed if appellant is in contempt of court.

1995—*Zadravecz v. Zadravecz*, 39 Conn. App. 28, 664 A.2d 303.

Scope of review of a decision interpreting a stipulated judgment is plenary and not limited by the clearly erroneous standards.

1995—*Viets v. Viets*, 39 Conn. App. 610, 666 A.2d 434.

Motion for review of trial court's denial of motion for articulation must be filed within 10 days.

1994—*Gibson v. Gibson*, 34 Conn. App. 139, 640 A.2d 145.

Amendment to appeal to challenge court's subsequent ruling must be filed within 20 days of the ruling. Improper matters included in appellate brief may be stricken.

1994—*Gorneault v. Gorneault*, 34 Conn. App. 923, 642 A.2d 734.

Appellate court cannot render a decision without specific findings of fact to determine the basis of the court's ruling.

1994—*Mulholland v. Mulholland*, 229 Conn. 643, 643 A.2d 246.

Contempt order for failure to pay child support arrearage during the appeal period was proper even though the child support order was reversed on appeal before the contempt order was entered.

1994—*Bryant v. Bryant*, 228 Conn. 630, 637 A.2d 1111.

Order of contempt and requiring a payment plan were appealable.

1993—*Madigan v. Madigan*, 224 Conn. 749, 620 A.2d 1276.

Order is appealable if it terminates a separate and distinct proceeding or so concludes the rights of the parties that further proceedings cannot affect them.

1993—*Tessitore v. Tessitore*, 31 Conn. App. 40, 623 A.2d 496.

The court must consider statutory criteria in awarding counsel fees pending appeal.

1992—*Ippolito v. Ippolito*, 28 Conn. App. 745, 612 A.2d 131.

The motion to strike the reply brief was proper.

1992—*Maguire v. Maguire*, 222 Conn. 32, 608 A.2d 79.

Clerical error is a failure to preserve or correctly represent in the record the actual decision of the court and can be corrected by the court at any time.

1992—*Billington v. Billington*, 27 Conn. App. 466, 606 A.2d 737.

Credibility findings by trial court are not reviewable on appeal.

1991—*Salaman v. Salaman*, 25 Conn. App. 563, 595 A.2d 909.

Court will not consider an issue unless it was raised at the trial court.

1990—*Bucy v. Bucy*, 23 Conn. App. 98, 579 A.2d 117.

Court ordered defendant to reimburse plaintiff for psychologists expenses she paid for their daughter—because further orders were necessary as to timing of reimbursement, the appeal was untimely.

1990—*Rostain v. Rostain*, 213 Conn. 686, 569 A.2d 1126.

Supreme Court remanded case requesting trial judge to articulate specific questions regarding inherited asset.

1989—*Koper v. Koper*, 17 Conn. App. 480, 553 A.2d 1162.

Judge cannot change his decision via a motion for articulation but rather a motion to open it.

1989—*Sunbury v. Sunbury*, 210 Conn. 170, 553 A.2d 612.

Court's error in calculation of income required reconsideration of not only alimony but all other financial orders.

1989—*Schott v. Schott*, 18 Conn. App. 333, 557 A.2d 936.

Appellate court cannot order attorney fees.

1989—*Broderick v. Broderick*, 20 Conn. App. 145, 565 A.2d 3.

Appeal may be dismissed if appellant is in contempt of court.

1989—*Main v. Main*, 17 Conn. App. 670, 555 A.2d 997.

Motion for sanctions under Practice Book § 2036 was proper for a frivolous appeal.

1988—*Hurtado v. Hurtado*, 14 Conn. App. 296, 541 A.2d 873.

Formal objection to evidence must be made on the record to be considered on appeal.

1987—*Boland v. Catalano*, 202 Conn. 333, 521 A.2d 142.

It was error for trial judge to refuse to correct record.

1987—*De Teves v. De Teves*, 2 Conn. App. 590, 481 A.2d 92, *aff'd*, 202 Conn. 292, 520 A.2d 608.

Trial court cannot extend time in which appeal may be filed beyond 40 days.

1987—*Lefflbine v. Lefflbine*, 12 Conn. App. 638, 533 A.2d 576.

Grounds for new trial based on newly acquired evidence.

1986—*Jones v. Jones*, 199 Conn. 287, 507 A.2d 88.

Record was inadequate to review decision that opened dissolution judgment and equally divided a pension. Trial court found "substantial mutual mistakes," determined that a "manifest injustice would occur" but did not specify what "substantial" meant, and provided no legal analysis in support. Accordingly, the record was inadequate for review.

1985—*Lashgari v. Lashgari*, 197 Conn. 189, 496 A.2d 491.

Statements of fact must be found in memorandum of decision.

1985—*Tischbein v. Tischbein*, 4 Conn. App. 459, 495 A.2d 716.

Review was limited to determining whether trial court could reasonably conclude as it did; claims must be included in preliminary statement of issues.

1985—*Timm v. Timm*, 195 Conn. 202, 487 A.2d 191.

Appeal cannot be based on mistake made during trial that could have been corrected at that time.

1984—*Markarian v. Markarian*, 2 Conn. App. 688, 483 A.2d 276.

Case was remanded for articulation of basis of trial court's decision.

1984—*Pascal v. Pascal*, 2 Conn. App. 472, 481 A.2d 68.

Final orders are appealable.

§ 15.02 Abuse of Discretion

2019—*Dufresne v. Dufresne*, 191 Conn. App. 532, 215 A.3d 1259.

Trial court abused its discretion by sua sponte issuing order terminating child's relationship with her therapist. Father's motion did not request to terminate child's therapy or joint custody. Neither party had been given notice that trial court intended to address child's therapy. The issue was for mother, who has sole custody, to decide.

2019—*In re Skylar F.*, 191 Conn. App. 200, 215 A.3d 750.

Trial court did not abuse its discretion in denying motion to open default judgment rendered at case status conference where father did not provide a good defense: He did not address the concerns trial court previously expressed about his substance abuse and domestic violence. He did not show his failure to appear was result of mistake, accident, or other reasonable cause or provide a reason why he did not appear. He did not assert that he lacked notice of the case status conference which had been scheduled at a particular time for his convenience. It was his burden to inform trial court, his attorney, and Department of Children and Families of his whereabouts and intentions with respect to exercising responsibility for his child. Also, father did not abide by the requirement that his motion be verified by oath as required by the applicable rule of practice.

2019—*Merkel v. Hill*, 189 Conn. App. 779, 207 A.3d 1115.

Trial court abused its discretion in a child custody matter by adopting custody and parental access plan recommendations contained in an outdated report. The expert explicitly stated she could not make any present recommendations because she would have nothing on which to base such recommendations, and that she "would be doing a disservice to the minor child to say that" her recommendations were still valid at the time of the hearing.

2018—*Krahel v. Czoch*, 186 Conn. App. 22, 198 A.3d 103.

Trial court properly sanctioned defendant by precluding him from testifying about his personal and business finances where defendant failed to produce records pursuant to a court order.

2018—*Keusch v. Keusch*, 184 Conn. App. 822, 195 A.3d 1136.

Trial court erred in awarding unallocated alimony and child support that was not modifiable upon each child attaining the age of majority.

2017—*O'Brien v. O'Brien*, 326 Conn. 81, 161 A.3d 1236.

Trial court did not abuse its discretion in adjusting asset distribution to remedy wife's loss; decision to value stocks as of date of new trial was not arbitrary or irrational.

2017—*Lederle v. Spivey*, 174 Conn. App. 592, 166 A.3d 636.

Trial court abused its discretion in finding the defendant's claims in prior appeal were entirely without color and awarding fees based on that conclusion.

2015—*Schneider v. Schneider*, 161 Conn. App. 1, 127 A.3d 298.

Denial of husband's request for reimbursement of mortgage payments was an improper modification of dissolution judgment.

2015—*Anderson v. Anderson*, 160 Conn. App. 341, 125 A.3d 606.

Evidence sufficient to support award from husband's retirement account of $43,158.

2015—*In re Ariana S.*, 159 Conn. App. 513, 123 A.3d 463.

Denial of motion to reopen, based on insufficient notice, was not an abuse of discretion.

2015—*Keller v. Keller*, 158 Conn. App. 538, 119 A.3d 1213.

The trial court did not abuse its discretion in finding plaintiff in contempt because plaintiff did not affirmatively comply with the clear order of the trial court requiring plaintiff to provide defendant with her address and all other required contact information after leaving the family home.

2015—*Parisi v. Parisi*, 315 Conn. 370, 107 A.3d 920.

The trial court's failure to clarify an ambiguous alimony buyout provision of the parties' separation agreement, and to enter an accompanying order of compliance, was an abuse of discretion.

2014—*Rostad v. Hirsch*, 148 Conn. App. 441, 85 A.3d 1212.

Refusal to apply Child Support Guidelines for three years prior to commencement of action pursuant to Conn. Gen. Stat. § 46b-215(a)(7)(A) was not an abuse of discretion where the payor made voluntary payments and the payee accepted.

2014—*Mekrut v. Suits*, 147 Conn. App. 794, 84 A.3d 466.

No abuse of discretion by holding the defendant in contempt for not paying alimony from his severance, and by denying a motion to modify. However, it was error for a second judge to grant a second motion for contempt without an evidentiary hearing.

2014—*Talbot v. Talbot*, 148 Conn. App. 279, 85 A.3d 40.

Award of post judgment and appellate counsel fees was proper.

2014—*Doyle v. Doyle*, 150 Conn. App. 312, 90 A.3d 1024.

Trial court did not abuse its discretion in applying legal principals of contract construction, rather than relying upon child support guidelines, in determining intent of parties as to payment of children's medical expenses under separation agreement.

2013—*Kupersmith v. Kupersmith*, 146 Conn. App. 79, 78 A.3d 860.

Abuse of discretion ordering counsel fees where the court found that the defendant's motion was entirely without color and that he acted in bad faith, but did not support its finding with a factual basis.

2013—*Traystman v. Traystman*, 141 Conn. App. 789, 62 A.3d 1149.

Abuse of discretion where the court found that attorneys' fees paid from HELOC were reasonable, but that withdrawals from HELOC in lesser amounts to pay the fees was contemptuous. No abuse of discretion for denial of a post judgment motion seeking disqualification of a judge. No abuse of discretion for restriction of discovery and permission to redact evidence.

2013—*Kasowitz v. Kasowitz*, 140 Conn. App. 507, 59 A.3d 347.

No abuse of discretion where the court found the defendant in contempt for partial compliance with past court orders.

2013—*Harris v. Hamilton*, 141 Conn. App. 208, 61 A.3d 542.

No abuse of discretion where the court allowed the plaintiff to present evidence which predated a prior parenting agreement during the course of a long hearing on PJ motions to modify custody.

2013—*Munro v. Munoz*, 146 Conn. App. 853, 81 A.3d 252.

Precluding all evidence of bad faith in connection with a post-judgment motion for attorney's fees was an abuse of discretion because it denied the filing party the opportunity to present evidence that was material to proving her claim for fees.

2013—*Tuckman v. Tuckman*, 308 Conn. 194, 61 A.3d 449.

Court abused its discretion by awarding child support without determining net income and considering the child support guidelines. Court failed to properly determine whether taxable income of S corporation, attributable to one party as a shareholder, was available for child support purposes.

2013—*Szynkowicz v. Szynkowicz*, 140 Conn. App. 525, 59 A.3d 1194.

No abuse of discretion where the court awarded all of the parties' real property to one party. No abuse of discretion where the court awarded alimony and the memorandum of decision did not make a specific net income finding.

2012—*Allen v. Allen*, 134 Conn. App. 486, 39 A.3d 1190.

No abuse of discretion where plaintiff was found in contempt for failing to make any meaningful effort to refinance or sell the former marital home and for failing to pay household expenses.

2011—*Von Kohorn v. Von Kohorn*, 132 Conn. App. 709, 33 A.3d 809.

Abuse of discretion where the trial court changed the duration of a lifetime alimony award to an eight-year award by way of a motion for clarification.

2011—*Bruno v. Bruno*, 31 A.3d 860.

Trial court improperly failed to value assets as of date of dissolution when effectuating the property division.

2011—*Vanicky v. Vanicky*, 128 Conn. App. 281, 18 A.3d 602.

Trial court did not abuse its discretion when it entered financial orders at the time of dissolution.

2010—*Campbell v. Campbell*, 120 Conn. App. 760, 993 A.2d 984.

No abuse of discretion by refusal to delay hearing on defendant's motion for contempt where defendant had marked ready and then asked for continuance and plaintiff had cancelled trip to Florida to attend. No abuse of discretion by finding plaintiff not in contempt of the alimony order where evidence of plaintiff's cash payments was presented.

2010—*Bento v. Bento*, 125 Conn. App. 229, 8 A.3d 531.

The trial court abused its discretion by equally dividing responsibility for a corporate debt without making any findings of fact or law. Neither party's financial affidavit had listed the corporate debt as a liability, and there was no finding that either owed the debt. This issue was severable and did not impact the mosaic of financial orders. The

Appellate Court remanded with direction to vacate the order dividing the corporate debt.

2010—*Adamo v. Adamo*, 123 Conn. App. 38, 1 A.3d 221.

Trial court did not abuse its discretion when it looked to housing law "for guidance" to resolve defendant's claim that plaintiff willfully or negligently damaged a house.

2009—*Gamble-Perugini v. Perugini*, 112 Conn. App. 231, 962 A.2d 192.

Trial court's financial orders were not abuse of discretion nor is it bias to accept plaintiff's proposed property division without modification. Consonance of views is not bias, defendant was, "perhaps, the least credible witness the (trial) court had confronted in nearly two decades." Further, the court made some adjustments to the plaintiff's proposed property division.

2005—*Gervais v. Gervais*, 91 Conn. App. 840, 882 A.2d 731.

Abuse of discretion not to consider ex-wife's financial affidavit when deciding ex-husband's pending motion for termination of alimony.

2005—*Greco v. Greco*, 275 Conn. 348, 880 A.2d 872.

Abuse of discretion to award wife 98.5% of marital property, $710 per week in alimony and order former husband to maintain two insurance policies for wife's benefit.

2004—*Greco v. Greco*, 82 Conn. App. 768, 847 A.2d 1017, *cert. granted*, 270 Conn. 907, 853 A.2d 524.

Abuse of discretion and an incorrect application of law by the trial court to base financial orders on the gross income rather than net income.

2004—*Robelle-Pyke v. Robelle-Pyke*, 81 Conn. App. 817, 841 A.2d 1213.

Trial court abused its discretion in denying continuance.

2003—*Ragin v. Lee*, 78 Conn. App. 848, 829 A.2d 93.

Appeal by state was premature as it was not from "final decision" as required by Conn. Gen. Stat. § 46b-231.

2003—*Weinstein v. Weinstein*, 266 Conn. 933, 837 A.2d 807.

Trial court abused its discretion in denying motion to open judgment where wife learned that husband had a pending offer for the sale of his business during the divorce proceedings, which offer came to fruition. Husband fraudulently concealed his assets during the dissolution proceeding and if the court had known his true financial status, the outcome of the trial would likely be different.

2003—*Rosato v. Rosato*, 77 Conn. App. 9, 822 A.2d 974.

Trial court had no authority to order the plaintiff's pension be assigned to the parties' children. Trial court did not abuse discretion in dividing the pension as of date of dissolution.

2003—*Lambert v. Donahue*, 78 Conn. App. 493, 827 A.2d 729.

Trial court did not abuse discretion in modifying orders with respect to the child without first appointing an attorney or guardian ad litem where case did not involve allegations of neglect, sexual abuse or physical abuse, and neither party requested such appointment.

2003—*Jewett v. Jewett*, 265 Conn. 669, 830 A.2d 193.

Trial court did not abuse its discretion in excluding the irrelevant and speculative testimony of expert witnesses proffered by the defendant.

2003—*Gina M. G. v. William C.*, 77 Conn. App. 582, 823 A.2d 1274.

Fining plaintiff for her contempt and ordering her to pay counsel fees was not an abuse of trial court's discretion.

1999—*Smith v. Smith*, 249 Conn. 265, 752 A.2d 1023.

Court held that the trial court did not abuse its discretion in awarding plaintiff part of a settlement defendant had received from her former employer.

1999—*Milbauer v. Milbauer*, 54 Conn. App. 304, 733 A.2d 907.

Court held the trial court did not abuse its discretion in decreasing plaintiff's alimony award beginning from the date defendant filed the motion to modify where party's incomes, vocational skills, and employability were considered in making the ruling.

1998—*Ahneman v. Ahneman*, 243 Conn. 471, 706 A.2d 960.

Trial court's refusal to consider party's motion is appealable final judgment since it was functionally the equivalent of a denial of the motion.

1995—*Wolf v. Wolf*, 39 Conn. App. 162, 664 A.2d 315.

Standards for reversal of a decision on the basis of abuse of discretion.

1994—*Askinazi v. Askinazi*, 34 Conn. App. 328, 641 A.2d 413.

Appellate court will not place different weight on evidence or statutory criteria than the trial court.

1993—*Siracusa v. Siracusa*, 30 Conn. App. 560, 621 A.2d 309.

Seven-year payout to wife for her interest in the family business, plus alimony in excess of husband's income was not an abuse of discretion.

1993—*Puris v. Puris*, 30 Conn. App. 443, 620 A.2d 829.

Award of $276,000 per year was not an abuse of discretion.

1993—*Fahy v. Fahy*, 227 Conn. 505, 630 A.2d 1328.

Court's use of gross income and net income inconsistently to determine alimony modification was an abuse of discretion.

1993—*Tessitore v. Tessitore*, 31 Conn. App. 40, 623 A.2d 496.

The court must consider statutory criteria in awarding counsel fees pending appeal.

1992—*Watson v. Watson*, 221 Conn. 698, 607 A.2d 383.

Exclusion of inherited and gifted assets from marital assets was an abuse of discretion. Financial award was so low as to constitute an abuse of discretion.

1990—*Damon v. Damon*, 23 Conn. App. 111, 579 A.2d 124.

Award of 85 percent of marital assets to wife was not per se an abuse of discretion.

1990—*Bonelli v. Bonelli*, 22 Conn. App. 248, 576 A.2d 587.

Appellate court may disagree with trial court's result but may not overturn unless there is an abuse of discretion.

1990—*Brash v. Brash*, 20 Conn. App. 609, 569 A.2d 44.

A trial court's decision may be disturbed on appeal only when there has been an abuse of discretion.

1989—*Main v. Main*, 17 Conn. App. 670, 555 A.2d 997.

Abuse of discretion found when court ordered $25 per week child support where payor's income was $1,410 per week.

1989—*Blake v. Blake*, 211 Conn. 485, 560 A.2d 396.

Award of attorney fees to appellee when she had ample liquid funds to defend the appeal was an abuse of discretion.

1988—*O'Neill v. O'Neill*, 13 Conn. App. 300, 536 A.2d 978.

The award was logically inconsistent with the facts presented.

1987—*Misiorski v. Misiorski*, 11 Conn. App. 463, 528 A.2d 829.

Abuse of discretion found in amount of award of permanent periodic alimony.

1987—*Crocker v. Crocker*, 13 Conn. App. 129, 534 A.2d 1251.

Trial court had broad discretion in awarding alimony and dividing property as long as it considered the relevant statutory criteria.

1986—*Pisch v. Pisch*, 7 Conn. App. 720, 510 A.2d 455.

Failure to appoint counsel for minor child is not a clear abuse of discretion.

1986—*Carpenter v. Carpenter*, 7 Conn. App. 112, 507 A.2d 526.

In order to conclude that the trial court abused its discretion in making its financial awards, the appellate court must find that the trial court either incorrectly applied the law or could not have reasonably concluded as it did.

1985—*Timm v. Timm*, 195 Conn. 202, 487 A.2d 191.

Reasonable presumptions are given in favor of trial court.

1985—*Trivelli v. Trivelli*, 5 Conn. App. 488, 500 A.2d 244.

Court must either incorrectly apply law or could not reasonably conclude as it did.

1984—*Merritt v. Merritt*, 2 Conn. App. 425, 479 A.2d 255.

There was no abuse of discretion in the award or in the trial judge's proceeding with the trial, while the husband's attorney was on vacation.

1984—*Weisbaum v. Weisbaum*, 2 Conn. App. 270, 477 A.2d 690.

Trial court abused its discretion in permitting the use of the custodial funds for the purpose of discharging the husband's support obligations to his children.

1984—*Ehrenkranz v. Ehrenkranz*, 2 Conn. App. 416, 479 A.2d 826.

Trial court's financial awards to the wife constituted an abuse of discretion.

1984—*Mays v. Mays*, 193 Conn. 261, 476 A.2d 562.

Award of attorneys' fees was not abuse of discretion.

1984—*Vanderlip v. Vanderlip*, 1 Conn. App. 158, 468 A.2d 1253.

Court did not abuse its discretion by denying continuance and starting trial without wife.

1983—*Brown v. Brown*, 190 Conn. 345, 460 A.2d 1287.

Abuse of discretion in disproportionate support award.

1983—*Wolk v. Wolk*, 191 Conn. 328, 464 A.2d 780.

Financial orders in light of all the circumstances, cannot be said to be an abuse of the court's discretion.

1983—*Brown v. Brown*, 190 Conn. 345, 460 A.2d 1287.

Child support award was grossly disproportionate to the child's needs and imposing a constructive trust on the jointly owned home was error.

1983—*Anderson v. Anderson*, 191 Conn. 46, 463 A.2d 578.

Regarding attorney's fees on appeal, the court deems it appropriate for the trial court in the exercise of its broad judicial discretion to consider the statutory criteria set out in Conn. Gen. Stat. §§ 46b-62, 46b-82 and the respective financial abilities of the parties.

1982—*Carpenter v. Carpenter*, 188 Conn. 736, 453 A.2d 1151.

Trial court's financial awards to the wife were not abuse of discretion.

1982—*Cameron v. Cameron*, 187 Conn. 163, 444 A.2d 915.

Financial award and property division were vacated where the record disclosed a situation which raised a suspicion as to the fairness of the court's administration of justice.

1982—*McPhee v. McPhee*, 186 Conn. 167, 440 A.2d 274.

The trial court abused its discretion in establishing that alimony would terminate if the wife relapsed after treatment for alcoholism as a condition for receiving alimony.

1981—*Scherr v. Scherr*, 183 Conn. 366, 439 A.2d 375.

Trial court did not abuse its discretion in dissolving the 23-year marriage without an alimony award.

1981—*McGinn v. McGinn*, 183 Conn. 512, 441 A.2d 8.

Trial court did not abuse its discretion in ordering former wife to convey her interest in marital home to former husband.

1980—*Friedman v. Friedman*, 180 Conn. 132, 429 A.2d 823.

Despite the mother's failure to appear, the trial court did not abuse its discretion in awarding custody to her.

§ 15.03 Appeals Relating to Custody

2024—*S.C. v. J.C.*, 227 Conn. App. 326, 321 A.3d 427.

Where one of the parties' children reached age 18 during the pendency of the plaintiff's appeal of the order awarding full legal custody of that child to the defendant and, therefore, the defendant no longer had legal custody, the plaintiff's claim challenging the dispositional portion of that order was moot. The claim was dismissed as the Appellate Court could not provide any practical relief.

Also while plaintiff's appeal was pending, the parties' younger child filed a motion through an attorney appointed to appear on his behalf, seeking an order awarding the plaintiff sole legal custody and primary physical custody over him. Upon agreement of the parties, the trial court granted the motion. Because the defendant no longer had sole legal or primary physical custody, the Appellate Court could not grant any practical relief to the plaintiff with respect to her claim challenging the portion of the temporary custody order granting sole legal and primary physical custody of the younger child to the defendant. This claim was also dismissed as moot.

2023—*C.M. v. R.M.*, 219 Conn. App. 57, 293 A.3d 968.

The appellate court dismissed the appeal for lack of jurisdiction. The father, who had appealed from an order granting his motion to move to New York with the parties' minor children, did not have standing to appeal because he had not been aggrieved by the trial court's order. Conn. Gen. Stat. § 52-263 grants the right of appeal to a party who is aggrieved by the decision of the court or judge upon any question or questions of law arising in the trial. Aggrievement is a basic requirement of standing just as standing is a fundamental requirement of jurisdiction. The father did not have standing because he had not been aggrieved. Therefore, the appellate court lacked jurisdiction over his appeal.

2022—*Rek v. Pettit*, 214 Conn. App. 854, 280 A.3d 1260.

Plaintiffs, the legal guardians of a minor child, appealed orders requiring the child to suspend contact with his long-term personal counselor and engage with a new therapist with the goal of working toward resumption of visitation with Defendants, the child's maternal grandparents. Because the orders at issue were orders of visitation within the meaning of Conn. Gen. Prac. Book. R. App. P. § 61-11(c), they were not automatically stayed during the appeal.

2021—*In re Marcquan C.*, 202 Conn. App. 520, 246 A.3d 41.

The trial court's order that a mother participate in a psychological evaluation was an interlocutory order that was not an immediately appealable final judgment. The order for a psychological evaluation was not part of the judgment denying the mother's motion to revoke commitment of her child to the care and custody of the Commissioner of Children and Families, but instead a tool that could potentially benefit future reunification. The mother's appeal was dismissed.

2019—*Peters v. Senman*, 193 Conn. App. 766, 220 A.3d 114.

Plaintiff's claim that the trial court erred in denying her motions for declaratory rulings that under various provisions of the United States and Connecticut constitutions she is entitled, as a fit parent, to equivalent rights of access and decision making were meritless. Her arguments were based on a fundamental misunderstanding of when and how declaratory relief is available and her failure to recognize the difference between unwanted actions intruding upon the lives of intact families and the obligation of family courts to hear and decide cases brought by parent against the other.

2017—*In re Santiago G.*, 325 Conn. 221, 157 A.3d 60.

Appeal dismissed for lack of subject matter jurisdiction where intervening party did not have a colorable claim of intervention in termination of parental rights proceeding.

2009—*Watkins v. Thomas*, 118 Conn. App. 452, 984 A.2d 106.

Defendant mother cited no legal authority in support of her custody appeal and Appellate Court declined to review her claims.

2005—*Pritchard v. Pritchard*, 92 Conn. App. 327, 885 A.2d 207.

Judgment in child support enforcement proceeding that did not terminate a separate and distinct proceeding or conclude rights of parties is not an appealable final judgment.

2000—*Rosenfield v. Rosenfield*, 61 Conn. App. 112, 762 A.2d 511.

Denial of motion to dismiss is not a final judgment and therefore not immediately appealable.

1997—*Greene v. Bynum*, 46 Conn. App. 1, 698 A.2d 334.

Defective petition of appeal from family support magistrate deprives court of subject matter jurisdiction to hear appeal.

1997—*Taff v. Bettcher*, 243 Conn. 380, 703 A.2d 759.

Order precluding parties from filing any motions regarding custody or visitation of minor child for period of not less than one year is appealable final judgment.

1995—*Newman v. Newman*, 235 Conn. 82, 663 A.2d 980.

Guardian ad litem or friend of the court need not be appointed to take an appeal for the children if they are already represented by counsel.

1993—*Madigan v. Madigan*, 224 Conn. 749, 620 A.2d 1276.

Pendente lite custody orders are immediately appealable.

1988—*Hurtado v. Hurtado*, 14 Conn. App. 296, 541 A.2d 873.

The appellate standard of review in domestic relations cases is a very narrow one and the court will not reverse a trial court's rulings with regard to custody and financial orders unless the court incorrectly applied the law or could not reasonably have concluded as it did.

1986—*Cookson v. Cookson*, 201 Conn. 229, 514 A.2d 323.

Appellate court found that the standard used by the court comported with due process and served adequately to protect the various interests involved and found that it was implicit in the trial court's award that it was based on the statutory standard of the "the best interests of the child."

§ 15.04 Constitutional Issues

2024—*Kosar v. Giangrande*, 228 Conn. App. 749, 326 A.3d 266, *appeal denied*, 350 Conn. 930.

Trial court abused its discretion and violated the defendant's due process rights by allowing her only 15 minutes to present her case-in-chief at the hearing on the plaintiff's amended motion for contempt and motion for an injunction. The court's management of the hearing resulted in the plaintiff receiving several hours to present his case-in-chief while the defendant was afforded just a few minutes. The court's failure to allow the defendant more time improperly deprived her of a fair opportunity to present evidence on the contested issues. The judgment was reversed and the case was remanded for the limited purpose of determining whether the plaintiff was entitled to an award of attorney's fees. The defendant's requests for restitution related to the pendente lite order underlying the contempt proceeding and for a new trial on "all financial orders incident to the decree of dissolution" were denied.

2019—*In re Taijha H.-B.*, 333 Conn. 297, 216 A.3d 601.

Applying the due process balancing test employed in *Lassiter v. Department of Social Servs.*, 452 U.S. 18, 101 S. Ct. 2153, 68 L. Ed. 2d 640 (1981), appellate court determined that an indigent mother appealing termination of her parental rights has a constitutional right to appointed appellate counsel under the due process clause of the Fourteenth Amendment of the United States Constitution because she has a history of criminal activity, the trial court relied heavily on expert witness testimony, and she had serious mental health issues.

Appellate review counsel shall not be permitted to withdraw from representing an indigent parent who is constitutionally entitled to appointed counsel in a termination of parental rights hearing solely based on counsel's representation that he or she is unable to identify a nonfrivolous ground for appeal. Following *Smith v. Robbins*, 528 U.S. 259, 120 S. Ct. 746, 145 L. Ed. 2d 756 (2000), to vindicate the due process rights of the indigent litigant (1) the court must ascertain whether counsel has evaluated a potential grounds for appeal and brought the most promising; merely representing that upon review no grounds for appeal exist is insufficient; (2) the indigent parent must have opportunity to review counsel's conclusions and inform the court what he or she believes are appealable issues; and (3) the court must reach its own conclusion that appeal would be frivolous.

Practice Book § 79a-3, which dictates procedure for appointed appellate review counsel, does not violate the equal protection clause of the Fourteenth Amendment of the United States Constitution by imposing a higher legal burden standard on indigent parents seeking to appeal termination of parental rights. It does not impose a different, higher standard than rule 3.1 of the Rules of Professional conduct. The rules do not treat indigent parents and nonindigent parents differently.

2019—*Morera v. Thurber*, 187 Conn. App. 795, 204 A.3d 1.

Father was denied due process by the trial court, which did not offer him an adequate opportunity to review an expert's report or to present evidence in opposition to the report before the trial court ruled. The court remanded to afford him the opportunity, at a properly noticed evidentiary hearing, to present his own evidence and to cross-examine the expert.

2017—*Puff v. Puff*, 177 Conn. App. 103, 171 A.3d 1076.

Trial court properly canvassed the plaintiff at the hearing and was not required to canvass the plaintiff again after issuing its written decision memorializing the agreed-upon terms between the parties.

2017—*Medeiros v. Medeiros*, 175 Conn. App. 174, 167 A.3d 967.

Order of stayed incarceration, although vacated and thus moot, qualified for review under the capable of repetition yet evading review exception to the mootness doctrine.

2017—*In re Luis N.*, 175 Conn. App. 271, 165 A.3d 1270, *related proceeding at* 175 Conn. App. 307, 167 A.3d 476.

Any errors by the court in permitting the Department of Children and Families to meet with the minor children ex parte was harmless and was not a violation of the respondent's constitutional rights under *State v. Golding*, 213 Conn. 233, 567 A.2d 823 (Conn. 1989).

2011—*Lynn v. Lynn*, 130 Conn. App. 319, 23 A.3d 771.

Denial of due process where court did not address motions related to whether the defendant's failure to pay was willful or excused by a good faith belief or dispute.

2004—*Foster v. Foster*, 84 Conn. App. 311, 853 A.2d 588.

No constitutionally protected right to counsel in proceedings on custody and visitation.

2003—*Shapiro v. Shapiro*, 80 Conn. App. 565, 835 A.2d 1049.

Court's order was reversed because plaintiff's right to due process was violated.

2001—*In re Brianna B.*, 66 Conn. App. 695, 785 A.2d 1189.

Confidentiality order in juvenile court proceeding not violative of party's constitutional right to freedom of speech.

1997—*Taff v. Bettcher*, 243 Conn. 380, 703 A.2d 759.

A parent has no constitutional right to dictate how the best interests of her child should be legally represented and no standing to require counsel for minor child to be present at custody hearing.

1996—*Brubeck v. Burns-Brubeck*, 42 Conn. App. 583, 680 A.2d 327.

Constitutional claims do not have to be considered by the appellate court if they were not raised at trial.

1994—*Hill v. Hill*, 35 Conn. App. 160, 644 A.2d 951.

Court did not violate party's constitutional due process rights by proceeding to judgment in her absence or her attorney's absence.

1992—*Henin v. Henin*, 26 Conn. App. 386, 601 A.2d 550.

Conditioning the payment of a note secured by a mortgage on the spouse's remarriage is not unconstitutional.

1990—*Lehrer v. Davis*, 214 Conn. 232, 571 A.2d 691.

Court will not determine the constitutionality of a statute without sufficient facts.

1989—*Serrano v. Serrano*, 213 Conn. 1, 566 A.2d 413.

State law must do major damage to clear and substantial federal interests before the Supremacy clause will demand that state law be overridden.

1986—*Heiskell v. Heiskell*, 6 Conn. App. 471, 506 A.2d 151.

Court held that Conn. Gen. Stat. § 46b-81 is constitutional.

1982—*Lane v. Lane*, 187 Conn. 144, 444 A.2d 1377.

Court determined that Conn. Gen. Stat. § 48b-81 as not overly broad.

1980—*Seymour v. Seymour*, 180 Conn. 705, 433 A.2d 1005.

Connecticut custody statute's failure to provide guidelines for the exercise of the trial court's discretion do not make the statute unconstitutionally vague.

§ 15.05 Counsel Fees

2021—*Anketell v. Kulldorff*, 207 Conn. App. 807, 263 A.3d 972.

The trial court did not err in awarding the wife appellate counsel fees because it expressly found that she lacked the liquid assets to pay her attorney's appellate retainer. The trial court also specifically found that requiring the plaintiff to pay her attorney's $25,000 retainer would undermine the financial awards made in the dissolution judgment. The defendant did not demonstrate that such finding was unreasonable.

2020—*Ross v. Ross*, 200 Conn. App. 720, 239 A.3d 1280.

When the trial court's order must be reconsidered in its entirety on remand, its award of attorney's fees related to the underlying matter must also be remanded for reconsideration in light of the new order that will be issued at that time.

1993—*Cook v. Bieluch*, 32 Conn. App. 537, 629 A.2d 1175.

If no alimony is awarded, but counsel fees are, evidence relating to one but not the other must be identified.

1990—*Febbroriello v. Febbroriello*, 21 Conn. App. 200, 572 A.2d 1032.

Courts have knowledge of what a reasonable attorney fee would be an statement of attorney fees owed on financial affidavit was evidence of costs incurred.

1990—*Cabrera v. Cabrera*, 23 Conn. App. 330, 580 A.2d 1227.

The bill submitted post-trial by counsel was enough evidence to support an award of fees along with the court's knowledge of the proceedings.

§ 15.06 Error

2024—*Kosar v. Giangrande*, 228 Conn. App. 749, 326 A.3d 266, *appeal denied,* 350 Conn. 930.

The defendant failed to substantiate her claims that the trial judge committed plain error by presiding over the dissolution trial after previously holding a *Matza* hearing between the defendant and her prior counsel because accusations by her prior counsel made during that hearing had tainted the judge's view of her. On the basis of the record the defendant did not meet the stringent standard for relief pursuant to the plain error doctrine. She failed to demonstrate that the claimed impropriety was so clear, obvious, and indisputable as to warrant the extraordinary remedy of reversal. She had not asked the judge to disqualify himself and conceded that there are no cases holding that a judge is required to recuse himself under these circumstances. She essentially advocated for a per se rule that a judge be required to recuse himself from presiding over subsequent proceedings of a party if that party's counsel requests a *Matza* hearing.

2019—*Casablanca v. Casablanca*, 190 Conn. App. 606, 212 A.3d 1278.

Trial court erred in its determination that a retirement asset provision in proposed QDRO was unambiguous, as there were at least three possible interpretations of the provision. The court remanded for the trial court to determine the intent of the parties after consideration of "all available extrinsic evidence" and the circumstances surrounding the entering of the agreement.

2019—*Zaniewski v. Zaniewski*, 190 Conn. App. 386, 210 A.3d 620.

The husband was entitled to a new trial regarding the financial orders for child support and alimony because the trial court's memorandum of decision failed to set forth the factual basis for its financial orders. Generally, an inadequate record would foreclose appellate review; however, here the inadequacy of the record arose from the trial court's issuance of a memorandum of decision that contained virtually no factual findings that would permit review of defendant's appellate claims.

2019—*Nahlawi v. Nahlawi*, 189 Conn. App. 825, 209 A.3d 723.

Trial court erred in entering a final child custody and visitation order that incorporated a pendente lite parenting plan stipulation that had been superseded by a subsequent pendente lite parenting plan that had been agreed to by the parties.

2018—*Fredo v. Fredo*, 185 Conn. App. 252, 196 A.3d 1235.

Trial court erred in granting plaintiff's motion to dismiss defendant's motion for modification of child support for lack of subject matter jurisdiction where court had subject matter jurisdiction pursuant to General Statutes §§ 46b-1 and 46b-86(a).

2017—*Puff v. Puff*, 177 Conn. App. 103, 171 A.3d 1076.

Trial court did not err in finding the oral agreement of the parties, put on the record, to be an enforceable agreement where the parties demonstrated an intent to resolve the matter at the hearing and the material terms of the agreement were agreed upon by the parties.

2017—*Medeiros v. Medeiros*, 175 Conn. App. 174, 167 A.3d 967.

Court erred in awarding compensatory damages to the plaintiff without a showing that the plaintiff suffered any damages aside from attorney's and marshal's fees.

2017—*Grant v. Grant*, 171 Conn. App. 851, 158 A.3d 419.

Court erred in finding that the defendant had expended funds from his retirement account in violation of the automatic orders without identifying the specific expenditures that violated such orders; in ordering the defendant to pay the plaintiff $30,425.98 from his retirement account because the court did not make any findings pertaining to the defendant's ability to comply with the order, and in awarding plaintiff monies for contributions to property the court concluded the defendant was sole owner of, where court did not make any findings about the fair market value, location, or defendant's ability to comply with the order.

2017—*Rubenstein v. Rubenstein*, 172 Conn. App. 370, 160 A.3d 419.

Change in circumstances was not solely plaintiffs increase in income due to inheritance, but was the worsening circumstances of the defendant (thus *Dan v. Dan* was inapposite).

2017—*Watkins v. Demos*, 172 Conn. App. 730, 161 A.3d 655.

Denial of plaintiff's motion to open based on mutual mistake was not clearly erroneous.

2017—*Bauer v. Bauer*, 173 Conn. App. 595, 164 A.3d 796.

Any error committed by the trial court in excluding evidence related to the reduction in alimony obligation was harmless.

2017—*LeSueur v. LeSueur*, 172 Conn. App. 767, 162 A.3d 32.

Trial court did not err in declining to grant a child support overpayment credit retroactively to date of service.

2017—*Pressley v. Johnson*, 173 Conn. App. 402, 162 A.3d 751.

Trial court erred in denying her motion for contempt and finding that the defendant did not owe her an arrearage for the work related child care expenses she had incurred.

2017—*Richman v. Wallman*, 172 Conn. App. 616, 161 A.3d 666.

The court did not erroneously hold the plaintiff in contempt where the court did not rule on the defendant's motion for contempt.

2017—*In re Harmony Q.*, 171 Conn. App. 568, 157 A.3d 137.

Court's ultimate conclusion that the respondent failed to achieve sufficient rehabilitation that was not clearly erroneous.

2017—*In re Savannah Y.*, 172 Conn. App. 266, 325 Conn. 925.

Court did not err in ruling DCF had made reasonable efforts to reunify where multiple attempts were made by DCF but the respondent failed to respond or comply.

2017—*In re Luis N.*, 175 Conn. App. 271, 165 A.3d 1270, *related proceeding at* 175 Conn. App. 307, 167 A.3d 476.

Any errors by the court in permitting the Department of Children and Families to meet with the minor children ex parte was harmless and was not a violation of the respondent's constitutional rights under *State v. Golding*, 213 Conn. 233, 567 A.2d 823 (Conn. 1989).

2017—*Robinson v. Robinson*, 172 Conn. App. 393, 160 A.3d 376.

Courts finding of shared custody was not clearly erroneous where there was no set parenting in schedule and children came and went freely between both parents.

2016—*Nuzzi v. Nuzzi*, 164 Conn. App. 751, 138 A.3d 979.

The trial court erred by denying a party a de novo hearing on the basis of staleness, where the separation agreement required a de novo review of a support obligation and the moving party had filed a motion to modify four years prior but had failed to act on it.

1994—*Borkowski v. Borkowski*, 228 Conn. 729, 638 A.2d 1060.

A party is entitled to relief from the trial court's improper rulings only if one or more of the rulings are harmful; admission of improper evidence which favors the appellant cannot be grounds for error.

1993—*Cahn v. Cahn*, 26 Conn. App. 720, 603 A.2d 759, *aff'd*, 225 Conn. 666, 626 A.2d 296.

When claim is not made at trial, Appellate Court can consider it under the plain error standard.

1992—*Bartley v. Bartley*, 27 Conn. App. 195, 604 A.2d 1343.

Plain error found when court entered an order without a hearing, even though no party raised the error on appeal.

1990—*Sachs v. Sachs*, 22 Conn. App. 410, 578 A.2d 649.

Harmless error does not require reversal.

1990—*Brash v. Brash*, 20 Conn. App. 609, 569 A.2d 44.

Plain error rule can be invoked when error is not cited by complaining party during trial.

1989—*Ricciardi v. Ricciardi*, 18 Conn. App. 826, 559 A.2d 1193.

Appellant has the burden of showing error in judgment.

1989—*Main v. Main*, 17 Conn. App. 670, 555 A.2d 997.

Error in evidentiary ruling may be harmless.

1989—*Buchetto v. Haggquist*, 17 Conn. App. 544, 554 A.2d 763.

Assignments of error which are not briefed beyond a statement of claim will not be reviewed by court.

1989—*Breen v. Breen*, 18 Conn. App. 166, 557 A.2d 140.

Failure to grant a continuance because witnesses were late was not error.

1988—*DeVellis v. DeVellis*, 15 Conn. App. 318, 544 A.2d 639.

Failure to award alimony in a 20-year marriage was not error.

1987—*Voloshin v. Voloshin*, 12 Conn. App. 626, 533 A.2d 573.

Plain error rule can be invoked when error is not cited by complaining party during trial.

1987—*Cohen v. Cohen*, 11 Conn. App. 241, 527 A.2d 245.

Plain error not brought to the attention of trial court may be noted by Appellate Court.

1986—*Evans v. Santoro*, 6 Conn. App. 707, 507 A.2d 1007.

Error which does not affect result is harmless.

1985—*Levy v. Levy*, 5 Conn. App. 185, 497 A.2d 430.

No reversible error solely due to an inappropriate choice of words.

1985—*Solla v. Solla*, 3 Conn. App. 415, 489 A.2d 395.

Judgment will not stand if the error of fact is non-crucial.

1985—*Tomanelli v. Tomanelli*, 5 Conn. App. 149, 497 A.2d 91.

Error cannot be found without transcript.

1985—*Trubowitz v. Trubowitz*, 5 Conn. App. 681, 502 A.2d 940.

Foundation of court's judgment was not faulty.

1983—*Wolk v. Wolk*, 191 Conn. 328, 464 A.2d 780.

Appellate court held that defendant's testimony as to the valuation of plaintiff's jewelry was improperly admitted since the defendant was neither the owner of the jewelry nor an expert but that the ruling was harmless because there was nothing in the memorandum of decision to indicate that the court relied upon the defendant's valuation of the jewelry in making its financial awards.

1983—*Sands v. Sands*, 188 Conn. 98, 448 A.2d 822.

Claims of error will be considered if raised at trial.

CHAPTER 16

FAMILY LAW PRACTICE, FEES AND ATTORNEYS GENERALLY

SYNOPSIS

§ 16.01 Expert Testimony

2010—*Law Offices of Robert K. Walsh, LLC v. Natarajan*, 124 Conn. App. 860, 7 A.3d 391.

The trial court properly rejected a counterclaim for legal malpractice because it was unsupported by expert testimony.

2007—*McGuire v. McGuire*, 102 Conn. App. 79, 924 A.2d 886.

Report of physician retained for trial preparation only and not to provide treatment or expert testimony is not discoverable. Providing expert witness's report does not by itself satisfy Practice Book Sec. 220(d) disclosure.

2004—*Richards v. Richards*, 82 Conn. App. 372, 844 A.2d 889.

Expert testimony was not required.

2002—*Sowinski v. Sowinski*, 72 Conn. App. 25, 804 A.2d 872.

Court erred in admitting into evidence letter reviewed, but not relied upon, by expert appraiser.

1993—*Knock v. Knock*, 224 Conn. 776, 621 A.2d 267.

Expert is one who has a special skill or knowledge beyond the average juror, that, as properly applied, would be helpful to the determination of an ultimate issue; failure to request continuance after untimely disclosure of expert may prevent later objection to the witness' testimony; court has discretion to allow expert testimony despite failure to designate within time limits.

1993—*Ashton v. Ashton*, 31 Conn. App. 736, 627 A.2d 943.

Expert witness disclosed two days before trial was precluded from testifying.

1991—*Polomski v. Polomski*, 24 Conn. App. 491, 589 A.2d 378.

Court may accept or reject testimony of a real estate appraiser in whole or in part.

1990—*In re Barbara J.*, 215 Conn. 31, 574 A.2d 203.

An expert may base his or her opinions on facts or data not in evidence provided they are the type reasonably relied on by experts in a particular field; expert opinion that is partly derived from written sources is admissible.

1989—*Weinstein v. Weinstein*, 18 Conn. App. 622, 561 A.2d 443.

Test of admissibility of expert testimony is whether the witness has a special skill, knowledge or experience that would assist the trier of fact in determining an issue; whether a witness is qualified to testify as an expert is a matter that rests in the sound discretion of the trial court and, in this case, because expert witness had not examined documents that would enable him to value a business, there was no basis for him to render an opinion and the testimony was inadmissible.

1988—*Blake v. Blake*, 207 Conn. 217, 541 A.2d 1201.

Delay between expert's report and testimony affect its weight but not its admissibility.

§ 16.02 Attorney-Client Relationship

2019—*Dubinsky v. Riccio*, 194 Conn. App. 588, 221 A.3d 906.

In action to recover damages from defendant attorney for breach of contract and for legal malpractice in connection with defendant's representation of plaintiff in a divorce proceeding, trial court properly granted defendant's motion for summary judgment as to the malpractice claim.

2003—*DeLeo v. Nusbaum*, 263 Conn. 588, 821 A.2d 744.

Attorney-client relationship continues until the formal or de facto termination of that relationship for purposes of the continuous representation doctrine.

1994—*Hill v. Hill*, 35 Conn. App. 160, 644 A.2d 951.

Attorney leaving the courtroom without permission did not constitute a withdrawal of his appearance.

1993—*Matza v. Matza*, 226 Conn. 166, 627 A.2d 414.

There is no right to an evidentiary hearing on an attorney's right to withdraw.

1991—*Simms v. Simms*, 25 Conn. App. 231, 593 A.2d 161.

Attorneys have absolute immunity from claims of fraud and intentional infliction of emotional distress arising out of their conduct during proceedings.

§ 16.03 Attorney and Guardian ad Litem Fees

2024—*Hallock v. Hallock*, 228 Conn. App. 81, 324 A.3d 193.

Trial court did not apply an improper legal standard to the defendant's claim for attorney's fees. The court considered the factors in Conn. Gen. Stat. § 46b-82 and determined that an attorney's fees award was not warranted given its other financial orders and that those orders would not be frustrated in the absence of such an award.

2024—*Czunas v. Mancini*, 226 Conn. App. 256, 317 A.3d 843.

Trial court did not abuse its discretion in awarding $10,000 to the plaintiff to defend against this appeal because, pursuant to Conn. Gen. Stat. § 46b-62(a), the court based the award of attorney's fees on its determination that the defendant had substantial liquid assets that the plaintiff did not have. This determination was supported by the parties' financial affidavits.

2024—*Y.H. v. J.B.*, 224 Conn. App. 793, 313 A.3d 1245.

Trial court improperly awarded $40,000 in attorney's fees to the plaintiff. To the extent the award was imposed as a sanction for the defendant's contempt under Conn. Gen. Stat. § 46b-87, the award constituted an abuse of the court's discretion, which entitled the defendant to a new hearing as to the appropriate sanction for his wilful violation of the court's orders because the court did not cite any evidence in the record that the $40,000 of attorney's fees related to the plaintiff's three motions for contempt. To the extent that the award of attorney's fees was made pursuant to Conn. Gen. Stat. § 46b-62(a), this issue also had to be remanded for reconsideration in light of the new financial orders that would be issued on remand.

2023—*Simpson v. Simpson*, 222 Conn. App. 466, 306 A.3d 477.

Because the Appellate Court reversed the trial court's postjudgment financial orders challenged on appeal, it also had to reverse the trial court's award of attorney's fees related to those orders.

2022—*Seder v. Errato*, 211 Conn. App. 167, 272 A.3d 252.

Trial court did not abuse its discretion ordering defendant to pay towards plaintiff's legal fees for trial and appeal despite defendant's argument that plaintiff had sufficient funds. The court determined that the award of fees were warranted pursuant to Conn. Gen. Stat. § 46b-62(a) and because of defendant's litigation misconduct. The appellate court found no support in the record that the trial court had abused its discretion in ordering attorney's fees as it did. An abuse of discretion will be found only if the appellate court finds that the trial court could not have reasonably concluded as it did. *Misthopoulos v. Misthopoulos*, 297 Conn. 358, 386, 999 A.2d 721 (2010).

2022—*Taber v. Taber*, 210 Conn. App. 331, 269 A.3d 963.

Trial court did not abuse its discretion in ordering defendant to make weekly payments on the total arrearage of guardian ad litem fees. The court held a hearing to address the fees and heard testimony about defendant's financial resources and ability to pay bills. It also considered the parties' respective financial circumstances.

2022—*Zakko v. Kasir*, 209 Conn. App. 619, 269 A.3d 220.

Trial court abused its discretion in awarding plaintiff attorney's fees. An abuse of discretion in granting attorney's fees will be found only if the appellate court determines the trial court could not have reasonably reached this conclusion. *See Pena v. Gladstone*, 168 Conn. App. 175, 146 A.3d 51 (2016). Here, it was not reasonable for the trial court to conclude plaintiff did not have ample liquid funds after the court expressly refused to determine whether funds she received from her family were loans or gifts. Moreover, the trial court's factual finding that plaintiff had only $3,000 in bank accounts was clearly erroneous when she testified she had access to nearly $30,000 in an account she held jointly with her son.

2021—*McCormick v. Terrell*, 208 Conn. App. 580, 266 A.3d 182.

The trial court did not abuse its broad discretion in awarding the plaintiff $7,500 in attorney's fees because, pursuant to *Maguire v. Maguire*, 222 Conn. 32, 608 A.2d 79 (1992), it expressly found that failure to award fees would substantially undermine other financial orders of the court. The trial court was not required to make an explicit finding that the plaintiff did not have ample assets with which to pay her own attorney's fees.

2021—*M.S. v. P.S.*, 203 Conn. App. 377, 248 A.3d 778.

The Appellate Court affirmed an order granting the plaintiff's motion for attorney's fees pendente lite, finding that the trial court appropriately considered the experience of one of her attorneys in assessing the reasonableness of the fee request and the resulting fee award was not an abuse of discretion. Said attorney had represented the plaintiff in a restraining order hearing, but had not previously conducted a restraining order hearing. The trial court found that it was not unusual for more experienced attorneys at the firm to mentor this attorney, given her experience at the time, but certain billing entries by partners were excessive. The trial court identified on the record examples of billing entries it was reducing. It also found that although the fees were not easy to pay, the defendant had the assets to make the payment.

2019—*Peters v. Senman*, 193 Conn. App. 766, 220 A.3d 114.

Trial court did not abuse its broad discretion to award attorney's fees when it concluded that plaintiff was in a financial position to contribute to a portion of defendant's fees after considering all of the relevant statutory criteria, defendant's financial testimony, evidence and financial affidavit, evidence of the parties' lifestyle, and other credible evidence.

2019—*De Almeida-Kennedy v. Kennedy*, 188 Conn. App. 670, 205 A.3d 704.

The trial court abused its discretion in granting the mother attorney's fees without making a specific finding of bad faith. The court found no evidence that the defendant brought the motion for modification on bad faith, and reversed the trial court's award of attorney fees.

2018—*Brochard v. Brochard*, 185 Conn. App. 204, 196 A.3d 1171.

Trial court did not abuse discretion in denying defendant's motion for modification of a court order allocating guardian ad litem fees where defendant failed to prove a substantial change of circumstances since the entry of that order.

2017—*Lederle v. Spivey*, 174 Conn. App. 592, 166 A.3d 636.

Trial court abused its discretion in finding the defendant's claims in prior appeal were entirely without color and awarding fees based on that conclusion.

2017—*Rinfret v. Porter*, 173 Conn. App. 498, 164 A.3d 812.

Trial court did not find with adequate specificity that the plaintiff's actions were entirely without color justifying attorneys' fees.

2016—*Pena v. Gladstone*, 168 Conn. App. 141, 144 A.3d 1085.

A $75,000 award of counsel fees for future services was warranted, however, the inclusion of an award for past unrelated legal services was improper and remanded to be reduced by the amount awarded for such past services.

Trial court did not abuse discretion in refusing to award fees to a party who failed to make full and frank disclosure of his financial circumstances. Conn. Gen. Stat. § 46b-62 requires an analysis of the overall financial resources of both parties, and not the mere ability or inability to pay.

2016—*Szymonik v. Szymonik*, 167 Conn. App. 641, 144 A.3d 457.

Former husband's challenge of the trial court's characterization of guardian ad litem fees as being "in the nature of child support" was rendered moot, where former husband entered into a voluntary fee agreement with guardian ad litem.

2016—*O'Toole v. Hernandez*, 163 Conn. App. 565, 137 A.3d 52.

A family support magistrate did not err in awarding counsel fees to a party based upon a finding of contempt in magistrate's court.

2015—*Olszewski v. Jordan*, 315 Conn. 618, 109 A.3d 910.

Attorneys are not entitled to equitable charging liens on marital assets for fees and expenses incurred in obtaining judgments for their clients in marital dissolution proceedings.

2015—*Anderson v. Anderson*, 160 Conn. App. 341, 125 A.3d 606.

No abuse of discretion in awarding attorney's fees of $2,500.

2014—*Giordano v. Giordano*, 153 Conn. App. 343, 101 A.3d 327.

Pursuant to Conn. Gen. Stat. § 46b-87, a trial court may, in the exercise of its discretion, award attorney fees to the prevailing party in contempt proceedings.

2014—*Rostad v. Hirsch*, 148 Conn. App. 441, 85 A.3d 1212.

No abuse of discretion for $127,553 in attorney's fees under Conn. Gen. Stat. § 46b-171 where the fees were necessitated by the aggressive defense interposed by the other party, and interest on counsel fees was properly awarded.

2013—*Colbert v. Carr*, 140 Conn. App. 229, 57 A.3d 878.

Request for attorney's fees properly denied in paternity action where father acknowledged paternity and had provided financial support for the child but had not followed all formal requirements for acknowledging paternity.

2013—*Kavanah v. Kavanah*, 142 Conn. App. 775, 66 A.3d 922.

Sua sponte award of guardian ad litem fees was an abuse of discretion.

2012—*Richter v. Richter*, 137 Conn. App. 231, 48 A.3d 686.

There was no deprivation of plaintiff's right to a hearing in order to question the defendant's affidavit of fees before awarding fees where the court repeatedly attempted to schedule a hearing and plaintiff failed to participate.

2012—*Larson v. Larson*, 138 Conn. App. 272, 51 A.3d 411.

No abuse of discretion where the court ordered a party to pay counsel fees and the party did not challenge the reasonableness of the fees.

2012—*Berzins v. Berzins*, 306 Conn. 651, 51 A.3d 941.

Court's award of attorney's fees for litigation misconduct was outside the court's authority because there was no finding of bad faith.

2010—*Behrns v. Behrns*, 124 Conn. App. 794, 6 A.3d 184.

Trial court could properly award attorney's fees under Conn. Gen. Stat. § 46b-87 dating back to the filing of the motion for contempt nine years prior.

2009—*Buehler v. Buehler*, 117 Conn. App. 304, 978 A.2d 1141.

Trial court did not abuse its discretion by ordering fees for guardian ad litem and counsel for guardian ad litem, even though neither attorney had signed retainer agreement with plaintiff.

2008—*Gil v. Gil*, 110 Conn. App. 798, 956 A.2d 593.

Trial court did not abuse discretion by awarding counsel fees for legal work performed in a contempt proceeding and in an appeal. It could consider the plaintiff's litigation misconduct. The contingency fee agreement for legal services did not violate the Rules of Professional Conduct. The commentary to Rule 1.5(d) clearly permits such agreements for recovery of post-judgment balances due for "support, alimony or other financial orders."

2007—*Ramin v. Ramin*, 281 Conn. 324, 915 A.2d 790.

Despite each party having ample liquid funds, court can award attorney's fees to address litigation misconduct, where not doing so would undermine other orders.

2005—*Grimm v. Grimm*, 276 Conn. 377, 886 A.2d 391.

Award of $100,000 in attorneys' fees after lengthy action for dissolution upheld despite wife's possession of ample liquid funds where such award was necessary to avoid undermining trial court's other financial orders.

2004—*Marfo v. Hagan*, 83 Conn. App. 902, 853 A.2d 650.

Court ordered $50,000 in counsel fees to wife's attorney.

2003—*Lamacchia v. Chilinsky*, 79 Conn. App. 372, 830 A.2d 329.

Court's order to have plaintiff pay guardian ad litem 80% of present and future legal fees was reversed as too speculative.

2003—*Gina M.G. v. William C.*, 77 Conn. App. 582, 823 A.2d 1274.

Award of legal fees reasonable based on expenses incurred in connection with numerous post-judgment motions, all of which stemmed from plaintiff's violation of child support visitation order.

2003—*Jewett v. Jewett*, 265 Conn. 669, 830 A.2d 193.

Court ordered defendant to pay attorneys' fees for defendant's willful failure to comply with court order requiring him to produce financial business records for scheduled deposition.

2003—*Bee v. Bee*, 79 Conn. App. 783, 831 A.2d 833.

A $25,000 award of counsel fees was valid.

2002—*Esposito v. Esposito*, 71 Conn. App. 744, 804 A.2d 846.

Trial court's $500 counsel fees award in contempt motion upheld.

1990—*Febbroriello v. Febbroriello*, 21 Conn. App. 200, 572 A.2d 1032.

Courts have knowledge of what a reasonable attorney fee would be and statement of attorney fees owed on financial affidavit was evidence of costs incurred.

1996—*Durkin v. Durkin*, 43 Conn. App. 659, 685 A.2d 344.

Party's presence was not necessary for a motion for counsel fees on appeal.

1996—*Ottawa v. Ottawa*, 40 Conn. App. 458, 671 A.2d 854.

Party can waive right to hearing on issue of counsel fees.

1994—*Clement v. Clement*, 34 Conn. App. 641, 643 A.2d 874.

Counsel fees were awarded on appeal.

1994—*Farrell v. Farrell*, 36 Conn. App. 305, 650 A.2d 608.

Third parties are not required to pay counsel fees in a dissolution action.

1993—*Castro v. Castro*, 31 Conn. App. 761, 627 A.2d 452.

Court cannot award counsel fees without first conducting a hearing to allow the opposing party to challenge the reasonableness of the fees or the services rendered.

1993—*Tessitore v. Tessitore*, 31 Conn. App. 40, 623 A.2d 496.

Court must consider statutory criteria in awarding counsel fees pending appeal.

1993—*Miller v. Kirshner*, 225 Conn. 185, 621 A.2d 1326.

Attorney fees to defend appeal of paternity judgment can be awarded after the appeal; expert testimony is not required to prove the reasonableness of attorney fees awarded under Conn. Gen. Stat. § 46b-62 or Conn. Gen. Stat. § 46b-171.

1993—*Diamond v. Diamond*, 32 Conn. App. 733, 631 A.2d 1157.

Counsel fees cannot be awarded by judge for a prior hearing before a different judge without evidence.

1992—*Maguire v. Maguire*, 222 Conn. 32, 608 A.2d 79.

Court must find that an award of counsel fees was necessary in order to avoid undermining its other financial orders.

1991—*Monnier v. Monnier*, 24 Conn. App. 833, 591 A.2d 825.

Bills of attorney for minor child must be presented to determine reasonableness of fee.

1990—*Messina v. Messina*, 22 Conn. App. 136, 576 A.2d 579.

Court must look to financial ability of parties in awarding fees to defend an appeal from a contempt citation.

1989—*Schott v. Schott*, 18 Conn. App. 333, 557 A.2d 936.

Appellate court cannot order attorney fees.

1988—*Greene v. Greene*, 13 Conn. App. 512, 537 A.2d 537.

Post-trial award of attorney fees to defend an appeal is allowable; counsel fees of $5,000 awarded to defend appeal; total financial resources of the parties must be considered in awarding counsel fees.

1988—*Mailly v. Mailly*, 13 Conn. App. 185, 535 A.2d 385.

Fees and transcript costs awarded for appeal.

1988—*Mallory v. Mallory*, 207 Conn. 48, 539 A.2d 995.

Loan by parents to husband for attorney fees cannot be basis or order that husband pay wife's attorney fees on appeal.

1987—*Voloshin v. Voloshin*, 12 Conn. App. 626, 533 A.2d 573.

Trial court must consider the total financial resources of the parties in light of the statutory criteria in awarding attorney fees.

1987—*Costa v. Costa*, 11 Conn. App. 74, 526 A.2d 4.

Determination that spouse's counsel fees should be paid can be made without evidence, but evidence must be presented to set the amount.

1987—*Palazzo v. Palazzo*, 9 Conn. App. 486, 519 A.2d 1230.

Decision to award attorney fee should not undermine other awards.

1987—*Bielen v. Bielen*, 12 Conn. App. 513, 531 A.2d 941.

Attorney fees were awarded post-judgment without financial affidavits when no objection was raised.

1986—*Niles v. Niles*, 9 Conn. App. 240, 518 A.2d 932.

Court can rely on its own knowledge in determining reasonableness of attorney fees in the absence of evidence.

1986—*Jetmore v. Jetmore*, 6 Conn. App. 632, 507 A.2d 116.

Availability of cash to pay attorney fees is not an absolute standard.

1986—*Moll v. Gianetti*, 8 Conn. App. 50, 510 A.2d 1009.

Attorney fees were awarded in a custody action when the parents were never married.

1985—*Benson v. Benson*, 5 Conn. App. 95, 497 A.2d 64.

The court may order either spouse to pay the reasonable attorney's fees of the other in accordance with their respective financial abilities and the criteria set forth in Conn. Gen. Stat. § 46b-82; Conn. Gen. Stat. § 46b-1 includes family matters such as custody under the Uniform Child Custody Jurisdiction Act (UCCJA).

1981—*Arrigoni v. Arrigoni*, 184 Conn. 513, 440 A.2d 206.

A definitive award of counsel fees should not ordinarily be made until after a trial where evidence relating to factors such as the causes for the dissolution of the marriage, the age, health, station, occupation, amount and sources of income, vocational skills, employability, estate, liabilities, and needs of each of the parties, can be heard.

1978—*Marcus v. Marcus*, 175 Conn. 138, 394 A.2d 727.

Denial of a motion for counsel fees was not an abuse of discretion where the movant consented to the court taking the motion on the papers.

§ 16.04 Arbitration

2018—*Jenkins v. Jenkins*, 186 Conn. App. 641, 200 A.3d 1193.

Trial court properly denied plaintiff's motion to vacate arbitration award on the basis of the arbitrator's refusal to allow plaintiff's expert to testify and alleged bias where there was no record of the arbitration proceeding and expert's testimony was duplicative.

2018—*Toland v. Toland*, 179 Conn. App. 800, 182 A.3d 651.

Judicial review of arbitrator's ruling was limited to legal conclusions not findings of facts as stated in the arbitration agreement.

2016—*LaFrance v. Lodmell*, 322 Conn. 828, 144 A.3d 373.

Arbitration agreement entered into as part of prenuptial agreement was subject to statutory provision governing agreements to arbitrate in an action for dissolution of marriage. Superior Court properly determined the scope of the parties' agreement to arbitrate, and that it would be fair and equitable to arbitrate only those issues that were within the scope of the parties' prenuptial agreement.

2015—*Budrawich v. Budrawich*, 156 Conn. App. 628, 115 A.3d 39.

Under statute governing arbitration in dissolution of marriage actions, a court does not have the authority to order parties to submit issues to arbitration absent a voluntary arbitration agreement executed between the parties.

§ 16.05 Continuance or Adjournment

2023—*Anderson-Harris v. Harris*, 221 Conn. App. 222, 301 A.3d 1090.

Trial court did not abuse its discretion in denying Plaintiff's two July 2021 motions for continuance. To prove an abuse of discretion, an appellant must show that the trial court's denial of a request for a continuance was arbitrary. Plaintiff had several months to prepare for trial, the matter had been pending for about a year, and the issue of custody was not subject to a final resolution but had been deferred so that family relations could conduct a single issue evaluation as to whether Plaintiff was ready to assume a joint custodial role in her children's lives. On the basis of these facts, the trial court was within its discretion when it denied the motions.

2020—*Bevilacqua v. Bevilacqua*, 201 Conn. App. 261, 242 A.3d 542.

The trial court did not abuse its discretion in denying the defendant's motion for a continuance of trial. The long pendency of the case was a proper factor for the trial court to consider. The defendant's unsubstantiated claim that he could not miss more days of work was not compelling.

2016—*Mensah v. Mensah*, 167 Conn. App. 219, 143 A.3d 622.

Trial court's denial of a Motion for Continuance filed at 10:00 a.m. the morning of trial was not an abuse of discretion.

2014—*Cinotti v. Divers*, 151 Conn. App. 297, 94 A.3d 1212.

Trial court properly denied plaintiff's request for additional continuances of the trial date.

2009—*Tyler v. Shenkman-Tyler*, 115 Conn. App. 521, 973 A.2d 163.

Denial of continuance of dissolution trial until resolution of a criminal matter did not deprive husband of fundamental due process rights.

2009—*Dionne v. Dionne*, 115 Conn. App. 488, 972 A.2d 791.

Court did not abuse its discretion by granting a six week continuance of a contempt hearing, despite attorney's representation that check was in the mail. Obligor ultimately found in contempt for nonpayment during the previous six weeks.

2002—*Hammick v. Hammick*, 71 Conn. App. 680, 803 A.2d 373.

Court's refusal to continue trial due to wife's being 7-months pregnant upheld.

1987—*Atkins v. Atkins*, 13 Conn. App. 114, 534 A.2d 909.

Courts have sole discretion to deny a continuance and proceed with a hearing without the presence of a party.

CHAPTER 17

FINANCIAL AFFIDAVITS

SYNOPSIS

§ 17.01 Financial Affidavits and Duty to Disclose

2015—*Fulton v. Fulton*, 156 Conn. App. 739, 116 A.3d 311.

Trial court, in post judgment modification action, abused its discretion when it concluded that it was absolutely bound by the figures in ex-husband's financial affidavit submitted at the time of the dissolution judgment.

2013—*Mensah v. Mensah*, 145 Conn. App. 644, 75 A.3d 92.

There is a heightened duty to disclose in marital dissolution cases.

2012—*Brody v. Brody*, 136 Conn. App. 773, 51 A.3d 1121.

Defendant's refusal to produce financial records hampered the trial court's ability to calculate net income and therefore the trial court properly looked to the defendant's expenses and lifestyle when calculating the alimony award.

2011—*Brown v. Brown*, 130 Conn. App. 522, 24 A.3d 1261.

Trial court did not improperly exclude evidence regarding the husband's financial condition at the time of trial where parties stipulated that expert valuations of real estate investments would be as of a prior date.

2010—*Bento v. Bento*, 125 Conn. App. 229, 8 A.3d 531.

The trial court abused its discretion by equally dividing responsibility for a corporate debt without making any findings of fact or law. Neither party's financial affidavit had listed the corporate debt as a liability, and there was no finding that either owed the debt. This issue was severable and did not impact the mosaic of financial orders. The Appellate Court remanded with direction to vacate the order dividing the corporate debt.

2005—*Bartels v. Bartels*, 85 Conn. App. 772, 858 A.2d 879.

Outrageous discrepancies on defendant's financial affidavit adversely affected his credibility and court awarded defendant no alimony.

2005—*Weinstein v. Weinstein*, 275 Conn. 671, 882 A.2d 53.

Appellate court found that the husband intentionally misrepresented the value of the company to deceive his wife and reversed and remanded case.

1999—*Hayward v. Hayward*, 53 Conn. App. 1, 752 A.2d 1087.

Record for appellate review was adequate where court had one party's financial affidavit, a transcript of the hearing, and the trial court's memorandum of decision.

1993—*Ashton v. Ashton*, 31 Conn. App. 736, 627 A.2d 943.

Estimates on financial affidavit were properly relied on by court.

1990—*Cabrera v. Cabrera*, 23 Conn. App. 330, 580 A.2d 1227.

Court can enter financial orders even if plaintiff has not submitted a sworn financial affidavit as long as there was evidence of the plaintiff's financial condition.

1990—*Greger v. Greger*, 22 Conn. App. 596, 578 A.2d 162.

Court's finding that husband filed a fraudulent financial affidavit concealing 99% of his assets and that these assets probably would have affected financial orders required that the judgment be opened.

1990—*Sachs v. Sachs*, 22 Conn. App. 410, 578 A.2d 649.

Court's acceptance of a financial affidavit on the day of trial is a matter within the broad discretion of the court.

1989—*Kinderman v. Kinderman*, 19 Conn. App. 534, 562 A.2d 1151.

Case was remanded because value for marital home accepted by court was taken from an outdated financial affidavit.

1987—*Cohen v. Cohen*, 11 Conn. App. 241, 527 A.2d 245.

Information in wife's financial affidavit was sufficiently probative to support the court's order of periodic alimony.

1987—*Cuneo v. Cuneo*, 12 Conn. App. 702, 533 A.2d 1226.

Court must consider finances of parties at time of hearing following remand in fixing alimony and property orders.

1987—*Gelinas v. Gelinas*, 10 Conn. App. 167, 522 A.2d 295.

Diligence must be used to expose fraud.

1987—*Voloshin v. Voloshin*, 12 Conn. App. 626, 533 A.2d 573.

Court can draw adverse inferences as to party's credibility in areas other than finances when he files misleading financial affidavit.

1982—*Baker v. Baker*, 187 Conn. 315, 445 A.2d 912.

When it becomes clear to a trial court that an agreement has been concealed from it and that the parties had filed inaccurate and misleading financial affidavits, the court, at the very least, should order sua sponte that the judgment be opened for the purpose of rehearing the financial and property issues.

1980—*Pack v. Pack*, 180 Conn. 211, 429 A.2d 477.

The trial court had sufficient financial information before it upon which to base both its present and future alimony orders.

1980—*Friedman v. Friedman*, 180 Conn. 132, 429 A.2d 823.

Award of alimony is unsupported by trial court's finding where the record and briefs do not include evidence of the parties' financial circumstances such as financial affidavits.

CHAPTER 18

MISCELLANEOUS

SYNOPSIS

§ 18.01 Gifts

2019—*Nappo v. Nappo*, 188 Conn. App. 574, 205 A.3d 723.

Court correctly considered the income of ex-husband's current wife because it was relevant to his current expenses, a material factor in determining his current net income and, therefore, his ability to pay increased alimony. There was no evidence that the money was given as a loan, rather than as a gift.

2008—*Picton v. Picton*, 111 Conn. App. 143, 958 A.2d 763.

Trial court gave properly considered recurring gifts from wife's mother in alimony award.

2003—*Zahringer v. Zahringer*, 262 Conn. 360, 815 A.2d 75.

Financial assistance provided by spouse's parent to be considered in establishing alimony and support obligation. Trial court's finding that payments from parents were loans, not gifts, was not clearly erroneous.

1994—*Askinazi v. Askinazi*, 34 Conn. App. 328, 641 A.2d 413.

Evidence of periodic gifts to defendant from her family was properly relied on by the court.

§ 18.02 Debts and Liabilities

2022—*Lawrence v. Gude*, 216 Conn. App. 624, 285 A.3d 1198.

In an action for damages arising from a residential lease against married Defendants, the trial court erred by failing to impose joint and several spousal liability as to Wife, who had not signed the lease, pursuant to Conn. Gen. Stat. § 46b-37(b) and improperly found that she was not liable. Husband and Wife had admitted they were married and were occupying the premises as their primary residence. Wife was liable regardless of whether had she signed the lease. Therefore, Plaintiff was entitled to claim back rent and use and occupancy under the lease from Wife, pursuant to § 46b-37(b)(3). Judgment was reversed as to Wife only and the case was remanded with direction to render a judgment against Wife in the amount the trial court had determined for back rent and use and occupancy. Judgment was affirmed in all other respects.

2011—*Kleinman v. Chapnick*, 131 Conn. App. 812, 30 A.3d 3.

Court did not create an ambiguity when it ordered that each party be responsible for liabilities on their respective financial affidavits.

2011—*Reizfeld v. Reizfeld*, 125 Conn. App. 782, 40 A.3d 320.

A premarital agreement that precluded either party from seeking "payment for liabilities from the other" in a dissolution action was unambiguous, and it precluded the court from awarding attorney's fees.

2011—*Perry v. Perry*, 130 Conn. App. 720, 24 A.3d 1269.

Post-judgment order that each party would be responsible for the liabilities listed on their respective financial affidavits was an improper modification of equitable division.

2010—*Bento v. Bento*, 125 Conn. App. 229, 8 A.3d 531.

The trial court abused its discretion by equally dividing responsibility for a corporate debt without making any findings of fact or law. Neither party's financial affidavit had listed the corporate debt as a liability, and there was no finding that either owed the debt. This issue was severable and did not impact the mosaic of financial orders. The Appellate Court remanded with direction to vacate the order dividing the corporate debt.

2005—*Fewtrell v. Fewtrell*, 87 Conn. App. 526, 865 A.2d 1240.

Trial court had jurisdiction to entertain post-judgment motion to modify where motion was to effectuate original order regarding assignment of debt.

2000—*Osakowicz v. Osakowicz*, 57 Conn. App. 807, 750 A.2d 1135.

The court could find nothing in the record to justify requiring plaintiff wife to assume debt that defendant husband may have incurred.

1996—*Celani v. Celani (In re Celani)*, 36 C.B.C.2d 58, 194 B.R. 719 (Bankr. D. Conn.).

Issue involved balancing benefit to debtor of discharging debt arising out of divorce decree against detrimental consequences to debtor's former spouse for purposes of discharge exception.

1991—*Trella v. Trella*, 24 Conn. App. 219, 587 A.2d 162.

Ordering husband to pay debts incurred by wife during pendency of action was in effect an impermissible retroactive modification of pendente lite alimony.

1990—*Holcombe v. Holcombe*, 22 Conn. App. 363, 576 A.2d 1317.

Judgment that was silent on which party had to pay a liability intended that the party whose name the debt was in must pay it.

1990—*Brash v. Brash*, 20 Conn. App. 609, 569 A.2d 44.

Capital gains tax liability split equally when property was split 75–25.

1989—*Schott v. Schott*, 18 Conn. App. 333, 557 A.2d 936.

A debt incurred solely by the plaintiff can be paid from the proceeds of the sale of the marital home.

1987—*Forsdick v. Turgeon*, 812 F.2d 801, 16 C.B.C.2d 452.

Bankruptcy court must determine whether debtor's obligation is in the nature of alimony or support in determining which debts to discharge.

1987—*Wanatowicz v. Wanatowicz*, 12 Conn. App. 616, 533 A.2d 239.

An inability to pay alimony due to indebtedness must not be brought about by defendant's own fault.

1987—*O'Bymachow v. O'Bymachow*, 10 Conn. App. 76, 521 A.2d 599.

Payment of loan not evidenced by note is totally within party's control.

1984—*Russo v. Russo*, 1 Conn. App. 604, 474 A.2d 473.

A judgment that a defendant must pay all of the liabilities listed on his financial affidavit and save the plaintiff harmless from any claims thereon is permitted pursuant to Conn. Gen. Stat. § 46b-81.

1984—*Champion Int'l Corp. v. Ayars*, 587 F. Supp. 1274.

A requirement that a wage execution be issued only by a court in the area in which the wages are earned would unreasonably burden creditors seeking payment of lawful debts and husbands and other debtors need only move out of state to escape payment.

1982—*Beede v. Beede*, 186 Conn. 191, 440 A.2d 283.

Requiring one party to assume the joint liabilities of the parties is authorized by Conn. Gen. Stat. § 46b-81, which permits the court to assign the property of the parties in a dissolution decree.

§ 18.03 Doctrines

2016—*Olson v. Mohammadu*, 169 Conn. App. 243, 149 A.3d 198.

"Law of the case" doctrine did not render order requiring payment of child care arrearages improper.

§ 18.04 Defenses

[1] Equitable Estoppel

2018—*Doyle v. Chaplen*, 184 Conn. App. 278, 194 A.3d 1198.

Trial court properly determined that mother was not equitably estopped from opening judgment of paternity where both parties mistakenly believed that the acknowledged father was the father, acknowledged father was not prejudiced, and child would not suffer emotional and financial detriment.

2011—*Dougan v. Dougan*, 301 Conn. 361, 21 A.3d 791.

Judicial estoppel applies if: (1) a party's later position is clearly inconsistent with its earlier position; (2) the party's former position has been adopted by the court in the earlier proceeding; and (3) the party asserting the two positions would derive an unfair advantage against the party seeking estoppel.

2003—*Bouchard v. Sundberg*, 80 Conn. App. 180, 834 A.2d 744.

Trial court improperly concluded that plaintiff was estopped from raising certain issues in breach of contract claim.

2001—*W. v. W.*, 256 Conn. 657, 779 A.2d 716.

Trial court did not abuse discretion in applying doctrine of equitable estoppel.

1984—*Brock v. Cavanaugh*, 1 Conn. App. 138, 468 A.2d 1242.

Equitable estoppel is the effect of the voluntary conduct of a party whereby he is absolutely precluded, both at law and in equity, from asserting rights which might perhaps have otherwise existed as against another person, who has in good faith relied upon such conduct, and has been led thereby to change his position for the worse.

1980—*Papcun v. Papcun*, 181 Conn. 618, 436 A.2d 282.

There are two essential elements to an estoppel: (1) the party must do or say something that is intended or calculated to induce another to believe in the existence of certain facts and to act upon that belief; and (2) the other party, influenced thereby, must actually change his position or do some act to his injury which he otherwise would not have done.

[2] Laches

2013—*Kasowitz v. Kasowitz*, 140 Conn. App. 507, 59 A.3d 347.

Trial court rejected a claim of laches and found the payee's delay in filing motions reasonable where the payor claimed he was unaware of a $100,000 arrearage which had accumulated over 10 years.

2008—*Fromm v. Fromm*, 108 Conn. App. 376, 948 A.2d 328.

Laches barred collection of a decade old alimony and child support arrearage.

2000—*Burrier v. Burrier*, 59 Conn. App. 593, 758 A.2d 373.

Laches defense was unsuccessful.

1984—*Brock v. Cavanaugh*, 1 Conn. App. 138, 468 A.2d 1242.

Absent a finding of prejudice to the defendant, a trial court does not err in concluding that the plaintiff is not guilty of laches by virtue of her eight-year delay in seeking payments.

1980—*Papcun v. Papcun*, 181 Conn. 618, 436 A.2d 282.

Laches is a defense to payment of alimony arrearage and consists of two elements: (1) there must have been a delay that was inexcusable; and (2) that delay must have prejudiced the defendant as the mere lapse of time does not constitute laches.

[3] Waiver

2013—*Carpender v. Sigel*, 142 Conn. App. 379, 67 A.3d 1011.

Court improperly found laches, waiver and estoppel applied to reimbursement of expenses for extracurricular activities where the party incurred expenses seven to eight years before filing a motion for contempt and the court made no factual findings with respect to the holding.

2010—*McKenna v. Delente*, 123 Conn. App. 146, 2 A.3d 38.

Waiver of spousal benefits under pension plan was valid, both under premarital agreement and later modification of that contract.

2002—*Ford v. Ford*, 72 Conn. App. 137, 804 A.2d 215.

Trial court properly held that father owed alimony notwithstanding his claim of waiver, and his claim that parties had an agreement that he not pay.

§ 18.05 Due Process

2024—*In re T.-W.*, 223 Conn. App. 571, 309 A.3d 394.

Trial court improperly dismissed a father's motion to open judgment previously entered terminating his parental rights. The father was not present at the hearing on his motion and was not afforded an opportunity to participate remotely by telephone or video conferencing. Nothing in the transcript indicated that steps were taken to provide him with a meaningful opportunity to participate and be heard at the hearing; it simply states that counsel told the court that the father was incarcerated in the state of Washington. The father's due process rights under the 14th Amendment to the U.S. Constitution art. I, § 10 were violated because he was not given a meaningful opportunity to participate and be heard on his motion.

2023—*Buchenholz v. Buchenholz*, 221 Conn. App. 132, 300 A.3d 1233.

Defendant's federal and state due process rights were not violated by the lack of notice that Plaintiff would introduce testimony supporting the ground of intolerable cruelty. Plaintiff did not allege intolerable cruelty as the grounds for dissolution of their marriage, she did not amend her complaint to add that allegation, and the judgment was not based on that ground. Plaintiff's testimony about incidents of abuse was relevant to the issue of fault in the irretrievable in the breakdown of the parties' marriage. Defendant had sufficient time to conduct discovery and to prepare a defense with respect to Plaintiff's testimony regarding the abuse. His trial counsel did not object to her testimony and had the opportunity to cross-examine her. With the trial occurring over six months, Defendant had several months after Plaintiff first testified about incidents of abuse to offer additional evidence and witnesses or to file a motion for continuance to conduct discovery.

2023—*In re Gabriel S.*, 347 Conn. 223, 296 A.3d 829.

Trial court did not violate a father's due process rights to adequate notice when it allowed the Commissioner of Children and Families to amend its petition to allege a different ground for termination pursuant to Conn. Gen. Stat. § 17a-112(j)(3) after the initial ground was shown to be unviable. As a matter of law, Father's due process rights were not violated because he received actual notice of the grounds for the termination provision and an opportunity to respond. The record showed that although Petitioner's counsel indicated he would add § 17a-112(j)(3)(B)(i) as a ground for termination when he made the oral motion, he clarified the specific basis for termination the next day when he filed the amended summary of the facts, stating that he was relying on ground § 17a-112(j)(3)(B)(ii), and again in his written motion to amend the petition, which superseded the oral motion. After the trial court granted Petitioner's motion to file an amended petition and granted a six-week continuance to allow Father to prepare a response, Father could not reasonably have believed there was any real possibility that when the trial resumed, Petitioner would again proceed under the previous ground that had already been shown to be unviable. Nor could Father reasonably have been unsure as to whether Petitioner intended to proceed under ground (B)(i) or (B)(ii) when the written filings following and superseding the oral motion made it clear that Petitioner intended to proceed under ground (B)(ii). Father expressed no surprise or confusion at the continuation of the trial when Petitioner's counsel indicated that he was seeking termination of his parental rights pursuant to the amended summary of the facts, which was premised on ground (B)(ii). Father testified on his own behalf about his attempts to comply with the specific steps that had been provided to him to facilitate the return of his child to his custody, which evidence was relevant only to ground (B)(ii).

2023—*A.D. v. L.D.*, 220 Conn. App. 172, 297 A.3d 568.

The trial court did not deny the father's due process rights by applying the preponderance of evidence standard of proof to the mother's motion to custody. While in a hearing on a petition to terminate parental rights, due process would require the state to prove statutory criteria by clear and convincing evidence, this modification proceeding was substantially different. Similarly, he failed to demonstrate that the modification of the custody orders violated his federal constitutional right to family integrity. The father's argument that his parental rights had been effectively terminated without any means to ensure reunification or reinstitution was not persuasive. The modification orders suspended the father's access to his minor children but they also established a mechanism for him to reunify with them. He had the opportunity to have dinner with them each week. They were permitted to contact him. Their mother was required to make sure they met with a reunification therapist to assess the possibility of reunification and to keep the father reasonably informed of her decisions regarding the children. The father was also permitted to file a motion to modify the custody and visitation orders once he completed the Department of Children and Families' Intimate Partner Violence Program, giving him a course of action to reestablish his parenting access and contact with his minor children. Further, the trial court found that the father's lack of relationship with the children was due to his own actions, not the actions of their mother. The court also specifically found that the mother had encouraged the children to visit with their father after they refused to visit with him.

2022—*In re Aisjaha N.*, 343 Conn. 709, 275 A.3d 1181.

Because the record was largely silent regarding the nature of respondent's participation in a virtual trial, the record was inadequate to review her unpreserved claim that she was denied due process of law under the Fourteenth Amendment when the trial court failed to ensure that she was present by two-way video technology. The respondent did not demonstrate that the inability of parties to meaningfully participate in virtual child protection trials via two-way videoconferencing technology was a pervasive and significant problem requiring intervention by the instant court's supervisory authority over the administration of justice; neither respondent, her counsel, nor her guardian ad litem asked for technical assistance or accommodations from the trial court.

2022—*In re Annessa J.*, 343 Conn. 642, 284 A.3d 562.

The appellate court properly found that the record was inadequate for review of the mother's confrontation claim because, during the trial, the Commissioner of Children and Families and the trial court were never put on notice that the mother objected to the virtual nature of the termination of parental rights trial on the basis that it violated her right to confront the Commissioner's witnesses.

2022—*In re Ivory W.*, 342 Conn. 692, 271 A.3d 633.

The trial court did not deny mother's due process rights under the either the federal constitution or the state constitution when it denied her motion for continuance of the trial on petitions to terminate her parental rights pending conclusion of a related criminal proceeding. The mother argued that she could not testify in her own defense in the termination proceeding without jeopardizing her fifth amendment right not to incriminate herself in the criminal proceeding.

The trial court's decision to terminate her parental rights were based exclusively on clear and convincing evidence from the Commissioner of Children and Families that she had failed to rehabilitate with respect to both of her children and that as the result of her conduct in distributing sexually explicit photographs of Ivory, the child had been denied the care, guidance, or control necessary for her well-being. Further, the mother was not prevented from presenting evidence in her own defense. The only penalty she suffered as the result of her choice to invoke her fifth amendment rights was her inability to testify in her own defense. Although she had a difficult choice between invoking her fifth amendment rights and exercising her due process right to testify in her own defense, she could not cite a single case in which a court concluded that when the interests at stake in a civil proceeding are sufficiently important, the frustration of an individual's desire to testify in her own defense as the result of her choice to invoke the fifth amendment, in and of itself, is a sufficiently severe penalty to constitute compulsion under the fifth amendment.

In *State v. Geisler*, 222 Conn. 672, 684–86, 610 A.2d 1225 (1992), the appellate court set out the six factors to be considered in construing the Connecticut state constitution: (1) persuasive relevant federal precedents; (2) the text of the operative constitutional provisions; (3) historical insights into the intent of our constitutional forebears; (4) related Connecticut precedents; (5) persuasive precedents of other state courts; and (6) contemporary understandings of applicable economic and sociological norms, or as otherwise described, relevant public policies. None of the *Geisler* factors supports the respondent's claim that the trial court's denial of her motion for a continuance of the termination of parental rights proceedings pending the conclusion of the criminal proceedings violated her due process rights under the Connecticut constitution.

2021—*McNamara v. McNamara*, 207 Conn. App. 849, 263 A.3d 899.

The trial court did not violate the defendant's rights to due process when it denied her motion for continuance of the hearing on plaintiff's motion to modify custody. The defendant failed to satisfy the second prong of *Golding* because she did not meet her burden to prove that the denial of the requested continuance was of claim of constitutional magnitude.

The plaintiff sought modifications to parenting time and holiday parenting time, modifications to the method and frequency of communications between the parents, and an order that the plaintiff be awarded final decision-making authority regarding the medical, dental, orthodontic, and educational needs of the parties' children. The defendant provided no authority that denial of her requested continuance of the postjudgment hearing between two parents with joint legal custody and shared physical custody of their children is directly linked to her constitutionally protected interest in the care, custody, and control of her children.

2021—*Coleman v. Bembridge*, 207 Conn. App. 28, 263 A.3d 403.

The trial court did not violate the plaintiff's rights to due process in ordering joint physical custody because the plaintiff sought broad relief and custody was the primary contested issue at trial where the plaintiff testified, elicited testimony from a family relations counselor, cross-examined the defendant, and offered exhibits into evidence. On the basis of the evidence before it, the trial court concluded joint physical custody was in the best interests of the parties' child. Under these circumstances, particularly where the plaintiff herself requested broad relief from the court, the Appellate Court was not convinced she did not have fair notice and a reasonable opportunity to be heard as to the court's award of joint physical custody.

2021—*In re Skylar B.*, 204 Conn. App. 729, 254 A.3d 928.

A father appealed a trial court judgment terminating his parental rights, claiming the court violated his right to substantive due process guaranteed by the Fourteenth Amendment because transferring guardianship to relative foster parents was a less restrictive means to achieve permanency than terminating his parental rights. The Appellate Court declined to review the merits of his claim. Because he did not provide an adequate record for review, his claim failed the first prong of *Golding*.

The father unsuccessfully contended that the record was adequate for review under the first prong of *Golding* because his counsel had argued during closing arguments that the court should transfer guardianship to the relative foster parents instead of terminating his parental rights. However, he had not filed a motion seeking to transfer guardianship. None of the relevant parties had notice that he would argue for an alternative disposition. Only a proper motion provides requisite notice to all interested parties and the court of such an alternative disposition and evidence that is particularly relevant to a disposition of a transfer of guardianship, as opposed to evidence that would be relevant to a termination of parental rights and adoption.

2021—*In re Angela V.*, 204 Conn. App. 746, 254 A.3d 1042.

In proceedings adjudicating her three children neglected and her two older children abused, and placing the children in the temporary custody of the Department of Children and Families, the mother appealed claiming the court violated her due process rights when it denied her motion for permission to call the two older children. The trial court had two separate and independent grounds for denying the motion, one of which the mother did not challenge on appeal, rendering her challenge to the other independent ground moot. The Appellate Court was unable to provide any practical relief.

2021—*In re Riley B.*, 203 Conn. App. 627, 248 A.3d 756.

A mother's claim that the judgment terminating her parental rights violated her substantive due process rights guaranteed by the Fourteenth Amendment failed under the first prong of *Golding* because the record was inadequate for review. The record was devoid of any evidence that a maternal relative was amenable to guardianship to support the mother's claim that transferring the child to the guardianship of her relative in New Jersey would have been a less restrictive means to meet the government's goal of protecting the child and giving her permanency. In the absence of this "factual predicate" the record was insufficient for the Appellate Court to review the substantive due process claim.

2021—*In re Kiara Liz V.*, 203 Conn. App. 613, 248 A.3d 813.

The trial court's judgment terminating a father's parental rights was affirmed. The

Appellate Court declined to review the father's claim that the trial court improperly denied his request for a continuance because he did not preserve his claim at the time of trial and failed to satisfy the first prong of the test for whether an unpreserved claim may be reviewed on appeal set out in *Golding*, which requires that the record must be adequate to review the alleged claim of error. The record had scant details regarding his absence from the final day of trial; his reason(s) for failing to attend were vague and unclear.

2021—*In re Miyuki M.*, 202 Conn. App. 851, 246 A.3d 1113.

In her appeal of a judgment terminating her parental rights, a mother could not prevail on her claim that the trial court violated her Fourteenth Amendment right to due process when the court failed to canvass her regarding a written stipulation of facts before accepting it into evidence, a claim she had not preserved by objecting to the stipulation when it was offered during the termination trial. Although the record was adequate for review, her claim was not of a constitutional magnitude. Moreover, the trial court properly canvassed the mother at the start of the termination trial. It was not required to give a separate canvass before her attorney made a tactical decision not to contest the exhibits offered by the Commissioner of Children and Families.

2020—*Davis v. Davis*, 200 Conn. App. 180, 238 A.3d 46.

Where the parties had filed a litany of post judgment motions in the eight months following the entry of their judgment of dissolution and the trial court had issued an order indicating that all of the pending motions would be heard on a particular date, the defendant received adequate notice in satisfaction of his due process right that the court would decide the plaintiff's pending motion to modify alimony.

2020—*In re Aisjaha N.*, 199 Conn. App. 485, 237 A.3d 52.

The trial court did not deny a mother's procedural due process rights when it denied her motion for a continuance of a neglect proceeding where the mother was incompetent and her attorney and her guardian ad litem had advocated zealously on her behalf. The guardian ad litem does not replace mother at trial. However, the potential value of a continuance was lessened by the presence of the guardian ad litem and the previous finding that the mother was incompetent.

2020—*In re Geoffrey G.*, 196 Conn. App. 316, 229 A.3d 1203.

Appellate court confirmed a trial court order terminating a mother's parental rights. The mother claimed for the first time on appeal that the trial court violated her due process rights by failing to order, sua sponte, an evaluation of the mother's competency to assist her counsel at trial. Due process does not require a competency hearing in all termination cases, but only when the parent's attorney requests such a hearing or the conduct of the parent reasonably suggests that to the court, in its discretion, that it would be desirable for it to order such a hearing without a request. The trial court did not abuse its discretion by declining to order a competency hearing for the mother because the record reflected that the mother exhibited a present ability to assist her counsel with a rational understanding of the proceedings against her at the time of trial.

2019—*In re Adrian K.*, 191 Conn. 397, 215 A.3d 1271.

Father's substantive due process rights were not violated by denial of his motion to dismiss an order of temporary custody his infant child who had been adjudicated neglected. Trial court had ongoing jurisdiction to rule on order of temporary custody though neither a new neglect petition or nor a motion to modify had been filed in a timely manner as prescribed by the applicable rule of practice, which cannot confer or circumscribe the court's jurisdiction.

Trial court's decision to allow filing of motion to modify one day late did not deprive father of procedural due process or create substantial risk of erroneous deprivation of his private interest. Father had notice of ex parte order of temporary custody in advance of preliminary hearing, was represented by counsel, and had an opportunity to be heard and fully contest order of temporary custody and motion to modify before the court sustained the order of temporary custody and modified the disposition commitment.

2019—*In re Skylar F.*, 191 Conn. App. 200, 215 A.3d 750.

Father conflated alleged due process violation in rendering of default judgment at case status conference with denial of his motion to open from which he appealed.

Father was not denied due process when trial court denied his motion to open default judgment of neglect rendered after father failed to appear at case status conference. By filing the motion to open, father had invoked his right to due process, specifically, his right to be heard as to why he had failed to appear and whether he had a good defense. He was afforded a hearing and thereby exercised his right to due process.

2019—*Morera v. Thurber*, 187 Conn. App. 795, 204 A.3d 1.

Father was denied due process by the trial court, which did not offer him an adequate opportunity to review an expert's report or to present evidence in opposition to the report before the trial court ruled. The court remanded to afford him the opportunity, at a properly noticed evidentiary hearing, to present his own evidence and to cross-examine the expert.

2016—*Szymonik v. Szymonik*, 167 Conn. App. 641, 144 A.3d 457.

Trial court violated the parties' due process rights when it issued new, post-dissolution financial orders, including an order for child support, without first holding an evidentiary hearing.

§ 18.06 Exclusive Use of Family Home

2012—*Lynch v. Lynch*, 135 Conn. App. 40, 43 A.3d 667.

Trial court properly granted the defendant's post-judgment motion for exclusive possession of the family home as a way to protect the best interests of the minor children.

§ 18.07 Fraud

2022—*Conroy v. Idlibi*, 343 Conn. 201, 272 A.3d 1121.

The appellate court properly affirmed the trial court's denial of defendant's motion to open the dissolution judgment on the basis of fraud. Defendant claimed the trial court improperly denied his motion to open without first giving him an opportunity to present certain evidence that plaintiff had lied under oath about certain topics during the dissolution proceedings. The trial court expressly found that even if the allegations were true, it would have likely had the exact same result. Moreover, because plaintiff had admitted to lying in an interrogatory response, it was reasonable to infer that her lie did not impact the judgment. Making every reasonable presumption in favor of the trial court's ruling, the Supreme Court found no error in the appellate court's assessment.

2018—*Reinke v. Sing*, 186 Conn. App. 665, 201 A.3d 404.

Trial court did not improperly place burden of proof on plaintiff, the party alleging fraud, or improperly determine that defendant, who underreported his income and assets, did not commit fraud.

2018—*Reinke v. Sing*, 328 Conn. 376, 179 A.3d 769.

The trial court properly opened a judgment based on the oral agreement of the parties without a finding of fraud, in order to reassess the financial orders.

2017—*Sousa v. Sousa*, 173 Conn. App. 755, 164 A.3d 702.

A party seeking to open a judgment beyond the passage of the four-month limitation period from its rendering provided by General Statutes § 52-212a under an exception for judgments procured by fraud, bears the burden of proving fraud in all of its elements by clear and convincing evidence.

2017—*Cimino v. Cimino*, 174 Conn. App. 1, 164 A.3d 787.

Defendant did not commit fraud or misrepresentation re: pension; his testimony was credible that he had disclosed all he knew about the pension.

Defendant did not commit fraud or misrepresentation where at the time of dissolution the defendant had no present interest in gifts received post-dissolution.

2016—*Gaary v. Gillis*, 162 Conn. App. 251, 131 A.3d 765.

There was no fraud where a party had disclosed a pending litigation at the time of prior litigation, but had not disclosed the amount of settlement because it had not been determined at the time of the hearing.

2016—*Reinke v. Sing*, 162 Conn. App. 674, 133 A.3d 501.

The Appellate Court instructed the trial court to dismiss a motion to open judgment based upon a lack of subject matter jurisdiction, where the court made no finding with respect to fraud and, upon hearing the evidence, the moving party failed to prove fraud.

2003—*Weinstein v. Weinstein*, 266 Conn. 933, 837 A.2d 807.

Husband fraudulently concealed his assets during the dissolution proceeding and if the court had known his true financial status, the outcome of the trial would likely be different.

1991—*Billington v. Billington*, 220 Conn. 212, 595 A.2d 1377.

A party is not required to exercise diligence in discovering the other party's alleged fraud as condition of opening judgment concerning financial aspects of dissolution on basis of that fraud. The concept of fraud on the court is properly confined to situations where both parties intentionally conceal material information from the court.

§ 18.08 Judges

2024—*Karen v. Loftus*, 228 Conn. App. 163, 324 A.3d 793, *appeal denied*, 350 Conn. 924, 325 A.3d 1094.

In denying the plaintiff's motion to open the judgment for the limited purpose of allowing discovery, the trial court improperly determined that the plaintiff failed to meet her preliminary burden of demonstrating probable cause existed to warrant discovery and an evidentiary hearing as to her allegation that the arbitration award, which subsequently was incorporated into the judgment of dissolution, was obtained by fraud. The plaintiff presented evidence satisfying the probable cause standard that the defendant had made false statements or failed to disclose facts regarding the details of the end of his employment and his formation of a new company in an effort to deprive her of money she may have been entitled to under the terms of the parties' prenuptial agreement.

2016—*D'Amato v. Hart-D'Amato*, 169 Conn. App. 669, 152 A.3d 546.

Trial judge's re-statement of guardian ad litem's testimony at a post-judgment hearing did not establish bias sufficient to warrant his recusal.

§ 18.09 Life Insurance

2018—*Steller v. Steller*, 181 Conn. App. 581, 187 A.3d 1184.

Life insurance can be reduced in the same manner as alimony in a "second look" hearing.

2014—*Torla v. Torla*, 152 Conn. App. 241, 101 A.3d 275.

Upon entry of default against named beneficiary of former husband's life insurance policy on claim brought by former wife under terms of divorce decree that former husband maintain life insurance for benefit of minor children, and beneficiary's failure to file notice of defense or appear at wife's subsequent hearing on damages, allegations in wife's complaint were deemed admitted, and beneficiary's liability was conclusively established.

2013—*Szynkowicz v. Szynkowicz*, 140 Conn. App. 525, 59 A.3d 1194.

Trial court could reasonably have found that defendant had not met his burden to show that he was unable to secure life insurance.

2013—*Sagalyn v. Pederson*, 140 Conn. App. 792, 60 A.3d 367.

Court properly found that a life insurance order was not a property order and thus could be modified.

1999—*Papa v. Papa*, 55 Conn. App. 47, 737 A.2d 953.

Trial court improperly ordered defendant to pay life insurance without any evidence of defendant's insurability.

1999—*Cordone v. Cordone*, 51 Conn. App. 530, 752 A.2d 1082.

Trial court is not required to secure alimony order with life insurance.

1999—*Carroll v. Carroll*, 55 Conn. App. 18, 737 A.2d 963.

Trial court properly ordered defendant to provide $100,000 life insurance policy.

1998—*Lake v. Lake*, 49 Conn. App. 89, 712 A.2d 989.

Court cannot order life or medical insurance in absence of evidence of availability or cost.

1995—*Wolf v. Wolf*, 39 Conn. App. 162, 664 A.2d 315.

Court cannot order additional life insurance without evidence of cost and availability.

1993—*Michel v. Michel*, 31 Conn. App. 338, 624 A.2d 914.

Life insurance cannot be ordered to be purchased by a party without evidence of insurability, availability of the insurance, its cost, or whether party was insurable. Reversal of order to maintain life insurance necessitated a remand of all financial issues.

1988—*Mauro v. Mauro*, 16 Conn. App. 680, 548 A.2d 471.

Award of life insurance is within the court's equitable powers.

1984—*Arseniadis v. Arseniadis*, 2 Conn. App. 239, 477 A.2d 152.

Support for a minor child extends to age 18 years only and, absent a written agreement, a court had no jurisdiction to render orders that require the supporting spouse to name adult children as the irrevocable beneficiaries of life insurance policies.

1980—*Broaca v. Broaca*, 181 Conn. 463, 435 A.2d 1016.

A court order requiring a parent with the duty of child support to name his child as beneficiary of an insurance policy on his life is an appropriate order for the maintenance of that child, however, any order of child support purporting to extend beyond a child's 18th birthday is outside the jurisdiction of the superior court and of no force and effect.

§ 18.10 Civil Action for Emotional Distress

2009—*Davis v. Davis*, 112 Conn. App. 56, 962 A.2d 140.

Court affirmed summary judgment granted in civil action for intentional infliction of emotional distress and after the dissolution former husband's conduct allegedly caused the plaintiff upset. Trial court improperly concluded that mutual release provision in separation agreement barred a tort action.

2004—*Carrubba v. Moskowitz*, 81 Conn. App. 382, 840 A.2d 557.

Claims that defendant had negligently or intentionally caused emotional distress were dismissed.

§ 18.11 Collateral Estoppel

2018—*Shirley P. v. Norman P.*, 329 Conn. 648, 189 A.3d 89.

The trial court's property division award, which was based on the defendant's criminal conviction, was reversed following the reversal of the defendant's criminal conviction. Reversal of the criminal conviction deprived that judgment of any preclusive effect that it had in dissolution action.

2018—*Kimberly C. v. Anthony C.*, 179 Conn. App. 856, 182 A.3d 106.

Court's finding that wife's claim of abuse in a restraining order hearing was credible but made no finding of abuse sufficient to issue a restraining order was not collateral estoppel in a subsequent dissolution of marriage trial.

§ 18.12 Motion to Dismiss

2019—*Fleischer v. Fleischer*, 192 Conn. 540, 217 A.3d 1028.

While trial courts have wide discretion in determining whether to dismiss an action for failure to prosecute with due diligence, the sanction must be proportional to the misconduct. Trial court here improperly dismissed defendant's motions to modify alimony and for contempt for a one-time delay after defendant's counsel had been diagnosed with a Parkinson's disease, which was disclosed in defendant's opposition to plaintiff's motion to dismiss. There was no evidence that defendant was ever ordered to prosecute the motions more expeditiously during the delay or that defendant disregarded such an order. Hearing on the merits of the motions to dismiss was the first time defendant was confronted with potential dismissal. Delay caused by the illness of defendant's counsel did not justify the severe sanction of dismissal. Trial court made no findings that it considered lesser sanctions and found them to be inadequate before deciding to dismiss the motions. The dismissal appeared to be punishment for defendant's refusal to waive a claim that any reduction in alimony should be retroactive to the date the motion to modify was filed.

§ 18.13 Mediation and Arbitration

2020—*Blondeau v. Baltierra*, 337 Conn. 127, 252 A.3d 317.

Where the arbitrator had fulfilled her obligation to interpret and to apply the parties' arbitration agreement, the trial court erred in ruling that the arbitrator's award exceeded the scope of the parties' submission. The arbitration award relating to the division of equity in the marital home did not constitute an egregious or patently irrational rejection of clearly controlling legal principles constituting a manifest disregard of the law that would permit a court to vacate the arbitration award. However, Conn. Gen. Stat. §§ 46b-66(c) and 52-408 prohibit the inclusion of issues related to child support in arbitration. The portion of the arbitration award related to child support must be vacated.

2020—*Yun Zhou v. Hao Zhang*, 334 Conn. 601, 223 A.3d 775.

Supreme Court affirmed the trial court, holding that it properly ruled that an agreement the parties had entered during an unsuccessful attempt at mediation, which purported to revoke their postnuptial agreement, was unenforceable. The defendant husband's understanding was that the revocation agreement would not be binding unless the parties reached a full and final settlement of the disputed issues. His position was supported by the mediator's representations to the defendant on the mediator's website, in the mediator's email to the parties during mediation, and in the mediation agreement. The trial court's finding that the defendant's understanding was based on those representations was amply supported by his testimony. Accordingly, the revocation agreement was unenforceable because a full and final resolution of the issues during mediation was a condition precedent to the enforcement of the revocation agreement, and it was undisputed that no such resolution ever occurred. There was no merit to the plaintiff wife's claim that the trial court's consideration of the mediators representations on his website, in the email to the parties, and in the mediation agreement for the purpose of ascertaining the defendant's understanding and intent with respect to the revocation agreement violated the parol evidence rule because that rule does not prevent a party from relying on extrinsic evidence to establish the existence of a condition precedent to the formation of a contract. The trial court properly considered parol evidence in evaluating the defendant's claim that the revocation agreement was not binding in the absence of a final settlement agreement.

§ 18.14 Motion for Reassignment

2020—*Budrawich v. Budrawich*, 200 Conn. App. 229, 240 A.3d 688.

The trial court erred in denying the defendant's motion for reassignment. Because the defendant had timely filed his motion for reassignment and there was no evidence in the record to support a finding of consent to an extension or waiver of the 120-day filing deadline, the trial court was required to order that the matter be reassigned to another judge.

TABLE OF CASES

[References are to sections]

A

[References are to sections]

TABLE OF CASES

[References are to sections]

C

[References are to sections]

[References are to sections]

D

[References are to sections]

E

[References are to sections]

F

G

[References are to sections]

[References are to sections]

L

[References are to sections]

[References are to sections]

M

M.B. v. S.A., 194 Conn. App. 721, 222 A.3d 559. .13.02
M.B. v. S.A., 194 Conn. App. 727, 222 A.3d 551. .12.02
M.C. v. A.W, 226 Conn. App. 444, 319 A.3d 183 . . . . 9.01
M.M. v. H. F., 194 Conn. App. 472, 221 A.3d 523. . . . . 11.04[2]
M.S. v. M.S, 226 Conn. App. 482, 319 A.3d 223. . . . . .10.08; 12.02
M.S. v. P.S., 203 Conn. App. 377, 248 A.3d 778. . . . . .8.08; 11.08[2]; 16.03
M. S., In re, 226 Conn. App. 857, 319 A.3d 833. . . . . .11.08[5]
Machado v. Statewide Grievance Comm., 93 Conn. App. 832, 890 A.2d 622. . . . .11.05
Madigan v. Madigan, 224 Conn. 749, 620 A.2d 1276 . . . . 15.01; 15.03
Maguire v. Maguire, 222 Conn. 32, 608 A.2d 79 . . . . 15.01; 16.03
Mailly v. Mailly, 13 Conn. App. 185, 535 A.2d 385. . . . . .16.03
Main v. Main, 17 Conn. App. 670, 555 A.2d 997. . . .10.03[1]; 11.11[3]; 15.01, 15.02; 15.06
Mallory v. Mallory, 207 Conn. 48, 539 A.2d 995 . . . . 12.01[2]; 12.06; 16.03
Malpeso v. Malpeso, 140 Conn. App. 783, 60 A.3d 380 . . . . 6.02; 8.07[3]; 8.09; 10.07
Malpeso v. Malpeso, 165 Conn. App. 151, 138 A.3d 1069 . . . . 6.04; 8.09; 10.07
Malpeso v. Malpeso, 189 Conn. App. 486, 207 A.3d 1085 . . . . 10.10[2]
Manaker v. Manaker, 11 Conn. App. 653, 528 A.2d 1170 . . . . 1.03
Manndorff v. Dax, 13 Conn. App. 282, 535 A.2d 1324. . . . . .1.01[4]; 4.01
Manter v. Manter, 185 Conn. 502, 441 A.2d 146. 11.10[1]
Manzi v. Manzi, 134 Conn. App. 333, 38 A.3d 1247. . . . . .15.01
Marcil v. Marcil, 4 Conn. App. 403, 494 A.2d 620. . . . . .12.01[2], [3]
Marcquan C., In re, 202 Conn. App. 520, 246 A.3d 41 . . . . 15.03
Marcus v. Cassara, 223 Conn. App. 69, 308 A.3d 39 . . . . 10.07
Marcus v. Marcus, 175 Conn. 138, 394 A.2d 727. . . . . .16.03
Marfo v. Hagan, 83 Conn. App. 902, 853 A.2d 650. . . . . .16.03
Mark v. Mark, 40 Conn. App. 171, 669 A.2d 579. . . . . .15.01
Markarian v. Markarian, 2 Conn. App. 14, 475 A.2d 337 . . . . 8.06
Markarian v. Markarian, 2 Conn. App. 688, 483 A.2d 276 . . . . 15.01
Marmo v. Marmo, 131 Conn. App. 43, 26 A.3d 652. . . . . .8.06; 8.08
Marrocco v. Giardino, 255 Conn. 617, 767 A.2d 720. . . . . 10.03[2]
Marshall v. Marshall, 119 Conn. App. 120, 988 A.2d 314. . . . . .8.07[11]; 8.08
Marshall v. Marshall, 151 Conn. App. 638, 97 A.3d 1. . . . . .8.03[8]
Marshall v. Marshall, 200 Conn. App. 688, 241 A.3d 189. . . . . .8.04[1]
Marshall v. Marshall, 224 Conn. App. 45, 311 A.3d 235. . . . . . . .8.03[3], [8]; 10.03[1]
Marsico v. Marsico, 195 Conn. 491, 488 A.2d 1248. . . . . .6.03
Martin v. Martin, 101 Conn. App. 106, 920 A.2d 340 . . . . 9.05
Martocchio v. Savoir, 156 Conn. App. 224, 112 A.3d 211 . . . . 15.01
Martone v. Martone, 28 Conn. App. 208, 611 A.2d 896 . . . . 4.03; 8.03[2]
Martowska v. White, 149 Conn. App. 314, 87 A.3d 1201. . . . . .11.12
Mason v. Ford, 176 Conn. App. 658, 168 A.3d 525. .10.07
Masters v. Masters, 201 Conn. 50, 513 A.2d 104. . . . . .6.02; 10.10[1]
Mathis v. Mathis, 30 Conn. App. 292, 620 A.2d 174 . . . . 8.03[9]; 8.06
Matles v. Matles, 8 Conn. App. 76, 511 A.2d 363 . . . . .8.07[3]; 8.09; 10.04[1]
Maturo v. Maturo, 296 Conn. 80, 995 A.2d 1 (2010). . . . . 10.03[1], [3]
Matza v. Matza, 226 Conn. 166, 627 A.2d 414. . . . . .16.02

[References are to sections]

[References are to sections]

N

[References are to sections]

O

[References are to sections]

Q

R

S

TABLE OF CASES

[References are to sections]

T

[References are to sections]

U

V

W

X

Y

Z

[References are to sections]

INDEX

[References are to sections.]

A

C

[References are to sections.]

[References are to sections.]

[References are to sections.]